The Politics of Dialogic Imagination

CHICAGO STUDIES IN PRACTICES OF MEANING

Edited by Andreas Glaeser, William Sewell, and Lisa Wedeen
Published in collaboration with the Chicago Center for Contemporary Theory
http://ccct.uchicago.edu

ALSO IN THE SERIES

The Genealogical Science: The Search for Jewish Origins and the Politics of Epistemology
by Nadia Abu El-Haj

Questioning Secularism: Islam, Sovereignty, and the Rule of Law in Modern Egypt
by Hussein Ali Agrama

Neoliberal Frontiers: An Ethnography of Sovereignty in West Africa
by Brenda Chalfin

Ethnicity, Inc.
by John L. Comaroff and Jean Comaroff

Inclusion: The Politics of Difference in Medical Research
by Steven Epstein

Political Epistemics: The Secret Police, the Opposition, and the End of East German Socialism
by Andreas Glaeser

Producing India: From Colonial Economy to National Space
by Manu Goswami

The Moral Neoliberal: Welfare and Citizenship in Italy
by Andrea Muehlebach

American Value: Migrants, Money, and Meaning in El Salvador and the United States
by David Pedersen

The Making of Romantic Love: Longing and Sexuality in Europe, South Asia, and Japan, 900–1200 CE
by William M. Reddy

Laughing at Leviathan: Sovereignty and Audience in West Papua
by Danilyn Rutherford

Bengal in Global Concept History: Culturalism in the Age of Capital
by Andrew Sartori

Additional series titles follow index

The Politics of Dialogic Imagination

Power and Popular Culture in Early Modern Japan

KATSUYA HIRANO

The University of Chicago Press   Chicago and London

Publication of this book has been aided by a grant from the Hull Memorial Publication Fund of Cornell University.

KATSUYA HIRANO is associate professor of history at the University of California, Los Angeles.

The University of Chicago Press, Chicago 60637
The University of Chicago Press, Ltd., London

Printed in the United States of America

23 22 21 20 19 18 17 16 15 14   1 2 3 4 5

ISBN-13: 978-0-226-06042-2 (cloth)
ISBN-13: 978-0-226-06056-9 (paper)
ISBN-13: 978-0-226-06073-6 (e-book)

DOI: 10.7208/chicago/9780226060736.001.0001

Library of Congress Cataloging-in-Publication Data

Hirano, Katsuya.
The politics of dialogic imagination : power and popular culture in early modern Japan / Katsuya Hirano.
pages ; cm. — (Chicago studies in practices of meaning)
Includes bibliographical references and index.
ISBN 978-0-226-06042-2 (cloth : alkaline paper) — ISBN 978-0-226-06056-9 (paperback : alkaline paper) — ISBN 978-0-226-06073-6 (e-book) 1. Arts, Political aspects—Japan—History—19th century. 2. Popular culture—Government policy—Japan—History. 3. Human body in popular culture—Political aspects—Japan. 4. Human body—Political aspects—Japan. 5. Japan—Cultural policy—History—19th century. 6. Kabuki—Government policy—Japan—History. 7. Japanese wit and humor—Political aspects. 8. Japan—History—Tokugawa period, 1600–1868. 9. Japan—Politics and government—1600–1868. I. Title. II. Series: Chicago studies in practices of meaning.
NX180.P64H57 2014
306.0952'09034—dc23

2013006823

♾ This paper meets the requirements of ANSI/NISO Z39.48-1992 (Permanence of Paper).

Contents

Acknowledgments

This project has been enabled by so much inspiration and encouragement offered by a number of teachers, colleagues, and friends. Special thanks go to Tetsuo Najita, Bill Sewell, Jim Ketelaar, and Tim Screech. During the process writing the book, Harry Harootunian, Bill Sewell, Vic Koschmann, Naoki Sakai, Brett de Bary, Ryūichi Narita, Minoru Iwasaki, Robert Stolz, Richard Reitan, T. J. Hinrichs, Duane Corpis, Gavin Walker, Bill Marotti, Maki Fukuoka, Hirotaka Kasai, Ichiro Tomiyama, Jonathan Zwicker, Wendy Matsumura, Jin-Han Park, and Gyewon Kim all helped me in a way that I cannot thank enough. I received invitations to present parts of the argument and got helpful comments and criticisms from the faculty at many institutions, including Chicago, Columbia, Harvard, Michigan, UC Berkeley, UCLA, and Virginia. In particular, very helpful comments were provided by Andrew Barshay, Daniel Botsman, Herman Ooms, Anne Walthall, Leslie Pincus, Ken Ito, Suzan Burns, Carol Gluck, and Mary Elizabeth Berry. Richard Reitan, Robert Stolz, Derek Wolf, Maki Fukuoka, Tanya Maus, Jun Yoo, Sho Konishi, Juliette Chung, Patti Kameya, and Tong Lam extended their friendship during my years in the graduate program in Chicago. Dan Mackie kindly shared his impressive Edo print collection for this book. Sujin Lee generously offered her help to compile the bibliography and index despite her busy schedule in Cornell's graduate program.

The project has benefited from much help and support from Cornell`s Society for the Humanities, the Mellon Foundation, and Michigan's Japan Program, where I was fortunate to teach and conduct my research as a Toyota Visiting Professor.

Thanks are also due to the publishers for allowing me to use the following materials. Parts of chapters 1 and 3 appeared as "Politics and Poetics of the Body in Early Modern Japan," *Modern Intellectual History* 8, no. 3 (2011): 499–530; parts of introduction and chapter 3 appeared as "Dialectic of Laughter and Tosaka`s Critical Theory" in *Tosaka Jun: A Critical Reader*, edited by Ken Kawashima and Robert Stolz (Ithaca, NY: Cornell East Asian Series, forthcoming); and parts of chapter 2 appeared as "Edo no Asobi to Kenryoku" *Misuzu* 565 (Tokyo: Misuzushobō, 2008).

I also want to extend many thanks to the group of very competent editors at the University of Chicago Press: David Brent, Elissa Park, and Mary Gehl, as well as promotions manager Ryo Yamaguchi. It was a pleasure to work with them.

Lastly, Bellette Lee and Yuhki Hirano did more than I can acknowledge. I thank them for making my life so much happier and joyous.

Needless to say, all errors and shortcomings are mine alone.

Introduction

In Marxist theory, to say that contradiction is a motive force is to say that it implies a real struggle, real confrontations, precisely located within the structure of the complex whole; it is to say that the locus of confrontation may vary according to the relation of contradictions in the structure in dominance in any given situation; it is to say that the condensation of the struggle in a strategic locus is inseparable from the displacement of the dominant among these contradictions.

LOUIS ALTHUSSER, "ON THE MATERIAL DIALECTIC," *FOR MARX*

Since the deluge of poststructuralist discourse swept the academic world in the past several decades, it has become customary for historians and other social scientists, who are self-reflexive about their epistemic procedure of interpretation, to profess their own interpretive positionalities and to explain what theoretical perspective(s) shaped their works. However ritualistic or banal such a practice may have become now, it still seems extremely valuable because any historical inquiry, I believe, invariably presupposes a certain perspective and involves a methodological standpoint. Put differently, theory is internal and integral to the ways in which historians formulate and address a specific kind of historical question. "The methodological starting point" as Fredric Jameson lucidly puts it, "does more than simply reveal, it actually creates, the object of study."[1] This does not mean, however, that the interrelationship of the historical and the theoretical is a one-way street. Rather it is a continual reciprocal interaction and feedback loop. Historians work through this process of the historical and the theoretical in dealing with the fragmentary masses of extant documents and images, and bubbles of heterogeneous voices.[2] Dialectical and dialogical reflections between the material traces of infinitely complex historical realities and a conceptual grasp of these realities lead eventually to the possibility of formulating questions that historians judge to be worthy of inquiry.

The questions central to this work are no exception. Through a seemingly endless reciprocal process of historical and theoretical reflections, I conceived and hold the questions to be capable of bringing a new perspective not only to the understanding of the history of cultural politics during the time of great significance for the understanding of Japan's modern revolutionary change but also to a more general study of the relationship of politics and culture for a comparative inquiry of early modern and modern times.

Some readers who are acclimated to a more empirical approach may ask for further "evidence" and "materials" or a broader coverage of geographical areas for my claims. Or some may argue that my selectivity of texts and visual materials limits and lessens the credence of my analysis. It should be noted, however, that this study is never intended to present a general survey of early modern Japanese history or the study of Edo popular culture itself that helps create a more comprehensive picture of a place called "Japan." Its objective is to address a particular set of questions that are designed to historicize *and* theorize the *dialectical logic of the political* in the sphere of cultural and social formation—what Jameson once called "perpetual cultural revolution"—in the context of early modern Japan.[3] In this sense, the scope of the book is more focused and selective, and I would like to see it not as an insufficiency but as an indication of new and original interpretive intervention. What follows hereafter is the exposition of this project and its interpretive positionality and strategies by way of comparing them with the previously available interpretive paradigms.

The main questions I address in this study are as follows: Why did the sustained control of the urban popular culture of Edo (present-day Tokyo) occupy, especially since the late eighteenth century, such a central place in the Tokugawa state's efforts to maintain social order and public mores, and ultimately to defend its own political and ideological legitimacy? What aspects of popular cultural practices provoked the sustained concern and interference of the authorities? Why did the new Meiji state continue with its predecessors' policies of regulating the popular culture as a focal point of its program of remaking the country into a capitalist nation-state? Were there any differences in the way state regulations and the ideological rationales for these regulations operated between Tokugawa and early Meiji? If there were, what were they? And what are the implications of those differences for an understanding of Japan's modern transformation?

Humanists and social scientists working on this period have either dismissed the political significance of popular culture by calling it a benign and apolitical realm of escapist activity—ephemeral play and pleasure—or tried to argue for the presence, if limited and discreet, of a political consciousness in the culture by drawing on a facile concept of "cultural resistance," particularly "resistance of a decentered sort—those dispersed acts" of mockery and satire that expressed ordinary townspeople's resentment of the ruling samurai.[4] These perspectives have failed to provide a cogent explanation of how and why the putatively apolitical realms of play and pleasure or the dispersed cultural representations were a constant source of concern for officials and intellectuals. Furthermore, these studies fail to analyze why the new Meiji state continued with its predecessors' policies of regulating popular culture as a focal point of its program of remaking the country into a modern capitalist nation-state. In this regard, my interest in theory really originates from a desire to be able to effectively deal with this particular set of historical questions and thus to explore a new way of understanding how early modern politics (both Tokugawa and early Meiji) operated in relation to the problem of popular culture. (I will return to this historiographical and theoretical question in the next chapter.)

To approach the questions above, this study focuses on the interface between the distinct forms of popular literary, visual and theatrical representation and the configuration of social order (the status hierarchy and the division of labor), as well as moral and ideological discourses that were conducive to the reproduction of the order. Central to the forms of representation in Edo popular culture was the overarching literary and artistic principle, which I call "dialogic imagination," a phrase adapted from M .M. Bakhtin's work on Fyodor Dostoevsky.[5] By creating a dialogical interaction of divergent voices and perspectives, Edo popular culture created pluralized, contentious image of Tokugawa society, an image that underlined contradictory realities that had become widely discernible around the turn of the eighteenth century. The most salient of all the contradictions was the growing disjuncture between the ideological premise of social and economic hierarchies and their actual reversals. The primacy of the rice economy that sustained the samurai's wealth was overshadowed, even superseded by the ascendancy of a money economy controlled by merchants who were at the bottom of the formal status hierarchy—just above people of outcast status. The culture of popular entertainments (e.g., theaters, pleasure quarters, print culture, and street performances), which was closely associated with the outcasts and patronized by the townspeople (merchants and artisans), became the magnetic center for cultural innovations and unbounded social interactions, often involving people of samurai status. The dialogic imagination captured and accentuated the fluid and dynamic social interactions that threw the formal arrangements of social order into disarray, and the widely perceived tensions originating from these interactions, by supplying images that sharply contrasted with those that the Tokugawa authorities worked hard to foster and defend: of a harmonious, self-contained, and perfectly functioning society. The dialogic imagination visualized the disintegration of the totality and presented new understandings of divergent social realities. This study therefore analyzes the ways in which the inversion of hierarchies within the socioeconomic structures was interrelated with emergent contestations in the cultural domain by focusing on the interface of the production of cultural forms and of the socioeconomic circuit of power.

Crucial to our understanding of the relationship of culture and the socioeconomic is the contestatory meanings and divergent functions of the body between official (including dominant intellectual discourse) and popular discourses. This study shows that the Tokugawa government constructed the mechanisms of rule based on a fundamental distrust of the body—its desire and excesses—and sought to confine the body to the function of productive labor serving the operation of the rice economy. Imposing through sumptuary laws and decrees austerity and simplicity as the highest moral virtues for commoners to observe, the authorities vilified the body that defied this function as "idle" and "immoral" and subjected it to punitive or disciplinary measures. Popular culture, nonetheless, celebrated the idle body associated with the culture of urban/commercial entertainments, thereby transmuting the body into the site of an almost inexhaustible source for the production of new identities, sensibilities, and imaginations that had not existed within the ideological limits set by the founders of Tokugawa Japan. Wealthy merchants and ordinary townspeople patronized this new form of culture while peasants and farmers were drawn to its allure and began to migrate to Edo, abandoning their duties in the village. It is no coincidence that the explosive appearance of the new bodily images as a predominant subject matter in popular literary and artistic production occurred simultaneously with the government's aggressive control over the idle body as an attempt to maintain the moral order, public mores, and economic productivity. By the late eighteenth century, the body had become the primary battleground, both symbolically and materially, where the power and popular culture contended over the representation of social reality.

What made the popular culture's celebration of play and pleasure—the sphere of "idleness"—a problem for the Tokugawa authorities was that it represented a "weakest link," to borrow Lenin's words, or "conjunctural moment," of the social totality as it produced and amplified the sense of the "dissolution of (the existing) unity" through its brazen disregard for the moral imperatives of status identities and socioeconomic functions.[6] Literary and visual representations of the divergent images of the idle body came to signify the strategic nodal position that posed a serious challenge to the social order.

The representations of the idle body were certainly related to new socioeconomic conditions surrounding popular culture, but they were also derived from the dominant ideological discourse on the mind-body relationship during the Tokugawa period. The body was viewed as having its own dynamics not only independent of but also counter to the command of reason or mind, creating constant mental disjuncture, tension, and negotiation. For those who were concerned with the steady operation of established social relations, the body signified a potential locus of unruly energies and excesses to be contained. This ideological standpoint called for governmental policies of regulating popular media and entertainments that appeared to incite corporeal desire (e.g., censorship against "erotic" and "frivolous" prints, relocating popular entertainment and entertainers to the city's margin, preventing entertainment culture from entering the countryside, and occasional punishment of transgressors) as a measure necessary for preserving the status hierarchy, the division of labor, and public mores. It also worked as a powerful ideological tool with which to explain common people's proclivity for corporeal pleasure and relative lack of moral and intellectual capacity—the need to restrain them under the moral authority of the ruling elites. However, this view also inadvertently generated, through its assertion of the distinct dynamics of the corporeal, a contestatory perspective that prompted the articulations of new identities, subject positions, feelings, and values that could not be assimilated into "fixed [semantic] forms" or "received interpretations" embraced by the people of elite statures.[7] Depictions of the idle body brought to the foreground the possibility of life, work, and social relations outside the established social order. Not only can the duality—the contradictory interpretations and representations of the idle body—of the prevalent discourse of the mind-body relationship be understood as a primary locus of *ideological* contradiction, but the ideological contradiction constituted a nodal site where socioeconomic contradictions were "*condensed*."[8] This "overdetermination of a contradiction" in the ideological domain signified more than a symbolic struggle: it actually revealed the disintegration of the unity of the structures, or the displacement of Tokugawa power as a whole.[9] By examining the ways in which popular cultural representations articulated through the various bodily images these contradictions in multiple structures, this work seeks to unpack the hitherto overlooked dynamics of politics in late Tokugawa society.

This book also probes the implications of the drastic shift in social, economic, and ideological structures after 1868—a shift brought about by Japan's first modern state, the Meiji government. Under the slogan of "Civilization and Enlightenment," the state swiftly dismantled the Tokugawa social order and erected a new rule of social organization based on the idea of individual rights to equality and freedom. This new liberal principle was intended to promote incessant competition—or "industrious ethos," as a Meiji leader put it—for the purpose of advancing the country's strength and prestige in the global system of capitalism and nation-states. Accompanying the new ideological orientation was a drastic reconfiguration of the mind-body relationship underpinning the Tokugawa view of the subject. The policy called "Reform of Popular Culture and Customs" and the moral discourse underpinning the policy denied the Tokugawa view of the antagonistic relationship between the body and the mind, and in doing so, stripped the body of its agency, rendering it as an epiphenomenon of the interior space of mind. A correct mind-set would manifest itself, according to this new discourse, in demeanor and action. The Meiji state established compulsory education to instill correct values in pupils' minds, disclosing a centralizing and homogenizing impulse that had not existed in the previous age.

This book's first chapter explores the ideological and socioeconomic structures constructed by the founders of the Tokugawa government as the mechanism of rule capable of sustaining the newly unified polity after century-long civil war and strife. It then examines the dramatic transformations of socioeconomic structures around the beginning of the eighteenth century, and how those transformations brought about popular articulations of a new sensibility or "structure of feeling," to use Raymond Williams's phrase, and how it in turn led to a profound sense of dissonance with the ideological structure in place. The structure of feeling manifested itself in the word *ukiyo,* or the floating world, which denoted the sense of ontological indeterminacy or in-betweenness and was often used in and to refer to the eighteenth- and nineteenth-century artistic and literary genres—puppet theater, kabuki, popular fiction and ukiyo-e (e.g., woodblock illustrations of courtesans, kabuki actors, and scenes from the everyday life of commoners). To examine the use of this term, *ukiyo*, I focus on the literary and theatrical genre called the "story of double suicide," which depicted the tragedy of forbidden love between townsman and courtesan. The popularity of the genre was such that ordinary townspeople began to copy the suicides. The authorities responded by imposing bans on the performance of the genre. Those who attempted suicide were classified as criminals and subjected to humiliating public display, as well as hard labor as part of outcast communities. The chapter probes the implications of this criminalization as a case that demonstrates the crucial interface of governmental power and popular culture.

Chapter 2 shifts the focus from tragedy to a new literary and artistic form, parody. Although tragedy continued to be a popular genre among townspeople, parody became a more prevalent form of literary and artistic practice from the middle of the eighteenth century. I argue that Edo's distinctly urban atmosphere of fluid and heterogeneous social interactions gave rise to the predominant status of parody in popular art and literature, for the dialogical form of parody—engendering new and surprising perspectives by juxtaposing and melding incongruities such as high and low, old and new—could encapsulate the dynamic of the emerging social formations. To show this dynamic, the chapter also explains the social space of literary and print culture through which a coterie of cultural producers was formed and the reading public emerged.

Chapter 3 focuses on the particular form of parody, which I call comic realism (*kokkei*), with which the writers and print artists created a literary and artistic method called *ugachi* that was capable of generating humorous and satiric effects and laughter. It was the most commonly used form of parody to accentuate the prevalent sense of social stagnation and rigidity, the lack of innovative spirit, and the culture of corruption and hypocrisy epitomized by the obstinate defenders of the status quo, samurai and elite intellectuals. Comic realism generated these effects through symbolic inversion (*sakasama*), a visual and verbal operation that reversed the relations of binary opposites—high and low, mind and body, rice and money, productivity and idleness, propriety and impropriety, and elites and commoners—by celebrating the lower terms of the diacritical pairings. And the vulgar materialism of the body—farting, defecating, carnal desire—played the pivotal role in producing *sakasama* effects by valuing cheerful vulgarity over solemn propriety and dignity. With symbolic inversion, comic realism defamiliarized the values and distinctions that supported the established social hierarchies and foregrounded hitherto unarticulated perspectives on the prevailing truth of the established reality.[10]

Chapter 4 turns to another form of parody, grotesque realism (*iyō* 異様 or *kikai* 奇怪), which became widespread from the early nineteenth century into the early Meiji period. Compared to comic realism, this form resulted in a more affirmative negation of the given order of things by not simply inverting but deconstructing the binary classificatory categories and systems. The body in this form appeared not as the figure of cheerful vulgarity, but that of disfigurement that represented the moral bankruptcy of ruling elites. Revealing the sharp disjuncture between the elites' self-image of righteousness and benevolence and their actual deeds, the grotesque bodies of monsters and ghosts visualized elites' supposed moral and intellectual superiority as an ideological expression that helped naturalize social hierarchies and division of labor. This semiotic operation of the grotesque body echoes Bakhtin's characterizations of the grotesque in medieval Europe: it frequently foregrounded the ways in which ideology naturalized the mechanisms of domination by concealing their actual conditions. To understand the grotesque as a form of symbolic deconstruction, however, is not to define its role as a prerequisite for contestation. Rather it is to acknowledge that the grotesque *tended to operate* as a critique of a dominant symbolic order that had set the terms of "reality" by exposing fundamental disunity and contradictions in lived social realities. It was the grotesque's potential to unsettle the rules of inclusion, exclusion, and domination that made this form of parody vexing to the authorities.

Chapter 5 examines why and how the new Meiji government made a much more concerted effort to regulate the popular culture as a focal point of its program of remaking the county into a capitalist nation-state. It focuses on the early Meiji policy called "Reform of Popular Culture and Customs" (*fūzoku kairyō* 風俗改良) implemented in the 1870s and 1880s through a series of decrees and educational reforms. This policy was devised in conjunction with the government's swift decision to dismantle the Tokugawa social order and erect a new one based on the liberal ideological principle of individual rights to equality and freedom. The new political leaders believed that a competitive ethos of self-motivated individuals was the key to Western nations' dominance in wealth, military strength, and technology, and that Japan's successful transformation into a modern nation-state worthy of the respect of Western counterparts depended on the creation of such an ethos at home. On the basis of this conviction, the government launched a universal education program in 1872, arguing that the country's stability, prosperity, and strength depended entirely on the degree to which common people, not select men of intelligence, are civilized. The announcement of the program defined the public schools' ultimate goal as supplying every individual with the most basic "capital" to "establish oneself, acquire one's means of life, and prosper in one's vocation."[11] It also stipulated the "establishment of oneself" (*mi o tateru* 身を立てる) by way of learning as a "duty of every human being [*hitono tsutome* 人の務め], regardless of gender and class," and reasoned that "homelessness, poverty, downfall, and degradation" were the natural consequences of the individual's deficiencies in living up to this duty.[12] By attributing individuals' success entirely to their personal aptitudes and efforts, the Meiji state sought to implant in every individual citizen competitiveness and self-responsibility, not only as a new way of life to accept but also as a positive value to embrace, so that each citizen would become an industrious and productive subject for capitalist modernization. Accordingly, Edo-style popular culture and its forms of representation were all reconfigured as the markers of negative traces of the past—backwardness and ignorance—and a serious impediment to the nation's drive for modernization. This chapter examines the implications of this reconfiguration, reflecting on Meiji power's effects on subject formation.

What I hope to accomplish in this study is therefore twofold: to provide a textually thorough and convincing as well as theoretically well-reasoned account of the Tokugawa social order and how varied forms of cultural representation articulated underlying contradictions and vulnerabilities of the order; and to provide a new way to conceptualize the momentous historical change from Tokugawa to Meiji by outlining a general theory of the transformation in modes of subject formation during this period.

Historiography and Theoretical Perspective

When Louis Althusser wrote in 1962 that "one phantom is more especially crucial than any other today: the shade of Hegel," he was struggling to overcome the pervasive presence of the Hegelian concept of contradiction that had turned Marxist thought and praxis into a metaphysic or an idealism that it proclaimed to dispel.[13] Hoping to "drive the phantom into the night," Althusser set to work to offer a new materialist theory of contradiction—the now well-known concept of overdetermination.[14] He was not particularly thrilled by the concept itself, but he found it to be a useful "index" to show that he was dealing with "something *quite different from the Hegelian contradiction.*"[15] The source of his objection to the Hegelian contradiction was the presumption about Reason as the universal essence of consciousness that cut through the entirety of human history regardless of history's irreducible heterogeneities. This presumption ignored or dismissed the fact, complained Althusser, that "all historical societies are constituted of an infinity of concrete determinations, from political laws to religions via customs, habits, financial, commercial and economic regimes, the educational system, the arts, philosophy, and so on."[16] Thus, even though Hegelian contradiction appeared to be a complex form of dialectic, it actually meant a rather simple self-referential process in which consciousness gravitated toward its own internal essence, merely taking on different spiritual forms and appearing to overcome the preceding one through the different passages of time. The essence itself, thus, never transformed. Althusser wrote:

> If it is possible, *in principle, to reduce the totality,* the infinite diversity, of a historically given society . . . to a *simple internal principle, this very simplicity* can be reflected in the contradiction *to which it thereby acquires a right.* . . . This reduction itself . . . , the reduction of *all* the elements that make up the concrete life of a historical epoch . . . to *one* principle of internal unity, is itself only possible on the *absolute condition* of taking the whole concrete life of a people for the externalization-alienation of an *internal spiritual principle,* which can *never definitely be anything but the most abstract form of that epoch's consciousness of itself: its religious or philosophical consciousness, that is, its own ideology.*[17]

If the phantom of Hegelian idealism cast an overwhelming shadow over Marxist politics in Europe during the 1950s and 1960s, its presence was equally strongly felt in contemporary Japan—though not in Marxist but rather in liberalist politics. A most celebrated and charismatic intellectual in postwar Japan, Maruyama Masao (1914–96), offered an influential Hegelian interpretation of Japanese cultural and intellectual history in wartime Japan, and set a decisive tone for intellectual debates about Japan's modernity that ensued immediately after the war.[18] As is well known, Maruyama's interpretation was propelled by his desire, laden with a grave political concern, to construct a narrative about the incompleteness of Japan's modernity against the increasingly prevailing intellectual discourse of "overcoming modernity" under the rising tide of Japanese fascism in the early 1940s. He claimed that there was an "anomalous" intellectual development peculiar to Japan from early modern to modern times that led to the stillbirth of the modern political subject—the Hegelian subject—which professed to build a firm basis for the fuller realization of freedom.[19] The sorry dearth of a proper intellectual evolution and of the formation of the subject stemmed largely from early modern Japan's failure to nurture the archetypal bourgeois class exemplified by that in Western Europe. Comparing Tokugawa townspeople with European bourgeoisie, Maruyama argued that Tokugawa urbanites never attained "self-consciousness" or understood the "freedom of Spirit" as the "essence of man" that was supposed to propel Japan into the trajectory of "Universal History."[20] (Clearly, Maruyama was drawing on Hegel's theory of sublation—*aufheben*—as the decisive moment of dialectical leap toward a higher stage of history in order to argue that this moment never came in Japanese history.) Nor did they develop the "spirit of capitalism" (Max Weber) that thrust their European counterparts onto the stage of bourgeois revolutionary politics.[21] They instead embraced an epicurean attitude devoid of "the progress of the consciousness of Freedom" through which to forgo politics and indulge themselves in "petty satisfaction in ephemeral private freedom." In Maruyama's own words,

> (R)ather than seeking to raise the social power they acquired through their wealth into political power, many townsmen sought refuge in a world of sensual pleasure. And in the dark corners of "indecent gay quarters" they found petty satisfaction in ephemeral private freedom, or else merely sneered cynically at the existing relations of political authority. Here too there was no sign of any conscious will to take an active responsibility for the political order.[22]

Then he concludes,

> The townspeople themselves accepted the status assigned them in the social order and, arguing that because they had been driven outside the ethical realm they were justified in adopting any means at all to satisfy their personal greed, they freely adopted the mentality of the outcast.[23]

Here, Maruyama clearly projects his logic of the incompleteness of Japan's modernity, or more specifically fascism, back onto premodern history, determining the culture of preindustrial society to be an origin of the foundering of a liberal democracy—and ultimately the rise of Japanese fascism. Following this logic, Maruyama later developed the theory of cultural substratum, a distinctly "Japanese" form of irrationalism without Reason, which he regarded as always already having existed as the deep undercurrent of Japanese thought since ancient times, and worked as the fundamental impediment to the healthy development of the political subject capable of fighting for liberation and freedom.[24]

Maruyama's adoption of the Hegelian subject, a subject equipped with self-consciousness of the timeless essence—Spirit—with which he/she is able to objectivize and actively transform any given historical conditions in pursuit of greater freedom, not only served as a strategic intellectual intervention into Japan's clamorous march to militarist fascism but also reflected his "unwavering faith in the Universal History of mankind."[25] His critique that Edo townspeople passively and uncritically accepted the externally imposed social and political environs, not only being unable to objectivize them but also escaping to the petty epicurean world, came precisely from his embrace of this universalistic assumption about Spirit, Reason, and History. For him, the unfolding of "the essence of man," that is, "Spirit," which was "governed by Reason," as Hegel put it, signified the normative, even ideal progression of history, and politics was an artful means by which individuals actively sought to make history with their own free will.[26]

The way this idealist view of politics and political subjectivity influenced the interpretation of Japanese history left important yet profoundly problematic legacies. It certainly worked as a much-needed alternative paradigm to modernization theory—a functionalist theory that conceptualized history as the universal process of teleological progression toward capitalist civilization—that dominated Japanese Studies in the American academia from the late 1950s to the 70s. As argued by many, under the accelerating tension between the capitalist and communist worlds during the Cold War era, this theory was intended to supply a competing model against the Marxist revolutionary theory of social change by downplaying the concepts of contradiction, struggle, and conflict, which were most fundamental to the Marxist understanding and formulation of historical dynamisms, as an aberration from, even a detriment to, the peaceful transition to society built on the market and the liberal democratic model. To counter the Marxist model of social change, it promised to provide prescriptions for propelling non-Western societies, especially former colonies that had undergone or were undergoing the traumatic passage of decolonization, into the historical path where their political stability and economic growth—material wealth and prosperity—were guaranteed. What this promise practically meant was that, in Harry Harootunian's words, "(w)hile marketization invariably swelled the wealth of a minority, democratization enfranchised whole populations only to put control back into the hands of elites (often linked to the rich)."[27] The theory's claim of political stabilization and economic growth not only justified the developmental dictatorships in the Third World by concealing its devastating consequences for the locals but also silenced the critical analysis of social change or historical transformation that paid close attention to contradictory and conflictive processes as expressed in class struggles and their ideological contestations.

Although Maruyama always reminded his readers that his work was distinct from Marxist literature, his epistemic assumption about the "universal force" of historical development resembled orthodox Marxism, the target of Althusser's defiant criticism with regard to the specter of Hegelian idealism mentioned earlier. If orthodox Marxists privilege(d) the Economy "as a secret of intelligibility in the same spirit that Christianity offers God and Divine Providence . . . at the very moment (it) claims to be annihilating all varieties of idealism," Absolute Spirit assumes the same status for Maruyama.[28] For both the Marxists and Maruyama, it was the idea of Hegelian sublation—the universal process of dialectical unfolding of the Spirit (or the Economy, for the former)—that propelled history toward progress.

Interestingly enough, Maruyama's view of history as a dialectical progression, a view shared by orthodox Marxists, served as an important corrective to the modernization theory. Maruyama rejected the theory's nondialectical view of history that negated the importance of contradiction and conflict by reducing human thought to a mere utilitarian value—a variable of modernization.[29] Yet at the same time it became increasingly clear that Maruyama, the Marxists, and modernization theorists all converged on the unilinear and teleological view of historical change, which functioned as the epistemic basis for their comparative historical studies. Maruyama's comparative approach was based on the privileging of the particular experiences of Western Europe as the universal measure against which Japan's particularity was imagined and judged to embody an incompleteness of the modern. Because Maruyama saw universal values in Europe's particularity by conceiving it to be the site of the originary modernity, he lamented that Japanese experiences represented no more than a deformed variation of that modernity.

This mode of comparative approach that took Europe as the normative reference was also at the heart of Thomas Smith's influential essay "Japan's Aristocratic Revolution" written in 1961. Smith declared, in a manner similar to Maruyama, that the Meiji *Ishin* was a revolutionary event, but not in the same way as the English and French cases.[30] Their dissimilarities originate from the fact that the former was a revolution by the aristocratic class (samurai) itself, whereas the latter was a prototypical bourgeois and democratic revolution by the rising middle class allied with the aristocracy to overthrow monarchy, one which eventually abolished the privileges of the aristocratic class. Through this comparative perspective, Smith tries to explain the samurai's seemingly irrational decision to dismantle the system that sustained their own rule and privileges for more than two centuries. Three reasons are presented: (1) the rapid impoverishment of samurai, especially of the lower ranks; (2) enormous socioeconomic differences (differences in privileges) between the high-ranking and low-ranking samurai; and (3) alienation of average and low-ranking samurai from land ownership and political power.[31] What these three reasons amount to is that the low-ranking samurai differed fundamentally from the European aristocracies in their being bereft of resources and facing greater impoverishment and alienation, and these difficult socioeconomic conditions made them the agent of revolutionary change. Put simply, they had nothing to gain from the existing political order and something to gain from revolutionary change.[32] Rather than being irrational, then, this particular group of discontented samurai acted along the perfectly rational line of reflection on pros and cons of their existing living conditions. They judged that the demolition of the status hierarchy and land ownership, as well as the creation of a centralized government, would better serve their own interests.

There are two deeply troubling implications in Smith's views. First, there is an unstated assumption about human thought and action derived from classical liberalism: human beings or their actions are always motivated by self-interest. Society is invariably projected as an agglomeration of autonomous individuals each seeking his/her own gains by increasing his/her pleasures and decreasing his/her pains. Smith's reduction of human thought and action to the universal law of self-interest and rational calculation clearly differed from Maruyama's approach in that it paid no attention to cultural and intellectual dimensions of social change—how the "spiritual essence," an aspiration for freedom, moved society. Smith downplayed the role of ethos, which Maruyama considered central to the unfolding of history, as less crucial. In this regard, Smith's approach bore more resemblance to modernization theory than to Maruyama in its reification of self-interest and its presupposition of rational calculation as the ultimate driving force of human action (modernization theory also posited self-interest and rational thought as the universal essence of man that enabled human progress). But, at the same time, the distance between Smith and Maruyama disappears in their shared epistemic assumption that there is a universal essence of humanity and that it is to be used as the basis for comparative analysis. That essence is, needless to say, Rationality for Smith and Spirit for Maruyama. And both accepted that, to borrow Althusser's words, "this essence is the attribute of each single individual who is its real subject."[33] As Althusser perceptively observed, this essentialist assumption intrinsic to humanism presupposes "an empiricist-idealist world outlook." Althusser wrote:

> These two postulates [a universal essence of man and the essence being the attribute of each single individual] are complementary and indissociable. But their existence and their unity presuppose a whole empiricist-idealist world outlook. If the essence of man is to be a universal attribute, it is essential that *concrete subjects* exist as absolute givens; this implies an *empiricism of the subject*. If these empirical individuals are to be men [and women], it is essential that each carries in himself [or herself] the whole human essence, if not in fact, at least in principle; this implies an *idealism of the essence*.[34]

It is based precisely on this idealism of the essence that both Smith and Maruyama universalized Western Europe as the absolute standard for the comparative study of history and discovered signs of difference or anomaly in Japanese history. Europe empirically represented the originary instance of Rationality (a genuine bourgeois and democratic revolution) and Spirit (a full materialization of Freedom), whereas Japan provided a unique instance of the unity of modernity (revolution) and tradition (samurai as the revolutionary agent) or a deformed variation of Europe (incompleteness). Whether one sees Japanese politics as unique or distorted, both perceptions operated on the idealism of the essence in the guise of the empiricism of the subject.

This empiricism of the subject, which makes imaginary unitary subjects, such as European, French, British, and Japanese, the real object of comparative studies, extends to the second implication of Smith's, as well as Maruyama's, view of politics of the early modern period.[35] Echoing Maruyama, Smith reinforced the view that townspeople were the empirical proof of the peculiarity of Japan's modern transformation: they remained politically passive for they never translated "many instances of private resentment" into "a great principle of struggle," a coherent "ideology," or a new vision of a future Japan.[36] "They were seemingly content with a secondary political role," Smith writes, "finding apparent satisfaction in moneymaking, family life, and the delights of a racy and exuberant city culture."[37] In short, they harbored no true aspiration for fundamental change. For Smith, this lack of public (political) consciousness reflected Japan's unique historical condition under which townspeople tallied greater benefits in holding on to the status quo, whereas, for Maruyama, as stated above, the stillbirth of the modern political subject. Despite their differences in evaluating the implications of Japan's "difference," Smith was in agreement with Maruyama's view that there was no bourgeois revolution and thus no sprout of the archetypal liberal democratic society in Japan.[38] Thus, politics existed only among a few elites.[39]

Against this prevailing intellectual current, one of the most significant theoretical and historiographical interventions came from the volume edited in 1982 by Tetsuo Najita and J. Victor Koschmann, *Conflict in Modern Japanese History: The Neglected Tradition.* This anthology marked a major scholarly reorientation not only in that it explored conflict as the essential driving force of social change in the manner that somewhat resonated with Maruyama's view of idea or idealism as the constitutive force of struggle but also in that several essays, together with the introduction and conclusion, presented the possibility of going beyond Maruyama's paradigm with novel articulations of history and historical consciousness derived from structural anthropology and poststructuralism. Najita's introduction unequivocally challenged modernization theory, as well as Smith's and Maruyama's paradigms, all of which presupposed history, according to Najita, as "a process in the homogeneous chronological time" and thus as an unfolding of a universal essence or the lack thereof.[40] The problem with historical narratives based on these models is, for Najita, their tendencies to exclude or neglect otherwise diverse and heterogeneous experiences and an equally wide variety of others (losers, occupants of the fringe, and the marginal) as being "abnormal," thus suppressing "all the social energies which seem to act in a way contrary to the demands of the norm, and to ignore all the social energies not included in the sphere embraced by the norm."[41] According to Najita, "The dimension of conflict, dissent, and in general, the turbulence that one sees over the course of that history was [therefore] treated as an aberration of the true course. Voices of dissent were seen as those of marginal figures, sure losers lacking demonstrable influence."[42] Citing Hayden White's words, Najita asserts that "we require a history that will educate us to discontinuity more than ever before; for discontinuity, disruption, and chaos is our lot."[43] Then a new kind of history, neither being trapped in the universal essence of humanity nor guided by the linear temporality of progression, is capable of attending to many different forms of temporality in ways explored by anthropologists such as Victor Turner. The exploration of heterogeneous temporalities enables us to grasp the "occupants of the fringe" as those who communicate "frequently the most articulate conscious voices of values. . . . These liminal voices include poets, philosophers, dramatists, novelists, painters, prophets, peasant rebels, and shamans."[44] Perceived in this way, "an event is not simply political or institutional action, struggle among competing interests, factional rivalry, coup d'etat, or assassination." Nor is it a "single act or cause that intervenes in a linear series of events. It is a totality of challenges and contestations through which a society with its diverse layers and segments acts on itself."[45] Thus, conflict can be also theorized as constituting "part of a dialectic of social self-reflection and action, of a society consciously acting on itself and on the history it has received."[46]

What Najita proposes here can be summarized as a new historical analysis and narrative that attend to the following: (1) discontinuity engendered by a wide variety of conflicts, not as an aberration but as the generative components of history; (2) the infinite diversity and complexity of historical reality embodied by the multiplicity of temporalities and actors; (3) conflict as the dialectic of agency in terms of the continuous reworking of social self-reflection and action (of thought and practice), as well as the interplay between a society working on itself and on the history it has received (between society's self-transformation and the transformation of the received history that constitutes the basic conditions of the society). Although these proposals clearly presented a much-needed intervention in the field and a fundamental break with the previously available interpretive paradigms, with their devastating deconstruction of the Eurocentric mode of comparative history as well as of its consequential logic of "difference" (anomaly, backwardness, and incompleteness) and politics without politics (nothing much happening in politics except for people's conformism to the status quo or aristocracy's revolutionary actions), some ambiguities remained.

First and foremost, despite Najita's compelling advocacy of attending to the multiplicity of social actors and the multilayered aspects of conflict, because *Conflict in Modern Japanese History* still delimited conflict, or politics, as originating generally from the *conscious* voices of dissent and protest in *major* events, thinkers, and ideologies, it paid little attention to much less conspicuously "political" voices and practices in popular culture and everyday life. "Dramatists, novelists, painters, prophets, and shamans" were not given much attention in the volume, contrary to Najita's important suggestion. Did their absence indicate that they could not be considered, after all, a meaningful constituent of politics? Was it because, after careful examinations and considerations, they turned out not to represent "the most articulate conscious voices of values"? Furthermore, if we follow Najita's advice that these occupants of the margins are to be taken seriously, how should their voices and practices that did not seem consciously and conspicuously political, yet were actually taken to be seriously political by the Tokugawa authorities, be understood as comprising the dialectic of agency?

These ambiguities appear to result from two crucial issues that need to be addressed in a rigorous way: first, how to define politics. More specifically, should politics be understood exclusively in terms of conscious thought and practice? Or should everyday matters such as fashion, appearance, demeanor, sexuality, taste, consumption, and play, as well as their representations in a variety of media (popular novels, prints, theaters, and so on), be considered a crucial part of politics? Second, what does "values" ("articulate voices of values") mean? More specifically, does it exclusively refer to commonly recognizable political values such as justice, freedom, equality, and resistance? Or does it include values articulated or represented in those popular cultural spheres mentioned above? *Conflict in Modern Japanese History* certainly marked a great theoretical and historiographical leap from the old paradigms of historical analysis haunted by the shade of Hegel and modernization theory by introducing a more social, (post)structural understanding of politics and conflict, but these ambiguities might have left a lacuna for Maruyama's interpretation of politics to persist, even to remain influential in the study of early modern cultural politics to this day.

Among the most recent works, Nam-lin Hur's *Prayers and Play in Late Tokugawa Japan* published in 2000 serves as the case in point. Hur's work in many ways is a rich description of the social history of the cultural environs of Asakusa, in particular the Sensōji Temple, a hub of the popular culture of play and prayer in Edo. Its analysis of the socioeconomic system that allowed for the curious coexistence of commercial and religious practices certainly makes an important contribution to our understanding of the structure and dynamic that shaped a characteristic of late Edo society. But when Hur seeks to explain the political implications of the popular culture, Maruyama's language seems to return. Hur writes:

> Commoners sometimes engaged in critiquing the feudal system when they played with the deliberate satire of "mad poetry" (*kyōka*) or short verse (*senryū*), or when they lent disproportionate importance to the different and exotic, thus relativising the importance of hierarchy of Tokugawa society. . . . Through play, autonomous individuals could distance themselves from the culturally imposed social status. . . . Understandably, however, the disengagement from public ideology engendered by the consumption of *asobi* [play] commodities never resulted in a direct collective challenge to the Tokugawa system. . . . It is, therefore, not surprising to find that people's obsession with self-indulgence and self-satisfaction while engaging in their isolated cultural pursuits

was often tinged with gloom and pessimism, for they could not affect the larger social system. . . . In the end, *asobi* activities were an escape from, not a solution for, the discontents feudal society engendered in commoners.[47]

The explanatory model of politics offered by Maruyama unmistakably finds its imprints in Hur's arguments. The ideas of "disengagement" as "escapism," popular culture as the arena of "self-indulgence" and "self-satisfaction," and cultural pursuits as "isolated," and thus "tinged with gloom and pessimism," demonstrate the degree to which Hur's arguments still draw, whether consciously or unconsciously, on the idealist or humanist theory that posits the individual subject born with critical Reason as the basis for politics. Politics, for Hur, is measured exclusively in terms of the individuals' will and ability to "affect," influence, or change social systems. The conscious act of active critique and struggle for greater freedom becomes the absolute horizon for the interpretation of politics, reinforcing Maruyama's characterization of popular culture as an apolitical domain where ordinary people sought "petty satisfaction in ephemeral private freedom." The understanding of the location of culture in Tokugawa politics remains trapped within the language of deficiency, passivity, gloom, pessimism, defeatism, and escapism.

Although Japanese historians of early modern popular culture have approached the above problematic more independently of Maruyama's influence, they seem to have not yet worked out a genuinely novel perspective liberated from the phantom of Hegel.[48] Because many of these scholars are by training students of literature and art, they tend to concentrate exclusively on the textual analysis of burlesque, parody, and satire. They share Hur's observation that there was a widespread literary and visual culture of polished wit and poignant satire directed against the people in power and elites, but they diverge from the judgment that such a culture represented a passive attitude of townspeople's escapism and pessimism. By looking at language and images alone, they posit discontent and criticism expressed in them as the sufficient qualification for the political, without an attempt to understand it in relation to the ideological, socioeconomic and political structures, and their transformations. This isolation of the textual from its social milieus or "built environment" finds itself in the realm of Hegelian idealism, for claiming the politicality of the culture without locating textual form and content in relation to the complex material reality, the diverse structural determinants, is to act out "Hegel's pure principle of consciousness" that reduces the "infinite diversity of history to the singular and universal essence."[49] Politics remains trapped in the abstract concept of consciousness.

Before moving on to a new interpretive perspective that presents an alternative to the idealist/humanist theory, it is critical to clarify that my attempts to problematize the dominant interpretive perspectives are not motivated by a desire to prove that ordinary people were more progressive, independent, or politically conscious than Maruyama and others have allowed. Vindicating ordinary people as the subject of history is not the objective of this study. In fact, to posit the people as the given subject of history and to organize a historical narrative around their progressive image would simply repeat the populism of "history from below" or what Japanese historians call "people's history" (*Minshūshi*). The populist reading of history wishes to decouple history from an elitist standpoint by demonstrating that "it is the people's fundamental vitality that moves history."[50] But to claim that ordinary people also possess the active agency, or that they are the ones who really move history, is simply to reinforce the paradigm of "an empiricism of the subject," for it merely problematizes its elitist assumption, but not its fundamental epistemic assumption that grounds politics on the Hegelian idealism of human essence, namely, the Spirit's journey toward greater freedom. The polarization of elites and masses ironically legitimizes the vision of politics conceptualized exclusively on the basis of how—and how much—self-consciously active individuals influence or change existing social systems. The reversal of the polarity is no more than an attempt to afford unsung "heroes" their place in the pantheon of history next to the luminaries and victorious generals. It is merely an expression of desire spurred by the Hegelian vision of history to overcome the Hegelian polarity of the plenitude of history (the universal, the West, and the elite) and the lack thereof (the peculiar, the non-West, and the subaltern) by realigning the popular to the former of the bipolar. Any historical inquiries, as Gayatri Spivak reminds us in her penetrating critique of Subaltern Studies, need to reckon with the untenability of naïve empiricism, the impossibility of recovering the "lived experience" of the nameless (figures vanished from the master narratives of the past).[51]

I would like to turn to the insight presented in 1937 by a prewar cultural critic and Marxist thinker Tosaka Jun (1900–1945) as a way to suggest a new approach to the historical analysis of early modern cultural politics. To cite Tosaka's somewhat lengthy formulations:

> Popular custom [or culture] is a product of the fundamental structure of society, but it is not vice versa. . . . The essences of social structure obtain exuberant or ugly flesh and skin and finish the final task of putting on costumes through popular custom. . . . But it is never simply a society's custom, convention, or consensus in the ordinary

sense of these words. Nor is it what is generically called trend. Popular custom not only designates the fact that the majority of the people tend to do a certain thing together, but it also reveals that this very fact works as a regulatory force, as a moral and ethical authority, and thus incites the pleasure of conformity among those who follow it. . . . Fashion, demeanors, appearance, sexuality, and mannerism of ladyship and gentlemanship are all connected consistently with the ritualism and solemnity of ruling power. They all carry specific moral implications. . . . This is why the disruption of popular custom is seen as anti-social . . . and it raises great concerns for political moralists and police authorities. . . . It is dangerous to accept the common assumption that popular custom is an expression or a manifestation of the [collective] thought of nation or "nationality" as if it were a seamless whole organically formed by an agglomeration of individuals. . . . In other words, the point I am making here is a seemingly commonsensical conclusion that popular custom carries with it a moral essence and constitutes a particular form of thought.[52]

Tosaka's insistence that popular custom or culture should be understood as a distinct product of social structure's formation is of great importance. By arguing against the commonly held view that popular culture constitutes a natural basis for collective thought and national community, Tosaka rejects the organicist theory of culture and proposes a social understanding of it. If the organicist theory renders popular culture into a foundation of national community, into a reified category of collective identity, Tosaka seeks to locate it in a complex ensemble of social relations or structures to underscore the regulatory force the culture exercises via its moral and ethical authority. Tosaka's observation of the close link between popular culture and "the ritualism and solemnity of ruling power," as well as his formulation of the culture as carrying "with it a moral essence and constitute[ing] a particular form of thought" that "incites the pleasure of conformity among those who follow it," comes very close to the ideological effects theorized by Antonio Gramsci and Louis Althusser. (I will return to this point in a moment. It suffices to say that ideology for Gramsci and Althusser does not mean a form of deception, lie, or false consciousness about the reality, but rather both discourse and practice that work as a constitutive material force of the reality—the "lived experience.")

The unique reality of popular culture is exactly the way in which a specific configuration of social relations not only appears but also actually reproduced and lived—as it provides social structures with "exuberant or ugly flesh and skin" and helps them "finish the final task of putting on costumes through fashion, demeanors, appearance, sexuality, and mannerism of ladyship and gentlemanship"—as the given reality in the form of "common sense" (Gramsci) or "the unconscious" (Althusser).[53] In other words, popular culture is a complex field where relations of power—"essences of social structure"—not only manifest themselves as a surface phenomenon but also are actually lived by people on a daily basis as an unconscious or commonsensical reality.

Yet, according to Tosaka, this outwardly given reality of popular culture does not always remain self-evident as it is constantly "disrupted"—evaluated and reconceived—through diverse and divergent literary and artistic representations of the culture, especially its moral authority. Tosaka continues to write:

> But this conclusion alerts us to the unique characteristic of the social reality of popular custom—a characteristic that not only calls attention to a social and historical nature of the popular, but illuminates the theoretical importance of the logic and function of literature with regard to the concepts, representations, and categories [the literature deploys]. . . . The attractiveness of romance novels, for instance, stems from the realistic tone that the narrative of the story creates. This realism speaks to how the narrative represents the reality of popular custom. . . . The attractiveness of literary representation is determined by the ways in which the representation disrupts or reinforces the widely received morality.[54]

For Tosaka, art, especially literature, has a special place in popular culture for playing a dual, contradictory role of affirming and transforming and reinforcing and disrupting the received moral authorities inscribed in the culture. (This position is identical with those of Raymond Williams and Fredric Jameson. Again, I will elaborate this point below.) Tosaka's formulation of popular culture as the site of contradictory social formation—both regulatory and transformative—points to the important materialist concept of politics. Neither does the monadic individual's will toward consciousness of freedom nor the collective spirit of individuals constitutes the foundation of the possibility for politics. But politics emerges from the sphere of popular culture and custom, that is, an everyday social formation of structural relations where the dialectic of power unfolds: it both generates its regulatory effects via moralizing discourse and practice and weakens its ground through non- and antinormative literary and artistic imagination and representation. The popular culture and custom reveal contradictory attitudes toward dominant values and conducts by simultaneously reinforcing and disrupting them. The unity of society in this sphere not only can never be assumed but also is incessantly confronted with its own disunity and fragmentation.

This concept of social formation of power is critical for my analysis of the politics of Edo popular culture because it was, I argue, the culture's conscious and unconscious articulation (especially in its literary and artistic forms) of the "ruptural unity," or "a "fusion of an accumulation," of contradictions in and of dominant ideological and socioeconomic structures that made itself a salient symptom of "crises" widely felt from the middle of the Tokugawa period onward.[55]

This view is obtained from my appropriative reading of Tosaka's theory of popular culture and custom, especially his idea of the duality of the culture, via Althusser's elucidation of contradiction as a historically overdetermined condition, Volosinov's concept of sign, William's discussion of the role of art and literature, and Jameson's symptomatic reading of cultural politics. Let me conclude here by briefly explaining this interpretive perspective intended to offer an alternative to that of liberal humanism. Overdetermination, according to Althusser, is "the effect of the contradictions in each practice constituting the social formation on the social formation as a whole, and hence back on each practice and each contradiction, defining the pattern of domination and subordination, antagonism and non-antagonism of the contradictions in the structure in dominance at any given historical moment."[56] In other words, overdetermination explains the historical contingency of the social formation as determined by multiple contradictions, especially in the dominant structure (the structure in dominance). But this dominant structure is only one of many structures, each of which has its own dynamics of contradiction, constituting the infinitely complex whole, and it is not fixed but varies according to how and how much the contradictions in and of the dominant structure are overdetermined by other contradictions and how their uneven development (i.e., domination and subordination, antagonism and nonantagonism) unfolds. The structure is displaced by a crisis or revolutionary change occasioned by the "condensation" and the "ruptural unity" of contradictions.[57] Such an occurrence depends on whether a condensation of contradictions remains at the level of "antagonism" or whether the ruptural unity of contradictions reaches its "explosive" level. In the state of "normalcy," the overdetermination of a contradiction remains dispersed and thus has yet to congeal into such a nodality. These different phases do not follow the chain of any particular causal law or developmental path. An understanding of crisis in any given space and time, for Althusser, requires a *historical* analysis of "many conditions of the existence of the complex whole itself."[58] Here, there is neither dogmatic division of base and superstructure nor the privileging of the former over the latter, as the orthodox Marxist paradigm often posits. "Each practice" that constitutes a structure engenders a distinct logic of contradiction in the complex whole, but by the virtue of constituting part of the complex whole, it is the condition of existence of all other practices that have their respective forms of contradictions. In this regard, his concept of structure is different from the Hegelian totality that "presupposes an original, primary essence that lies behind the complex appearance that it has produced by externalization in history; it is a structure with a center."[59] For Hegel, each element constituting the whole exists simply as a phenomenon or an epiphenomenon of the universal essence (Spirit), thus expressing always the organic totality. Althusserian structure or totality, on the contrary, is constituted by the *uneven and transformative relations*—or *mediation*—that exist among practices and elements, revealing many sites of contradictions, thus with no center, only a dominant element.[60] And those relations (mediations) are neither defined by the logic of homology nor regulated by a timeless essence and a telos. Instead, they are historically formed. This is why Althusser warns that, while his theory of the difference of contradictions is crucial to the understanding of the complex whole as constituted by the multitudes of contradictions and their uneven development, it does not lead us to the conclusion that social reality is infinitely random or "equivocal."[61] What the materialist reading of history can achieve then is to unpack multiple sites of contradictions and their uneven relations that generate a social formation and that provoke the transformations of structure(s).

What is valuable about Althusser's conception of overdetermination for my analysis of Edo popular culture is the perspective that enables me to explain the centrality of culture as a political issue and analyze it as a nodal point (functioning both as effect and catalyst) of the whole complex of relations of contradictions, as a site where contradictions are *condensed* (effect) and *articulated* (catalyst). Not only does this concept forsake the reductive understanding of culture within the law of economic determinism—whether the economy is the sole determinant in any given historical formation—as simply reflecting or expressing the economy (i.e., a reductive concept of class consciousness), but it suggests a way to think of culture as a distinct yet deeply interrelated structure with other structures, especially the structure in dominance (i.e., the Tokugawa system that consisted of social, economic, political, ideological, and legal structures). It is precisely this theoretical perspective of overdetermination that makes it possible to probe the politicality of culture beyond the idealist/humanist definition of the free-willed individual subject—the abstract subjectivity—as the foundation for the possibility of politics.

But my formulation of the analysis of (Edo popular) culture based on the concept of overdetermination requires one important qualification: the problem of *articulation*–how what Tosaka called the duality of culture unfolds at a certain historical conjuncture—in the Althusserian paradigm. How do the multitudes of contradictions, their ruptural unity, their uneven relations, and the tensions and conflicts stemming from those contradictions get articulated? How is articulation itself overdetermined by contradictions and their uneven relations? Although Althusser never delved into these questions, there are some clues in his discussion of ideology as to how these questions may be approached within the logical parameter of overdetermination. Althusser understands ideology in a dual sense: it is "a structure essential to the historical life of societies" (unconsciousness)—"not an aberration or a contingent excrescence of History"—yet one that can be simultaneously transformed "into an instrument of deliberate action on history" through "the recognition of its necessity" (consciousness).[62] For Althusser, "[i]t is *in* ideology," *in* the *un*conscious, that humans "*become conscious* of their place in the world and in history."[63] His recognition of the duality of ideology—as the "perceived-accepted" structure into which humans are born and live their world and as the instrument that humans mobilize to act on history—opens up the possibility of conceiving of ideology as an overdetermined field of signification, especially as a field wherein signification gives rise to divergent and contestatory articulations of society as a complex whole.[64] It is in accordance with this logic, I believe, that Althusser defined ideology as the "overdetermined unity of the real relation and the imaginary relation between (men) and their real conditions of existence." "In ideology," argues Althusser,

> the (real) relation (between men and their real conditions of existence) is inevitably invested in the imaginary relation, a relation that *expresses a will* (conservative, conformist, reformist or revolutionary), a hope or a nostalgia, rather than describing it. It is in this overdetermination of the real by the imaginary and of the imaginary by the real that ideology is *active* in principle, that it reinforces or modifies the relation between men and their conditions of existence.[65]

The problem of Althusser's formulation is his tendency to associate the active forces of ideology, or the variant forms of articulation,—"expression," "reinforcement," or "modification"—exclusively with the ruling class and the ruling ideology. It does not offer how such an overdetermined interplay between the real and the imaginary in the articulation of "lived experience" ("the way people live the relation between them and their conditions of existence") may inadvertently produce divergent and contestatory articulations.[66] For Althusser, ideology remains a monolith as well as a privileged site for dominant power. In other words, his theory is, in Terry Eagleton's words, "too monistic, passing over the discrepant, contradictory ways in which subjects may be ideologically accosted—partially, wholly, or hardly at all—by discourses which themselves form no obvious cohesive unity." [67]

The theory of language by M. M. Bakhtin/V. N. Volosinov supplements the problem of articulation seen in Althusser's formulation of ideology, thus providing a theoretical acumen to Tosaka's idea of the duality of culture.[68] Volosinov conceptualizes signification, or the practice of meaning, as "a function of the sign," "the expression of a semiotic relationship between a particular piece of reality and another kind of reality that it stands for, represents, or depicts."[69] And the expression of a semiotic relationship is not univocal but creates multiple "social accents,"[70] or various value orientations, because the sign is "itself a material segment of reality" that is inseparably linked with "concrete forms of social interaction" conditioned by "the pressures of the social struggle."[71] In other words, each sign is inevitably invested in overdetermined social realities ("contradictions and their uneven development" in Althusser's words) and thus conveys conflicting and contentious social values and perspectives as reflected and refracted in the complex and contradictory conditions of existence. Volosinov calls the multiplicity of accent of a sign the "multiaccentuality of the ideological sign."[72] Based on this concept, Volosinov sees idioms, jargons, and rhetoric (i.e., curse, praise, irony, satire, parody, and mockery as in the case of Edo popular culture), as well as visual images (i.e., iconography), as constituting the site where "differently oriented accents intersect in every ideological sign."[73] "As a result," Volosinov states, "sign becomes an arena of the class struggle," or more broadly social conflict.[74] He concludes:

> In actual fact, each living ideological sign has two faces, like Janus. Any current curse word can become a word of praise, any current truth must inevitably sound to many other people as the greatest lie. This *inner dialectical quality* of the sign comes out fully in the open only in times of social crises or revolutionary changes.[75]

The concept of multiaccentuality supplements Althusser's overdetermination in that it elucidates the sign, whether literal, verbal, or visual, as a form of overdetermination of *meaning,* which is capable of articulating overdetermined social realities. Volosinov's formulation of social accent points to the understanding of society as composed of a multitude of enunciations of contradictions and their uneven relations. But, more importantly, it helps explain how these enunciations of contradictions are always accompanied by voices of *contention* and *contestation* over the conditions of social reality.

I believe that Raymond Williams developed in *Marxism and Literature* the now well-known concept of "the structure of feeling" based in part on Bakhtin/Volosinov's discussions of language in order to theorize the moment of emergent articulation. Williams uses this concept to elucidate the social process in which "practical consciousness" or "lived experience" finds a form/sign that can articulate it in a most persuasive way. Practical consciousness refers to "the experiences to which the fixed *forms* do not speak at all, which indeed they do not recognize."[76] It is, according to Williams, "often indeed not yet recognized as social, but taken to be private, idiosyncratic, and even isolating, but which in analysis has its emergent, connecting, and dominant characteristics."[77] This consciousness soon finds a language first "through *forms* and *conventions* in art and literature."[78]

Williams's theory suggested a novel way to consider the social formation of articulation by establishing the dynamic link between sign/form and consciousness, but it overlooks Bakhtin/Volosinov's crucial insight about the reciprocal relation between sign and overdetermined social realities. Williams's exclusive emphasis on the problem of consciousness could be considered a return to an idealist/humanist tradition, and indeed, he has very little to say about the relation(s) among political, economic, and cultural formations. In this regard, Fredric Jameson's work on postmodernism provides a useful model for how to approach this problematic.[79] By identifying distinctively postmodern aesthetic forms of representation in various media, Jameson shows the interface between postmodern cultural formations and the logic of late capitalism. "The base," as Jameson puts it, "in the third stage of capitalism, generates its superstructures with a new kind of dynamic."[80] Through his repeated emphasis on the postmodern's distinct place in history, Jameson makes the postmodern moment an exemplary case of what Althusser calls the "great lesson of practice (history)," which is that "if the structure in dominance remains constant, the disposition of the roles within it changes; the principle contradiction becomes a secondary one, a secondary contradiction takes its place."[81] Indeed, Jameson draws on Althusser's "structure in dominance" in reference to capitalism and uses his insistence on a certain "semi-autonomy" of the various elements of the structure, including theory, ideology, and politics, from the realm of the economic to explain the shift in the principle contradiction. In fact, Jameson seems to view, following Williams's claim, the contradictions within the cultural or aesthetic world as the principle contradiction of our time (of course, "our" here refers to those who live in societies of late capitalism), insofar as they shape and prefigure any political praxis. His observation of mediatic art forms as the site of principle contradiction is based on his conviction that they urge us to reflect on the conditions of existence under late capitalism both "positively and negatively all at once."[82]

Jameson's observation of aesthetic practice as playing a crucial role in stimulating dialectical reflections on the historicity of late capitalism echoes, as explained earlier, Tosaka's theory of popular culture and the way I see the unique roles played by popular cultural forms (parody, comic realism, and grotesque realism) in late Tokugawa politics. I ague that it is through analytic attentiveness to and rigorous examination of *forms* and *their symptomatic implications* that we may begin to understand the complex relation between culture and politics in early modern Japan, and overcome the idealist assumption of (individual) consciousness as the absolute horizon for politics.[83]

ONE

Strategies of Containment and Their Aporia

Ideologies and mystifications are based upon real life, yet at the same time they disguise or transpose that real life.

HENRI LEFEBVRE, *CRITIQUE OF EVERYDAY LIFE*

The appearance of an alternative symbolic universe poses a threat because its very existence demonstrates empirically that one's own universe is less than inevitable.

PETER L. BERGER AND THOMAS LUCKMANN, *THE SOCIAL CONSTRUCTION OF REALITY*

The Tokugawa shogunate (1603–1868)—the shogun and his top echelon of advisers and officials—had since its establishment considered domesticating the body as an integral part of the complex set of strategies required to construct and maintain social order. Within two decades of its rise to power, the shogunate implemented a series of policies aiming to regulate popular practices and spectacles that threatened to subvert a specific meaning and function it sought to endow on the body. Kabuki dancing (*kabuki odori* 歌舞伎踊り)—the early form of female kabuki performance initiated by Okuni of Izumo and her troupe—was outlawed because its transvestism and "unduly" erotic choreography were viewed as inciting "debaucheries among high and low" and for perturbing core moral values that the shogunate exalted to consolidate new social order.[1] A new form of kabuki (*wakashūu kabuki* 若衆歌舞伎) that used male youths in place of banned female dancers met with the same repressive measures. Tokugawa authorities judged the youths' erotic female impersonations to be "corrupt," "perverse," and "licentious," and accused the young actors of enticing their patrons to commit the "irremissible sins of male-male love."[2] The *kabuki-mono* (かぶきもの, which, in its literary sense, meant a person with idiosyncratic appearance and unrestrained or nonconformist behavior), from whom the term kabuki was said to be derived, also became targets. These men and women roved the streets of castle towns with ostentatious appearances and, at times, insolent behavior and were apprehended by the authorities for spreading "lawlessness" and disrupting "public morals."[3] Other entertainers such as itinerant female shamans, dancers, blind street diviners, fishmongers, and puppeteer-prayer nuns, who made a living by offering both religious and sexual services and thus bore very little social stigma during the medieval period, were also forced to settle as "prostitutes" in fringe areas of castle towns, transportation nodes, or commercial routes as part of the shogunate's policies of delineating palpable social boundaries for the construction of "proper" mores.[4] By the mid-seventeenth century, all these itinerant entertainers and "delinquents" would be incorporated as bottom rungs in the social hierarchy: as outcasts called *hinin* (nonhuman), a status equivalent to that of beggars and vagrants. They would be confined within the walls of prisons or such specially designated areas as entertainment districts located at the margins of cities, so that "their perilous influence on the larger social whole" could be controlled and contained.[5]

Despite the Tokugawa authorities' incessant attempts to segregate and contain the undesirable body, by the early eighteenth century, there emerged through popular literary and visual imaginations in major castle towns, in particular in Edo (present-day Tokyo), a variegated, novel representation of the body, which was antithetical to the official conception of the ideal body. The popular imagination foregrounded "unproductive," "idle" bodies immersed in the culture of pleasure and play associated with various forms of entertainment, including kabuki, that had been regulated, if not proscribed, and reviled by the shogunate for diffusing "follies" and "debaucheries."[6] The authorities took punitive measures, albeit fitfully, against those who produced, disseminated, and consumed the new forms of culture and entertainment, but people in Edo continued to explore and celebrate the new possibilities that these playful and provocative bodily images presented.

But what were the historical implications or connotations of the proliferation of a novel representation of the body that defied the officially prescribed body? Did it suggest that the shogunate's earlier strategies of building and maintaining social order through the domestication of the body had lost their efficacy? Did it also then represent a new historical situation in which the mechanism of the shogunate's power and domination was rendered obsolete? If so, what were the historical conditions that contributed to the waning potency of Tokugawa rule? Furthermore, did the new representation of the body constitute part of the growing historical consciousness that recognized the increasingly conspicuous and irreparable disjuncture between the ideological premise and the ongoing social and economic transformations of Tokugawa Japan, a consciousness articulated by critically minded intellectuals from the early eighteenth century onward?[7] If so, how did popular cultural imaginations of the body communicate such a consciousness?

Tokugawa Ideology: Configuring the Body in the New Social Order

What guided the Tokugawa regime's strategies during its early formative years to contain the undesirable body epitomized by kabuki, kabukimono, and semireligious itinerant entertainers was its commitment to creating a populace whose daily endeavors would be devoted to the task of contributing to the preservation of social harmony, a task that the regime proclaimed to be the most fundamental moral duty for every single person living in Tokugawa Japan. The means through which one was expected to perform this duty varied, depending on one's designated place in society. During Tokugawa times, every individual was born with a predetermined status (*mibun* 身分) and a particular occupation (*shokubun* 職分or *yaku* 役) that corresponded to that status within the matrix of hereditary social relations. From the womb to the tomb, individuals carried supposedly unalterable markers, or "social tattoos," reflected in their speech, appearance, and habitation, which signified their permanent belonging to a given group and social function.[8]

This highly rigid classificatory system was devised to institute and perpetuate the hierarchical arrangement of authority and to facilitate the interdependent relations of material production. Peasants and artisans were allotted manual work and merchants served a distributive function, while the ruling samurai status groups held bureaucratic responsibility for monitoring and regulating the mechanisms of production and distribution. In practice, of course, these distinctions were not always observed with strict consistency; functions of commerce and material production were more frequently merged in the same person from the eighteenth century onward.[9] But the general distinction was not on that account to be overlooked.[10] The classificatory scheme set up by the founders of Tokugawa Japan to organize people into different status categories and to require them to perform assigned productive functions constituted an essential part of the system of rule designed to lubricate the social hierarchy's interdependent relations.

Given this reproductive configuration of social relations of production, the shogunate swiftly discerned that the body—especially that of the common person—should be understood exclusively in terms that were both moral and utilitarian: the body was valuable only as an instrument satisfying through its productive function the moral imperative to preserve social unity. Measuring commoners' existential worth by how—and how much—they contributed through industrious devotion to the social whole, the shogunate placed peasantry engaging in the most laborious work higher than artisans and merchants in the status hierarchy and relegated the merchants whose work was considered to be least onerous, even "parasitic" by some, to the bottom of that hierarchy.[11] And, "outside of" or "beneath" the formal structure (*seigaisha* 制外者 or *jingaisha* 人外者), there was the populace—entertainers, prostitutes, and vagrants—bearing the outcast status of "nonhuman" whose activities were considered to be utterly unproductive by the shogunate. The status hierarchy therefore reflected the Tokugawa government's core ideological value that the productiveness of one's body was the prerequisite for one to be accredited with moral worth and "humanity."

It is no coincidence that around the same time the shogunate set out to contain the undesirable body—the early seventeenth century—influential ideologues such as Suzuki Shōzan (1579–1655) and Yamazaki Ansai (1618–82) began extensively writing and promulgating their deprecating views of the body. Suzuki, an ex-samurai Zen Buddhist monk and ardent spokesperson for the shogunate, theorized the body in an absolutely negative light and limited its meaning and function to an idea of duty that called for selfless and industrious devotion to the well being of the whole. In his essays, Suzuki pressed the idea that the cardinal truth for humans to recognize and accept was the utter worthlessness of their bodies. "If one knew how impure the body is," Suzuki wrote, "how could one ever attach any importance to it? It is a conglomeration of filth, that is, fluids of eyes and nose, urines and feces, the five entrails—not one of these is clean." Furthermore, he continued, "the body is compounded of suffering," but people "believe it to be a source of pleasure. . . . Where does suffering come from? Only from love of the body."[12] For Suzuki, the body was not only impure and filthy but also plagued by desires and passions, and this disturbing truth was the underlying cause of human beings' distressing conditions: "It all too often happens that the sensual self becomes the fortified headquarters of the desires. Then the mind becomes an unenlightened master [that produces] bad karma and destroys the self. Such a mind is our enemy. This body is a bag of desires."[13] Low and useless as filth, the body should never be perceived in a positive light unless it strived to fulfill the moral duty of contributing to the whole through hard work. Peasants, according to Suzuki, must not think that they "need leisure to pray for Rebirth" because "people realize Buddhahood only by tormenting both body and mind in their quest for enlightenment." For Suzuki, only by "work[ing] painfully hard as [they] assault body and mind," could peasants keep their mind "untroubled" and thereby reach the state of Buddhahood.[14]

As for merchants, Suzuki went on to explain, they must "[b]ear clearly in mind that in the business of buying and selling [they] fear this [heaven's punishment for their selfish and greedy deeds], and only in casting off all personal desire, can [they] function as an officer entrusted by heaven with assuring free flow [of goods] throughout the land." "Offer this body to the world," Suzuki implored merchants, "and make up your mind that what you do is only for the sake of the land and of the whole."[15] For both peasants and merchants to effectively perform their public duties, Suzuki concluded, they must succeed in regulating, even negating the corporeality of their existence, that is, "forgetting the body."[16] Ascetic life realized through rigorous self-discipline was thus a prerequisite for every Tokugawa subject to follow.

Similarly, Yamazaki Ansai, a synthesizer of Shinto and Neo-Confucianism and a principal contributor to the formation of Tokugawa ideology, advocated the strict regulation of the bodily self. Placing an exclusive emphasis on the virtues of "reverence" (*kei* 敬), by which he meant "restraint, discretion, deference, prudence, and self-control," as a way to keep the purity of one's mind, Yamazaki told his followers that reverence "dominates the entire life of the mind because it regulates all activities and disciplines the body."[17] When facing difficulties in keeping the whole of the bodily self under the mind's control, "one must struggle through quiet sitting to the point of spitting blood."[18] Yamazaki's formulation of repressive rigorism was the normative basis of Tokugawa Neo-Confucian thought: for the purpose of subduing what Neo-Confucians viewed as the disturbing human reality—the animality of the body, it advocated, in a manner similar to Zen Buddhists, such mottoes as "abiding by stillness," "abiding in oneness without motion," and "control of the floating mind," and resorted to "quiet sitting" (*seiza* 静座), or "meditation," as a means of self-discipline or "self-cultivation."[19]

Underpinning the official conception of the body, as expressed in writings by both Suzuki and Yamazaki, was language that drew a sharp distinction between the mind and the body. Abstract thought and moral cultivation were regarded as the expression of the individual's higher self and the higher reality, while sensual or corporeal experience was an inevitable yet lower reality—a shifting, uncertain, disorderly world of appearances, ephemeral and uncontrollable. This binary formulation divided the world into a high mental reality and a low material reality, stripping the mortal body of its spiritual truths and assimilating it into the mass of things. Yet, because humans were schematized as beings possessing minds, who thus occupied a status superior to that of animals, they were figured as residing in an ambivalent place between the mental and the material. If the mortal body was completely assimilated into the mental, human reality was sacred, but that reality was profane insofar as the mental was held captive by the sensual. Thus, the ideologues of the Tokugawa shogunate insisted that the higher reality of the mind had to vanquish the body and its senses—or at least regulate them by subordinating them to its sovereignty.[20]

These stark binary oppositions of body and mind paralleled the ideological notion that the ruling class embodied the higher realm of the mental self, whereas commoners belonged to the lower realm of the corporeal self. Much as the mind was given a sovereign position from which it could make the body conform to its commands and its truths, the samurai class assumed a position enabling it to rule and regulate the common classes. Suzuki Shōzan, in the treatise discussed above, adamantly maintained that "[o]rdinary people must first recognize that they are sick. . . . the diseases of greed and wrong views abide there [within their mind], as do those of laxity and iniquity." "So do not undertake the means," Suzuki warned, "which goes beyond your capacity and your station in life. . . . Horses are horses, cattle are cattle, and fowl are fowl; and each has its own role." Only those who are capable of attaining "victory over the teeming thoughts" should "ride above all things. . . . Such a man is not an ordinary man but a man I call a follower of the Way [samurai]."[21]

Similarly, Yamaga Sokō (1622–85), a samurai turned Confucian scholar who wrote one of the earliest theoretical treatises on the samurai's distinctive role and identity titled *The Way of Samurai* (*Shidō* 士道), offered a clearer definition of the relationship between ruler and subject as follows: "should there be someone in the three classes of common people [peasants, artisans, and merchants] who transgresses against these moral principles [loyalty, duty, and respect], the samurai summarily punishes him and thus upholds proper moral principles in the land. . . . The three classes of common people make him their teacher and respect him. By following his teachings, they are enabled to understand what is fundamental and what is secondary."[22] In this characteristic depiction by samurai intellectuals, commoners were represented as incapable of moral conduct, self-discipline, and self-reliance, and must therefore obey the moral and intellectual injunction of the ruling elites.[23]

It was this official rhetoric of commoners' lack of moral competence and of their troubling propensity toward corporeal pleasure that allowed the shogunate to claim the mandate to impose stringent regulations on the body and to make it serve the social whole as a productive instrument. The mind-body binary opposition thus legitimated the logic of not only absolute social hierarchy but also the division of labor between the ruling samurai and common people: because of their superior moral and intellectual faculty, the samurai were suited to rule through mental labor, whereas the commoners must abide by their rulers' directives through manual labor—material production and distribution—due to their intrinsic moral and intellectual shortcomings. The ideological discourse providing a rationale for the legitimization of a static, frozen social hierarchy worked to anchor nonsamurai subjects to an instrumental body required to perform, through the punctilious observance of frugality and discipline, a singular duty: providing the material conditions necessary for the samurai's existence and dominance.

Daniel Botsman's elucidation of the symbolic function of the body in "the complex set of strategies of ordering society and exercising power" affirms the significant status given to the body within the ideological structure of the Tokugawa polity.[24] By setting up a multilayered system of corporeal punishments, including the public display of criminals' severed heads, Botsman argues, the shogunate aimed to domesticate the body to have it reflect the social order and public morality positively in its appearance and conduct. When the body hovered over or traversed the boundary between order and disorder, the shogunate took the prompt and extreme measure of stamping on it the brutal marks of punishment so as to bring it back into conformity with the expectations of "appropriate" behavior. Thus, the horrifying spectacle of tortured and executed bodies realized the dual effect of maintaining social order and valorizing the moral authority and physical power that the samurai regime held over the rest of society. The body, in short, played the decisive role in reproducing the normative order as a concrete sign through which order and disorder in their oppositional nexus played against each other. Botsman perceptively calls this mechanism of social control the shogunate's "system of bodies-as-signs."[25]

What needs to be added to Botsman's semiotic analysis of the body is the question of how the "system of bodies-as-signs" was intertwined inseparably with the moral imperatives of the productive body. The samurai regime's rendering of the body as a physical manifestation of norms and rules reflected the keen awareness that the regime's long-term survival depended on the extent to which the body could be successfully conceptualized and mobilized as a productive force. For example, through its obstinate and sustained efforts to enforce the ideals of simplicity (*shisso* 質素) and frugality (*ken'yaku* 倹約), as well as loyalty-duty (*chūkō* 忠孝), via sumptuary laws and decrees, the shogunate aimed not only to uphold the symbolic relations of status but also to ensure steady material production through the body's reification of austerity and discipline.[26] Given the fact that representations of rigid binary oppositions such as mind/body, reason/passion, order/disorder, and ruler/subject were all linked closely to the representation of another binary, mental/manual labor, it is essential to interrogate the complex relations of the symbolic and the material for our understanding of how social order was organized and power was exercised during the Tokugawa period.[27]

To probe further the implications of the new bodily images that emerged against the discursive economy of Tokugawa ideology and the shogunate's strategies of containment, it would be useful here to recall Fredric Jameson's dialectical formulations of ideology. Jameson draws in part on György Lukács's concept of ideology as a form of synecdoche, a form that takes the part for the whole, that is, that renders a partial, limited view as representing a totality. This view of social totality that prevails among the bourgeoisie is, for Lukács, a dire effect of socioeconomic conditions—reification or commodity fetishism—that structurally constrain that class's imagination and practice by dislocating and fragmenting its experiences.[28] Lukács's theory of ideology differs from that of an orthodox Marxism in that it defines ideology as a symptom of the objective circumstance called reification rather than as a form of false consciousness in the sense of a lie or an illusion about the reality in which people live. In other words, for Lukács, ideology is an integral part of established reality in that it is immanent in and an essential condition for the functioning of reality. Jameson draws on Lukács in taking ideology not as simply a lie or an illusion but "as the approximation of some [partial] truth about the totality that, given the limitations always imposed by the historical process, stands in for the deeper truth it exists to deny."[29] But Jameson takes a further step, by following an Althusserian notion of history, to reconceive Lukács's idea of the totality/history by defining it as an "absent cause," too complex an entity to be encapsulated or captured by any forms of representation.[30] In this regard, any sweeping claim to the complete intelligibility, or any ideal representation of it, is an ideological gesture. Indeed, for Jameson, ideology always seeks to put a closure to the incertitude and indeterminacy of history and to contain it within the limits of its own terms of absolute coherence while "repressing the unthinkable which lies beyond [those limits]." Jameson thus defines ideology as "strategies of containment."[31]

These strategies of containment can be in turn, according to Jameson, "unmasked by confrontation with the ideal of totality," that is, thinking through the unthinkable, or imagining through the unimaginable, because the limitations of the ideal are made visible (and thus denaturalized) only when what the ideal represses (the unthinkable/the unimaginable) is articulated.[32] What makes Jameson's theory of ideology particularly valuable for my interpretations of the cultural politics of late Tokugawa Japan is his recognition of totality as an uncanny effect of representation whose ideal projection is a constitutive element of social order and yet one that simultaneously remains vulnerable to threats posed by what the projection represses or marginalizes—often material realities of socioeconomic overdetermination and cultural forms articulating such realities that fundamentally contradict the representation's internal logic of coherence. This theorization of ideology helps us understand why the shogunate viewed the blatant celebration and valorization of "idle" bodies—an essential figure of the unthinkable—in Edo popular culture as impairing its projection of Tokugawa society as a harmonious, self-enclosed, perfectly functioning universe.

In Tokugawa Japan, the ideal of totality was explicated through a politically composed version of the theory of "cosmic-human unity" (*tenjin sōkan setsu* 天人相関説). Referring to Hayashi Razan (1583–1657), a Neo-Confucian scholar who contributed to the early construction of Tokugawa ideology, Herman Ooms summarizes his theory of the social order as follows: "The order. . . . is a hierarchical social order where the upper and the lower, the exalted and the vulgar, keep their place, just as in nature, where Heaven is above and Earth is below. The Sage Kings who received Heaven originally defined this hierarchical stability as the fundamental principle of Heaven and Earth, the will of Heaven."[33] Assuming an uninterrupted continuum between extraterrestrial and earthly worlds, the ideologues of the Tokugawa state projected timeless, inviolable, and harmonious images of the cosmos onto the human social order, and thereby presented the new order of things as naturally given. This strategy was intended to purge any possibility of social mobility and transformation or the consciousness of such a possibility by effecting a "genesis amnesia," in which the accidental and treacherous formations of the new polity were consigned to oblivion.[34] The founders of the state, having emerged from the plight of extreme social fluidity and fragmentation called *gekokujō* (the lower supplanting the upper) characteristic of the Warring States periods that had lasted for a century, were haunted by the terrifying possibility of everlasting civil warfare and were therefore determined, by enacting the self-occultation of its historical origins, to establish an incontestable system of perpetual power under the name of "Great Peace" (*taihei no yo* 太平の世). Bringing peace and stability to the war-torn society provided the Tokugawa regime with a politically and ideologically viable ground for proclaiming its rise to power to be a Heavenly mandate. By approximating the unprecedented achievement of unifying the country, the new state fashioned itself in the image of inviolable, righteous, and benevolent ruler who faithfully followed direct injunctions from Heaven. Accordingly, the new hierarchical configuration of social order was transposed onto a cosmic plane, which aided in restructuring the postwarring society in such a way as to make individual subjects understand or imagine their lives or experiences in relationship not to the process of social formation, but to transpersonal and immutable realities that existed beyond the vicissitudes of history. The theory of the cosmic-human unity offered, in short, a totalizing vision of society in which corporeal realities were reified as part of Nature, and history was thus denied or repressed.

The shogunate's attempts to build the new system of totality through the projection of eternal time and natural order were bound up with the assumptions it held about economy. First, the shogunate considered that the accumulation of wealth was "a zero-sum game" because "wealth could only be redistributed, not created."[35] Second, wealth could consequently be accumulated only through coercive means such as taxation or self-disciplinary means such as hard work and thrift. And lastly, given the view of wealth as limited and scarce resources, wealth must be redistributed not on the grounds of an egalitarian principle but in line with the hierarchical arrangement of authority. This restrictive view of economy was most clearly elucidated in 1725 by Ogyū Sorai (1666–1728), a renowned Confucian scholar who served as an advisor to the fifth shogun Tokugawa Tsunayoshi (1646–1709) and wrote extensively about politics in the last decade of his life:

The amount of goods to be produced is generally limited. How much rice can be produced in the entire land of Japan? How much millet can be produced? How much lumber can be made available? Every good in this world has limited quantity. Those of fine quality in particular are few, while coarse goods are many. Therefore, it would be perfectly logical to establish institutions whereby one has people of venerable status use the fine goods (from clothing, to food, to housing) and those of base status the poor goods because the number of the former by nature is small while that of the latter is large, that is, the fewer people use the fewer things and the more numerous people use the more numerous things. All the things available in this country will be used to the full extent by all the people to satisfy their respective needs.[36]

The only way the shogunate could legitimize the idea of this fundamental unevenness in wealth and its distribution and consumption was to naturalize it by transposing hierarchical social relations onto a cosmic plane and representing them as immune from forces of historical change. In other words, it could justify the disproportionate economic relations only by supplying a normative dignity (cosmic-human unity) to the hierarchical arrangement of social relations.

Furthermore, what enabled the shogunate to reinforce its claim on "natural" or "inevitable" unevenness was the official discourse that moralized the observation of the given hierarchies. Leading intellectuals, as seen above, helped elaborate on the notion that upholding the hierarchies was the highest ethical conduct required of every Tokugawa subject, and in doing so, they were instrumental in naturalizing and universalizing unevenness in socioeconomic relations. The ruling samurai elite's demand for heavy taxes, hard labor, and subservience from lower status groups was thus rationalized as a wholly lawful act on a moral ground.

It comes as no surprise that based on this economic principle the Tokugawa authorities regarded conspicuous or exorbitant consumption—the most emblematic of "idleness"—by people of lower status as a clear indication of anarchy and governmental failure, as well as a direct cause of social conflict. Sorai summarized this view in the same treatise:

If our institutions [whereby wealth is distributed according to the status hierarchy] fail, a vast number of lowly people will start acquiring fine goods, which will result in a dramatic increase in the price of commodities. . . . Furthermore, because it brings confusion to the order of high and low, it will open up a path to conflicts from which all kinds of vices will be born. . . . Without institutional [arrangement and authority] the world becomes sumptuous as it is people's natural sentiment to relish extravagance.[37]

Because the Tokugawa state and its advisors understood economy primarily as conservation and distribution of limited resources by way of reproducing given social relations of production and saw undue expenditure not as beneficial but as inimical to the economy, they understood sumptuary regulations as the most logical and efficacious measure to retain the equilibrium of production and consumption. Edicts were regularly issued to curtail waste or excess by urging people to exercise "self-discipline in all matters of consumption" and to retain the level of production vital for the well-being of society by demanding that they "maximize labor available through cooperation" within a community.[38] For example, all sumptuary laws implemented in villages during the Tokugawa period were based on the premise that peasants produce as much as possible while consuming as little as possible. A Tokugawa injunction of 1642 stipulated that "peasants should use as food the miscellaneous grains, and should not eat much rice," "wear straw capes and hats" instead of cotton rain capes or umbrellas, and refrain from using "leather-soled sandals, and combs and bodkins with metal ornamentation or of tortoise shell."[39] They were allowed to have only a house of limited size, without floor mats, paper-covered sliding doors, or verandas. In some rural areas, silk, pongee, bleached cotton summer kimonos, bleached cotton towels, striped materials, tunics, trousers, sash materials, wooden clogs, mirrors, nail scissors, capes, incense, drums, blankets, lacquered chopsticks, swords, bows and arrows, spears, and books were all prohibited.[40] The prohibition of swords, bows and arrows, spears, and books reflected a view of the ruling class that the possession of these weapons and the acquisition of literacy would inspire insubordination among peasants or interfere with their agricultural production.[41] Even wedding and New Year's banquets were regulated in rural areas in such a way as to be limited "to one soup, one viand, and one hors d'oeuvre, and to be concluded before dark."[42]

The level of luxury permitted to townspeople was much higher than for ordinary farmers or peasants. Yet, they were not allowed to wear wool capes and elaborate silk kimono or to dress in splendid clothes or to have a presumptuous appearance. Wearing long swords or large short swords was also banned. Their household articles must not have gold lacquer decorations and their houses were limited to a two-story structure without gold and silver leaf in it. They were warned against conspicuous display at weddings, funerals, and memorial services. Entertainments by and for townspeople, such as kabuki and puppet theaters (*ningyō jōruri* 人形浄瑠璃), were also ordained to keep their simplicity: no fine costumes and adornments permitted.

By promoting frugality, simplicity, and communal loyalty-duty as the foundational virtues for commoners' everyday conduct and enforcing these virtues through decrees and punishments, the Tokugawa authorities intended to purge the "unnecessary expenditures" or "waste" represented by activities honoring pleasure and play, such as spectacles, fashion, street vogue, and popular art and literature, which in their view "have no end beyond themselves."[43] They hoped that commoners would grasp and abide by the idea that consumption was acceptable only if it took place within the limits of justifiable utilitarian ends—consuming no more than the volume necessary for their subsistence without upsetting maximum productivity, and that transgressing the limits meant a serious deviation from and disruption to the moral imperatives of social harmony.

Forestalling the body's fall into the world of unwarranted expenditure was crucial, therefore, to the shogunate for its success in sustaining social order. That "[t]here should be no idle people within and without the four classes" was an axiom advocated widely by leading Confucian and Buddhist intellectuals, including Suzuki, Yamazaki, and Ogyū, as well as by state officials.[44] Allowing the real or imagined body to defy its moral imperatives implied a pernicious contradiction to the shogunate's ideological postulate—or "the ideal of totality," in Jameson's words—fashioned to sustain the mechanism of rule.

From the mid-eighteenth century onward, the Tokugawa shogunate was indeed steadily, if not continuously, faced with the possibility of losing the power to sustain the mechanism of rule, with the emergence of bodies that flouted the moral duty of productivity. The burgeoning material allure and relative freedom of urban life, which contrasted sharply with the growing misery of rural areas resulting from famines and heavy taxes, impelled peasants to flee their villages. This led to the formation of large vagrant populations in the major castle towns, especially Edo, consisting of beggars, peddlers, unlicensed prostitutes, and street entertainers. In 1692 the official number of vagrants in Edo was 5,366; that number grew to 13,266 by 1837.[45] As the total population of Edo reached over one million by the mid-eighteenth century and as 60 percent of this figure consisted of common people, the increase in the vagrant population indicated that approximately one out of fifty or sixty commoners was identified categorically as a vagrant in the early nineteenth century. From the late 1780s onward, when the number of vagabonds coming to Edo increased dramatically due to the devastating Tenmei famine (1782–87), Matsudaira Sadanobu (1758–1829), the senior counselor for the shogun at the time, embarked on an aggressive policy of repatriating vagrant peasants to their native lands (under a law entitled "Order for the Return of Unregistered and Wild Beggars to Their Former Native Places") and created the Stockade of Labor, a workhouse in which vagrants and criminals were classified as one and the same—a common threat to social stability—and put into a program of "rehabilitation" to be molded into fully functional workers. "All inmates at the workhouse were paid for their labors" and were required to "deposit one-third of their wages in their individual savings accounts maintained at the accounting office," so that they would learn to value the rewards of labor and understand the importance of saving and financial independence.[46] The shogunate also obliged every inmate to attend thrice-monthly lectures by eminent Confucian and the Mind Studies School (*shingaku* 心学) scholars on the morality of diligence and social conduct. The combination of work, discipline, and moral (re)training for the "rehabilitation" program was exactly what the shogunate viewed as an effective measure to diminish idle bodies and resuscitate mechanisms of social control. However, it succeeded neither in bringing a halt to the inflow of fleeing or displaced peasants into Edo from nearby villages nor in regulating or containing the allure of pleasure and play that urban popular culture exuded and disseminated beyond the borders of Edo. Officials' frustrations and anxieties were well conveyed in the following order issued at the time of two major ideological and political campaigns—in 1799 soon after the Kansei Reform of 1787–93 and in 1839 just before the Tenpō Reform of 1841–43:

> Under the pretext of holding annual fairs and festivals, some people in villages perform plays imitating kabuki and make a profit. In addition, there are villagers who invite itinerant traders, who bring in goods [comic books and ukiyo-e prints] that are wasteful of both time and thrift and are detrimental to the morality of village life. Others, who invite outcasts [itinerant entertainers] spreading through lascivious mirth and levity the undesirable influences of pleasure and play, must also be punished. This sort of transgression naturally encourages peasants to cease their cultivation and to create more wasteland, and eventually leads them to impoverishment. As a result, peasants are forced out of their villages and migrate to cities. Urban performances such as kabuki and *jōruri* [puppet plays] must therefore be strictly prohibited in villages.[47]

This statement not only confirmed the Tokugawa rulers' most basic ideological proposition that morality and productivity formed in conjunction the basis of social unity but also revealed officials' fear of the challenge to the established order of things posed by the new, proliferating forms of urban culture and entertainment. Characterizing urban popular culture as intrinsically immoral due to its propensity to foster a penchant for pleasure and play over the venerable virtues of thrift and hard work, the edict was aimed at containing the "vice" of popular culture within the city proper to keep it out of the countryside. The language of the Tokugawa authorities unequivocally condemned urban popular culture, with its power to entice people out of their assigned stations and social functions, for throwing into disarray the mechanism of reproduction of social relations.[48]

The shogunate's repeated attempts to halt declining productivity and reclaim social control through the discourse of moral and economic discipline proved futile. Indeed, villagers and townspeople alike often ridiculed the ineffectiveness of sumptuary laws in the derisive saying, "three days law" (*mikka hatto* 三日法度), because the laws appeared absurdly irrelevant to rapidly changing realities and were so often disregarded. Buyō Inshi (dates unknown), presumably a retired samurai in Edo or a samurai turned Confucian scholar residing in the city, observed in the second decade of the nineteenth century that the ruling class's ability to manage social control through the discourse of morality diminished significantly and that the distinction between the rulers and ruled was not merely blurring but actually disappearing:

> Even though townspeople and city idlers are said to be filthy and inferior, they are so only in name. They are in reality the winners of our time, for they enjoy the fruits of unprecedented prosperity and continue to influence every aspect of our social life with their culture of debauchery. . . . It is increasingly common for samurai to choose to become townspeople, willingly renouncing their status and opting to live among these lowly people. Even peasants, violating our sacred law, leave their home villages for larger cities to live like townspeople. . . . The entire world has fallen into the hands of the townspeople. From samurai to peasants, everyone imitates their lifestyles, manners, and appearance. Who could have anticipated such a dramatic dissolution of our sacrosanct moral order at the time of the Tokugawa system's founding?[49]

The new historical realities of a world turned upside down engendered by urban culture provided the social conditions for Edo commoners to forge a subculture that flouted—even negated—the official discourse of the social hierarchy's inviolability. It was in this very context that literary and visual representations of the idle body surged forth in the popular imagination, signaling an exigent state in which the "empty formalism" and untenable logic of the "ideal of totality" were exposed.[50]

Urban Space and the Heterogeneous

It is of great importance that these new bodily images sprang from the "low" city, as officials called it, an urban space where the culture of "unwarranted" expenditure—production and consumption of pleasure and play—drove economic life. In popular entertainment places such as Asakusa and Ryōgoku, comic storytellers, street musicians, animal entertainers (with monkeys, snakes, elephants, and tigers), jugglers, dancers, actors, mimes, puppeteers, acrobats, food vendors, barbers, diviners, itinerant shamans, souvenir peddlers, and teahouse girls offered large crowds of people of all social statuses the delights of "bizarre," "obscure," and "vulgar" spectacles.[51] They made a living out of nothing but their skills and bodies, which could not be made into an instrument to serve the moral imperatives of material production. Authorities denounced the entertainers and their festive vulgarity as the source of dissipation and disorder, relegating them to the outcast status categories of "idlers" and "nonhuman."

Yet, it was these "unproductive" spaces that began to function as magnetic centers, to an unprecedented scale, for the vital cultural production and consumption that occurred during the latter half of the eighteenth century. These spaces consisted of such an intensely heterogeneous commingling of all kinds of people (from samurai to townspeople to outcasts) and goods (from provincial products to exotic foreign items) that one contemporary observer marveled, "So many different styles and customs, and such diverse faces, in crowds too dense to push through—has Edo emptied the houses of the [other] provinces?"[52] These riotous gatherings and in-mixings of "high" and "low" and "the familiar" and "the strange" transgressed the social boundaries designed to mirror the official logic of status distinctions, encouraging forms of discourse that fostered the interaction of divergent and competing values and perspectives. The transgressive excitement of the market and entertainment districts for the subordinate classes was therefore not a result of their "otherness" or "marginality" to official discourse, despite the claims of some theorists of subculture who often posit this marginality as a warrant for countercultural innovations. Rather, it should be understood as an effect of hybridization or what M. M. Bakhtin calls the "carnival."[53] The districts were sites that engendered the interpenetrating interaction or dialogical encounter of divergent views, values, perspectives, and habits. This interaction fostered a complex process of dislocating and defamiliarizing Tokugawa norms and customs.

What contributed more to the effect of defamiliarization were the ruling elites' ambivalent and contradictory attitudes toward the culture of pleasure and play. Despite their moralistic condemnation of urban culture, samurai were also drawn to its allure. As Buyō's remark cited above shows, the spaces of popular entertainments and the lifestyles associated with them engrossed not only the townspeople but also the samurai to such an extent that many chose to renounce or jeopardize their social status by indulging in them. In the same treatise, Buyō added that "feeling envious of the townspeople who gratify themselves in profligacy, samurai plunge into the lifestyle of the lowly and forget their proper stations in society. As a result, some of them go so far as to throw themselves into financial difficulties and ruin their lives and posterity."[54] Moreover, shoguns or shoguns-to-be made frequent visits to the Sensōji Buddhist Temple located in the Asakusa area, which functioned as a popular hub of both prayer and play, as Nam-lin Hur has shown, despite the Tokugawa ideologues and Confucian critics' condemnation of the intermingling of these seemingly contradictory activities.[55] Matsudaira Sadanobu, mentioned above, an architect of the Kansei Reform of the 1790s that tightened control over townspeople's sumptuousness and popular entertainments in places like the Sensōji Temple and Ryōgoku (another popular hub where prayer and play coexisted), vilified them for corrupting the minds of both high and low with moral debauchery, dissipation, and idleness.[56] Yet Tokugawa Ienari (1773–1841), the eleventh shogun under whom Sadanobu implemented the reform, cherished the places as one of Edo's great attractions and as sources of Edo's vitality and creative energy. Ienari made regular visits to the amusement sites of the Sensōji Temple to see a wide variety of entertainments. In 1803, after the resignation of Sadanobu because of his failed and unpopular Kansei Reform, Ienari accompanied his son to the temple and spent a day enjoying a freak show, an acrobatic performance, street music, mimes, and a magic show. Moreover, before ascending to the position of shogun, Ienari visited the Asakusa area around the temple at least twice a year from 1784 to 1787.[57] It was also a common practice for shoguns' wives or concubines to organize day trips to Asakusa. Ienari's wives and concubines frequently visited the temple and its entertainment places, usually accompanied by thirty to fifty attendants. Samurai of lesser status were also drawn to these vibrant parts of Edo. Matsudaira Kanzen (1767–1833), a lord of the Wakasa domain, was presumably a most enthusiastic Asakusa goer. He completed a multivolume history of the Sensōji Temple and its environs in 1813, recording in great detail the shops, shopkeepers and their famous delicacies, and entertainers. It is clear from these volumes that Kanzen took great joy in visiting the two hundred eighty shops and tasting all their popular products. The diary of Sakai Hanjirō, a samurai retainer serving the lord of Kishū, described his tour around the Asakusa and Ryōgoku areas in 1860:

> We arrived at the Sensōji Temple in the afternoon, and after praying to Kannon [a Buddhist deity of compassion], we saw a famous ghost show. As a brief evening shower passed by, we popped into a store and ate a dish of broiled eels, yams, and octopus with sake. In Yoshiwara, we saw the procession of a stunning Oiran [a courtesan of the highest rank] for the first time, and then enjoyed watermelon. We headed to Ryōgoku, where we saw a wicked show [of male-female intercourse]. It was fun.[58]

These examples of samurai's ambivalent and contradictory attitudes toward the spaces of "idleness" demonstrated the ruling class's inability to retain clear demarcations between high and low, sacred and profane, or mind and body as a mode of social control.

Contributing further to the shogunate's inability to implement a draconian policy toward popular culture was the dilemma it faced in coping with a large number of Edo's poorest commoners. Implementation of strict sumptuary measures (1818, 1820, 1823, 1828, and so on) and edicts banning unlicensed prostitution, pornography, gambling, alcohol, and entertainments always resulted in economic recessions affecting the poorest stratum of urban commoners. Popular cultural spheres constituted an important source of income for this group of people; therefore, the authorities could not adopt a radically repressive measure against them. Clearly, what the shogunate vilified as unwarranted expenditure actually constituted an indispensable part of the productive economy in late Tokugawa society.[59] The "low" city's culture of play thus signified to the samurai class both repulsion and fascination, excess and necessity, twin poles of a self-contradictory process that undercut that class's claims of inviolability and immutability for the principle of distinction and exposed its ineptitude in regulating the culture of the townspeople within the limits of the totality it hoped to project and institute.

The ruling class's ineffectiveness or lack of consistency in social control did not suggest, however, that the interaction between high and low in these entertainment districts dissolved completely the power relations delineating social hierarchies. Rather, such interaction offered rulers one of the rare opportunities to exalt their power and authority in front of urban commoners through the pompous display of privileges.[60] Whenever the shogun and his family made a visit, the Sensōji Temple was overhauled and redecorated, and special rituals were performed under the name of protecting the polity from calamities and misfortunes. The time-honored Buddha statue, usually kept sealed in the main hall, was made available for public prayer and viewing only on the occasion of their visit. The privileges attached to their excursions worked to endow them with a divine and magnanimous aura, invoking their putative superiority as the ultimate ruler of the realm. Furthermore, while touring the entertainment sites, the shogun and his family remained shielded from the gaze of commoners, viewing both entertainers and townspeople from inside their splendidly decorated palanquins. Their contact with the townspeople was distinguished by symbolic physical distance, a position from which they might gaze on the populace, but not gazed on, inducing a sense of distinction and reverence. The carefully calculated spectacle of the shogun's absent presence was a common tactic, as Timon Screech reminds us, frequently used by the shogunate to heighten the mystique of the ruler.[61] The interaction of high and low thus promoted both a liberation from and a permeation by power. The "pleasurable play of shifting solidarity with others" was liberating, as if the heterogeneous gatherings and interactions in the entertainment and market districts had dispensed with the hierarchy separating the rulers from the ruled.[62] Yet the districts also provided the ruling elites with strategically opportune moments to further consolidate the principle of distinction between high and low.

It was these spaces of multilayered, dynamic, and contradictory social intercourse that inspired the producers of popular culture to visualize imaginary situations where the values and perspectives of high and low came into direct contact and conflict with one another. Drawing on the districts' "low" languages, performances, and gestures, which radiated the energy of cheerful vulgarity riding roughshod over ruling-class civilities, popular writers, woodblock artists, and playwrights forged a culture of comic, satiric, and grotesque forms that pitted bodily excess—or "filth," in Suzuki Shōzan's terms—against dominant norms and authoritarian words. This vulgar materialism of the body became a foremost principle for late Tokugawa literary and artistic imagination and representation, subjecting piety, humility, servility, and loyalty to parody, ridicule, and blasphemy.

Ambiguities of Power and Unintended Consequences in Early Tokugawa Times

The analysis of Tokugawa ideology thus far may give an impression that it worked as a unitary, rigid, and fixed system of idea and practice, lacking any plasticity, heterogeneity, and adaptability. However, its primary purpose is to distill the logic that informed the construction of social order and the institutional arrangement and implementation of power under the Tokugawa shogunate, as well as to show its lacuna and aporia that arose from the rapidly changing social realities brought on by urbanization and the permeation of money, exchange, and consumer culture in the eighteenth century. As Herman Ooms has shown, Tokugawa ideology consisted of many different intellectual currents (Buddhism, Neo-Confucianism, and Shintō, as well as a multitude of positions within each of these "currents"). But what Ooms and others such as Bito Masahide have also presented is the common ideological assumption—which resembles what Michel Foucault calls an episteme—that cut across those diverse voices.[63] Ooms demonstrates that the mind-body relation was understood as necessarily hostile and hierarchical, and this conception of the mind-body worked as a way to condemn either different forms of excessive desire—for example, sexual or consumptive—or new ways of life that exalted expenditure and exorbitance over austerity and material production to valorize the pleasures of the body. Underlying this official condemnation of undue desire and pleasure was the preservation of a restricted economy based on agricultural production (rice) against the rapid commercialization of the economy (money). Despite some admittedly important differences in language and mode of articulation, the diverse voices constituting Tokugawa ideology assumed this fundamental logic of the mind-body relationship that supplied legitimacy to social order.

An analysis of the episteme of Tokugawa ideology does not lead therefore to the conclusion that the mechanism of power actually functioned in perfect harmony with the "ideal of totality" as envisioned by the founders of the Tokugawa shogunate.[64] In fact, the historical conjuncture presented by the proliferation of the new representation of the body in eighteenth-century popular art and literature was both the direct and the indirect consequence of ambiguities and chasms that had existed within the mechanism of power from the very beginnings of the Tokugawa era. Originary unison or oneness of social whole purported in the official discourse of the "cosmic-human" unity was after all a theory, not a reality itself, contrived to lend legitimacy or a normative integrity to the rule-by-status imperative. Tokugawa society in reality stood to a great degree on ambiguities that resulted from the multiple layers of disjuncture between theoretical premises and empirical realities, or discourse and corporeal experience, in three basic domains of everyday life: governance, economy, and leisure.[65] Nowhere were these ambiguities more discernible than in Edo, the administrative, commercial, and entertainment center of Tokugawa Japan.

In "Governing Edo," Kato Takashi makes the important point that the city's governance must be understood in terms of its duality: "as a concept that spread from above but that was exercised in no small part from below."[66] Indeed, despite the fact that Edo's system of governance was managed on the foundations of an autocratic assumption that the shogunate held the monopoly of ultimate legislative, policing, and executive powers and of means and use of violence (swords, arrows, and guns),[67] "the actual operations of urban institutions that most affected the lives of the ordinary residents of the city were left to the people themselves."[68] This duality was the result of the chronic shortage of administrators and police—a result caused by the hereditary system's denial of social mobility—relative to the population that grew exponentially until the early eighteenth century. The shogunate worked long and hard to ensure not only that its laws, ordinances, decrees and proclamations would be communicated expeditiously to the residential quarters of merchants and artisans or to their families directly but also that they would be observed unfailingly by the townspeople. An integrated chain of command and authority was devised in such a way that common people assumed a crucial role in transmitting the shogunate's orders and will and in realizing universal compliance. The chain extended from city magistrates (of high-ranking samurai status) to the city elders (townspeople) to the neighborhood chiefs (townspeople) and then to the monthly representatives of the five-family groups (townspeople).[69] The shogunate made the city elders, the neighborhood chiefs and the representatives of the five-family groups responsible for mediating and resolving conflicts in neighborhoods or within families, as well as watching and reporting on crimes, vagrants, and entertainers to city magistrates. Clearly, the shogunate hoped to maintain order by holding a firm grip on society at the very microlevel through the centrifugal system of command and authority. But it was precisely this centrifugal organization of politico-administrative process that, placing an emphasis on persuasion as much as on coercion, allowed merchants, artisans, and even outcasts broad latitude in managing many significant aspects of urban life in their own ways. The townspeople often negotiated with city magistrates to transform to their own advantages the ways in which the shogunate organized and controlled their residential and commercial spaces. The "widened street" (*hirokoji* 広小路) at the one end of the Ryōgoku Bridge was, for example, initially constructed by the shogunate as a firebreak after the great fires of Meireki in 1657 had caused more than a hundred thousand deaths, but townspeople transformed it within several decades into one of the most famed hubs for popular entertainment. Even when the shogunate threatened to pull the Ryōgoku Bridge down in the 1730s due to frequent damage caused by the seasonally rapid currents and high waters of the Sumida river, the merchants and entertainers, expressing their concerns that their business would be significantly impaired, managed to persuade the shogunate to save it in exchange for their promise to cover the maintenance cost of the bridge.[70] James L. McClain, in discussing cases similar to the Ryōgoku, calls "the appropriation of the space, institutions, and cultural motifs of the city by its merchants and artisans at the expense of the government and the ruling samurai status group" the "chōninization of Edo,"[71] which aptly describes the unintended consequences of the ambiguities of Edo's governance. As argued earlier, no matter how the Tokugawa authorities tried to curtail the growing influence of popular culture, spaces of pleasure and play increasingly became an integral element of urban life for the majority of Edo's population and an essential means of living for the lower classes. The particular style of the shogunal governance can certainly be described as a kind of autocracy for its ultimate political and administrative powers and monopoly of violence, as well as its adamant defense of status-based society, but one cannot overlook the fact that people in Edo constantly negotiated this autocracy.[72] In this sense, it is safe to assert that the shogunal governance was less concerned with social control than the maintenance of order itself. In other words, control hardly constituted the objective of governance and instead served the need of order. Therefore, the authorities demonstrated plasticity and adaptability in deploying different means of governance for the ultimate objective of ensuring the sustenance of the established order.

If the systemic disjuncture of shogunal governance led to the chōninization of Edo, certain ambiguities built into the structure of Tokugawa economy had much to do with that development as well. Although Tokugawa society was established on the assumption that agricultural production held primacy over commercial activities, it depended largely on the foundations of a certain level of market economy.[73] Shogun and domainal lords' wealth was calculated for all arable lands in terms of standard crop yields in rice. They levied on peasants in their own domains annual taxes that were based on the principle of payment of a fixed percentage of the parcel's potential productivity in rice even if certain land parcels were not used for rice cultivation. Taxes were paid not by individual peasants but by each village as a whole. Each domainal lord, by selling rice to merchants in Osaka, supported his enormous expenditures to perform the requirement of an alternate attendance system imposed by the shoguns. Under this policy, each domainal lord was not only obliged to divide his residency and thus make extensive trips between his home domain and Edo every other year but also had to sustain a sufficient financial basis for his family in Edo as they were required to live in the city as virtual hostages when he returned to his domain.

This ritualistic repetition of alternate attendance by domainal lords brought an unparalleled economic impetus to Edo's transformation from backwater to bustling commercial center. Far from their home domains, nearly two hundred and seventy lords and over one hundred thousand of their retainers required cash to sustain their lives while living in Edo. According to Constantine Vaporis, "roughly 25 to 30 percent of Edo's population traveled from the domains to take up residence in the more than six hundred domain compounds found across the city, and their numbers were continuously replenished from the castle towns through the migrations of alternate attendances."[74] While the retainers tended to live a humble life due to their limited stipends and increasing financial difficulty, their lords led opulent lifestyles in large mansions. But both increasingly relied on wealthy merchants and moneylenders to acquire cash as a loan against their stipend (rice) or through the sale of their stipend. As a result, by the turn of the eighteenth century, money prevailed in Edo as the predominant medium of economic exchange and transaction. "Everything is money," Dazai Shundai (1680–1747), a preeminent student of Ogyū Sorai, observed in his *On the Political Economy* (1729). He went on to write,

> [L]arge and small expenses are all paid for from one moment to the next so that the people of today value money one hundred times more than in ancient times. Indeed, though one may have adequate food and clothing today, one will find it difficult to make his way in society if short on money. Not only is this true for poor commoners, but also for the aristocracy [samurai], including domainal lords.[75]

The implication of this shift to a money economy was probed a decade earlier by Shundai's mentor, Ogyū Sorai, in his aforementioned political treatise, *Seidan* (*On Politics*):

> Nowadays [around the 1710s], samurai are forced to live in castle towns in discharge of their duties. Living away from home, in a manner similar to travelers seeking lodging, requires cash for sustenance. They must sell rice for cash, and purchase their daily needs from merchants. In this way, merchants become masters while samurai are relegated to the position of customers, unable to determine prices fixed on different commodities. In olden days when samurai lived on their lands, they had no need to sell

their rice, and under such circumstances, samurai remained masters and the merchants their customers.[76]

Sorai's observation revealed the disturbing truth to the authorities that a market economy originally established to assist the operation of the rice-based economy began to dictate the mode of economic exchange and transaction whereby the hierarchical relationship between samurai and townspeople was jarred, even reversed. But, more importantly, it points to one of the most fundamental ironies of eighteenth-century Tokugawa society: it was the sumptuous consumption by the ruling samurai class, not by townspeople or peasants, which marred the economic foundations of social order. Put differently, the regime built on the premise of a restrictive management of economy—enforcing minimum consumption and maximum production—was responsible, through its own exorbitant expenditures, for reshaping the economy into a consumption-led economy. Through this transformative process, as Sorai put it so eloquently, the ruling class demoted itself to the status of customers, whereas subordinate groups were promoted to that of masters. This world-turned-upside-down situation was obviously an unintended consequence for the people in power, for they never anticipated their political rituals to play the pivotal role in making consumption a driving force of Tokugawa economy while rendering agricultural production secondary to the dictates of market logic. Nor did they expect this economic transformation to allow people to thrive in a manner that threatened to undermine the economic basis of their monopoly on power. This inversion in power relations could be observed most vividly in the case of the townspeople called "rice brokers" (*fudasashi* 札差), ninety-some agents who received a commission for delivering rice (stipend) from the shogunate's granary to the direct retainers of the shogun. By the early eighteenth century, they had remade this duty into a business of lending money to samurai with high interest rates and taking rice as security. The shogunate had authorized their business by according them the right to form a guild in 1724, but after witnessing the deteriorating financial conditions of its samurai retainers, it ordered in 1791 that all their debt to *fudasashi* was to be canceled. Despite the shogunate's interventions to mitigate the samurais' financial predicament, *fudasashi* continued to accumulate an unprecedented scale of wealth.[77]

As seen in the cases of governance and economy, a great degree of ambiguity had subsisted in the organization of everyday life since the establishment of Tokugawa society, and it yielded unintended consequences that amplified deep dissonances between the ideological projection of a totality and ongoing historical transformations. The dissonances surfaced as a grave concern not only because they demonstrated the functional deficiencies of ideological representation but also because they brought to light the paralysis and disintegration of the mechanisms of social order. The government endowed the townspeople with a certain degree of responsibility for governance for the purpose of communicating the ruler's will to each and every individual and thus of achieving universal compliance. It also acknowledged the importance of the money economy in terms of its subsidiary role in ensuring the steady management of the rice economy. It was not at all anticipated, certainly not desired, that townspeople began to exert some power, backed up by their lately acquired economic potency, to appropriate and manage their residential and commercial spaces or that the principle of market economy began to reconstitute Tokugawa society in place of that of regulated economy.

If the shogunate authorized the semi–self-governance and money economy as a necessary yet auxiliary mechanism for the stability and sustenance of social order, it also accepted the installation of an enclave for a certain kind of leisure for the same rationale. Although "carnal" leisure such as pleasure quarters and kabuki theater were vilified as decadent entertainment (pleasure quarters and theater districts were called "evil places"), they were legally permitted to exist as a fixture and the nucleus of Edo popular culture since they were believed to be capable of offering momentary diversion that helped prod the townspeople to work productively within the confines of assigned duties and functions. In other words, they were officially sanctioned as a "safety valve."[78] It may seem inconceivable for the government, which regarded a contribution to social stability and harmony through productive work as the highest moral duty, to sanction this type of leisure, for nowhere were unproductiveness and thus immorality more signified than in the body sold and bought for pleasures and spectacles. But if the shogunate truly believed that the presence of the depraved and worthless body could avail the productive body by supplying an outlet for momentary diversion, the authorization of the former seems logical, at least, from the vantage point of the government's self-interest. Such logic can be called the economy of culture. How many times were the words of warning, "Do not let oneself be consumed by evil play," reiterated in popular literature, storytelling, or Buddhist and Confucian sermons from the late seventeenth to the early eighteenth century? It was indeed also in the eighteenth century that "to not plunge into the excess of play" became one of the prevalent norms among dandies (*tsūjin* 通人) who were said to be "specialist[s] in the knowledge of pleasure."[79] "The real players," writes Harry Harootunian summarizing

Edo popular writer Santō Kyōden's (1761–1816) characterization of the dandy, "understood the proper behavior and when to stop, unlike the poor wretches who were destined to remain semiplayers the rest of their lives."[80] The shogunate hoped that the integration of the noneveryday of carnal pleasure into the order of the everyday would strengthen the foundations and working of the latter as long as it succeeded in setting clear limits for the former and in separating it from the spaces of work and discipline. The "evil places" were therefore allotted the land located at the margin of the city proper, and making a visit to them was a daylong (for kabuki) or an all-night (for the pleasure quarters) affair. The ruling power's authorization of popular leisure as a "necessary evil" indicated another layer of ambiguity subsisting in the system of Tokugawa rule.[81]

But was this stasis or rather the hierarchical relationship between work and play sustainable? In other words, did the culture of pleasure and play officially sanctioned as a means of lending support to the established social relations of production continue to operate according to the envisioned role? As discussed earlier in this chapter, from the middle of the eighteenth century on, the popular culture in Edo began to articulate alternative images of social realities, overpowering official counterparts. This new historical situation was perspicaciously captured by Buyō Inshi's observation that "the contemporary [popular] theaters no longer imitate the world, but the world imitates them because they have captivated people's hearts."[82]

The widely perceived reversal of the given order of things was marked more clearly in the informal sector of makeshift entertainments flourishing in commercial districts and in the precincts of temples than in the licensed enclaves of pleasure and play. Springing up outside of institutional frameworks, these entertainments were not considered a "proper" occupation under the Tokugawa system of the division of labor. Nor did the entertainers, called *gōmune* (ごう胸), possess "proper" status identities. In fact, they bore the dual identity of an outcast or nonhuman, in terms of their occupation, and of "proper" townspeople, nonoutcasts, in the official registry.[83] This duality is important because it revealed again the shogunate's ambiguities toward the salient presence of popular culture in Edo: street performances as an occupation deserved a pariah status because they embodied no moral values, yet entertainers must not be discriminated against because the repression of their businesses would eradicate an important means of livelihood for a large number of poor urbanites. While keeping this dual policy toward the street entertainers, the Tokugawa authorities decided by the early eighteenth century that their businesses be placed under the supervision of the head of the outcast groups *Danzaemon* (弾左衛門). This decision was meant to ensure their grip on the otherwise transient and elusive existence. Indeed, this group of townspeople often managed to evade the requirements of taxation and temple registry (every individual was required to report the temple of his/her birth, death, address, and religious affiliation). In addition, the vibrant informal economic sector posed a serious challenge to the official notion of economic productivity: what the shogunate condemned as frivolous endeavor and wasteful expenditure—the production and consumption of spectacles—actually constituted a substantial segment of Edo economy. This recognition threatened the important distinction between work and play, or discipline and diversion, a distinction that the shogunate saw as crucial to the successful operation of the mechanism of social order. Many late eighteenth- and early nineteenth-century intellectuals such as Buyō saw with an acute sense of crisis the undermining effects of the proliferating informal economic sector on the institutional frame of social relations of production.

> There are no limits to the popularity and prosperity of countless spectacles such as puppet shows, acrobatic shows, magic shows, impressions, storytelling, etc. They all use fine costumes for their performances. In recent years, large-scale spectacles that cost one or two thousand pieces of gold for their elaborate settings and performances have appeared. They amaze and dazzle the spectators and rob them of a lot of money for their vulgar performances. With their titillating effects on the public, they weaken the way of loyalty and filial piety, being a complete adversary to the old customs of promoting good and chastising evil. It is hard to estimate exactly how many people—more than tens of thousands of people at least—are making their livings in this business. Are they not the true idlers, in that they evade taxes and social responsibilities and lead their lives according to selfish desires? Are they not the true idlers, in that they spread wasteful expenditure, the confusions of high/low distinctions, and sins of libidinal indulgence? There are no limits to their prosperity. They must to be stopped.[84]

Despite the censorious charges by the ruling elites, this new group of "free" floating and unclassifiable people continued to grow in number and popularity and began to flout and jar the official rhetoric of status distinction and appear as a chief motif in popular literature and visual materials from the late eighteenth century. For instance, *jōruri* or *gitayū* (an entertainment in which a female performer "sang" a melodramatic ballad with the instrument, *shamisen*, by personifying multiple characters with varying voices) became so popular in Edo by the end of the eighteenth century that a number of samurai followed the female entertainers to learn the skills of singing and playing the instrument and the Edo city magistrate had to ban the practice in 1798 by calling the cross-status interaction "a grave concern" for public mores and the art form "vulgar" and "immoral."[85] In 1831, the authority reissued the ban on female *jōruri* performance, yet a reference to it continued to appear in romantic love stories by Tamenaga Shunsui (1790–1843) and a flier containing the ranking of performers was circulated in Edo in 1837.[86] (I will return to this subject matter in chapter 4.)

What can be concluded from the above examinations of the deep ambiguities in the three domains of everyday life is as follows. Everyday life during the Tokugawa period consisted of what might be called first- and second-order realities: the former denotes the formal structure of governance (autocracy), economy (rice), and work (productive labor assigned to each individual according to his/her status); the latter refers to quasi-institutional practices of self-governance, economy (money), and play (licensed theaters and pleasure quarters). The dual reality was contrived to make the second order serve the needs of the first order, just as merchants were expected to assist samurai, through the distribution of goods, in accumulating and managing their wealth, or as a certain kind of leisure was supposed to function as a momentary means of escapist pleasure to ensure stable social order and economic productivity. But the eighteenth century witnessed the reversal of this order. The provinces of experience that would otherwise remain auxiliary within the realm of everyday life became conspicuously primary to the privileged provinces of autocracy, work, and productivity. Sorai's and Shundai's observations of economy or governance cited earlier openly acknowledged that the primacy originally given to the first order reality was shifting rapidly to the second order in the early eighteenth century. But, most importantly, what made the eighteenth century more distinct from the preceding century were unintended consequences engendered by this reversal: townspeople's power to negotiate with authorities for the appropriation of urban spaces (e.g., Ryōgoku and Asakusa), the burgeoning of consumer economy as the primary mode of people's livelihood (entertainment), and the creation of informal sectors of play and pleasure (literature, art, and performances linked to entertainment). These new provinces of reality joined to form a new space of cultural production and consumption, which could not be easily classified within the institutional frame of the first- and the second-order realities. They constituted an indefinable and inarticulable terrain within the reality of everyday life, ipso facto signifying the threshold of the Tokugawa shogunate's hierarchical cognitive schema. The shogunate's application of ambiguously generic categories such as "idler," "vagrant," or "nonhuman" to lump the people associated with this terrain indicated not only its desire but also its desperate efforts to integrate the unidentifiable existence into any conceivable reality. That is to say, the regime's use of these categories evinced the fact that it found it exceedingly difficult to configure these people within the set terms of status order because all available language defining status order and relations of production based on the order could not supply clearly intelligible identities to them. But that the regime made sustained efforts, despite the difficulty, has important implications here: the rise of the unidentifiable existence as a new and inassimilable reality signified to the authorities the most acute threat to taken-for-granted, routinized existence within the established order. The derogatory and discriminatory imports of "idler," "vagrant," and "nonhuman" clearly conveyed, however generic these terms might be, the shogunate's view of such existence as a real peril and its resolution to marginalize it by rendering it as pernicious Other.

The authorities' concerns about the increasingly vibrant and influential presence of this new cultural space were not entirely grounded in paranoia but in some discernible realities. The producers of urban popular culture paid no heed to the shogunate's strategies of calumniation and containment in their accentuating and espousing the positive connotations of living a "useless" life within the institutionalized realities by adopting language such as "madness," "eccentricity," and "trickery" as a metaphorical description of their lives and works. Most of the cultural figures, who are discussed in this chapter or the other chapters, invariably assumed this sort of metaphorical self-identification. Recollecting his life, Chikamatsu Monzaemon (1653–1724), a highly acclaimed popular playwright for *ningyō jōruri* (ballad drama using puppets), described himself as a "phony" (*magaimono* まがいもの) in his dying words written in 1724. Similarly, a distinguished poet, Ōta Nanpo (1749–1823) referred to himself as a "useless person" (*muda mono* 無駄者) and, an eminent woodblock artist, Katsushika Hokusai (1760–1849) called himself a "mad" painter (*gakyōjin* 画狂人), whereas a bestseller comical writer and satirist, Hiraga Gennai (1728–1779), was known as a "trickster" (*yamashi* 山師) or an "eccentric" (*kijin* 奇人). From the perspective of the functional logic of status identity, those who embraced and lived on the domain of a new reality certainly embodied a liminality of existence, as expressed in metaphors such as "phonies," "madness," "uselessness," or "eccentricity," for they did not supply or extol the kind of societal contribution—the preservation of social harmony through productive work—required of every Tokugawa subject. Renouncing stable identities within the matrix of the given social hierarchies and stratification, they immersed themselves in the liminal spaces of cultural production and brought to the foreground the presence of a reality inassimilable to the dominant norms and discourses safeguarding the authority of the putatively unalterable reality. Metaphorical signifiers such as "madness," "uselessness," and "eccentricity" posed a threat precisely because their very existence demonstrated empirically not only that normative realities were less than inevitable but also that everyday life was a field of changing and divergent—not static and monolithic—experiences irreducible to the symbolic representation of the ideal of totality.

The Structure of Feeling: Floating World (Ukiyo) as Being-In-Between

How did the widely perceived reversal of power relations in socioeconomic life in eighteenth-century Tokugawa Japan affect the townspeople's understanding of their own stations within the Tokugawa status order? How was this self-understanding related to the phenomenon in which many cultural producers came to assume those metaphorical liminal identities? Nishikawa Joken (1648–1724), a Nagasaki townsperson and a renowned scholar of international studies and astronomy, published his meditations in 1719 on the status of townspeople in fast changing Tokugawa society, and his views disclosed a novel understanding of what it meant to be *chōnin* (townspeople), a term originally invented by the ruling samurai status groups as an administrative category to govern and tax common people (artisans, merchants, and outcasts) living in castle towns. Nishikawa compared *chōnin* to samurai as follows:

> Samurai have to sell their bodies and lives to their masters: even when society is in peace, they must keep in mind that in any circumstances, they should be ready to do anything necessary to avoid the defamation of their masters. This is why they have no choice but to sacrifice their lives willingly [for their masters] with a smile, albeit a bitter one. Townspeople have no master, but only father and mother. How fortunate we are to be born as townspeople.[87]

Nishikawa embraces the relative "freedom" enjoyed by townspeople over the samurai's distinctive values of self-sacrifice and unconditional loyalty, which the latter valorized as the source of their pride and moral superiority. It would be a mistake, however, to construe his bold statement as an expression of a "slave" mentality that sought to reverse the master-slave relations by degrading the samurai's alleged superiority. Rather, further examination of Nishikawa's text reveals a much more ambivalent perception of the place occupied by townspeople in Tokugawa society:

There are five statuses in the human world: emperor (*tenshi*), regional lords (daimyo), their followers with official ranks (*hatamoto*), those without them, and the people . . . Among the people, there are four kinds: low-ranking samurai, peasants, artisans, and merchants . . . When these four kinds of people do not exist, the principle of five statuses shall cease to exist. This is why there is no place in the world which does not require four kinds of people . . . Among these four, artisans and merchants are called *chōnin.* Although *chōnin* are located at the bottom of the order, since our society witnessed the shift from a barter economy to a monetary economy in recent years, the wealth has fallen into the hands of *chōnin.* Nowadays, *chōnin* are more frequently called to the nobles' presence. It looks as though they stand above farmers in the status order . . . But *chōnin* should not seek to surpass those above them, they should not envy the power of those above them, and they should observe simplicity and frugality. Above all, they should accept what is given to them with pleasure, as in the saying "as long as cattle flock together, they shall live happily forever."[88]

In this passage, Nishikawa carries out a deliberate and innocuous assessment of the status hierarchy under the Tokugawa rule. While suggesting the increasing economic power of *chōnin* and its potentially subversive implications for the status structure, he was adamant in reminding his readers (presumably his fellow townspeople) that *chōnin* must live within the bounds of the given stations in society. This assessment was accompanied, however, by a rather contradictory statement:

Though one may be born into a family of outcasts, when brought up by a noble and wealthy family, one will learn writings and literature. Some may even win fame for their scholarship in these subjects. In a discussion of such inner human qualities as courage and cowardice, the high-low distinction has no place . . . In a word, there is no such distinction as high and low in the human world. The difference only originates in one's upbringing. Why then should there be the distinction between high and low? Even one who lives in a lowly shack has a spirit as noble as anyone else.[89]

Here we encounter a resolute insistence on an egalitarian view of humanity, a position that contradicts the vertical organizations of Tokugawa society that Nishikawa himself urged his fellow townspeople to comply with in the previous citation. This statement even articulated a view that went directly against the thrust of the ruling ideology that posited the samurai's domination of the other groups as a natural consequence of their inherent moral and intellectual superiority. For Nishikawa, the distinction between high and low was not natural, but artificially contrived. One's moral and intellectual capacities were not innate, but were to be nurtured a posteriori regardless of her/his status. Then, Nishikawa asked, why should there be hierarchical distinctions among people?

The coexistence of the contradictory views in Nishikawa's writing spoke of the very historicity of the townspeople's self-understanding of their conditions of being under the Tokugawa system. In the same work Nishikawa repeatedly evoked the importance both of being cognizant of the bounds of status-defining *chōnin*'s "proper" conduct and ways of life—"*chōnin mizukara no bunsai wo shirubeki nari*" (町人自らの分際を知るべきなり)—and of not overplaying their rise in the socioeconomic relations with their superiors. Such a caution stemmed from the recognition that the townspeople's survival was conceivable only in accepting, if not necessarily believing in, the existing social hierarchies (the presumed hierarchical relationship between the first and the second order realities) because it was this social relationship that enabled townspeople's rise and prosperity (the ruling samurai groups being the most powerful and resource-rich consumer in the entire realm). But this strategic thinking was never easily reconciled with the irrepressible awakening of their sense of self-esteem and egalitarian perspective. The paradox—the acceptance and negation of the existing social hierarchies—led townspeople like Nishikawa to view the status identity, *chōnin*, both as necessary and as constrictive for their conditions of being. While *chōnin* signified a way of identification by which ordinary people in castle towns were guaranteed their rise and prosperity through their performance of duties and responsibilities, it also meant that they were permanently reduced to a position of low and ancillary existence. The awakening of the egalitarian perspective grounded in their growing confidence not only in socioeconomic but also in cultural endeavors resulted in Nishikawa's assertion that there was no such distinction as high and low in the matters of inner human qualities. And this assertion was accompanied by a potentially subversive implication that status identities such as *chōnin*, samurai, peasants, or outcasts were neither the reflection of the cosmic order nor the manifestation of innate differences in moral and intellectual capacity, but were simply names given to people, who were otherwise irreducibly heterogeneous, for the purpose of organizing and stratifying a society. In other words, the subject called *chōnin*—be it artisans, merchants, or outcasts—came to be perceived as a site of overdetermination suffused with ontological ambiguities and contradictions in terms of its being both the condition necessary for ordinary urbanites' survival and the condition constricting the new domain of reality felt in their daily experiences.[90]

The sentiment of the overdetermined reality so well elucidated by Nishikawa echoed one expressed in early eighteenth-century popular literature and theater, although the areas of their concerns did not exactly correspond to each other. If Nishikawa's essay grappled with ontological tensions originating from the unbridgeable chasm between the presumed relationship of the first- and the second-order realties and the reversal of the relationship in reality, the artistic representations dealt with the same tensions stemming from sharp discord between norms and corporeal realities. The latter employed the widely used semantic opposition of norm (*giri* 義理) and passion (*ninjō* 人情) to illuminate this sense of in-betweenness. What was brought forth in this conflictive depiction of the relationship between norms and passions was a consciousness of the irrepressibly powerful effusion of passion against the stricture of the normative reality (both the first- and the second-order realities). Chikamatsu Monzaemon dramatized this new sensibility in a compelling manner in the genre called "double suicide" story (*shinjūmono* 心中物). Many of his tragedies followed a plotline in which heroes (townsmen) and heroines (low-ranking prostitutes) were torn between moral norms and uncontainable passion for forbidden love (love between those unequal, in particular, that between male commoners and female outcasts such as prostitutes, was viewed not only as dishonorable to the men's families but also as detrimental to their prosperity and posterity), and they would eventually take a desperate and fatal measure of double suicide to end their otherwise everlasting agonies. Those implicated by their forbidden affairs included the lovers' families, relatives, and friends, and Chikamatsu's plot brought together these people's contending multiple voices, all of whose positions oscillated between norm and passion. This dialogical composition meant that his stories were primarily concerned with exploring social, if not personal, implications of friction brought about by the conflictive negotiation between moral imperatives and unbridled feelings. The normalcy of social relations would be eventually restored with the demise of the transgressive actions that opened the tabooed zone of social life. But this closure of transgression was hardly a closure as "Chikamatsu neither praised nor condemned his heroes" and heroines for their hopeless and helpless involvement with forbidden love, or as his stories often ended with a tone sympathetic to the lovers, announcing that death was the only resolution permitted to them to remain "truthful" to their feelings.[91] Instead of negating transgressive action with the language of moralistic condemnation, the story of double-suicide left the haunting imageries of "true" love or desired life that could be affirmed only by way of negating life. This compelling articulation of tragedy separated Chikamatsu's narratives from conventional literary forms that portrayed the Tokugawa world through the prism of the good-evil dichotomy.

In his theoretical essay on the method of artistic representation, Chikamatsu contended that spectators would find themselves drawn emotionally to the fictional world of a puppet theater should it be effective in arresting the reality in which people incessantly hovered on the border between the determinate and the indeterminate.[92] One's efficacy in communicating reality depended on whether the difference between the real (*jitsu* 実) and the unreal (*kyo* 虚) was rendered in its subtlety. The "real" here referred to the sphere of the determinate, that is, a precise depiction of society in terms of the ways in which differences in behavior, speech, and appearance were organized and represented according to status identities and norms anchored to the identities, whereas the "unreal" denoted the domain of the indeterminate, that is, a fictive representation of nebulousness made possible by ellipsis and hyperbole of meaning and action. It was essential to ascertain, Chikamatsu contended, that the "real" never dictated the entire performance despite its paramount presence in reality, so that it could bring forth some nebulousness (*oomaka* おおまか) capable of conjuring up the indeterminacy of life. These two spheres should interact in such a way that things omitted and exaggerated (the unreal) interrupted and transformed the ostensibly determined life (the real), while at the same time that determined life continued to put limitations and inhibitions on the possibility of such an interruption and transformation. Spectators' emotional responses would be provoked, according to Chikamatsu, precisely at the moment when this artistic method successfully attended to the fine layer of difference between the real and the unreal and visualized their contending and mutually decentering interactions. When riveted by the power of this representational strategy, spectators "no longer recognize[d] the unreal simply as the unreal, nor [did] they perceive the real merely as the real"—*kyo ni shite kyo ni arazu, jitsu ni shite jitsu ni arazu* 虚にして虚にあらず、実にして実にあらず.[93] The demarcations between the real and the unreal became hardly discernible or even irrelevant, and this fuzziness made the fictional depiction of powerful and unpredictable feelings more "real" than the reality in spectators' eyes.[94]

Chikamatsu's artistic theory seemed validated by his extraordinary popularity as a playwright. His fame invited, not surprisingly, the Tokugawa authorities' charge that he was directly responsible for the dramatic increase in the number of double suicides among the townspeople in the early eighteenth century. His plays were banned for a short while in 1722 with the official pronouncement that "from now on it is prohibited to show remorse over the death of lovers who died in an act of double suicide by writing about it in illustrated books or by putting it into *jōruri* and kabuki performances."[95] The ban was accompanied by new regulations that insisted on two measures of punishment: first, by prohibiting the use of the term *shinjū* as a reference to "double suicide" and applying the criminal code "death by accomplice" (*aitaijini* 相対死に) instead, it outlawed the burial of the corpses of the lovers and ordained the exposure and abandonment of the bodies of those who had committed suicide;[96] second, if those lovers happened to survive their attempted double suicide, they were to be exposed to public spectacle for three days and would subsequently work under the people of an outcast status.[97] The shogunate's replacement of the term *shinjū* with "death by accomplice" demonstrated the disquieting implications the Tokugawa power saw in the concept of *shinjū*. Because *shinjū* meant an act that proved to be "truthful or loyal to one's feeling or heart," it valorized a violation of social norms—love between those unequal—as an enactment of honesty or sincerity. It also meant that only the self-destruction of one's existence could lead one to truthfulness in Tokugawa society. These implications clearly pointed to transgressive claims regarding the invalidity of the established moral order. Moreover, the shogunate's punitive measures inform us of the ways in which Tokugawa power operated. The fact that new laws revealed no intention to "reform" the mind and applied the harshest corporeal punishment indicates that the shogunate judged the causes of illegitimate passion to have originated from the body rather than the mind. In Tokugawa power's view, it was the body that affected—indeed "deranged"—the mind. This corresponded to Yamazaki and Suzuki's earlier view that the body was not easily tamable and even possessed disruptive influences over the power of reason/the mind. The effective containment of the bodily energies was indispensable, as Yamazaki and Suzuki described, for the successful governance of society. The shogunate's application of the harshest of punitive measures against double suicide, in particular its intent to fundamentally mortify the lovers through the negation of their corporeal dignity, and its subjection of them to gibbeting, putrefaction, or hard labor under outcasts, reflected this official conception of the mind-body relationship.

To further probe why the body of double suicide was met with the harshest punitive measures, I would like to return to one of the main arguments I have made in this chapter from the beginning: the Tokugawa shogunate saw the "unproductive" body, especially its valorization, as a serious moral aberration and a perilous offence against the public order.

There could be nothing more emblematic of life devoid of moral and utilitarian values upheld by the shogunate than the bodies of those involved in a double suicide since their failure to uphold moral imperative by regulating passions with their minds and their attendant self-destruction represented the extreme, even the most unthinkable, negligence with regard to the foremost duty under Tokugawa rule: contribution to the preservation of social harmony through assiduous and productive labor. The bodies from double suicide evoked in a most sensational fashion the consciousness, which the shogunate had worked long and hard to repress since its founding moments, that not only was the body inextricably bound up with the powerful effusion of passion but also this inextricable connection was what made the body impregnable and untamable by the sovereignty of mind. The body reemerged around the turn of the eighteenth century as a locus where norm and passion violently collided with each other in such a way that neither could reign over the other. In other words, the body was rediscovered as the zone wherein one would experience life defying the doctrine of stasis and encounter unknown possibilities and unpredictable consequences. The (re)discovery of body's heterogeneity not only eluded but also decentered the logic of status identity by unsettling and invalidating the alleged self-evidence of morality, duty, and responsibility prescribed according to this logic.[98] Chikamatsu's articulation of the body as the locus of the heterogeneous and townspeople's enthrallment with it pointed to the new recognition that corporeal experience in everyday life was neither representable nor comprehensible within the discursive economy of the "cosmic-human" unity. It was precisely the recognition of the gulf between the symbolic and institutionalized universe of reality and the newly felt corporeal reality that gave rise to Chikamatsu's perceptive view of the "real"—the unreal being more real than reality. And it was against the recognition and articulation of a new reality—the experience of the singular, heterogeneous, and unpredictable passage of life—that made the Tokugawa authorities anxious about and determined to contain the real or imagined "anomalous" body of double suicide, a figure that evoked the overwhelming presence of "dysfunctional"/ "immoral" life, by criminalizing its transgressive and self-destructive deeds and mortifying those who committed the deeds.

Raymond Williams has noted that at moments of great historical transformation tension frequently arises between the received semantic forms and practical experience. He calls this "thought as felt," "feeling as thought," or "structure of feeling." It refers to social consciousness whose formation is still in process, "often indeed not yet recognized as social, but taken to be private, idiosyncratic, and even isolating, but which in analysis has its emergent, connecting, and dominant characteristics."[99] This consciousness will soon gain some social ground, according to Williams, in a way that that the people feel that they share "the experiences to which the fixed forms do not speak at all, which indeed they do not recognize."[100] This feeling is often articulated first through forms and conventions—"semantic figures"—in art and literature.[101] Such was the case during the mid-Tokugawa period. Chikamatsu's representations of townspeople's lives as oscillating in the irresolvable rift between the determinate and the indeterminate marked one of the earliest enunciations of the formation of the new practical consciousness among ordinary urban inhabitants, and it signaled the sprout of a new province of experience irreducible to the world organized around the logic of status identities.

The consciousness that the logic of status identity could not speak to new experiences found an expression in the most commonly used semantic figure among the townspeople: the floating world (*ukiyo* 浮世). This term began to emerge as the denotation of eighteenth-century forms and contents of popular fiction, poems and the artistic genre called ukiyo-e, the woodblock illustrations of courtesans, kabuki actors, and scenes from the commoner's everyday life. *Uki* was written with the ideograph "float" and *yo* with that of "world," thus combined together, it connoted, as I argued above, the ontological indeterminacy arising from the state of "incessant flux" or "in-betweenness." Before it came to be commonly used in this way, however, *ukiyo* was written with the ideograph of "sorrow" or "lamentation" (憂き), which indicated that the term was firmly coupled with the Buddhist notion of insouciance (indifference toward the worldly existence) originating from its dualistic view of the world, a view that divided the world into a life-death dichotomy and opposed the ephemerality of this world to the absoluteness of the other world. The meaning of *ukiyo* in the Buddhist worldview, therefore, pointed to a transient view of life in the sense that people could and must not expect salvation except in the world after death.[102]

The sense of transience gained a new orientation in the eighteenth-century notion of *floating* world: it signified life-in-this-world not as a step toward real salvation and emancipation awaiting one in the next world, but a realm of hovering, like "bubbles," between two realities, the "established" and the "emergent," without any definitive recourse in the world of "now."[103] Meshed with the previous meaning, *ukiyo* metamorphosed into a new semantic figure that signified the incertitude of being, with a somewhat existential nuance, conceived of and articulated by the townspeople in Osaka and Edo through their various artistic and literary forms.

Ihara Saikaku (1642–93), an Osaka merchant and a renowned popular writer, might have been one of the earliest to begin to use *ukiyo* with this new connotation. While writing stories that underscored the importance of not transgressing given stations and duties as merchants, artisans, and peasants and thereby promoting the values of piety, humility, and diligence,[104] Ihara explored in some other stories the world of profligacy and the attendant crime of passions against the feudal laws that prohibited love between those of unequal status. In the latter attempts, he spoke to the potential moments of an alternative universe in which emotional intensities against the strictures of law were unleashed and led to tragic consequences. If Chikamatsu's tragic stories were concerned with consequences of defying social norms, Ihara's focused on those of transgressing law and order. Chikamatsu's protagonists took their own lives before laws could punish them, but Ihara's faced their demise as the result of criminal charges. In "The Story of Seijūro in Himeji" in *Five Women Who Loved Love* (*Kōshoku Godai Onna*; 1686), for example, Ihara's female protagonist, Onatsu, fell in love and eloped with an attractive and experienced gallant, Seijūro, who worked for her elder brother as a competent and trusted clerk. After being captured by the brother's apprentices, Seijūro was beheaded on the counts of seduction, kidnapping, and theft (he was falsely accused of stealing seven hundred pieces of gold from his master), and Onatsu would soon lose sanity and withdraw to a humble retreat in a deep valley. Life "drifts as light as bubbles in the Floating World," concluded Ihara.[105]

Conclusion

Since its formative years in the early seventeenth century, the Tokugawa shogunate had hoped to encompass all conceivable realities by representing and organizing everyday life according to the theory of cosmic-human unity. It sought to suppress the dynamics of historical contingency epitomized by uprisings, rebellions, and usurpations that were characteristic of pre-Tokugawa times by structuring society in such a way that the facticity of change and existential incertitude was to be purged permanently from popular consciousness. A status hierarchy was rationalized as the unerring reflection of the inviolable and immutable truth embodied in the structures of cosmic order and its preservation was established accordingly as the foremost ethical principle for all members of the new society to observe. A hereditary system was instituted throughout the realm and the perpetually repetitive enactment of given status and duty (i.e., practices that reproduced given social relations) was authorized as the practical basis of the ethical principle.

This particular configuration of society was meant in part to facilitate the Tokugawa shogunate's agrarian approach to economy. Despite the fact that money had already infiltrated into major cities such as Sakai during the pre-Tokugawa times as a universal equivalence for economic exchange, the shogunate decided to privilege rice as the universal measure against which all wealth was evaluated. However, because it was logically and practically untenable for rice to pose itself as a universal equivalent in the manner of money because it was itself a consumable product (i.e., it was anchored essentially to use value, not exchange value), the shogunate did recognize that money was necessary for enabling the circulation of goods including rice. Money was thus theorized as auxiliary to rice despite its universal function, just as merchants were given a status secondary to that of peasants in social hierarchy despite their indispensable role of distribution and exchange. By attaching a universal or an abstract value to rice rather than money and accepting exchange as a necessary means of circulation, if not that of wealth creation, the shogunate hoped to contain or curtail the power and influence of urban commoners, in particular merchants, who had once demonstrated fierce independence from and obstinate insubordination to samurai rule during the fifteenth and the sixteenth centuries. The agrarian approach to economy was therefore intertwined inseparably with the shogunate's efforts to rationalize and enforce the political system that instituted the principle of perpetual and circular repetition.

Reifying the conception of eternity was, however, not an easy task to execute. As the economic structure built on the primacy of rice economy began to expose the chasm of its own logic (i.e., making use value—rice—reign over exchange value—money—as if it represented a value of universal equivalent) while being subsumed by money economy, common urbanites were awakened to an actual expansion in the scope of existence which had been repressed or negated by the official ideology. New aspects of existence, once they were drawn into the sphere of literary and artistic visions and articulations, did not coexist harmoniously with normative elements of existence, but engaged them in struggle, reevaluated them, and brought about a recognition of corporeal reality unassimilable to the unity of the normative domain of reality. The registration of new meanings as exemplified by the etymological shift in *ukiyo* emanated from an old one and did so with its help in such a way that the new significations became more capable of communicating the "structure of feeling" that still remained largely unarticulated in the urbanites' world of the everyday. The new connotation registered in *ukiyo* accentuated ontological ambiguities and indeterminacies in terms of a sharp tension between norm and passion, the real and the unreal. The fluid and unpredictable dimensions of the newly felt reality came to constitute the main trope of literary and artistic representations, displacing the alleged immutability and universality of the given order of reality built around the status system.

It was not a coincidence that the body occupied the preeminent place both in the shogunate's efforts to create and sustain the social order and in the new consciousness that saw the emergent province of reality as inassimilable to that order. The state made attempts consistently to delimit the meaning and function of the body to the moral imperative of productive work based on its deep concern that the failure to regulate the body, especially its excessive desire, would result in people's awakening to the irrepressible presence of history. Indeed, as in the case of Ihara and Chikamatsu, the popular culture of the eighteenth century rediscovered the body as the locus that generated conflictive negotiations or dialogues of divergent values, feelings, and ideas. Their artistic method of tragedy called attention to the images of the body torn apart between norms—the symbolic universe of reality and its institutional embodiments—and widely felt corporeal realities under the Tokugawa rule, visualizing an irreconcilable rift between the two domains of reality. By the late eighteenth century in Edo, the representation of the rift would find a new form of articulation in the images of the body associated with the popular culture of play and pleasure. The form was a parody. It represented the rift in a manner that ridiculed, satirized, and debased social thought and practices that supplied authority and legitimacy to the assumed integrity of the established order of things. And the "idle" body suffused with earthy, folly, and grotesque images would offer powerful modes to the new form of representation. The next chapter will consider the form of this new representational mode and the historical conditions that gave rise to this mode.

TWO

Parody and History in Late Tokugawa Culture

Parody is indeed an ambiguous play.

TOSAKA JUN, "ON SATIRICAL LITERATURE"

Literary critics often observe that parody is a general feature of all discourses. Simon Dentith identifies two common characteristics of parody: it works as a conservative force "in the way that it is used to mock literary and social innovation, policing the boundaries of the sayable," but it can also be subversive in that it "attacks the official word, mocks the pretensions of authoritative discourse, and undermines the seriousness" through which domination is achieved.[1] But Dentith, at the same time, calls for a historically situated analysis of parody.[2] While paying attention to the generalities of the use and function of parody, this chapter examines it as a historically specific social form and phenomenon that was symptomatic of massive and fundamental transformations taking place in late eighteenth- and the early nineteenth-century Tokugawa Japan.

As the previous chapter indicates, there was an important shift around the middle of the eighteenth century in how Edo popular culture articulated the widely felt dissonance between the formal structures of Tokugawa society and ongoing socioeconomic and cultural transformations. In the early eighteenth century, the popular trope of tragic double suicide reflected this dissonance as an irresolvable tension between received moral norms and the effusion of passion in forbidden love between people of unequal status. From the middle of the century, however, parody also presented a new possibility of articulating the dissonance, through the performative repetition or appropriation of Tokugawa norms and customs. The parodic repetition forged satiric attacks on dominant social thought and practices that were conducive to the status hierarchy and division of labor, and in doing so, supplied literary and aesthetic forms—comic realism and grotesque realism, which I discuss in detail in the next two chapters—capable of articulating social and cultural contradictions felt or observed by Edo townspeople in their everyday life.

By the late eighteenth century, parody clearly superseded the tragic trope in the popular cultural practices in Edo, signaling a new concern and preoccupation with the "affairs of the here and now" (*genseno arisama* 現世の有様) or "affairs of the floating world" (*ukiyono arisama* 浮世の有様). This focus on the here and now should not be viewed as an instance of secularization—the universalized teleological narrative of transition from premodern to modern epochs—but as a shift in accent in the mode of signification, reflecting and refracting the "expansion of the evaluative purview" of the city dwellers.[3] New aspects of existence no longer coexisted well with dominant aspects of existence, but began to engage and reevaluate them in a critical light.

Money, Parody, and Production of a New Social Space

The new evaluative purview was occasioned by the pervasiveness of a money economy that advanced the juxtaposition and intermixing of the incommensurable—the hierarchically differentiated objects, people, and customs. The doctrine of the social hierarchy had been instituted to minimize social mobility, uproot political uprisings, and support a subsistence economy built on the primacy of agricultural production, especially rice. The Tokugawa shogunate's ultimate interest in privileging a rice economy over a money economy lay in its effective regulation and containment of the forces of commerce and market that had once empowered merchants and townspeople in free cities such as Sakai during the fifteenth and sixteenth centuries to declare and exercise fierce political and military independence from the samurai regimes. In order to recast society under its reign as the aggregation of self-contained and self-sufficient communities, the shogunate devised the hereditary system that divided people into discrete status groups, each with its supposedly homogeneous and corresponding moral and intellectual aptitude. No cross-status interactions such as marriage between the people of unequal statuses were permitted.

Money, however, knew no boundaries. By bringing products into the relations of equation, comparison, and evaluation not through a coercive means of distribution (levy) but through the sphere of exchange, namely, market, it cut across boundaries of status, labor, and domains. Money therefore exerted a corrosive effect on the mechanisms of hierarchy by promoting the dynamic flow and uninhibited interaction of goods, ideas, knowledge, customs, and people. Observing the development of commerce, as well as the vibrant flow of ideas, knowledge, and people that came with it, the samurai-turned–political economist Kaiho Seiryō (1755–1817) concluded in 1810 that all things from rice to vegetable fields to mountains to labor possessed exchange values and thus followed the law of exchange in their transactions. "Everything in the world," Kaiho declared, was an "exchangeable object" or a "commodity" (*shiromono* 代物).[4] Because townspeople knew this irrefutable truth, according to Kaiho, they were actually more suited to manage the polity than samurai. If samurai wished to survive, they must learn "the law of exchange."[5] Despite the shogunate's avowal of the primacy of agrarian economy over commerce, by the beginning of the nineteenth century, money had established itself as the principal motor force of Tokugawa Japan. The Tokugawa authorities and ruling elites' undervaluing of commerce and the market appeared to people such as Kaiho as an utterly insupportable ideological gesture contrived to vindicate and resuscitate the waning social values of eternity, stasis, and harmony.

The money economy was thus altering the fundamental structures and value systems of Tokugawa society. Fluid and heterogeneous social interactions formed through this new economy shattered people's restricted horizons and permitted a more extensive evaluative purview about social world. This situation particularly described social and cultural developments in Edo, the largest consumer castle town. The dissolution of the socioeconomic boundaries and status distinctions transformed the castle town—designed originally to reflect the social values of eternity, stasis, and harmony—into a dynamic urban space where heterogeneous people and things, fashions and customs, passions and desires, came and went incessantly. Nowhere was this transformation more observable than in Edo's popular streets and squares (*sakariba* 盛り場), such as Ryōgoku and Asakusa. The popular writer Hiraga Gennai (1728–79) described the crowd and hustling, bustling atmosphere of Ryōgoku:

> Monks mix with ordinary people and men with women, while gawking country samurai serving at the Edo mansions of domain lords mingle with stylish commoners wearing the latest long combs and short capes. The attendant of a lord's son carries a glass goldfish bowl, and a woman-in-waiting follows a lord's wife, dangling a brocade pipe sheath. . . . The amorous-looking woman pulling her sleeves stiffly away from the men who tug on them looks like a professional dancer who already has a lover, and that other stiff woman with an amorous look on her face must be a maid looking for love on a rare day off from the women's quarters in Edo Castle. And over there are the smooth body motions of a master swordsman; the steady movements of the bearers of a large palanquin; the relaxed humming of a blind masseuse who knows exactly where he's going; the two-colored formal robes of a merchant who sells to great lords; the old, ripped divided skirts of un unemployed samurai; the loose, light cape of a retired man; the leisurely strides of kabuki actors; the clipped motions of artisans; the long topknots of construction workers; the loose sidelocks of farmers, hunters coming, and woodcutters going.[6]

In this lively and rhythmic depiction of the crowd in the popular hub of Edo, an image of orderly society governed by the status hierarchy and the division of labor is utterly absent. Instead, Ryōgoku emerges as the melting pot of people with all sorts of social, economic, and cultural backgrounds. The dense crowd consisting of high and low, old and young, men and women pointed to a new mode of life based on fluid and transformative social relations, contrary to the presumed rigidity and verticality of the Tokugawa social order that insisted on the primacy of fixed dwelling, identity, and occupation. Edo's unique cultural stew generated a new mode of existence and served as the social condition for a new evaluative purview, a new horizon of signification. And it is precisely in this context that the rise of parody as a predominant literary and visual mode of representation in Edo popular culture needs to be understood.

As Gilles Deleuze reminds us, an effective parody in theory cannot be satisfied with being a good mimicry of the original, but it inverts the order of the original and imitation, and transforms cognitive boundaries that generate the values authorizing the order.[7] Parody therefore should not be considered to be a pure repetition of the original, but instead it exercises first and foremost the transformative potency of recomposing and reorienting preexisting authoritative texts or discourses by mimicking them in such a way that it places them under erasure. This parodic erasure of the original texts or discourses reevaluates and often displaces their central values and ideas so as to render them less self-evident or even absurd. Parody is, in other words, a form that performs the disfiguration of its object reevaluating the putative system of values that sustains the object's integrity and authority. Parody's deconstructive appropriation of the preexisting texts or discourses comes into play via its active dialogical engagement with diverse and divergent voices that often remain latent or repressed in original texts or discourses. M. M. Bakhtin hence calls parody a "double-voiced" discourse.[8]

This general theory of parody helps us to grasp the role and efficacy of parody in late Edo popular culture. Parody's distinct way of bringing together divergent voices and perspectives perfectly represented the confluence of the incommensurable engendered by the new economy. Parody captured the new social formations by foregrounding pluralized, contentious images of Tokugawa society, images that underlined contradictory realities that had become widely recognized by the late eighteenth century. The most salient of all the contradictions was, as discussed above, the growing disjuncture between the ideological premise of social and economic hierarchies and hierarchies' actual reversals. The primacy of the rice economy that sustained the samurai's wealth was overshadowed, even superseded, by the ascendancy of a money economy controlled by merchants who were at the bottom of the formal status hierarchy—just above people of outcast status. Popular entertainments (e.g., theaters, pleasure quarters, print culture, and street performances), which were closely associated with outcasts and patronized by merchants and artisans, became the magnetic center for cultural innovations and unbounded social interactions, often also drawing in people of samurai status. The dialogic imagination captured and accentuated the fluid and dynamic social interactions that threw the formal arrangements of social structure into disarray, as well as the widely perceived tensions originating from these interactions, by supplying images that sharply contrasted with those the Tokugawa authorities worked hard to foster and defend: of a harmonious, self-contained, and perfectly functioning society. The dialogic imagination visualized the disintegration of the totality and presented new understandings of social realities. Parody was therefore the salient symptom of the dissolution of established cultural and socioeconomic hierarchies—and a bellwether of the dissolution's larger implications for late Tokugawa Japan.

It was no coincidence that parody was brought into the center of cultural innovations by loosely associated writers and artists with extremely diverse social backgrounds. Indeed, status-crossing social relations were the group's defining feature. Two significant developments during the latter half of the eighteenth century—the expansion of literacy and the emergence of vibrant publishing and distribution networks—produced social spaces that encouraged this new kind of association.[9] These two closely intertwined phenomena helped to eliminate the distinction between author and reader, literati strata and masses. People from different segments of society, especially those with commoner origins, began to assume the roles of writer, artist, poet, and scholar, as well as reader and audience. This "democratization" of cultural formation, as Dominick LaCapra suggests in a different context, presupposed "the circular relationship composed of reciprocal influence between the high and low cultural spheres."[10] That is, commoners had to become familiar with idioms of the ruling class—and vice versa—before the culture of parody could come into being. As these forays across old boundaries primarily began in the realm of popular culture, our task here is to understand how communities mixing writers and artists of samurai and commoner backgrounds engaged collectively in the appropriation or defamiliarization of dominant discursive norms by infusing something new, strange, or incompatible into the norms.

The implications of these mixed communities can be understood by examining how the normative discourses responded to this new cultural practice. Makino Toshimichi (dates unknown), presumably a Confucian scholar, wrote in 1794 in *The Virtuous Lessons for the People of Four Statuses* (*Shiminzenkun* 四民善訓): "There is nothing more desirable than that samurai, peasants, artisans and merchants clearly understand their duties. As the saying goes, it is useless for people to read Confucian classics without understanding them. . . . We must seek the virtue of learning only in efforts to help ourselves understand our respective place in society."[11] Nakamura Hirotake (dates unknown), a samurai and Confucian scholar, remarked in 1811 in *The Lessons for Father and Child* (*Fushikun* 父子訓): "Learning does not refer to frivolous art or skill. . . . It aims at cultivating one's mind. Through learning, samurai, peasants, artisans and merchants should come to grasp their respective essences. Thus, the goal of learning is to understand how to respect and observe one's own place in society."[12]

What these responses to artistic alliances across social boundaries reveal is that widespread literacy among commoners clearly caused a great degree of anxiety among cultural elites, because it implied the rapid dissolution of the mechanisms of cultural distinction upon which the Tokugawa social hierarchy was maintained. Nakamura's reference to "frivolous art or skill" indicated his view of the community of popular writers and artists—which used parody to turn dominant ethical norms such as filial piety, duty, and loyalty into the object of mockery—as anarchic and thus detrimental to the public mores and the social order. For intellectuals and officials, the fact that the expansion of literacy had not resulted in educating common people about the norms and virtues that maintained the Tokugawa system was disconcerting and ultimately led to the Kansei Reform (1787–93) and the Tenpō Reform (1841–43), which sought to curb excesses of the popular culture.

The spread of literacy cannot be separated from the emergence of a commercial economy in publication and print business. Popular cultural texts were certainly a commodity, as Kaiho would put it, whose success depended entirely on market demand for and, thus, consumption of entertainment. Their subject matters were largely determined by short-lived trends, reflecting the astute and timely responses of artists, writers, and playwrights to the fashions expressed in streets, theaters, pleasure quarters, and market districts. Furthermore, unlike traditional literary and artistic works, whose value was derived from their exclusive, singular, and original existence, popular cultural texts were prized for their affordability, reproducibility, and transportability. Ukiyo-e woodblock prints, for example, were so inexpensive and ephemeral that people casually pasted them on paper-covered sliding doors (*shoji* 障子) for temporary appreciation. They were, together with the popular novella, the favored souvenirs for visitors to Edo. Itinerant merchants always carried these items with them to nearby villages and towns as among the most sought-after products. The social characters of these popular cultural texts generated a discursive space for producing, disseminating, and sharing images, knowledge, and ideas beyond the traditional social boundaries. In other words, these cultural media marked the emergence of the public as well as an early form of mass communication, or "information revolution," that dispensed with the principles of hierarchy and encapsulation.[13]

The publishing business brought together writers and artists of diverse socioeconomic and cultural backgrounds. One type of publishing entrepreneurship, the bookseller-publisher (*hon'ya* 本屋), selected and invited promising writers and artists, regardless of their social backgrounds, to publish and sell their works. According to one study, there were more than two hundred bookseller-publishers in Edo in the 1780s.[14] Suwaraya Ichibei (1726–1811), a pioneering entrepreneur in the Edo publishing business, equipped his store in the low city as a gathering place for the most innovative writers and artists. The list of the authors who published with Suwaraya's company is impressive: Hiraga Gennai (1728–79); Hezuku Tōsaku (1726–89), a samurai retainer and disciple of Gennai who was known as a *gesaku* writer; Ōta Nanpo (1749–1823), a samurai retainer and disciple of Gennai known as a "mad poetry" (*kyōka* 狂歌) master; Sugita Genpaku (1733–1817), a close associate of Gennai and physician who cofounded Dutch Studies; Takebe Sei'an (1712–82), a physician from northeastern Japan who exchanged ideas about medical knowledge with Genpaku; Hayashi Shihei (1738–93), a military strategist who warned of the imminent arrival of Western imperialism; and Kaibara Ekken (1630–1714), a samurai turned Confucian scholar who was not a contemporary of those mentioned above, but whose famous book published by Suwaraya posed grave doubts about Neo-Confucian dualism.[15]

Another prominent publisher who played an equally important role in creating a cross-status social space was Tsutaya Jūzaburō (1750–98). He specialized in the publication of *gesaku*, *kyōka*, and ukiyo-e prints created by Hiraga Gennai, Ōta Nanpo, and Hezuku Tōsaku, along with works by Koikawa Harumachi (1744–89), a samurai retainer and *gesaku* writer; Kitagawa Utamaro (1753–1806), a commoner and founder of the Kitagawa school of ukiyo-e art; Santō Kyōden (1716–1816), a commoner and best-selling writer; Kitao Shigemasa (1739–1820), a commoner and illustrator; Shiba Kōkan (1747–1818), a commoner and Gennai's associate who pursued the European method of painting; and Sharaku (dates unknown), an eccentric print designer who drew kabuki actors and sumo wrestlers in an unorthodox style.[16]

It is clear from these lists of names that the writers and artists who worked with Suwaraya and Tsutaya belonged to the same vibrant literary and artistic community. In the wake of the shogunate's Kansei Reform campaign, however, Suwaraya's and Tatsuya's businesses fell apart and their creative communities crumbled. The campaign promoted social, political, and ideological cleansing through programs imposing austerity, redressing popular culture, and regulating schools of thought other than Neo-Confucianism. The chief architect of the campaign, Matsudaira Sadanobu (1758–1829), vilified the producers of popular culture and the widespread taste for luxury, as well as unorthodox Confucian teachings. Along with the publishers, several writers and artists also fell victim to the campaign as well. In 1791, Santō Kyōden was heavily fined for "confusing the minds of commoners" through his "frivolous" novellas, some of which were banned. In 1792, Hayashi Shihei was imprisoned for criticizing the shogunate's potential weaknesses in preparing for the arrival of Western imperialism and died after receiving severe punishment by shogunate hands. Ōta Nanpo, after receiving a warning that he must live as a "proper" samurai, voluntarily stopped composing *kyōka* poetry. Koikawa Harumachi died mysteriously—perhaps a suicide—in 1789 after being summoned by the shogunate authorities.[17]

Another enterprise associated with the publishing business, which continued despite the Kansei Reform, was book lending (*kashihon'ya* 貸本屋). The book lenders contributed to the formation not only of status-crossing communities of writers and artists but also of a reading public. The lenders were peddlers who walked through the streets carrying numerous copies of popular fiction, erotica, and theatrical works on their backs. They were themselves rarely engaged in publishing. Instead, they purchased from bookseller-publishers a number of copies of the original works or made their own handwritten copies and then lent them to townspeople. This mode of book distribution expanded the literary underground, as the book lenders made and circulated books and prints classified as heretical by the authorities. Ōta Nanpo noted in his diary that, in his search for a banned book by Baba Bunko (1718–58) that reported with great sympathy on the peasant protest in the Mino domain (present-day Gifu), he used every available means, including inquiring with book lenders.[18] Nanpo's personal book list also shows that he possessed many banned books and handwritten copies, including Baba's other works, which were presumably obtained through book lenders.[19]

Book lending played a crucial role in the expansion of readership in the lower urban classes. Compared to purchasing books and prints, renting was far less expensive. For instance, it cost eight *monme* to rent illustrated books for five days, whereas the price for purchasing them was said to be ten times that amount.[20] Around 1840 a bowl of buckwheat noodles cost about sixteen *monme.* Such noodles were a common evening meal for the artisans of Edo, so illustrated books were being rented for only half the price of an inexpensive dinner.[21]

The shogunate was naturally vigilant about the greater accessibility of information to an expanded readership that book lending enabled. During the Kansei Reform, the shogunate attempted to divest book lenders of the right to handcopy and lend books containing "heretical rumors" (*ifū* 異風) or erotic content (*irogoto* 色事) by outlawing such activities. The lending business nonetheless continued to thrive, in part by providing a space for underground literary activity. Some historians estimate that by 1808 there were approximately six hundred book lenders within Edo alone and that this number grew to eight hundred in the 1830s.[22]

Book lenders' activities were not limited to the underground, however. In fact, the most popular kind of reading that lenders delivered to the townspeople—war tales—was officially sanctioned. The historian Nagatomo Chiyoji, whose *Kinsei Kashihon'ya kenkyū* (*Research on Early Modern Book Lenders*) is a seminal study in the field, argues that the popularity of books of war tales like the fourteenth-century *Chronicle of Great Peace* (*Taiheiki* 太平記) is attributable at first glance to their intended function of "enlightening" the commoners.[23] Enlightening here meant two things: making the commoners venerate the spirit of "praising good and condemning evil" (*kanzen chōaku* 勧善懲悪)—of course, the good here referred to heroic acts of samurai—and cultivating their proficiency in reading Chinese ideographs. But even the officially sanctioned genre of war tales failed to encourage commoners' unquestioning obedience because, according to Nagamoto, the commoners often ignored the intended significance of war stories and enjoyed them simply as books for amusement. After reading *Chronicle*, one anonymous commoner wrote this verse: "The Taiheiki, a story in which many samurai wither like flowers" (*Takusan ni bushi no hanachiru taiheiki* 沢山の武士の花散る太平記).[24] Another commoner reader composed the following poem: "After reading a military story, I deploy new strategies for making money" (*gunsho yomi zenino arateni semekaeru* 軍書読み銭の新手に攻め変える).[25] By reading the supposedly enlightening war stories, these commoners did not absorb the intended reverence for samurai. Instead, their readings forced these stories to transgress their own putative system of values. Commoners simply found the war tales startling and entertaining: startling because so many samurai had to die in vain like withering flowers and entertaining because military strategy as narrated in these stories appeared useful for thinking about new ways of making money. Converting the story of moral instruction into a source for the pleasure of money making and entertainment, the anonymous commoners also converted "reading" from a means of inculcation into a practice of subjective signification that nullified the primacy of prized virtues such as reverence and loyalty. For commoners, then, reading was not merely passive reception: it was a process of appropriation—dispossessing and transforming the signified into a new sign that could be meaningful in and for their everyday experiences. In Edo popular culture, reading meant an active engagement with what Paul Ricoeur calls "text" that permits the act of interpretation to "decontexualize" it in such a way that it can be "recontexualized" in new semantic directions.[26] As the example of *Chronicle* clearly demonstrates, the commoners' reading of such works betrayed a particular code inscribed in the works by the authors with the expectation that it would induce commoners' reverence for samurai heroes. The disquiet of the Tokugawa authorities—manifested in their stringent censorship policy—resulted precisely from the transformative quality of the interpretive act that came with the great expansion and flow of information. "Heretical" views could now be not only produced through rumor, books, and prints but also widely disseminated and translated into different social and political meanings by commoners.

The ways in which Edo townspeople interpreted the woodblock print by Utagawa Kuniyoshi (1797–1861), *Illustration of the Phantoms Generated*

2.1 Utagawa Kuniyoshi (1797–1861), *Illustration of the Phantoms Generated by Tsuchigumo at the Mansion of Lord Minamoto Yorimitsu*, 1843. Woodblock print, ink and color on paper. (Courtesy of Keio University, Tokyo)

by Tsuchigumo at the Mansion of Lord Minamoto Yorimitsu: figure 2.1), demonstrates the Tokugawa authorities' worst fear.[27] Kuniyoshi completed this work in 1843, just as the Tokugawa shogunate was conducting a new political campaign that was much larger in scale than the Kansei Reform during the 1790s. The Tenpō Reform of 1841–43 aimed to wipe out all "ostentations" of conspicuous consumption and wasteful expenditure by prohibiting commoners from enjoying street entertainments, comic novellas, makeshift theaters, and multicolored ukiyo-e prints, as well as relishing delicacies, luxurious clothes, elaborate accessories, and food delicacies. The Edo city magistrate punished a number of teashop owners, kabuki actors, prostitutes, storytellers, vagrants, abortionists, puppeteers, woodblock illustrators, and *gesaku* writers.

Kuniyoshi's picture depicted a horde of phantoms summoned by a legendary ancient tribe of cave dwellers, which was said to be conquered by the Yamato state (third to eighth century) and who are referred derogatively to as Earth Spider (*tsuchigumo* 土蜘蛛) in old mythistorical documents such as *The Record of Ancient Affairs* (*Kojiki* 古事記) and appeared in war tales like *Tales of Heike* (*Heikemonogatari* 平家物語) and *Chronicle*. Here, ghosts are summoned back to the world to take revenge on Minamoto Yorimitsu (Minamoto Raikō; 948–1021), a shogun from the clan that would later, in the twelfth century, establish the first samurai regime. The print caused much controversy, and Kuniyoshi was subjected to cross-examination by shogunate authorities. It is hard to determine what message Kuniyoshi meant to convey in his print, because he never acknowledged any intended political implication and thereby escaped punishment. Nonetheless, documents indicate that the townspeople interpreted Kuniyoshi's phantasmal images as the return of those who had been harmed during the shogunate campaign, thus reading the illustration as an expression of the common people's grudge against repressive shogunate deeds.

Like many popular illustrations from the Tokugawa period that ridiculed the authorities, Kuniyoshi's print made use of historical allegory as a parodic disguise based on shared popular knowledge; therefore, a reference to the Minamoto clan was actually a way to talk about the Tokugawa clan. Because the Minamoto clan was the founder of the samurai government, the Tokugawa clan consistently claimed that they had ancestral ties with the Minamoto, despite the lack of evidence supporting such a claim.

Kuniyoshi's print also parodied the customary representation of *tsuchigumo* in war tales. In an 1838 print triptych *The Earth Spider and Minamoto Raikō* (figure 2.2), this legendary outcast depicted as a barbaric and demonic creature, as in the *Tales of Heike* and *Chronicle*, was to be abhorred and purged by heroic warriors. But in the 1843 triptych, instead of depicting *tsuchigumo* as a symbol of evil, Kuniyoshi transfigured it into a legend who invoked and led the angry ghosts in seeking their revenge, subverting the order of customary vision purported to glorify the bravery and righteousness of warriors. Accordingly, the samurai figure identified in a cartouche in the later triptych as Minamoto Yorimitsu was rendered as the twelfth Tokugawa shogun, Tokugawa Ieyoshi (1793–1853), under whose reign the repressive Tenpō Reform campaign was implemented. Kuniyoshi rendered other samurai figures playing the board game *go* as Ieyoshi's advisers, and the phantoms as the townspeople persecuted during the campaign.

The presumed identities of the phantoms in Kuniyoshi's 1843 triptych are given in four records that were written by anonymous townspeople in the early 1840s. Minami Kazuo, a historian of Edo popular culture, has constructed a chart that compares the different interpretations of each phantom.[28] The female ghost with the figure of a deformed child on her head, for example, was read as an abortionist in one record and in others as a prostitute or a fortuneteller who claimed to have inherited the magical power of the legendary female dragon that was believed to have created within the premise of the popular Sensōji Temple a pool of healing for sick children. According to the moral teachings of Confucianism and Buddhism, abortion and prostitution were the most heinous evil acts. In addition, the ruling elite condemned popular belief in the legendary female dragon and her healing water as superstitions of the "stupid crowd" (*gumin* 愚民). The prostitute, abortionist, and fortuneteller all represented the world of outcasts condemned under the Tokugawa moral order, and individuals engaged in these occupations were purged during the 1840s campaign. Kuniyoshi's print was immediately banned, yet it continued

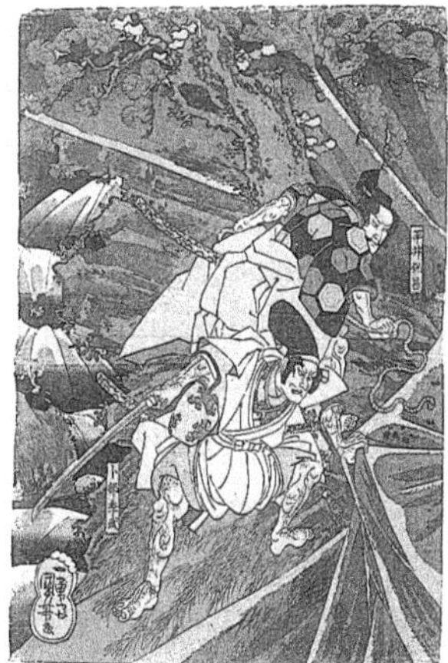
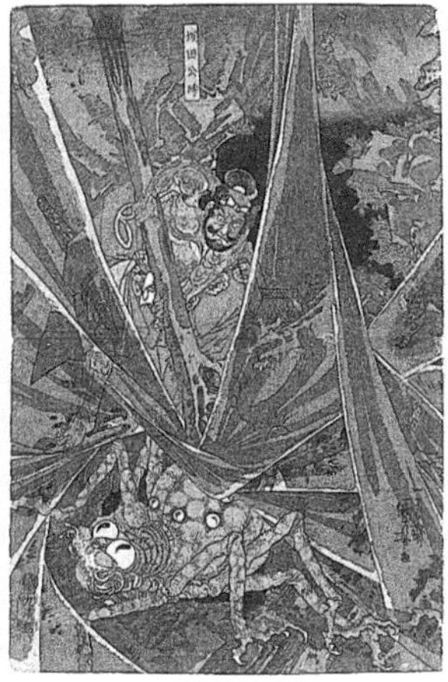

2.2 Utagawa Kuniyoshi (1797–1861), *The Earth Spider and Minamoto Raikō*, 1838. Woodblock print. (Courtesy of Japan Gallery, New York)

to be circulated widely within and without Edo through underground networks such as book lenders.[29] What the simultaneous emergence of cultural entrepreneurs, numerous media, and writers and artists in late-eighteenth-century Edo signified was the birth of a social space in which townspeople actively took part in in the networks of *interpretation*. Their interpretative acts brought force to the new often unanticipated articulation of feelings, emotions, aspirations and judgments related to commoners' everyday experiences—an unequivocal symptom of fundamental structural transformations that grew dissonant with normative discourses and practices that supported status distinctions and division of labor.

Parody and Representational Space

Tokugawa authorities referred to the marginalized urban spaces, where the "unproductive" people—vagrants, peddlers, entertainers, prostitutes, writers, artists, laborers, and déclassé samurai—dwelled, as the evil places (*akusho* 悪所) or the fringes of the world (*basue* 場末). It is tempting to conclude that these places worked as the major inspirational source for literary and artistic production, precisely because the shogunate's estrangement and containment of the "idlers" and their culture formed these places into a distinct symbolic universe, a locus for stimulating alternative conceptions of reality. Indeed, popular literature, prints, and theaters all drew heavily from the fantastic and idiosyncratic characteristics of these social spaces and their culture, which affirms Barbara Babcock's generic formulation that "(w)hat is socially peripheral is often symbolically central."[30]

But if the literary and artistic inversion of a center and periphery were effectively contained within the fringe spaces, apart from the everyday domains of productive work, these urban spaces' symbolic efficacy would also be limited to the role designated by the Tokugawa authorities: a safety valve. As long as the symbolic inversion did not prod people into disregarding their utmost duty of observing societal harmony and the virtues of simplicity and diligence, a temporary immersion in prodigality was acceptable. But, as seen in the previous chapter, in late Tokugawa Edo, the boundaries between work and play, the everyday and the noneveryday collapsed in such a way that the logic of the noneveryday pervaded the everyday, or the everyday folded into the noneveryday. "Idle" life became the daily means of sustenance for many, and social relations and ways of life associated with the culture of play and pleasure encroached on the official order by revealing heterogeneous realities that sharply contradicted the ideological premise of the order. Popular novellas, prints, and theatrical performances communicated realities excluded and concealed by the ruling ideology, reassessing and rearranging the familiar order of things and offering readers, beholder, and spectators alternative responses to the official reality. In this regard, the subversive implications of marginal spaces and their culture did not arise from their otherness to or detachment from the dominant reality: they sprung from their *dialectical* and *dialogical* relation to it. The various forms of literary texts and artistic representations sought to capitalize on this particular semiotic potency of the marginal and brought radically different views of reality to the center of consciousness in the symbolic universe of popular culture.[31]

The fringes of the world in Edo resembled what Henri Lefebvre calls "representational space." Lefebvre sees this space as "dominated" by power "and passively experienced" by inhabitants, yet a space where "imagination also seeks to change and appropriate."[32] This imagination, according to Lefebvre, "overlays physical space [by] making symbolic use of its objects," and then the space in turn need "obey no rules of consistency or cohesiveness for [being] redolent with imaginary and symbolic elements."[33] Thus, the space embraces "the loci of passion, of action, and of lived situations, and immediately implies time."[34] The fringes of the world in Edo were indeed dominated in the sense of their being denigrated and regulated as the space for momentary relief or flight, and yet popular imagination and lifestyles associated with the imagination sought to transform the official designation and thus gained a hegemonic status as an unremitting social practice not only among the ordinary urbanites but also among "Confucian scholars, samurai, Buddhist priests, and immigrant peasants."[35] "Everyone in the real world," in Buyō Inshi's words, came to "imitate idlers' frivolous arts, theater, and lifestyles, but not vice versa" in early-nineteenth-century Edo.[36] Images and words encapsulating "passions, actions, and lived situations" captivated people beyond social boundaries.

Symbols unique to the fringe spaces of Edo played a central role in popular cultural texts. For instance, the humorous and satirical stories written by Hiraga Gennai, which I discuss extensively in the next chapter, unfolded exclusively within popular entertainment districts such as Asakusa and Ryōgoku, and his heroes and heroines were all based on Edo's outcast inhabitants, including actors, entertainers, and courtesans. In *On Farting* (*Hōhiron* 放屁論), a peasant turned entertainer called the "fartist" demonstrates at a popular amusement site, Ryōgoku Bridge, his skill in manipulating the sound and rhythm of farts into music. In *A Rootless Weed* (*Nenashigusa* 根無し草), the protagonist who attracts the Judge of Hell (*En'ma*) was modeled on an actor who impersonated women in a kabuki theater of Asakusa. In *The Biography of Elegant Shidōken* (*Fūryū Shidōken-den* 風流志道軒伝), the hero was directly taken from the tales of the professional storyteller Shidōken, who entertained with vulgar stories and war tales in the Asakusa marketplace. These figures all in reality belonged to the lowest stratum of the social hierarchy and were characterized in the stories as social outsiders who had been exiled, abandoned, or despised by the establishment. But, as in the stories of a pre-Edo genre—*otogizōshi*—the underdog heroes and heroines of Gennai's stories were capable of eventually transcending—through wit, skill, satire, or physical attraction—and even teaching the world that had shunned them. *The Biography of Elegant Shidōken*, for example, ends with a scene where the hero, Asano Shin, is sent by Gennai's alter ego, a Taoist sage, to the Asakusa marketplace to be a popular storyteller for the purpose of "enlightening" and "guiding" the fellow commoners, taking the role played by Buddhist priests and Confucian intellectuals.[37]

Asakusa's heterodoxy was an essential motif for folk legends related to many of the popular sites in this area. According to one of the most popular versions of the legend, found in the Edo guidebook *Edo's Attractions* (*Edo meishoki* 江戸名所記; 1662), when Asakusa was still a desolate fishing village, three brothers caught an object carrying the image of the Kannon deity (bodhisattva of mercy and benevolence) in their nets. On the same day, after they had repeatedly snagged the object but failed to harvest any fish, they discussed with their relatives how to make sense of these miraculous happenings and what to do. On the following day, the three brothers built a humble shrine consecrated to worship and prayed to the deity for successful fishing. An unprecedentedly successful harvest followed. After making a large profit from fishing, they rebuilt the shrine into an edifice that would come to be known as the Asakusa Kannon or the Sensōji Temple. The three brothers were also deified as the guardian gods of Buddha. In this legend, Asakusa was represented as the place where the commoners could live under the protection of Buddha's mercy and compassion.[38]

Another legend about the origin of a deep pool called Old Lady's Pool (*Ubagafuchi* 姥ヶ淵) adjacent to the Sensōji Temple, which I have touched on in the discussion of Kuniyoshi's triptych, describes Asakusa as a lonely place where a man-eating dragon, disguising herself as an old woman, ran an inn with her daughter. One day, as the old woman continued to victimize wayfarers, the Kannon deity punished her by tricking her into eating her own daughter. Grieving her daughter's death, the old woman began to reveal her identity as a dragon and went back to her home country where she had once belonged. After the dragon vanished, the inn was transformed into a deep pool, which was said to heal sick children when people prayed to the pool by hanging a bamboo tube of sake on a branch of the tree alongside the pool. In this legend, Asakusa was a place where destruction was transformed into healing by the holy power of Kannon.[39] The depictions of marginal figures were suffused with remarkable power of redemption, metamorphosis, and healing—experiences that remained peripheral within the established order of the everyday.

Edo townspeople's vernacular language also worked as a representational tool. The everyday language of the townspeople differed greatly from that of samurai.[40] This difference corresponded to the geographical boundary between the high city, the residential quarters of samurai, and the low city, where the townspeople lived, so the samurai's language was referred to as the language of the high city (*yamate kotoba* 山手言葉), in contrast to that of the low city (*shitamachi kotoba* 下町言葉). Neither the language of the Edo commoner nor that of the samurai, however, was monolithic. There existed a complex heteroglossic diversity, the interaction of dialects, jargons, slangs, and accents, each of which reflected not only status, gender, and class differences but also the social context in which a word was spoken. For example, the wealthy merchants adopted the samurai language in their business dealings with samurai, while using in their daily life the commoners' ordinary language, which was heavily coded with gender distinctions. In contrast, artisans, small-shop owners, peddlers, samurai with the lowest status, and masterless samurai shared a "crude" language. In the early Tokugawa period, they began to form a particular speech style called *roppō kotoba* (六方言葉). It was a mixture of coarse yet colorful regional dialects and samurai language. In speaking it, they pronounced *ookii* (big) as *dekai*, *hiroi* (wide) as *dadabiroi*, *arekore* (this and that) as *nannokanno*, *iyada* (no) as *yada*, *nani* (what) as *ani*, *naze* (why) as *aze*, and so on.[41] This speech style was later adopted by kabuki plays that required the performance of rude behavior and abusive language. Courtesans also had their own language (*kuruwakotoba* 廓言葉). It was invented and spoken purposely to create the fantastic ambience of the pleasure quarter. Most courtesans came from poor farming families in the countryside, so in their private time, they spoke the dialects of their home villages.

This dynamic mosaic of languages, which was marked by various relations of prestige and authority, inspired cultural articulators to capture and create—often in comical ways—moments in which social tensions and contradictions surfaced at the intersection of diverse enunciative positions. Each of these positions accentuated a specific kind of valuation and feeling. In his popular *The Bathhouse in the Floating World* (*Ukiyoburo* 浮世風呂), for instance, Shikitei Sanba (1776–1822) introduced a scene in which a protagonist representing the townspeople of the low city reacted to the well-to-do merchants' practice of emulating samurai class's speech: "What the hell! How come they say *ogushi* [an honorific expression of "hair"]? When I hear that, I really wanna say, Shame on you! I can't stand it. Why don't they just say *kami* ("hair")? After serving samurai, they come to say *omaesama* [an honorific word for "you"]. . . . or things like that. Ah, to hell with them! The poor folk like us don't need to speak like that."[42]

Edo popular culture's preoccupation with the here and now signaled the important underlying artistic principle that shaped its forms of representation and subject matter. The popular works were predicated on a vision of the world as revolving around the same essential material element, "the single life energy" (*ichigenki* 一元気). Unlike the dualistic vision of the world (e.g., heaven and earth, high and low, reason and passion, and mind and body) held by officials and elite intellectuals, popular works did not devalue passion and emotion as the lesser attributes of humanity. They instead took them as a part of the single energy that ceaselessly generated the vitality of life. These works placed an enormous weight on the materiality of bodily experiences: making love, seeing, speaking, eating, farting, and drinking. Images of the new earthy subject based on the single life energy were most vividly illuminated in a series of pictures called *playful sketch* or *Drawing Things as They Come* (*manga* 漫画). Katsushika Hokusai (1760–1849), Utagawa Kuniyoshi, and Watanabe Kazan (1793–1841; a samurai literati, reformer, and Dutch Studies scholar), were all fascinated with scenes from townspeople's everyday world and, in particular, their ordinary corporeal movements. Tirelessly drawing bodily motions, including laughing and angry faces, stretched out and shrunken postures, and laboring and resting bodies, Hokusai, Kuniyoshi, and Kazan declared that their sketches aimed to "depict life as it is" (*shasei* 写生). Compared with mainstream official arts such as those by the Kano (狩野派) and Tosa (土佐派) schools or the literati art school the Nanshū (*Nangaha* 南画派), which represented nature and human beings in abstract, static and heavenly images, Hokusai's, Kuniyoshi's, and Kazan's aesthetic representations highlighted the materiality and ordinariness of the subjects they drew. The fullness of life was their foremost concern, which was to be found only in ordinary time and space. Kazan wrote in the prologue of his 1818 sketchbook, *Quick Sketches of One Hundred Postures* (*Issō hyakutai* 一掃百態), "It is a serious mistake to regard drawing commoners' everyday activities as a base art. Schools of art such as the Kanō and the Nanshū, which serve their samurai patrons, are all erroneous to disdain this sort of art."[43]

Drawing scenes from everyday life, especially bodies in motion, with extraordinarily deft and soft and purposefully exaggerated lines, Kazan used quick strokes to capture and celebrate the incessant flow of life energy (figure 2.3). Hokusai and Kuniyoshi shared the same artistic method and subject matter. Hokusai's *Happiness of Commoners* (figure 2.4), part of his famed *Playful Sketches*, depict happiness in eating, drinking, and respite through various bodily expressions. One of Hokusai's friends remarked of *Playful Sketches* that the "drawings capture the true intricacies and forces of people's everyday passions and motions."[44] Kuniyoshi's work from the 1830s, demonstrated in *Drawing One-Hundred Faces as They Are* (figure 2.5), realized a dramatic perspective on daily life. Interestingly, the images Kuniyoshi created were often described as weird (*kikai* 奇怪) or grotesque (*iyō* 異様) by the authorities and some literati,[45] but Kuniyoshi responded that the images best represented the concept of "depicting life as it is."[46] The bold and exaggerated lines with which Kuniyoshi drew facial expressions and bodily gestures brilliantly encapsulated the intensity of life-in-motion as figures peeked, washed hair, looked through a telescope, or looked up at the sky. Hokusai, Kazan, and Kuniyoshi all explored new aesthetic and social values—the incessant flow of life energy in the world of the ordinary—by prioritizing the con-

2.3 Watanabe Kazan (1793–1841), *Quick Sketches of One Hundred Postures* (*Issō hyakutai*), 1818. Woodblock print. (Owned by the author)

2.4 Katsushika Hokusai (1760–1849), *Happiness of Commoners*, 1840s, in *Hokusai Manga*. Woodblock print. (Courtesy of Dan McKee)

2.5 Utagawa Kuniyoshi (1797–1861), *Drawing One-Hundred Faces as They Are* (*Shasei hyakumensō*), 1830s. Woodblock print. (Owned by the author)

crete over the abstract, the earthly over the heavenly, and the ordinary over the sublime.

Hattori Yukio, an eminent historian of kabuki, argues that Edo culture's preoccupation with the here and now, as evident in literary and visual texts' valorization of concrete, earthy, and ordinary matters, also informed the central disposition of kabuki's plot and choreography.[47] Before the turn of the nineteenth century, according to Hattori, kabuki prized soft humors and easy and slow choreography, but, in the beginning of the century, the language and aesthetic of speed, sheer shock, and materialism came into prominence. Many historians of Tokugawa culture, including Hattori, refer to this shift as the emergence of realism (modernism) in the late Tokugawa period, an understanding of late Tokugawa culture that emanates from the preconceived teleology of the modernization theory, as discussed in the introduction. I would maintain that this shift actually represented the rise of a new kind of "structure of feeling": that is, an aesthetic form that seized and articulated the *historicity* of the here and now. Just as Gennai's depiction of the crowd at the Ryōgoku Bridge area showed an excitement about new social spaces, these cultural texts also took an intense interest and delight in rapidly unfolding changes—even ruptures—that began emerging in the late eighteenth century. The texts deployed many different means to articulate this rupture, but it was the form of dialogic imagination, parody, that gained the most prominent status in this cultural practice. This comes as no surprise, as mentioned earlier, since the dialogic imagination proved to be effective in expressing the newness of social reality by realizing a vision and trope of the dense mixture and interaction of heterogeneous voices in ordinary space and time. By encapsulating the moment in which various people, ideas, values, and perspectives interacted and collided with one another, parody articulated most vividly the singularity of the present.

Play as a Transformative Act

Play (*asobi* 遊び) generally denoted all kinds of activities for pleasure during the Tokugawa period, but, more specifically, it designated literary and artistic innovations referred to as "play-in-arts" or "immersing oneself in arts" (*geini asobu* 芸に遊ぶ) for the cultural producers of Edo.[48] According to the Edo literary historian, Nakamura Yukihiko, this concept of "play-in-arts" originated from the Chinese literati or gentleman scholar (*bunjin* or *wenren* 文人) tradition that began to take root around the middle of the seventeenth century, first in the Kyoto-Osaka area, and then later in Edo. Because Edo's popular cultural producers used the same term to describe their practices, Nakamura argues that they constituted part of the literati tradition. Nakamura outlines three sociocultural conditions that contributed to the formation of this tradition during the Tokugawa period. First, the imperative of the hereditary system and the status hierarchy impeded low-ranking samurai and nonsamurai with talent from realizing their ambitions in the public arena.[49] This alienation of talent from public life resulted in the widespread trend for self-fashioning of intellectual and cultural communities among low-ranking samurai and commoners. The Gansuidō Academy (Osaka's commoner academy) and the Kaitokudō academy (Osaka's merchant academy) were a case in point. Second, with the introduction of Chinese literati-style painting around the middle of the seventeenth century, the arts began to gain a new currency as the field in which talented individuals sought to express their individuality, unfettered by the constraints of the Tokugawa system.[50] This new outlet for self-expression shaped literati's adoption of "play-in-arts" or "immersing oneself in arts," which designated the cultivation of selfhood through aesthetic and intellectual activities. Third, a theory that supported and legitimized the position of play-in-arts gained influence among intellectuals.[51] In the orthodox Neo-Confucian paradigms of the time, art was regarded as the least important field of knowledge and practice, but eminent intellectuals such as Ogyū Sorai and his students altered this view by imparting great significance to artistic practice. Even though Sorai's idea about the importance of literature, poetry, and music were meant to encourage only small groups of elites, he and his students provided a theory that people with talent could use to justify their immersion in artistic activities.[52]

Nakamura's argument that the alienation of talents yielded a desire for self-realization through aesthetic and intellectual refinement seems to explain in part the emergence of Edo's artistic community. With a few exceptions such as Koikawa Harumachi, Ōta Nanpo, Ryūtei Tanehiko, and Watanabe Kazan, writers, artists, and playwrights were townspeople of the lower orders, outcasts, or samurai who belonged to the bottom rung of their hierarchy. Hiraga Gennai, for example, was born into a samurai family of the lowest rank, and chose to live as a masterless samurai among townspeople in Edo;[53] Hezuku Tōsaku was a low-ranking samurai serving his master in Edo; Santō Kyōden was a commoner who owned a tobacco shop; both Katsushika Hokusai and Utagawa Kuniyoshi were commoners; the eminent kabuki playwright Tsuruya Nanboku was born into a family of a kabuki actor; and Shikitei Sanba was a woodblock cutter.[54]

Nakamura's discussion fails to recognize, however, the critical difference between the literati and the producers of Edo's popular culture. For the literati, the practice of play-in-arts meant the self-stylized gesture of transcending the world that alienated them. Following the Daoist dictum that "leaving the mundane world behind is the only worthy way [to live]" (*zoku wo saruni hakano nori nashi* 俗を去るに他の法なし), the literati cherished the life of seclusion (*in'ton* 隠遁) and pursued elegance (*miyabi* 雅) or cultural refinement as the basis of their self-identity.[55] Their conscious indifference, or occasionally contemptuous stance, toward any worldly affairs shaped their distinct identity. Gion Nankai (1676–1751), a physician and Confucian scholar who worked for the lord of the Kii domain (present-day Wakayama), for instance, wrote that the literati ought to compose poems with the language of elegance to avoid "base and ordinary conversation, language used in casual letters and inferior fictions, words that referred to money, selling and buying, and indecent" matters.[56] Minakawa Sōen (1734–1807), a Confucian scholar who studied with Ogyū Sorai, noted that poetry required three essential components—style, strain, and spirit—and privileged spirit over the others as the most vital principle for composing poetry.[57] Echoing Ogyū Sorai's view of China's ancient times as the ideal and most creative moment in human history, both Gion and Minakawa advocated reciting and emulating the works of such ancient Chinese poets as Li Bai (701–62) and Cen Shen (712–70) as the way to attain the highest level of refinement. It comes as no surprise that their poems, essays, and artworks were filled with exclusive literary and visual codes that privileged ancient Chinese literacy and aesthetic taste. The literati's highly exclusive cultural practices fostered and exalted closed, monologic intellectual communities and thus epitomized the dominant normative values of self-containment and self-sufficiency.

Unlike the literati, the producers of popular culture did not ennoble seclusion from the world of the ordinary: they embraced the ordinary. Ōta Nanpo wrote in the late 1780s, "It givens me a great pleasure to be blamed for being vulgar by the people of refined taste, for the ordinary, which those people despise, interests me more than anything else."[58] For writers and artists of popular culture, play-in-arts meant not only a critical stance against the literati culture that held on to the high-low binary but also an active engagement with the ongoing transformation of the everyday by articulating feelings, aspirations, and experiences that emanated from that transformation. "Play" in this sense did not refer to the self-gratification of ego through the act of seclusion as demonstrated by the literati, but a conscious choice to embrace the here and now by becoming a witness and articulator of the transformative moment in history.

It was no coincidence that this world of play-in-arts distinguished itself from established arts, such as Noh theater and the tea ceremony, or the official Confucian academy, the Shōheijo, whose prestige and reputations were safeguarded by the hereditary system. If the hereditary system was meant to freeze everything in a given place, as it were, the world of play-in-arts prioritized action over status, becoming over being, and metamorphosis over immutability. This principle can be aptly explained in terms of Paul Ricoeur's notion of play: "Play is an experience which transforms those who participate in it. . . . In play subjectivity forgets itself; in seriousness, subjectivity is regained. . . . In play, there occurs . . . a metamorphosis, that is, both an imaginary transportation marked by the reign of figures, and the transformation of everything into its true being."[59] There are two correlated insights in this formulation to be considered: one is the idea that "play makes subjectivity forget itself," while the other is that the subject then experiences a "metamorphosis." We may understand the underlying existential possibility that connects these two moments of change or transformation as *potentiality*, a term that points to uncertain possibilities that remain latent and thus unnamable in the normative world. Under the normal circumstances, individuals are tied firmly to their social positions and identities, but in play they "forget" subjectivity and undergo "metamorphosis" to become something new, different, or unknown. This transformative process lifts the players out of the identitarian (*dōistsuteki* 同一的) world and leads them to a non-identitarian (*hidōitsuteki* 非同一的) terrain of experience, meaning, and self-realization.

Edo's popular cultural practices, especially parody or dialogic imagination, bore the same performative potency as play defined by Ricoeur. In fact, parody, in its many different manifestations, was called wordplay (*kotoba asobi* 言葉遊び) and visual play (*mitate asobi* 見立て遊び) during the Tokugawa period. It suffices to say here, as I elaborate on the implications of parody as wordplay and visual play in the next chapter, that the kernel of both lays in their performative potency to dislocate syntax and a familiar order of vision and perception. The defamiliarizing effect of parody unveiled new semantic and experiential terrains in front of readers and audiences and rendered the ideological premise of status identities and division of labor indefensible.

One might detect in this new social space of Edo popular culture the residual fragments, if not the unbroken continuity, of the sphere of autonomy (*muen* 無縁) that evolved in free cities such as Sakai or Buddhist temples in fifteenth- and sixteenth-century Japan.[60] The free cities and the temples, according to the historian Amino Yoshihiko, served as sanctuaries in which commoners of various social backgrounds could commingle in freedom and peace without intervention by military regimes. Yet with the entrenchment of the Tokugawa bureaucratic system, these places gradually lost their extraterritorial status and were eventually integrated into the structure of authority and accountability. The disappearance of the social spaces of sanctuary took place in parallel with the shift in the meaning of the term "public" (*kō/ku* 公). Before the end of the seventeenth century, "public" roughly denoted the "cooperation" or "association" (*kyōdō* 協同) realized in the spaces where autonomy from the secular authorities was the precondition for social interactions. By the early eighteenth century, however, when the Tokugawa regime began to take more aggressive control over the everyday world of the commoners, the ideograph for "public" also started to be replaced, or sometimes interchangeably used, with that of "suffering" (*ku* 苦), a homonym of "public."[61] This semantic shift helps us to understand the historical characteristics of the social space of Edo popular culture. Commoners came to view the public as the realm of "suffering," instead of "cooperation" or "association," as soon as the formal structure that had once demarcated their public life as the sphere where they coexisted in peace and freedom began to diminish.

Such a sphere of association reemerged in a radically different form under the different historical circumstances of the eighteenth century. It did not develop any formal political and economic structures that could guarantee participants' autonomy, nor was it capable of forging open and collective political confrontations against the Tokugawa regime. Rather, this new space of association consisted of dispersed cultural practices that hinged on a vibrant commercial economy. Individuals in Edo were connected through networks of artistic and commercial practices, and their associations, according to Victor Turner, materialized through "the interstices of [the dominant] structure, in liminality; at the edge of [the] structure, in marginality; and from beneath [the] structure, in inferiority."[62] Amino and Jinnai Hidenobu see this transitory and fluid liminal space in Edo as an instance of "communitas," Victor Turner's utopian concept of a spontaneous, ephemeral, and horizontal community that is formed by an "unmediated relationship between person and person, a relationship which nevertheless does not subsume one in the other but safeguards their identity in the very act of realizing their commonness."[63] But I would strongly argue that positing the world of play-in-arts as an unmediated and spontaneous, and thus ideal and authentic, community is simply to produce the reified—disembodied—conception of community. Edo's cultural forms and practices could have never come into existence in the way they did without the mediation of the dominant Tokugawa structures and their contradictory metamorphosis, as argued in the previous chapter. And most importantly, these cultural forms and practices must be understood in relation to material conditions that emerged from those structural transformations: commercial economy, publishing industry, and reading public. Without taking into account how these various material conditions mediated and determined Edo's cultural forms and practices, it would be impossible to comprehend the historical characteristic of the politics of Edo popular culture—namely, the ways in which the culture worked as a site where structural contradictions were most vividly articulated.

Parody as Relativism and Fetishism

I have argued that parody worked as the literary and artistic method that brought together diverse voices in contentious dialogue so as to foreground tensions, frictions, confrontations, contradictions, humors, and irony. My argument may seem to echo a prevalent tendency in recent scholarship to designate Edo cultural texts, in particular, the playful composition called *gesaku*, as the quintessential instance of what Bakhtin calls the polyphonic novel. Although I see some relevance and usefulness in this designation, I find the casual application of a Bakhtinian concept troubling because it tends to disregard the specific social and ideological features of the cultural texts by underscoring their random resemblance. A more rigorous examination of the form of dialogic discourse and its use in relation to specific historical contexts is needed if we are to understand popular art and literature as integral part of the rich historical drama of late Tokugawa Japan.[64]

The dialogic form was not the invention of any particular author. It was used extensively first in *gesaku*, especially in the late-eighteenth-century genre "yellow-covers" (*kibyōshi* 黄表紙). But the form I consider here as a true dialogism is essentially different from that of the common style of *gesaku*, which put several voices together to generate comic conversation about recent trends on the streets and in the pleasure quarter and often ended with simple moral and didactic messages. It refers to the specific method of parody that created antagonisms and collision of plural values and ideological stances, each of which reflected a specific social background. Comedy, irony, and satire were used as a means to express criticism against *any* discourse that exalted commonsense and authoritative words for the purpose of defending the dominant values and customs conducive to the status order.

It was perhaps Hiraga Gennai who first rose to prominence as a popular *gesaku* writer by using this method in his works. Gennai demonstrated an extraordinary ability, as seen above, to observe and describe the heterogeneous composition of crowds, their noises, and their movements and interactions in Edo's popular streets and entertainment districts. He drew heavily on the images of people and entertainers whom he observed in these places to create his own dialogical style. His works, as I will demonstrate in chapter 3, were structured by two diametrically opposing views: one defending the normative discourse and the other subverting it. Their disagreement would erupt into polemics filled with curses, mockery, satire, and irony. Although such a narrative structure clearly represented one type of dialogical form, it was limited in that the authorial voice—Gennai's own voice, representing the antiestablishment position—tended to dominate the polemics. In other words, Gennai's dialogue was never based on an even relationship between contentious voices but was designed to convey his own satirical criticism against the establishment. It was arguably Shikitei Sanba who, while retaining Gennai's use of curses, mockery, satire, and irony, pushed dialogic imagination in a new direction. By superimposing squabbling voices while sidelining the authorial voice, Sanba's works generated a polyphonic effect—a riotous confluence of contentious voices—as a way to undercut any dogmatic and authoritative discourse, including his own.

Sanba's *The Barbershop in the Floating World* (*Ukiyodoko* 浮世床) best demonstrates his method. Speedy and chaotic dialogue created by a riot of bickering voices delegitimates all authoritative claims and exposes the limitations, contradictions, and absurdity of authoritative words. One example is a scene in the barbershop where Master Kōfun—a member of the literati whose name is written with the ideographs 孔糞, which literally meant "shit of Confucius"—and regular customers come to realize after a series of absurd misunderstandings that they cannot communicate at all. Master Kōfun sees the world only through the lens of Chinese language, art, and literature. He relies on the phoneme of Chinese language and his knowledge of Chinese art and literature to attempt to participate in the customers' conversation about street fads. Master Kōfun continuously misconstrues names of popular actors as references to famous Chinese actors and genres of popular entertainments as references to Chinese art and literature. Unaware of his own misapprehension, he gives the other customers a long lecture about the greatness of Chinese civilization. The regulars listening to Master Kōfun's didactic talk make an attempt to understand him by superimposing their colloquial words and knowledge about the entertainments over his references. Master Kōfun gets frustrated with their debasing, albeit unintentional, of Chinese art, literature, and moral teachings to the level of "vulgar" art forms and daily affairs. The two worlds of language and knowledge never find common ground in communication.

Master Kōfun eventually expresses his frustration to the barber, "Oh, how helpless! I now see why Sages in old times were also troubled [by the ignorance of the common people]."[65] But then the customers instantly respond:

> Hey, I always thought that those fellows called Confucians were really smart and knowledgeable. But ain't they actually very stupid? They talk in delirium and sound arrogant, but they don't even know who Muraku and Karaku [popular Asakusa storytellers] are. Buddies, they cannot be trusted. They only know Confucius' teachings, but once asked about anything else, they look so lost. They have no idea about what common folks do. All they care about are things Chinese! They are all infected by a really bad disease. That fellow [Master Kōfun] is lesser than common folks.[66]

As both parties attribute the utter failure of communication to the other's ignorance and stupidity, these two conflicting worlds are never reconciled. Nor is there a third voice that arbitrates the two worlds. Instead, through confusions of linguistic meaning and cognitive process created by the collision of the two different worlds, social and ideological hierarchies such as high/low and cultured/uncultured are completely displaced. The authoritative dictum of Confucianism is brought down to the level of popular entertainments, and the uncouth customers inadvertently reveal a truth: that Confucians' teachings have absolutely no connection with people's everyday concerns and thus are nothing but self-satisfied and self-serving dogma. In this way, Master Kōfun's words are rendered nonsense, and his knowledge is desacralized.

This method of rendering words utterly nonsensical through the production of excessive and confusing meanings—which the scholar of Japanese literature Maeda Ai once called "canceling" or "nullifying" (*muka* 無化)—may seem to be applied exclusively against the antiestablishment in Sanba's stories, but Sanba in fact directs his fire against any authoritative and dogmatic truth claim. Thus, his satire and criticism should not be understood as operating within the binary structure of domination/

resistance, ruler/ruled, and elite/commoner. Townspeople routinely mock and curse each other for their foolishness and vanity in *The Barbershop*.

One example is a dialogue about the meaning of *tsū* (通)—a term that denoted being "sophisticated" in the matters of play, in particular, the Yoshiwara pleasure quarter. As a paragon of true player, the person of *tsū* (*tsūjin* 通人)—"a dandy, a dilettante, and a habitué of the Yoshiwara"—embodied the most valued cultural capital for the wealthy townspeople.[67] *Tsū* was a product of the rapid commercialization and commodification of social life among the townspeople, for most *tsūjin* were the newly rich: rice brokers who amassed wealth by loaning money to samurai, taking their rice stipends as security, or bordello proprietors who prospered from the popularity of the Yoshiwara pleasure quarter. Their flashy lifestyles, tastes, and bearings epitomized what the Tokugawa authorities vilified as "idleness" and "exorbitant expenditure."

In *The Barbershop*, barbershop customers discuss a poor yet exuberant old man, a barbershop regular, who lost his wife some years ago and lives a humble life alone. They praise him for his good nature and for having managed to bring up his son well on his own. They conclude that he must be an exemplary *tsūjin*, contrary to its received meaning:

> Those guys admired as *tsū* are actually pretty ostentatious. If you don't believe, take a careful look at how messed up they are [in their personal lives]. On the other hand, those fellows regarded as *yabo* (野暮) [poor bumpkins] are actually pretty decent folks. They are never slighted by others, and even often extend their help to the poor. I think this kind of fellow is a true *tsū*.[68]

Listening to these words, a presumptuous customer shouts, "I got it. I will cease to be *tsū* from this moment!" Then another customer immediately curses him, "Hey, who said that you are *tsū*!? You are a real stupid asshole!"[69] In this dialogue, the meaning of *tsū* is dislocated through praise of the poor and supposedly unsophisticated old man as a genuine *tsū*. Furthermore, the playful curse directed against the man who assumes he is *tsū* underlines this man's ignorance and self-conceit. The lively exchanges of curses, jokes, and mockery cancel the meaning of *tsū* and strip *tsūjin* of the badge of social distinction. Lower-class commoners—the barbershop customers who are usually mocked as *yabo* by *tsūjin*—ridicule and nullify the commonsense by inverting the cultural hierarchy of the townspeople.

The Barbershop repeats an endless loop of "canceling," while offering no profound philosophical or didactic moral teachings. This narrative feature is of great importance. Although many *gesaku* writers, such as Santō Kyōden, began to use moralistic language in their works after the Kansei Reform, Sanba's work did not follow the trend. *Gesaku* scholars tend to regard this literary stance as a sign of nihilism or escapism widely shared by writers and artists of the time. These authors' refusal to take a firm position about anything, however, is better read as symptomatic of the dissolution of established norms and mores in the social order of Tokugawa Japan. The consistent distrust in and negation of any authoritative words was a strategy of deconstruction deployed to announce and accentuate the bankruptcy of meanings and values that made up the social fabric of the Tokugawa system.

However, the power of parody to foreground social change remained ambiguous. It could lose its efficacy when these texts took the figures of "idleness" and "exorbitant expenditure" as a fetishistic object without any critical distance from them. *The Playboy Dialect* (1770), written by an anonymous author, is a story that mocks two samurai figures, one called the Man-About-Town, a middle- or low-ranking samurai representing the half-*tsū* (*hankatsū* 半可通) type, and another called Hira, a high-ranking samurai from the provinces representing the *yabo* character, for their vanity, rudeness, and lack of knowledge about Yoshiwara.[70] The story draws a sharp contrast between their foolishness and the behavior of The Youth, a son of a prosperous merchant family, who exemplifies *tsūjin* for his refined demeanor, lack of pretension, and sensitivity toward courtesans' feelings. The Man-About-Town believes himself to be a man of refined tastes, despite his utter ignorance of the unspoken rules—codes and idioms of behavior—that were peculiar to the pleasure quarters. The Man-About-Town's vain demonstrations of bravado earn him the proprietress's disdain, and he is shunned for this tactless treatment of the courtesans as mere commodities whose services can be bought, whereas The Youth is appreciated for his sincerity and respectfulness. The sharper contrast is highlighted between The Youth and Hira. Hira's apparent impudence in ignoring the Yoshiwara codes of manner—consuming too much sake and demanding sexual "service"—invites disgust and disdain from the courtesans. The fact that The Youth is the Man-About-Town's and Hira's nominal social inferior yet far surpasses them both in affluence and refined demeanor reveals the irony that, in order to gain acceptance in a world which revolves around the commodification of women and sex, a man has to prove his complete detachment from behavior based on commodity value. This irony of *tsū* shows that it was not solely the shogunate and leading intellectuals who recognized the immorality of libidinal pleasure in Edo's urban landscape. The notion of *tsū* could sustain its legitimacy only if it successfully inscribed the performance of morality in its aesthetic values to counteract or compensate for the underlying logic of blatant commercialism upon which the pleasure quarter operated. Commodity values certainly dictated the business of the pleasure quarter, for courtesans were indeed bought and sold for different prices according to the scale of their desirability. And it was the power of money that enabled wealthy urbanites to enjoy momentarily equalizing, inverting, or rearranging established social hierarchies within this confined world of play and pleasure. This materialism, however, was carefully countervailed by sensibilities and codes of behavior that rejected any display of monetary value, exchange, and commercialism. The overt evocation of materialism was a taboo of the first order and earned naive players opprobrium as *yabo*. The acquisition and seemingly natural enactment of "taste" was required to "humanize" the otherwise commodified world of fantasy. Fantasy would cease to be fantastic, after all, if the fundamental logic of commodification enabling the fantastic flight from the everyday was not kept dormant.

The pleasure quarter and its aesthetic of *tsū* was therefore a space of reification or a reified space under the new economic principle of commodity value. But in what sense could this reified world of play and pleasure be perceived as "transgressive"? Did it necessarily signify substantive challenges to authority in a way that materialized for Bakhtin the "temporal liberation from the prevailing truth and from the established order"?[71] The world of play and pleasure exemplified by Yoshiwara—in particular, literary and visual representations of it—offered an ambiguous, even contradictory, cultural logic toward the established order. Literary and visual works that celebrated carnal pleasure and "wasteful" expenditure were a clear marker of the type of "idleness" disdained by the shogunate authorities and intellectuals. Such works represented, in Harry Harootunian's words, "the challenge of a general economy of expenditure against the restricted economy of mere production."[72]

> What appeared in [late] eighteenth-century Edo was surplus, money to waste, glorious expenditure that increasingly displaced political authority altogether to the accumulation of wealth and extravagance. . . . Yet, this incidence of wealth and expenditure should not be seen as merely the sign of an emerging bourgeoisie, who would, according to the law of political economy, reinvest wealth on the expectation of a return. . . . Rather, what the new cultural practices were showing was . . . the apparent imposition of a dangerous libidinal economy, not utilitarian consumption, and this recognition

revealed the shape of a [new] social [formation] far more troubling to the Tokugawa than merely the appearance of commercial economy.[73]

What these popular cultural texts' overt commendation of *tsū* signified was "the apparent imposition of a dangerous libidinal economy" that was toppling down the restricted economy. Their transgressive character stemmed precisely from their symbolic function of propelling the recognition of the irreversible socioeconomic transformations. *The Playboy Dialect* exemplified it by promoting the radically different value system of libidinal economy and demonstrating the reversibility of the symbolic status hierarchy.

But when, unlike Sanba's *The Barbershop*, the cultural texts failed to articulate the historicity of *tsū*, or the aesthetics of commodity value, and reified its implicit logic of commodification as the principle of the new social order without maintaining any critical distance from it, their playfulness and delectation ended up affirming the bounds of "licensed transgression" rather than being a site of social disruption or a medium for message of change. Their relevance was confined, in other words, to the role of an expedient outlet for release with puns and fads, which enabled the continuance of the social order.

The 1785 story *Grilled And Basted Edo-Born Playboy* (*Edo Umare Uwaki no Kabayaki* 江戸生艶気樺焼) by Santō Kyōden (1761–1816) makes visible this paradoxical logic of *tsū*.[74] Enjiro, the son of the wealthy merchant, is an attractive young man who dreams of becoming the most celebrated *tsūjin* in Edo. One day, he sets about to acquire the reputation through a series of publicity stunts: he tattoos the names of fictitious lovers on his arm, pays a courtesan to beg his parents for permission to marry him, employs newspaper boys to distribute tabloid sheets about his exploits, hires a mistress to act jealous, and finally commits a fake double suicide with a courtesan from Yoshiwara. *Grilled and Basted* creates in Enjiro a stereotypical *yabo* who has no luck at being popular with the girls and courtesans; thus, he resorts to the power of his abundant wealth to realize his fantasy. Love, marriage, and double suicide are a pure performance that can be bought and sold with money. The story pushes the logic of *yabo* to its extreme to expose the fact, which the *tsū* aesthetic is designed to cover up, that the underlying structure of the world of play and pleasure is based on the commodification of social relations and bodily perceptions (love and pleasure). The story calls attention not only to the absurdity of *yabo* but also to the essentially commodified attributes of *tsū*. By representing love, marriage, and double suicide as an object of pure consumption, it shows that "the loci of passion, of action, and of lived situations that immediately imply time"—what Lefebvre calls "representational space"—could become the place for depthless and disembodied experiences. But *Grilled and Basted*'s strategy of crystallizing the concealed kernel of the *tsū* aesthetics came with no sense of irony, criticism, or satirical edge.

Although *Grilled and Basted*'s overt references to the fetishism of money differed from the Tokugawa regime's attitude toward idle expense, in its playful affirmation of commodity value as the organizing principle of social life and its tendency to assign commercial values to bodily and emotive pleasures without irony or criticism, the story ended up espousing a vision of eternity consistent with the fundamental ideological postulates of Tokugawa power. It is in this sense that Thomas Looser writes that the value of commodities worked as a new basis for eternity: "in the merchant economy eternity was no longer defined in terms of the perpetual cycles of nature, but rather in terms of the temporality of the value of a commodity."[75]

Touting money's omnipotence in transforming anything—whether tangible or intangible—into an exchangeable object might be viewed as a liberating disruption of a social order built on the premise of innate and fixed difference. Yet, the fetishism of money was a form of abstraction or reification; therefore, when parody relied on the fetishism without an ironic distance from it, it played no part in offering a critical commentary of the reification performed by the official ideology. It then reinforced, rather than subverted, the posthistorical vision of the social, which was held by the Tokugawa authorities. "Depthlessness," "flatness," "nihilism," and "gratuitous frivolity," common attributes noted by modernist critics such as Kitamura Tōkoku (1868–94), Abe Jiro (1883–1959), and Watsuji Tetsuro (1889–1960), in some of the playful writings and woodblock prints of the 1770s and 1780s, were probably the symptoms of a "posthistorical" consciousness evident in their tendency to reduce the social to commodity form.[76]

The problem of Edo parody that reified the value of commodity resembled what Fredric Jameson calls "pastiche" or "blank parody," as a reference to a postmodern form of aesthetics as distinguished from parody.[77] Jameson writes:

> Pastiche is, like parody, the imitation of a peculiar or unique, idiosyncratic style. . . . But it is a neutral practice of such mimicry, without any of parody's ulterior motives, amputated of the satiric impulse, devoid of laughter and of any conviction that alongside the abnormal tongue you have momentarily borrowed, some healthy linguistic normality still exits. Pastiche is thus blank parody.[78]

Put differently, pastiche produces the vision of a world without cultural hierarchies; "a depthless world in which the recourse to nature, or a past, or 'high' culture, as ways of getting the measure of the world, has been abandoned."[79] What dictates the postmodern sensibilities is then the endless loop of allusion to other styles in a continual reprocessing that echoes the unending commodity circulation of the absolutely extensive movement of capital. Although it is absolutely anachronistic to compare Edo society with societies of late capitalism, Kyōden's method of allusion in *Grilled and Basted* bore the essential feature of pastiche that mirrored the increasingly pervasive logic of the commodity fetishism in late Edo society. Not surprisingly, in reflecting his literary achievement, Kyōden expressed a nihilistic view by calling his works "the endless repetition of jest and parody—an utterly empty play" and self-mockingly warned his readers not to follow his example: "If you keep punning and joking about everything around you, you lose your mind and turn into something that nobody cares to recognize."[80]

Conclusion

Parody in late Tokugawa Japan could work as a critical force, as it self-consciously alluded to lived experiences—whether in the historical past or present—with varying degrees of irony that suggested the impossibility of ignoring or repressing those experiences. Its repetitive insertion of narratives about and images of the experiences into the contemporary moment evoked the historicity of the present or the singularity of the here and now; in doing so, it rendered the Tokugawa social hierarchy and its ideology as an empty formalism. Parody performed this particular function through a dialogic form wherein the "high," commonsense, and dominant norms were appropriated by and through the "low" or marginalized symbols, spaces, and experiences. But parody was never intended to replace or topple the existing structure of power. Rather, it was the mark of a gameful but productive relationship with a sense of the historical present that implied the persistence of the dominant structure, as well as the necessity of critical distance from it. When parody failed to sustain this critical distance, extreme relativism, which could be used effectively as a deconstructive strategy as in the case of Shikitei Sanba, became a form of fetishism, and the possibility of dialogical engagement with the historical present, as in the case of *Grilled and Basted*, was lost.

Unable to convey the stricture of norms and contradictions that surrounded ordinary urbanites, *Grilled and Basted* ended up representing the present as a random unfolding of sheer play, momentary flight of fads and excitement, which exactly mirrored the logic of money fetishism. Tensions between a rice economy and a money economy, a restricted economy and a general economy, which rose to the surface during the eighteenth century, did not automatically guarantee cultural conflict or struggles in the symbolic arena. These tensions simply provided the historical conditions for the possibility—not necessity—of such politics. And such a possibility should be understood in terms of "tendential alignment," a moment when the use of parody and the popular spurning of dominant norms and habits amalgamated into a form capable of delivering mordant wit and pungent satire and therefore invoking a sense of the historical present.[81] Replacing the natural order with money as a second nature could not produce this effect. The next two chapters focus on forms of parody that sought to perform the task of historicizing the present.

THREE

Comic Realism: A Strategy of Inversion

"Symbolic inversion" may be broadly defined as any act of expressive behavior which inverts, contradicts, abrogates, or in some fashion presents an alternative to commonly held cultural codes, values and norms, be they linguistic, literary or artistic, religious, social and political.

BARBARA BABCOCK, *THE REVERSIBLE WORLD: SYMBOLIC INVERSION IN ART AND SOCIETY*

Satire or satirical literature is engendered by the objective condition of a contradictory situation in which one feels compelled to rebel against the social order while having no choice but to remain within that order.

TOSAKA JUN, "ON SATIRICAL LITERATURE"

Let us pervert good sense and make thought play outside the ordered category of resemblances. MICHEL FOUCAULT, "THEATRUM PHILOSOPHICUM"

The preceding chapter has discussed how the particular cultural, social, and economic conditions of eighteenth-century Edo gave rise to the pervasiveness of parody as a distinctively popular form of visual and literary representation, a form that hybridized or dialogized the cultural realms of high and low that were otherwise held separate under the symbolic structure of the social order. This chapter shifts the focus from the question of the historicity of parody to a most commonly used form of parody—what I call "comic realism"—for the purpose of evaluating the ways in which, and the degree to which, the dialogization performed a specific function: the defamiliarization of binary classificatory systems that served as a support for the authoritative discourse on the established reality.[1] A close analysis of this form helps us reflect on the socioideological implications of a specific type of parodic operation and its performative efficacy in the context of late Tokugawa cultural politics.

In discussing how comic writers (*gesakusha* 戯作者) were guilty of "confusing people's minds and hearts," Buyō Inshi elaborated in 1816 on their use of parody as follows:[2]

> These writers distort and ridicule [authoritative] narratives of historically significant events and people, which have been handed down from old times, by inserting fictive or indecent elements into them. The purpose of their outrageous enterprise is to turn the narratives into stories that appeal directly to popular sentiments and tastes. They are keen on such vulgar affairs as male and female relations, theatrical plays, base arts and courtesans, and by mixing them with the narratives, they make the old and good customs and the eternal virtues of loyalty and filial piety into objects of comic mockery, thus encouraging depravity and spreading confusion among the ordinary people.[3]

Written with an acute sense of crisis, Buyō's treatise was a work devoted to the idea of returning to what he believed to be the originally seamless yet now fragmented moral substructure of the social unity constructed by the founders of Tokugawa Japan by identifying and analyzing the various causes of the degeneration. The reference to *gesakusha* in the above statement appeared as a major element of this problem, representing Buyō's grave concern about the unbridled and prevailing use of comic parody that appeared to be undermining the moral economy of Tokugawa life. Buyō's apprehension relates specifically to the way in which *gesakusha* "distorted" the veracity of purportedly important historical events and people: transforming truthful narratives into a comedy that "appeal[ed] to popular sentiments and tastes" by way of infusing "vulgar"—"fictive" and "indecent"—subjects into those narratives. A corollary of this parodic operation was, for Buyō, a debasement of "the old and good customs and the eternal virtues of loyalty and filial piety" and thus the fostering of "depravity" and "moral confusion" among the ordinary people. In other words, Buyō found the proliferation of comic parody very perturbing precisely because of its "perversion of good sense" nurtured and safeguarded by authoritative discourses on moral values and its marring of the discourses' positively constitutive relationship with the mores of Tokugawa society.[4] For Buyō, the problem of parodic composition seemed then to be twofold: not only did it recompose and "refunction pre-existing authoritative text(s) and/or discourses" in such a way that placed them "under erasure," but its modification or appropriation of the original texts/discourses reevaluated and refigured their central values and ideas so as to make them appear negligible, even negative.[5] "Parodic erasure disfigures its pre-texts," in Robert Phiddian's words, "in various ways that seek to guide our re-evaluation or re-figuration of them."[6] In this regard, as we have seen in the previous chapter, parody was never a form of simple imitation of the original but rather a form of "metafiction" (a fiction about fictions) or of dialogical deconstruction of the pre-existing texts.[7] By using someone else's words, parody conveyed values, thoughts, and perspectives that were disagreeable and hostile to those words. The hostility was usually directed against the higher terms of the diacritical pairings—high and low, center and margin, and morality and immorality—to produce the scurrilous relativization of those terms and to subject them to ridicule, humor, and laughter. In popular fictions, a protagonist representing the low or the marginal very often repeated the statement of the other protagonist representing the high or the center, and, according to Bakhtin, "investing it with new value and accenting it in his own way—with expressions of doubt, indignation, irony, mockery, ridicule and the like."[8]

Defining *Kokkei* (滑稽) or Comic Realism as a Form of Parody

This "double-voiced discourse" of parody was an immensely widespread popular cultural mode of representation from the mid-eighteenth century on. Popular writers and artists used this mode to produce comic effects. I use "comic" as a translation of the Edo term *kokkei* (滑稽), which was commonly used to refer to certain genres of urban literature and woodblock prints. Noting many instances in illustrated books, such as the *Book of Punning* (*Sharebon* 洒落本), *Book of Comics* (*Kokkeibon* 滑稽本), and *Yellow Cover* (*Kibyoshi* 黄表紙) of the Meiwa and Ansei periods (1764–80) where the compound *kokkei* was glossed as punning (*share* 洒落) and vice versa, Nakano Mitsutoshi, a leading historian of Edo literature, shows that punning at the time was synonymous with wordplay (*kotoba asobi* 言葉遊び), a meaning that was also identical to *kokkei*.[9] The interchangeability of these terms signifying the comic suggests that the essence of comic writings was a kind of witticism, a clever or humorous use of a word to elicit laughter from the readers.

Although Nakano's analysis helps explain the meaning of *kokkei* in literary genres, it overlooks the fact that the same analysis could be applied to the role of visual play in pictorial genres known as comical drawings (*manga* 漫画), playful drawings (*giga* 戯画), and crazed drawings (*kyōga* 狂画). If comic literature generated humor by drawing on punning or wordplay—a demonstration that words possess more than one meaning, or have different meanings, but sound the same—those drawings engendered the same effect by relying on the method called "visual punning" or "superimposition" (*mitate* 見立て)—a method that made an image represent more than itself or one meaning. Clearly, both wordplay and visual play occupied the same semiotic terrain in which *kokkei* worked as a form of parody.

The playful use of words and images was hence made possible by practices that prized and made full use of the polysemic and fluid quality of linguistic and visual signs as the foremost artistic principle. Such practices drew a sharp contrast with the official and intellectual discourse that, as examined in chapter 2, insisted on the univocality of language by suppressing its equivocal or multivocal possibilities as a disruptive excess. The celebration of the ambiguity of language must have made the Tokugawa authorities and intellectuals, like Buyō, perturbed. Viewed from their presumption that social relations were structured and sustained by the clarity of linguistic meaning or the perfect accord between names and things, wordplay (and visual play) would have appeared to be an anarchic disturbance and perversion of existing social relations. Language, for them, played the crucial role of taxonomic reference in designating unambiguously specific duties and statuses for individuals and therefore that of symbolic power that established the legibility and transparency of social fabric for effective governance of the polity. Keeping order in the taxonomy of status identity and labor was therefore thought to be a precondition for the regime's stability and longevity.

The playful disruption of the familiar order of signs was performed through the verbal and visual method of symbolic "inversion" called *sakasama* (さかさま). *Sakasama* generally referred to a mode of turning the order of things upside down, but, as a mode of comic parody, it involved more specifically two distinct semiotic operations. First, it "addressed the social classification of values, distinctions and judgments which underpinned" the established social hierarchies. Second, it systematically reversed the relations of binary opposites such as high and low, mind and body, and productivity and idleness, by celebrating the lower terms of the diacritical pairings.[10] The corollary of these two operations was often the foregrounding of hitherto unknown perspectives on established reality. The inversion, in other words, confronted and "reordered the terms of the binary pairs" that sustained the dominant perception of reality and, in doing so, called into question the alleged "irreversibility of the order of phenomena, the perfect singularity of a perfectly self-contained series" of perceptions.[11] Through a temporal retextualization of the perceived reality and thus a demonstration of its reversibility, this topsyturvydom recast the reality not as a simple given but as mediated and structured by a series of binary configurations that reduced the contradictory relations of overdetermined realities to their simplicity. And such recasting decentered the dominant reality by bringing the margin to the center, foregrounding it and giving it voice. This is not to say that the inversion worked necessarily as a transformative power that openly challenged the dominant reality. Neither did it redefine the terms of the order nor was it equipped to topple the order. The comic inversion's transgressive potentials were latent in, if not guaranteed by, its proclivity to unveil tensions and contradictions disregarded or concealed by the dominant representation of reality and thus to visualize the representation's partiality. *Sakasama* referred precisely to this type of symbolic operation.[12]

It is in reference to its capacity to negate the given reality that I understand inversion as a form of realism. Clearly, the literary and visual texts of comic parody discussed in this chapter were unreal in the ordinary sense of this word, especially given the metafictional character of their symbolic operation. The new perception and perspective created by the texts can therefore be called, at best, a "fictitious" reality. But following Herbert Marcuse, they were "'unreal' not because [they were] less, but because [they were] more as well as qualitatively 'other' than the established reality. . . . As fictitious world, as illusion, it contains more truth than [did] everyday [i.e. normative] reality."[13] It is precisely in this sense that Sigmund Freud also talked about negation as a form of realism in reference to the function of dream and fantasy. Negation, according to him, "is a way of taking cognizance of what is repressed; indeed, it is already a lifting of repression, though not, of course, an acceptance of what is repressed."[14] What is at stake in this Freudian negation is the logic of disclosure of the repressed. Just like Freud's celebrated concept of "the return of the repressed," negation brings to the fore what is repressed by lifting away the dominant perception of reality. This theory of negation adequately captures the essence of the reordering effect of inversion vital to Edo's comic parody: by removing the social classification of values, distinctions, and judgments that buttressed the hierarchical order of Tokugawa society, it made visible marginalized or repressed realities. In this sense, what I mean by realism refers neither to the objective description nor to the actual alteration of the terms of the given world of reality, but to the semiotic operation that provoked the literary and aesthetic imaginations of hitherto unarticulated perspectives. Realism in the sense of playful negation then consisted in the standpoint that "only in the inverted world [did] things appear what they [were]."[15] A brief remark by Ryūtei Tanehiko (1783–1843), a comic fiction writer, on the characteristics of his contemporary Katsushika Hokusai's (1760–1849) comical drawings captured precisely the essence of the realism performed by playful negation. He wrote, "Hokusai's [playful] drawings—*manga* 漫画—reflect the truthfulness of realities by virtue of their distance from the reality."[16] For Tanehiko, the (fictitious) form of Hokusai's art was capable of grasping reality more truthfully precisely because of its detachment and estrangement from the established world of reality. The dialectic of "reality" and "fictitiousness" in the articulation of the real was the essential logic of popular art forms in the late eighteenth century, a logic that enabled *sakasama* as a form of realism to rise to prominence.

The Techné of Inversion: *Ugachi* (うがち) or the Form of Mordant Indictment

What were the social conditions of the late eighteenth century that gave rise to inversion as a form of realism? Honda Yasuo, a historian of Tokugawa literature, argues that the popularity of parodic inversion indicated the degree to which the system of hierarchical classifications of subject positions—be it status, occupation, or gender—created rigidity and inelasticity in Tokugawa society: everyday habits and behaviors embodied stereotypical characteristics reflecting those subject positions. According to Honda, the unprecedented popularity of the entertainment of impersonation (*monomane* 物真似) was a clear indicator of the pervasiveness of this phenomenon. Impersonation was performed on a daily basis in the markets, streets, and theaters, and its style and content were frequently adapted into comic novellas.[17] Meticulously establishing the intertextual relationships between *monomane* entertainment and popular novellas, Honda claims that the possibility for the rise of playful writings, especially their enormous popularity for the extensive use of humor, satire, and parody, was attributable to the prevalent social phenomenon wherein people's manners and speech were conventionalized. This observation seems to echo Marius Charney's more generic claim that "comic convention postulates a society that is rigidly hierarchical."[18] According to the Tokugawa laws of decorum, carefully formulated by the official discourse of status distinctions, different social groups had their prescribed styles, both of manners and of speech. Representing a range of clearly delineated social types supported a concept of order that asserted its cohesion and totality by claiming to predict, know, and catalogue the behavior of all kinds and types of people. A parade of stereotypes afforded popular writers and artists the opportunity to poke fun at inelasticity and a lack of living pliability evident in normative discourses and behaviors prescribed to reflect the official values of eternal harmony, unity, and stability of society.

It does not suffice, however, simply to point out the high degree of rigidity or fixity of Edo society as the sole reason for the emergence of inversion as a form of realism. In order for stereotypes to become the object of ridicule and laughter, there must be a widely shared societal recognition of some degree of strangeness or idiosyncrasy about them. What made them humorous was the palpable presence of irrepressible incongruity between regulatory norms and lived experiences, as well as preposterous blindness and obliviousness to such an incongruity, which those stereotypes seemed to embody.

To underscore and mock the sense of strangeness, popular writers and artists used the particular techné of negation called *ugachi* (うがち). *Ugachi* was effective in dramatizing and accentuating the rigidity and inelasticity discerned in ritualism and conventionalized demeanor and speech and in mocking their oddity, even absurdity in light of rapidly diversifying and divergent realities. Three artistic methods—*henchiki* (へんちき), *chakashi* (茶化し), and *naimaze* (ないまぜ)—helped make the *ugachi* style of negation work.[19] They were all deployed to overturn the familiar order of moral and aesthetic judgments—true and false, good and evil, and the refined and the vulgar—and thereby to negate habitual ways of thinking and seeing. Hiraga Gennai (1728–1779), Ōta Nanpo (1749–1823), and Santō Kyōden's (1761–1816) contentions about the spirit of playful composition explains the intent of these tactics. According to Kyōden, for example, "the spirit [of *gesaku*] is not to promote the conventional theories that describe good as praiseworthy and evil as reprehensible from the perspective of the received truth, but to embrace *ugachi* which performs a farcical yet serious reassessment of received truths."[20]

Henchiki was the method of condensing incongruent multiple logics and images into one story or one pictorial representation. The effect of this condensation was to produce strange instabilities through utterly unexpected combinations of heterogeneous elements.[21] *Henchiki*, therefore, displaced the very terms of the established sign system. For instance, in his recurrent blemishing of Confucian scholars as uncreative simpletons for their uncritical devotion to the memorization and repetition of the same archaic aphorisms, Hiraga Gennai compared those scholars with the street entertainer called a "fartist," who entertained the crowd in

Ryōgoku with varying rhythms and melodies of flatulence, to praise the latter over the former for innovativeness and artistry. The juxtaposition and comparison of the refined and the vulgar denaturalized the general perception of the putative boundary between the two. The comical sense of strange instability stemmed not only from the way farting—"a most palpable symbol of filth and waste," as Gennai puts it—was placed on the same plane with the privileged world of reason and knowledge but also from the way the self-evident hierarchy that existed between the fartist and the intellectuals was scandalously inverted. Once the well-established norm of hierarchy between the two incongruent existences was overturned with the praise of the lower body over the upper, then the inversion changed into a form of negation: it negated the type of knowledge produced by Confucian scholars by holding them responsible for intellectual stagnation in the face of growing socioeconomic problems, such as famine, natural disasters, urban riots, and peasant protests.[22] We shall return to this text on flatulence for more extensive discussion in the next section.

The method of *henchiki* was also effectively applied in Katsushika Hokusai's illustration entitled *Privy* (figure 3.1; 1810s). In this, the juxtaposition of incongruities is realized in Hokusai's choice of subject matter: a samurai of respectable rank in the privy. Like Gennai's essay on flatulence, an obvious tactical effect of this juxtaposition is the profanation of the powerful—the samurai in this case. Observing such an effect, Peter Duus has argued that this illustration conveys the message that "despite their affectation of superiority, at some basic level (in the privy, for example) the samurai were no different from commoners."[23] Clearly, this scatological profanation of the samurai works to impair the principle of social hierarchies by demystifying the samurai's noble attributes and recasting him in a most basic quotidian scene. The fact that three retainers serving him must wait patiently for their master appears to attest to this samurai's superior power, but such power is dramatically profaned by this scatological scene of the privy, as Duus observes. This illustration, however, possesses more than humorous profanation. The critical edge, allied with the comic spirit, originates from the way in which Hokusai drew the retainers' ludicrous efforts to endure the seemingly unbearable stench coming from their master. The image invites its beholders to ask, "Why don't they leave, or keep at least more distance from the privy?" Hokusai's illustration reveals the absurdly inelastic behavior embodied by these samurai retainers, an obvious instantiation of samurai's dogmatic ritualism. It was a law, albeit an unwritten one, in Tokugawa society that the hierarchical relationship between the lord and his retainers was

3.1 Katsushika Hokusai (1760–1849), *Privy*, 1810s. Woodblock print. (Owned by the author)

unconditional and inviolable. The retainers were expected to enact the code of absolute loyalty to their lords under *any* circumstances. Hokusai tried to demonstrate the absurdity of the rigid ritualism and hierarchical values through this profane instance. In this illustration, the retainer on the left holds a traveling trunk containing his lord's clothes. The middle retainer is the sandal bearer. The man in black holds the highest rank of all, and is responsible for protecting his master, as indicated by his two swords. The iconography of the supposedly reverential behavior of loyalty to the master turns into that of the ridiculousness, even irrationality, of that "virtue," once represented in such a profane context as the *Privy*.

The second artistic method that helped to facilitate the *ugachi* style of negation, *chakashi*, referred to the way in which unexpected logical inversion produced the *ugachi* effect. Hiraga Gennai's *Rootless Weeds* (*Nenashigusa* 根無し草; 1763) is an illuminating example of the *chakashi* tactic. It is a story in which the world of Hell falls into chaos as the Judge of Hell (*Enma* 閻魔) gives up his duty as a guardian of the "good" for the sake of pursing a beautiful female impersonator in a kabuki performance. The *chakashi* tactic lies in showing the contradiction between the axiomatic norm that the Judge of Hell is responsible for punishing those who transgress official moral codes, such as the prohibition of the pleasure of male-male love, and his irresistible carnal desire for the very act of transgression for which he condemns human beings to hell. This contradiction is most vividly presented in the following comical moment: during the interrogation of a Buddhist priest on the matter of his male-male love disposition, the Judge of Hell confiscates a portrait of a beautiful female impersonator from the priest, but as soon as he sees the image depicted in the portrait, he finds the impersonator's beauty so alluring that he loses control, falls off his chair, and faints. After becoming conscious again, he declares himself no longer the Judge of Hell and confesses his desire to join the human world in order to spend a night with the female impersonator. The *chakashi* tactic calls attention to a contradiction or disparity between the requirement of established order and deeds diverging from it. The Judge of Hell is supposed to be punishing "evil" instead of falling into it; he is supposed to behave majestically instead of losing himself, falling off his chair, and fainting. The ironic sense stemming from this *chakashi* depiction was further augmented by the fact that *Rootless Weeds* was "a satire of the scandalous infatuation by Mizoguchi Naonori, a castle lord from Echigo [now Niigata], with the real [impersonator] Kikunojō."[24] Just like the Judge of Hell, the eminent lord failed to live up to the official norm and duty of "chastising evils." The sense of the comic, which is engendered by the unexpected logical inversion of the normative sense of order, becomes here meshed with that of caustic satire of the ruling elite's hypocrisy in condemning the urban popular culture (*ugachi*). Cultural producers often applied this tactic to expose the contradictory discrepancy between principles and realities in the lives of ruling elites and authorities.

The third method, *naimaze*, designated the way of suggesting unexpected congruencies between incongruities.[25] Cultural texts using *naimaze* made visible unacknowledged similitude among qualitatively different matters by intermixing them. This tactic bore resemblance to metaphor—it connects difference by way of suggesting similarity. *Naimaze* was effective in pointing out profane aspects in images of the high and the sacred and in discovering sacred elements in images of the low and the profane. The result of this operation was to dissolve terms of binary oppositions. The opening of Shikitei Sanba's *The Bathhouse in the Floating World* (*Ukiyoburo*; 1809–13) provides an example. Sanba finds the mundane scenes of bathing in the public bathhouse to be a manifestation of all five fundamental Confucian virtues—benevolence, righteousness, propriety, wisdom, and faithfulness. By identifying, for instance, the spirit of propriety (*rei* 礼) as best represented in the people's casual exchanges in the bathhouse like "Hey," "What's up?" and "You call me a lout? What the heck!," Sanba displaces the normative concept of decorum: what is seen as rude can be seen as an instance of propriety, depending on the context. Likewise, *The Bathhouse* finds bathing to be exemplary of the Buddhist practice of purifying the spirit (*jōka* 浄化) for the following reason: "to be naked for taking a bath is the law of Heaven and Earth; Buddha, Confucius, a maidservant and manservant all without exception turn into the unselfish shape by removing every possession from their bodies; then after washing away the dirt of greed and lust, master and servant can no longer be differentiated from each other: what they have in common are only naked bodies."[26]

It is this witticism performed through the discovery of similitude in difference that effectively displaces the normative understanding of decorum and spiritual purification. By intermixing casual exchanges of words and the Confucian concept of propriety, as well as public bathing and the Buddhist notion of spiritual purification, *naimaze* pulls moral and spiritual matters down to the level of earthly activities. *The Bathhouse* collapses the familiar distinction between high and low and deprives intellectuals and priests of the carefully guarded authority in which their putative superiority resides.

The function of all three methods of *ugachi*-style negation was to precipitate a perceptual and aesthetic event that opened up the moment of negation of the familiar. Displacing or dissolving the familiar meant to call into question the palpability of unitary identities, such as samurai, peasants, artisans, merchants, outcasts, and intellectuals, and to invalidate the moral and aesthetic categories of social classification on which such identities were conceived. In the cases of *henchiki* and *chakashi*, the negation took place in such a way that common assumptions of the subject's identity were fractured by the discovery of its immanent contradiction and heterogeneity. In the case of *naimaze*, this was realized when two putatively incompatible subjects were put together and seen as comparable through the discovery and mediation of unthinkable similitude between them.

It was through this clash of heterogeneous and contradictory images and meanings unveiled in the commonly held notions of unitary subjects that the producers of popular culture were able to negate the figures of the powerful. The clash fragmented the assumed integrity of identity, with which the powerful forged their authority, and drew attention to the untenability of that assumption.

In practice, we find all these methods combined together as an intricate ensemble of *ugachi* performance. Let us take Hiraga Gennai's *The Biography of Elegant Shidōken* as the final example to examine how the *ugachi* effect was generated. Gennai begins this comical biography of a storyteller named Shidōken (modeled after an actual eccentric and a friend of Gennai who entertained by telling vulgar stories in the Asakusa market) with a characterization of his sermons as *waizatsu kokkei* (猥雑滑稽) (see figure 3.2).[27] *Waizatsu*, a term meaning "vulgar" or "indecent," and *kokkei*, meaning "comical" or "humorous," supports my analysis of inversion as a rhetorical and visual device for defamiliarizing the prevailing norms and the dominant sense of reality. By using these terms to describe Shidōken's sermons, Gennai defamiliarizes the conventional notion of the sermon (*dangi* 談義), a narrative form commonly used by both writers and storytellers in Tokugawa Japan to convey the moral messages of Confucius's and Buddha's teachings to the general populace.

The following two phrases further complement my analysis of how Gennai created the effect of inversion. He describes the manner in which Shidōken gives his sermons to the audience as "*tottemo tsukanu hanashi no kuchi wo kuishibari sokora darake ga shiwa darake naru kao* . . . (取っても付かぬ歯なしの口をくいしばり、そこらだらけが皺だらけなる顔 . . .)." *Tottemo tsukanu hanashi no kuchi wo kuishibari* roughly means "clamping shut his

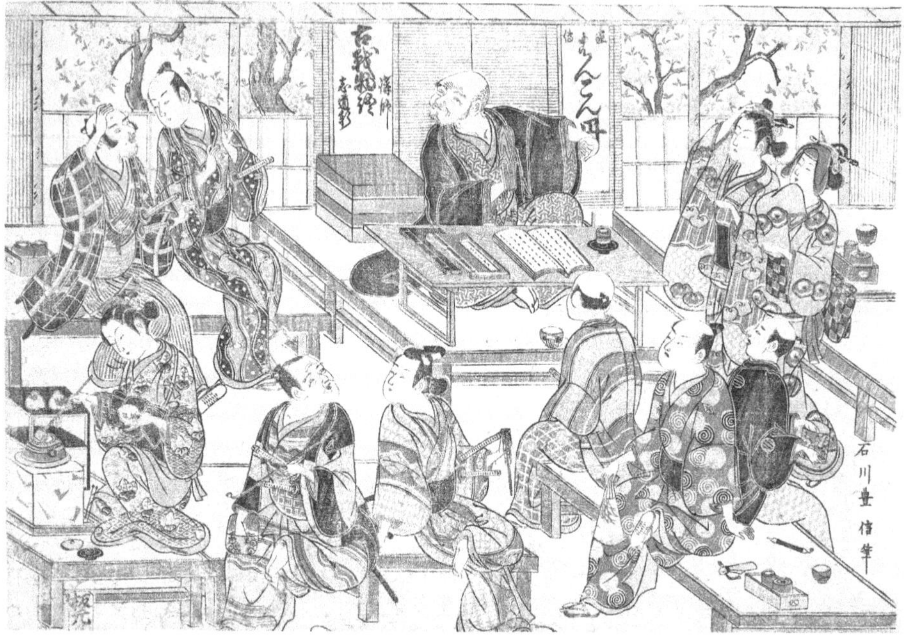

3.2 Ishikawa Toyonobu (1711–85), *Fukai Shidōken Lecturing* (*Kosen monogatari kōshi Shidōken*), 1750s. Ishikawa Toyonobu's print depicts the performance of Shidōken in the Ryōgoku area. It captures the cheerful and ebullient atmosphere of Shidōken's storytelling. Woodblock print. (Photograph © 2013 Museum of Fine Arts, Boston)

toothless mouth that bites in vain."[28] *Hanashi no kuchi* literally means "toothless mouth," and *tottemo tsukanu,* "you cannot get it however you try." *Sokora darake ga shiwa darake naru kao* means "wrinkles all over the face." This literary reading reinforces the "vulgar" image of Shidōken in terms of appearance and the manner in which he gives his sermons. Yet, once a reader allows the equivocal reading of this phrase to work against the literary reading, these words elude the latter and suggest alternative meanings. Since the sound of *hanashi* (toothless 歯なし) is the same as that of the term meaning "story" (話) and *tottemo tsukanu* could be rendered "empty" or "meaningless," these words and phrases could combine to mean an "empty or meaningless story." Accordingly, this second reading makes it possible to suggest an alternative rendering of *sokora darake*—all over the place—as "disorderly." The adjectives of "meaningless" and "disorderly" point to the nature of Shidōken's sermons as "nonsense." Thus with these two possible readings the entire phrase carries a double message with regard to the features of Shidōken's appearance and story. These double characterizations condensed and conveyed in a single phrase effectively reinforce the "absurd" nature of Shidōken's performance. This message of "absurdity" is further confirmed by Gennai's subsequent description of Shidōken's somewhat "eccentric" and "grotesque" manner of storytelling: "this ugly skinny man whose age might be between eighty and ninety imitates the seductive gestures and voices of female impersonators while giving his sermons."[29] With the absurdity highlighted, Gennai's narrative parodies supposedly serious sermons in its continuous description of Shidōken's oral entertainment in the following manner:

Sono tokutokoro wa, shin ju butsu no zakuzaku jiru, rōsō no karashinuta, kōri no suimono, inabikari no aburaage, atomo katachimo nai. (其説くところは神儒仏のざくざく汁、老荘の芥子ぬた、氷の吸物稲光の油あげ、跡も形もない.)

His lectures are a philosophical minestrone of Shintoism, Confucianism, and Buddhism, poisson cru vinegared with Lao Tzu and spiced with Chuang Tzu, served with hot ice soup and deep-fried tōfu with lightening, none left over, not a trace.[30]

Indeed the illogicality of this sentence appears to accentuate the frivolous character of Shidōken's lectures. The phrase *atomo katachimo nai* literally means "leaving nothing behind" or "leaving no traces," implying the emptiness of the story. However, another possible reading is "exhaustive." What is "exhaustive" is to be read as Shidōken's artful mastery of Shintoist, Buddhist, and Taoist philosophical discourses. This second reading becomes more feasible in conjunction with the term *zakuzaku jiru*, which literally means "mixed soup," or minestrone, but it alternatively means a mixture of all sorts of philosophical teachings. Though "mixture" could be rendered as "mess," an alternative reading can mean "eclectics." The meaning of the passage as a whole begins to show two paradoxical and competing readings—one affirming the absurdity of Shidōken's sermons, and another offering a completely inverted semantic landscape where his nonsense sermons are in fact full of unconventional wisdom masterfully created through a fusion of diverse philosophical discourses.

This rhetorical play of paradoxical opposites—absurd and insightful—further culminates in Gennai's biographical description of Shidōken. When a Taoist sage suddenly appears and instructs Asano Shin (Shidōken's original name) concerning his future course of action, he begins by expounding on the ludicrousness of popular belief in life after death in Buddhist doctrine and the corruption of Buddhist priests. Asano Shin, as a devout priest convinced by the sage's view, asks what Way he should follow, if not the Way of Buddha. Condemning samurai officials as parasites, Confucian scholars as hopelessly dim-witted, and the samurai world of pomp and decorum as corrupt, the sage first contends that the decadent state of all these establishments originates from a lack of sincerity that prevents them from understanding the "real"—human feelings and passions. He then gives Asano Shin the following sermon: "Draw the ordinary people to you through your humor and wit, and teach them through the secular examples that are found in their everyday lives."[31] This rhetoric suggests that the seemingly "absurd" story is not only an insightful "philosophical" teaching but also a form of social, moral, and intellectual criticism of the Tokugawa establishment. The sage encourages Asano Shin to leave the secluded priesthood and to immerse himself in the world filled with human feelings and passions. The first destination of his journey is the pleasure quarter. As the story goes, when all possibilities of sexual titillation in Japan have been exhausted, Asano Shin embarked on a voyage to foreign lands using his magic fan to fly through the air. These "foreign lands" parody the various segments of the Tokugawa establishment: people in the land called the Land of Play seem to allude to top-ranking samurai officials in contemporary Tokugawa society since nobody bothers to work until calamity strikes the land and the folly of the ruler is openly acknowledged. Asano Shin also visits the Land of the Blockheaded Bumpkins where dull-witted scholars—presumably Confucian scholars—enjoy their privileges without making much contribution to improving the livelihood of the poor.

After Asano Shin's voyage is over, the sage suddenly reappears and gives him a second sermon: "My instruction to you was that once you had leaned about human passions throughout the world you were to dispatch yourself from society through the medium of humor (*kokkei*) . . . This floating world is like a dream. Seventy years have already passed since I saw you last. Now it is time to go back to the ordinary people and tell them what you have seen and experienced."[32]

Gennai's description of the ending scene where Shidōken is about to start his sermons suggests again the multifaceted implications of this story.

Shougi ni koshi wo uchikakureba sono matsutake nite tsukue wo tataki, ton ton ton toto ton ton ton tonda hanashi no hajimari. (床ぎに腰を打ちかくれば、彼松茸にて机をたたき、トントントントントントトトントン、とんだ話の始まり始まり.)

He seated himself upon the mat and beat the dais with that matsutake mushroom—bam, bam, bam, the beginning of a most unthinkable tale!

Tonda (とんだ) denotes "most unthinkable." It can be read either as "unthinkably nonsensical" or as "unthinkably illuminating." The two paradoxical renderings of the term—"nonsense" and "illuminating"—can be accommodated in this phrase for there is no word following the term *tonda*, which makes it impossible to determine its precise meaning. The tale is "nonsense" because of its persistently irrational, vulgar, and grotesque disposition (especially with the *matsutake* mushroom being a phallic symbol), but it is at the same time "illuminating" because of its "insights" drawn from Shidōken's unconventional humor and wit. The final judgment of its meaning appears to be left to the readers, for the simultaneous presence of negation and affirmation within the statement simply forbids a fixed interpretation. Indeed this passage epitomizes the heterogeneous nature of *gesaku* writing. However, when such a paradox is bracketed and the story is read as a form of social criticism, the seemingly paradoxical meaning of the story begins to reveal a very clear indictment—it is written as a satirical attack on the establishment. The paradoxical characterization of Shidōken's tale is to be read as a statement that even the most vulgar and nonsensical storytelling may offer more illuminating wit and insight than the orthodox teachings of Confucianism, Buddhism, and Shintoism. Thus, "how useless these teachings are!" wrote Gennai.[33]

His travesty was plotted in an absurd rhetoric, divorced from reason—an upside-down rhetoric. This does not signify, however, that it was devoid of rhetorical form. Rather, the form was designed to invert and confuse the established rhetoric in which the official conception of the "real"—sense, logic, meaning, and truth—was demarcated. It was predicated on the structure of a dialogical interaction that played out between two contradictory signifiers: "serious" indictment and the delectation of "absurdity." And Gennai's writing could sustain this structure of paradoxical representation only by following a particular conception of language, which is best encapsulated by V. N. Volosinov: "[m]eaning does not reside in the word or in the soul of the speaker or in the soul of the listener, [but it] is the effect of interaction between speaker and listener," and writer and reader.[34] In other words, "meaning is realized only in the process of active, responsive understanding" and thus a product of *social, dialogic* interaction; and "[a]ny true understanding is dialogic in nature."[35] This conception aptly explains the compositional characteristic of the comical texts of Edo in general. Writers and artists presupposed the cooperation of readers and beholders and created the plane of a plurality of interpretive choices open to them. Facing multiple ways of understanding the meanings of words and images, readers and beholders made a series of interpretive choices that, even though not infinite, were, however, more than one.[36] Indeed, this multiplicity did not imply random and boundless chains of signifiers, as a deconstructionist reading might suggest, but the possibility of *dialectical* interpretations of verbal and visual signs. When readers and beholders discerned and accepted the presence of two paradoxical meanings as they were presented within a single narrative or visual form, a sense of humor was evoked. This was because humor was an effect of going along with the existence of paradox rather than that of reading critical implications into the paradox. But when the readers and beholders attended more to negative connotations in the paradox, then the paradox transmuted itself into the form of mordant satire and indictment (*ugachi*). The polysemy and equivocality of linguistic meaning and visual perception was deployed exactly in this way so that it could work as a method of producing the varying degree of comic parody and of carrying out the negation of authoritative discourse.

The Body that Performs *Ugachi*

If the playful use of the polysemy of sign was central to comic realism's creation of mordant wit and humor, the body, especially its vulgar materialism, constituted the central motif of that playful use. Hokusai's *Privy*, Sanba's *Bathhouse*, and Gennai's *Rootless Weeds* and *Shidōken* all converged on the materiality of corporeal functions or desire. This materialism was aimed at augmenting comic and satirical countermeanings against moralistic discourses that advocated, on the basis of the presumed primacy of mind over body, the inevitability of hierarchical divisions of status and labor as the matrices of social organization. Wordplay and visual play valorized the vulgar body to overturn the mind and body hierarchy, and in doing so, it called into question the legitimacy of that advocacy. The works of the best-selling satirist Hiraga Gennai, such as *The Story of a Secluded Little Phallus* (*Naemara Inishuden* 痿陰隠逸伝; 1768), *On Farting* (*Hōhiron* 放屁論; 1774), and *On Farting, Part Two* (*Hōhiron kōhen* 放屁論後編; 1777), exemplified most clearly the use of the vulgar materialism of the body.[37] In these stories, the phallus and/or the fart appeared as the dominant motifs in the stories. In particular, *The Story of a Secluded Little Phallus* took on the style of an autobiography of a male sexual organ with the name of Godōken. With the scandalous personification of the phallic symbol as the protagonist, the story violated literary decorum and conventions. Phallic symbol signified an assault on and thus a full-fledged negation of the received notions of wisdom, majesty, knowledge, truth, and, ultimately, power.

Comprising only some four or five pages, *The Story of a Secluded Little Phallus* was a parodic account of Japanese history where legends, luminaries, and historic events were all reduced to the level of sexual activity. The erect phallus represented the mainstream establishment whereas the soft, withered phalluses represented the excluded or forgotten figures, including the phallus-narrator, Godōken. The story begins with a vulgarized restatement of the influential cosmological theory in the *Book of Changes* that human life comes into being as the result of the interactive movement of *yin/in* (陰) and *yang/yō* (陽), or aspect of *qi/ki* (気), the material ether that generates all life forms.[38] Like their Chinese counterparts, Neo-Confucian scholars in the Tokugawa period also relied on this theory for their formulation of the dualism of Principle (*li* 理)—the universal Idea or Reason—and the material ether—the uncertain and ephemeral material reality, as well as the generative energy. Gennai's endorsement of this theory in vulgar terms represented the scandalous appropriation of the theory, because it took the form of a scatological assault on the conception of *li*. The parentage and the birth of a "child" are narrated as follows:

> Its father is called *he* [fart], its mother is called *onara* [a genteel word for fart]. Noisy [farts] are yang, smelly [farts] are yin. When yin and yang intersected, being emerged out of the void and gave birth to this thing [penis]. This is how the Principle of nature is manifested.[39]

Gennai's parodic rewriting of the birth of human life perverts the Neo-Confucian cosmological theory. Neo-Confucians believed that *li* was invisible and became manifest only when there was the active movement of the yang and the quiescence of yin.[40] By substituting farts for the dialectical interaction of yin and yang, *A Secluded Little Phallus* renders the generative moment of human life into flatulence and *li* into that which is made manifest through the birth of the "penis." This thoroughly materialist deconstruction brings down the working of cosmological order to earthy images and assails the integrity of the Neo-Confucian metaphysics of Principle. Such a deconstructive rendering of Neo-Confucian cosmological theory is followed by the representation of luminaries in history as variations of the archetypal phallic form. Parodying official histories written customarily in a manner that glorifies the powerful, Gennai makes them into a history of desire and carnality. He writes:

> There are a great variety of penises not only in shape, but also in virtue, talent and wit. For instance, the sages and gentlemen's pricks all must shine like rainbows for they are stuffed with Confucian teachings. Buddha renounced the world probably because he was so smitten by his prick's impotence. In our country, the penis looked gentle and amicable in the age of the gods, but in the age of men the penis came to be imbued with evil thought. First Kawakaminotakeru, and then the rebellious phalluses of Azuma Ebisu were cut down by the sword-phallus of Yamatotakerunomikoto. As a result this sword began to stink (*kusai* 臭い) thereafter, and he was therefore named *Kusa*naginomikoto (stinky prince) . . . [Down to the fourteenth century], the penises of Nitta Yoshisada and Ashikaga Takauji vied with one another, and after Kusunoki Masashige was castrated at Minatogawa, Emperor Godaigo's loincloth got pulled askew and divided the country into a North and a South Head, allowing another penis to rule the former. The long-lived penis of the Ashikaga finally withered, and then Toyotomi Hideyoshi advanced his penis abroad for nothing. This turned out to be the mere exhaustion of its energy. There are indeed countless numbers of stupid and impotent penises [in the history of Japan].[41]

The images of an erect phallus symbolize the naked pugnacity and aggressive ambitions of these legends and luminaries. The metaphorical use of the phallic symbol poses itself as a poignant attack on the mainstream historical narratives that tend to embellish the rulers with a sagacious and benevolent aura, intellectuals with a gentlemanly image, and spiritual leaders with an inviolable stature. For Gennai, these narratives serve the purpose of muting or hiding the truism that the conducts of historic figures consisted in nothing but a clamorous and aggressive pursuit of power. These erect phalluses are actually "stupid" and "impotent" for not only do they have no interest in but are incapable of serving the well-being of the people. But once adorned with the exalted words, they are immediately turned into "compassionate" and "righteous" luminaries. Through language, the clamor of personal ambitions was muffled and the virtue of righteous intents to serve the public realm was concocted. "On the contrary," Gennai writes, "the decent and ethically motivated phalluses like Godōken who wished to serve the people were vanquished from historical memory." As forgotten beings, the story ends, "they must wither and seclude themselves from the public life."[42]

Gennai's profanation of Japanese history unveiled the ways in which language and knowledge served as a tool for mystification. Making visible the performative nature of representation in the sense of obscuring a certain reality to form another, Gennai's carnalized narrative rejected the view of language grounded in the theory of *The Rectification of Names*. Language was never a transparent medium of expression and a carrier of truth: it neither transmitted nor reflected things as they were, but was always already mediated by a certain ideological orientation, thus carrying with it, in Volosinov's words, a "specific accentuality of meaning."[43] Furthermore, by carnalizing the deeds of major historic figures in the image of phallic symbols, Gennai's rhetoric exposed the fallacy of the moralistic tone underlying the "official" history and thus foregrounded the actual *impotence* of the powerful as rulers. The more the nakedness of these figures' power was demonstrated through the phallic symbol, the more their impotence was accentuated. "It is in this precise sense," as Slavoj Žižek once wrote about the phallic signifier, "that the phallus is the signifier of castration . . . This is the logic of the phallic inversion which sets in when the demonstration of power starts to function as a confirmation of a fundamental impotence."[44] The conventional reading of Gennai's assault on mainstream history as an expression of his personal grudge against or his victim mentality toward the dominant power structure that denied him a respectable position within the establishment does not reveal social meanings of rhetoric as a symbolic act. Its message was an indictment of this structure for the duplicitous disguise of its absolute impotence.

On Farting (*Hohiron*; 1774) and *On Farting, Part 2* (*Hohiron Kohen*; 1777) were arguably the best-known of all of Gennai's satirical works exploring themes related to the vulgar body and its transgressive implications. *On Farting* portrayed a spirited dispute between a samurai and Gennai himself over a peasant turned popular entertainer called the "fartist" (*heppiri otoko* 屁っぴり男), a real historical figure who amused the crowds with his "artistic" manipulation of flatulence in Ryōgoku, one of Edo's most popular market and entertainment districts during the late 1770s, as portrayed in figure 3.3 (1774), which was included in Gennai's *On Farting*.[45] The fartist of the story appears as a quintessential figure of the many late-eighteenth-century migrants to Edo who, as discussed in chapter 1, fled their villages to find a new means of survival in the city's thriving popular culture and came to constitute a major segment of society officially classified as "vagrants" and "idlers." The entertainer's background and means of subsistence imply the possibility of a life antithetical to and disruptive of the official paradigm of productivity as moral. By accentuating the fartist's symbolic value, Gennai deploys him as a metaphor that effectively calls into question a fundamental premise of Tokugawa ideology—the primacy of mind over body.

3.3 Fartist in Ryōgoku (owned by the author). Illustration that appeared in Gennai's short story *On Farting*, 1780s.

The dialogue between Gennai and the samurai begins with the issue of propriety. The samurai objects:

This man sets up shop in the midst of a public place and positively flaunts something that most normal people are deeply ashamed of. Utterly disgusting! . . . You should recall what the true sages have taught us in the classical texts. . . . We should not so much as overhear or witness indecencies from afar, let alone commit them—that is what the true sages teach us.[46]

Gennai replies:

All things that lie between heaven and earth array themselves naturally into categories of high and low, lofty and base. Among them, surely the lowest of low, the basest of the base, are urine and excrement. In China they have various pejorative figures of speech in which things are compared to "ordure," "coprolite,"etc., while in Japan we simply say of things we don't care for that they are "like shit." Yet, this loathsome filth, we should not forget, is turned into fertilizer and thereby nourishes the millions. Farts are different in this respect, it is true, being but the extraneous by-products of the perpetrators' quest for progressive relief from intestinal distress.[47]

He continues:

Not even fit for fertilizer, they [farts] are totally useless, if a wonderfully apt attribute to confer on corrupt scholars, as indeed Shidōken [a real historical figure and popular storyteller who entertained the people with vulgar stories and gestures] has done, with considerable originality, in his epithet "the Conpyewcianists" [*heppiri jusha*, or farting Confucians]. But to take this thing that is, beyond all else in the world, utterly useless and make of it such a great success that, aside from the main theaters, other shows have had to shut down for the lack of spectators—it is no mean feat, and ample proof of the little fellow's powers of invention in having arrived at all those intricate variations on a single theme.[48]

Gennai applauds the fartist's ingenious innovation to argue against the samurai's conviction that theatrical performances should be instruments for mollifying the people and for publicizing the proper relations between ranks in the social hierarchy. Whenever a spectacle portrays a deviation from established righteousness and propriety, the samurai argues irately, it must do so as a stern admonition and a cautionary tale that such a deviation will be met, without exception, with retribution or severe punishment. This is the sole reason, asserts the samurai, "why our government allows popular entertainments to exist."[49] Despite the samurai's agitated remarks, Gennai—with no pretensions of moral condemnation—continues to praise the fartist's use of flatulence as a form of legitimate art, thus refusing to support an authoritarian conception of spectacle.

In this dialogue, Gennai uses farting and the fartist to pit conflicting values against one another. For the samurai, they represent a serious offense against the official conception of propriety and social order, whereas for the character representing Gennai they embody wisdom and creativity. The two agree that a fart is nothing but a useless discharge, even in comparison with excrement: it certainly does not qualify as the kind of physical work officially sanctioned as productive, let alone as the mental work vital for the governance of Tokugawa society. However, they diverge sharply on what the fartist's use of the discharge implies. For the samurai, it signifies the antithesis of what the "true sages" taught as human decency and etiquette. But for Gennai, the great success of this "little fellow" is nothing other than a triumph of wisdom and creativity, for he has made a useless excess into music with "intricate variations on a single theme" and into a legitimate means for survival. Gennai's windy rhetoric aimed to expose and accentuate the problematic nature of official decorum and the system of classification dividing society into high and low. By claiming to discover ingenuity and creativity not in the enactment of societal duty but in the fartist's utterly unproductive spectacle, he sought to dislocate the perceived legitimacy of the establishment's conventions, subverting the official logic of social distinctions upheld in the normative discourse.

As the story unfolds, it becomes clear that the targets of Gennai's satire are the various domains of "high culture," its custodians, and its mode of reproduction. Gennai first questions what he sees as the problem of the reproductive mode of aesthetic practice in high culture. By declaring that the fartist's flatulence functions as a new kind of language—an alternative to words as sounds shaped and enunciated from the mouths of musicians—Gennai seeks to undermine the authority of tradition given to various schools of vocal art:

> Plenty of pupils join up, equipped with proper mouths and proper vocal chords; they dutifully receive from their teachers direct transmission of the tradition. . . . They may cackle and caw with abandon like so many crows and herons on their nightly fray and faithfully mouth the stanzas they have been taught, but their renditions fail to bring a single spark of life to the old ballads. . . . This man here, however, without benefit of any mentor or any oral transmission, has had to create his art through his ingenuity alone. From that inarticulate orifice, and out of undifferentiated flatulence, he has mastered breathing, diction, and phrasing, and he has contrived to reproduce the varied effects of vocal coloring and all of the twelve classical scales. He has, then, incomparably greater talent between his buttocks than these third-rate musicians have between their lips.[50]

Gennai's logic is that, although a fart by itself may seem useless, the fartist has developed it into a far more creative musical instrument than the voice. The fart becomes a new and commendable nonverbal form of articulation, actually preferable to established oral forms of language. This new language consists not of words, but of inventive rhythms and melodies of flatulence: things in which the traces and burdens of convention are absent. For Gennai, this language manifests genuine innovation precisely because it is unfettered by the command and authority of norms, through which elite culture legitimizes and reproduces itself. By contrast, pupils who abide by the established rules of the musical schools are unable to break conventions and bring life to their singing.

Gennai's provocative rhetoric was probably a parody of the Confucian theory that held music to be one of the essential means for cultivating the spiritual self. Ogyū Sorai, referring to Confucius's remarks on music, wrote in his *Clarification of Names*, "Music is for bringing order to one's inner nature and passion."[51] For Sorai and Confucian scholars in general, music as a method of realizing internal harmony was an integral part of a larger discourse on effective statecraft: namely, how to preserve an orderly society without resorting to coercive and oppressive measures. By comparing the Confucian notion of spiritual cultivation to the most vulgar kind of activity and praising the latter, Gennai displaced the instrumentalist idea that music was a means to achieve societal harmony through its self-disciplinary or self-regulatory effect on the corporeal self. Through this inversion of the upper and lower strata of the body—fart superseding voice, and the fartist "singing" better through his anus than established musicians through their mouths—Gennai effectively undermined the authority of the intellectual discourse on the primacy of mind over body and demonstrated how the mind-body binary functioned to legitimize the official view of social cohesion as the highest moral goal.

Gennai's argument with the samurai then extends into the problematic state of knowledge production in late Tokugawa society:

This favorable comparison holds up not only with respect to musicians, but vis-à-vis a number of incompetent wretches in other fields of contemporary endeavor. The scholars buried in cast-off scraps of continental learning; the philologists who dabble in classical Chinese poetry and prose, cloaking themselves in the most threadbare shreds of Han Yu or Li Tsung-yuan, which they mistake for the full robes; our nativist poets who travel nowhere in search of inspiration, preferring to sit back and wait for grains of rice to stick to the soles of their feet. Then there are the doctors, whether of the old school or of the latter-day post-Sung Faction, powerless to cure the diseases they claim to treat; who, whenever influenza strikes, can only stand by idly as all their patients die.[52]

Gennai asserts that Sinophiles, nativist scholars, poets, and physicians—being unimaginative, inflexible, and, above all, uncreative—can only turn to the received authority of the ancients or to the futile medical knowledge of the more recent past. For Gennai, the real problem is their uncritical immersion in conventions of learning that are utterly incapable of meeting the practical needs of the people. Gennai consistently argued that true creativity means a compassionate capacity to save others from suffering in such difficulties as the famines, poverty, and illnesses that were rampant during the late Tokugawa period. In another essay, *Slandering* (*Soshirigusa* そしり草) written in 1777, Gennai vehemently denounced defenders of high culture, such as samurai leaders, Confucian scholars, Buddhist monks, and physicians, for indulging themselves in "empty theories" and "meaningless polemics" without effectual measures against the increasing woes of ordinary people.[53] In *On Farting, Part 2,* after describing the samurai's role in society as killing, cheating, and robbing, Gennai went so far as to call samurai worn-out "parasites" whose survival depended entirely on the labor—that is, the creative work—of artisans, peasants, and merchants, whom they exploited. He also described them as "robbers" who stole money from commoners in the guise of taxation (*zei dorobō* 税泥棒).[54] With his symbolic use of the "idle" body and commendation of its "productivity," as opposed to the ruling elite's impotence and immorality, Gennai suggested that the assumed primacy of mind over body, the mental over the corporeal, provided the Tokugawa establishment not only with a rhetorical tactic to justify their dominant place in society but also with an alibi to hide the reality of their dysfunctional, paralytic, parasitic, and illegitimate existence.

Kitagawa Utamaro's illustrated story, *The Future* (*Sorekara Iraiki*; 1784), which depicted an encounter between a samurai and a beggar in his "hut" in Ryōgoku (figure 3.4), took up a subject closely related to Gennai's *On Farting*. It calls attention to the ruling elites' "flawed" and "hypocritical" high-low distinction by exposing, through visual and verbal representations of inverted relations of high and low, the classes' dependency and dysfunction. The beggar is clearly marked as an outcast sandal repairer called *setta* (雪駄). During early modern times, the shogunate classified *setta* as nonhuman vagrant outcasts, for they were often fugitives from poverty stricken villages and thus belonged to the class of unwanted idlers.[55] The samurai visiting the beggar's hut to repair his sandals appears to be a typical retainer living in Edo in order to serve his master. In contrast to the caption, "A beggar's hut," the illustrated hut appears to confirm the beggar's prosperity, as it is a modest but respectable dwelling decorated with flowers and a scroll painting. The beggar, wearing poor

3.4 Kitagawa Utamaro (1753–1806). Illustrated page from *The Future* (*Sorekara Iraiki*), 1784. Woodblock print. (Owned by the author)

and tattered clothing, nonetheless occupies a position superior, being placed visually higher to the well-dressed samurai, who is kneeling down to ask for his help. The samurai uses honorific language to ask the *setta* respectfully if it would be possible for him to mend the sandals today, and if not, if one of his disciples might do it. In typical samurai language, the *setta* replies, "I am extremely busy these days, so I will find you a disciple who can meet your request."[56] The samurai expresses unlimited gratitude to the *setta* for his kindness and compassion.

The inverted hierarchy of the samurai and beggar is clearly delineated by their upended language and manner of interaction. The comical and scandalous disjunctions between their appearance and substance accentuate the realities of the parasitic existence of samurai in the arena of material production and everyday survival. The samurai cannot ensure his sustenance without relying on the labor and production of commoners of the lowest status. The story questions the Tokugawa shogunate's ideological premise positing the primacy of mind over body, as the samurai's privileging of the mind and thus his exemption from material production are rendered as the basis of his utter incompetence and parasitic dependency on the very commoners he disdains. The precise logic that allows the samurai to claim superiority here operates as a reason for relegating him to a subordinate position in the social hierarchy. The title of the story, *The Future*, reinforced the biting tone of the satire as it implied the ruined prospects of the ruling elites.

Utagawa Kuniyoshi's illustrated *Asahina's Adventure in the Islands of Little People* (*Asahina Kojima Asobi*; 1847) offers another transgressive, dialogic encounter between samurai and commoners in a "low" district of Edo, Asakusa (figure 3.5). Kuniyoshi's illustration renders the procession of the daimyo (lords of domains) as a parade of "little people," as the caption says, in front of the giant figure of a popular legendary warrior called Asahina. Widely popularized through war tales such as *Azuma Kagami*, Asahina was originally an iconic warrior of extraordinary physical strength and bravery in kabuki plays and ukiyo-e prints in the eighteenth century. One play characterized him as "possessing extraordinary power like a god, and once attacked by enemies, leaving none alive."[57] Asahina's popularity grew in the early nineteenth century, especially through the wide circulation of adventure stories in which he became a Gulliver-like figure traveling all over the world, even to imaginary places such as the island of "little people." Taking this theme for his illustration, Kuniyoshi depicted the warrior hero as a *yakko* (奴), an outlaw and occasionally a laborer working primarily for the samurai class. The *yakko*'s origins could be traced back to the seventeenth century, when these mercenaries enjoyed a commanding presence as "social bandits" who organized bands distinguished by their outlandish appearance and violent, antisocial behavior.[58] Some historians argue that the *yakko* was a kind of *kabuki-mono* "かぶきもの," which, in its literary sense, meant a person with idiosyncratic appearance and unrestrained or nonconformist behavior, who be-

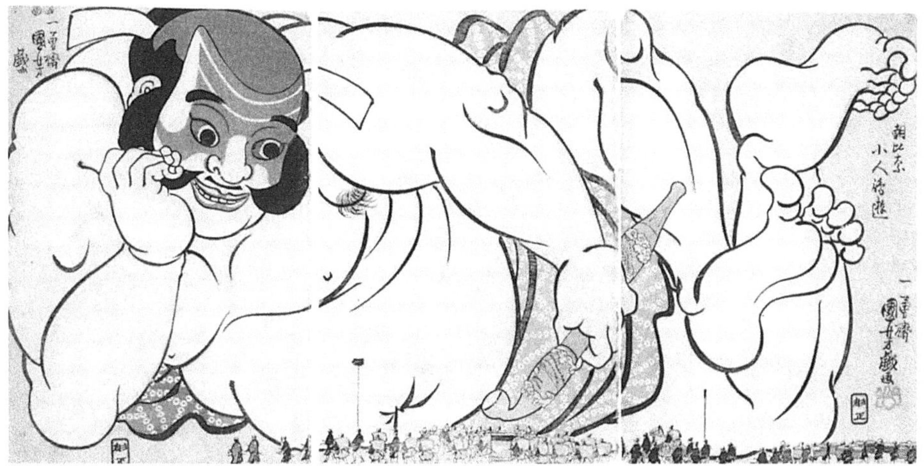

3.5 Utagawa Kuniyoshi (1797–1861), *Asahina's Adventure in the Islands of Little People* (*Asahina Kojima Asobi*), 1847. Woodblock print, ink and color on paper. (Courtesy of the Museum of Salt and Tobacco, Tokyo)

came the target of the shogunate 's strategies of containment during the first half of the seventeenth century.[59] In any case, their gang activities and fearless demeanor supplied kabuki playwrights and woodblock print artists with ample inspiration for popular stories and images of iconic *otokodate* (男伊達): "gallant, valorous young men of common origins who stepped forth in times of trouble to defend fellow merchants and artisans against injustice."[60] By the early nineteenth century, cultural representations of *yakko* as brave, righteous, and compassionate had been widely accepted among lower-class commoners.

The spectacle of *Asahina-yakko*'s body lying rudely in front of the high-ranking samurai's procession (*daimyō gyōretsu* 大名行列) and his comical and jolly demeanor, indicating that he thinks of the procession as a toy to play with, insults the respectability of samurai, in a manner that resonates with Gennai's depiction of the fartist. Asahina's gigantic pipe is pointing, in a gesture of ridicule, directly at the daimyo hidden and protected in the palanquin. In contrast to *Asahina-yakko*'s playful motions and animated expressions, the daimyo's retainers walk methodically, with a homogeneous appearance and posture, as though they are trapped in lifeless uniformity without pliability or adaptability. This insult is further accentuated by the *yakko's* grotesque and imposing physicality, which manifests, underscores, and affirms the symbolic meanings of *otokodate*—bravery, righteousness, and compassion—associated with *Asahina-yakko* and not with the daimyo. It seems not too far-fetched to

3.6 Sadahide, *Giant Asahina*, 1847. Woodblock print, ink and color on paper. (Courtesy of the Museum of Salt and Tobacco, Tokyo)

imagine that, embodying these values, *Asahina-yakko* is about to chasten the samurai for their injustice and wrongdoing.

Kuniyoshi's fantastic representation of inversion and subversion was not entirely a product of his ingenuity as an artist of comic images.[61] It was based on an actual event, in which a high-ranking samurai demanded that the townspeople remove a giant bamboo doll of Asahina exhibited in the fairground of the Sensōji Temple when the figure interrupted his excursion to the area (see figure 3.6).[62] The townspeople did obey the samurai's order, but their frustration with the higher authority's intervention lingered. Kuniyoshi's illustration was an attempt not only to recapture this moment of collision between high and low but also to suggest an imaginary scene that placed samurai and commoners in a dialogic encounter. The representation of this encounter obviously distorted the relative sizes of *Asahina-yakko* and the samurai, and it was precisely this distortion of their bodies that enhanced the illustration's effect of inverting the received order of things. The illustration brilliantly executes the conflation of the real event and the imagination to effect a symbolic inversion. The physically imposing hero embodying the popular values of righteousness and compassion looked down upon the "little" samurai. This imaginary encounter transformed the procession ritual, a spectacle of distinction that normally served to emphasize the high-ranking samurai's splendor, into an object of the hero's mockery. In Kuniyoshi's visual representation, the pageantry of the ruling elites became the subject of comedy and derision. By imagining the world turned upside down, Kuniyoshi's *Asahina-yakko* ridiculed the ruling class's putative superiority and dominance and hinted at its injustices.

In Tokugawa times, as briefly mentioned in chapter 1, daimyo processions were an everyday spectacle that demonstrated the most splendid pageantry of a high-ranking samurai's power and status. Pictorial art normally represented them as such. Utagawa Hiroshige's (1797–1858) illustration of a daimyo procession entitled *Okazaki* (1833), for example, effectively executes the iconography of the daimyo's power (figure 3.7). The daimyo's invisible presence seems strange at first sight in this illustration, but it is his invisibility that engenders the mystifying effect in representing power: it precludes the desacralization of the daimyo's image by shielding his body from the gaze of the beholders (note that it

3.7 Utagawa Hiroshige (1797–1858), *Okazaki*, 1833, from the *Tōkaidō* series. Woodblock print, ink and color on paper. (Tokyo Metropolitan Museum)

was for this reason that portraying the daimyo himself was unlawful in Tokugawa times). The actual procession was also always staged in such a way as to carefully conceal his physical presence within an extravagantly decorated palanquin. Instead of the daimyo's visible presence, it was the splendor of the procession—its metonymical effect of representing his absent presence—that produced the overwhelming impression of his power, authority, and status.[63] In Hiroshige's illustration, this metonymic strategy of the representation of power is also deployed, endowing different kinds of exterior features, such as the bridge, the castle, and the mountains, the role of creating the exalting and mystifying effect. The invisible end of the long and magnificent bridge makes the procession appear endlessly extensive, and this seemingly infinite horizon of the procession lends an air of eternity to the daimyo's power. The castle, the likely destination of the procession, prominently stands above the common people's red-roofed houses. Its dominant presence is nothing but a reminder of who rules the region. The beautiful mountains standing behind the castle serve to create the perception that the daimyo's castle and his political realm are blessed by nature's heavenly power. The tranquility and harmony of the landscape through the uniform and harmonizing use of color reinforces the sense that this community is in peace under the daimyo's rule.

Clearly, Kuniyoshi's *Asahina's Adventure* is a satirical parody of the aesthetic conventions in representing the powerful, which is exemplified by Hiroshige's *Okazaki*. Instead of furnishing the procession with visual metaphors for splendor, glory, and eternity, it trivializes it by subjecting it to comic ridicule.

What needs to be underscored here is that the "lowly" bodily motifs in all the examples discussed above played the specific function of inverting the order of high and low that underpinned the established social hierarchy of Tokugawa Japan. In particular, the affirmative rendering of the "idle" body that sprang from the culture of spectacle—"unproductive expenditure"—violated or displaced the most fundamental official assumption about "productivity": the primacy of the mind over the body as the site of the most prized labor that contributed to the preservation of societal harmony. In Gennai's *On Farting*, the ex-peasant performer who renounced the duty of labor in the village and made a living out of "waste" and "filth"—farting—in the city featured not only as the principal prong of an assault on the established morality of thrift and hard work but also as a categorical negation of the ruling class's cherished self-image as the custodian of mind, morality, and knowledge. Utamaro's

The Future exposed the parasitic existence of a samurai by making him grovel before the lowly outcast to repair a pair of broken sandals. And Kuniyoshi's *Asahina* called into question the presumed righteousness and superiority of the samurai by dwarfing their bodies in front of the body of the outlaw.

The political potency of these representations of an inverted world resided in their symbolic power to unhinge and deconstruct, through their articulation of the unthinkable, the Tokugawa regime's transcendental claims of high and low distinctions. By pronouncing heterogeneous meanings and images of the body that were irreducible to the paradigm of the productive body as moral, popular literary and visual texts disrupted the perpetual and inviolable images of the official order. At the same time, they generated the novel perspective that the categories of social classification were not sacrosanct, but *arbitrarily* constructed for a particular purpose, that is, to naturalize, legitimize, and universalize the worldviews representing the interests of the ruling class. Gennai's vehement attack on the elite for their ineptitude and lack of creativity, Utamaro's eloquent depiction of the samurai's parasitic existence, and Kuniyoshi's biting satire of the samurai's self-congratulatory grandeur constructed a critical perspective that, underneath the ostensible truth of social hierarchies, the ruling class was fundamentally illegitimate.

Laughter and Its Symbolic Meanings in Edo Popular Culture

The pungent wit and poignant satire of comic realism provided *gesaku* readers and ukiyo-e lovers with the pleasure of contestation and transgression through the extensive use of profanities, improprieties, and cheerful vulgarities that were capable of mocking the inelasticity of official norms and hierarchies, as well as the prohibitions of moralizing idioms. When they recognized lampooneries implicit in paradoxical messages of comic writings and prints by Gennai, Hokusai, Kuniyoshi, Sanba, and Utamaro, humor captivated their minds and imaginations and, most probably, culminated into a chorus of laughter. Laughter then signified the moment when users of those cultural texts made interpretive choices in deciphering built-in messages of idiosyncrasy, absurdity, contradiction, and hypocrisy in the structure of signs. It was, in other words, their active participation in the process of signification that made laughter possible. *Ugachi* could become an *ugachi* only when there was collaboration between the producers and users of a certain set of signs.

During the political and ideological campaigns of the Tokugawa shogunate in the early 1790s and early 1840s, a number of *gesaku* and ukiyo-e works using the methods of *ugachi* to elicit laughter became the targets of suppression by the authorities. In 1842, for example, an edict was issued to proscribe the selling and buying of books containing satire and mockery of the regime and high-ranking officials together with prints of popular kabuki actors and erotic images. The Edo magistrate's reasoning for this was that these materials "undermined public mores and respect for the social order and fundamental virtues—loyalty, propriety and filial piety."[64] This edict reflected the concern that these texts provoked their users to ignore or defy the requirement of conformity to conventions, etiquette, civility, and respectability—values central to the official discourses of the social order. Laughter was viewed as a symptom of dissipation and disorder.[65]

Identifying in laughter the ability to triumph over dogma and prohibition in medieval Europe, M. M. Bakhtin writes:

> [S]erious aspects of class culture are official and authoritarian; they are combined with violence, prohibitions, limitations and always contain an element of fear and of intimidation. These elements prevailed in the Middle Ages. Laughter, on the contrary, overcomes fear, for it knows no inhibitions, no limitations. Its idiom is never used by violence and authority.[66]

Bakhtin goes on to argue that "[festive folk laughter] means the defeat of power, of early kings, of the earthy upper classes, of all that oppresses and restricts."[67] Although the historical experience of medieval Europe differed from that of late-eighteenth-century Edo, Bakhtin's analysis of laughter holds some relevance to our understanding of the socioideological implications of laughter in Edo popular culture. I have argued that one of the ideologically significant aspects of *gesaku* and ukiyo-e was their ability to negate, via comic effect, the representations of the hierarchical social order. If this proposition has been well established and accepted by now, then we can argue that the authorities' sensitivity about these genres had something to do with this very ability. Can this ability then be understood exactly in light of Bakhtin's claim that laughter is capable of overcoming fear, knows no inhibitions and limitations, and thus means the defeat of power? Or are there any other explanations that can illuminate the politico-ideological implications of laughter, which were specific to the context of late eighteenth- or early nineteenth-century Edo?

In the discussion of inversion above, I have shown that *ugachi* referred to the satirical criticism of disparities between conventionalized norms and behavior and overdetermined lived experiences. It targeted in particular the reproductive practice of "common sense"—received norms, demeanor, and knowledge—that gave rise to a sense of social stagnation.

Analyzing the essence of laughter, Henri Bergson identifies rigidity and inelasticity of this sort as the major catalyst for laughter. He writes, "The laughable element . . . consists of a certain mechanical inelasticity, just where one would expect to find the wide-awake adaptability and living pliableness of a human being."[68] When *gesaku* writers like Gennai or Sanba mocked Confucian scholars, Buddhists, physicians, nativist poets, and so on for their uncritical devotion to antiquated knowledge and disjoined sensibilities, they were referring precisely to this "mechanical inelasticity." Or when Hokusai satirized the preposterous observation of the hierarchy between the samurai master and his retainers in *Privy*, and when Kuniyoshi mocked the splendor of the daimyo procession in *Asahina's Adventure*, the absence of "living pliableness" was also the central theme. Bergson elaborates further on this: "gestures would never repeat themselves . . . [they] become imitable only when we cease to be ourselves . . . our gestures can only be imitated in their mechanical uniformity, and therefore exactly in what is alien to our living personality. To imitate any one is to bring out the element of automatism he has allowed to creep into this person."[69]

Bergson's insight is applicable to our analysis of Edo laughter in that it spells out social conditions that brought forth laughter in Edo popular culture: laughter was a marker of the recognition of "automatism" or the lack of "living personality"—the morbid symptom of the rigid rules, regulations, and rituals that sustained the Tokugawa order.[70] Cultural producers often observed the absence of "living pliableness" and "living personality" in the automatism that predominantly existed in the establishment: in particular, its adherence to antiquated forms of decorum and its lack of adaptability, flexibility, and creativity in the domain of knowledge production. Although the Bergsonian theory of laughter offers a clue to understanding the social conditions that gave rise to the literature and art of laughter in late Tokugawa Edo, it does not shed light on why the authorities saw laughter as a source of dissipation and disorder. To understand this, we need to turn to the formulation put forward by Tosaka Jun (1900–1945), a Marxist thinker and cultural critic in prewar Japan. Tosaka argues that humorous laughter is the product of an indeterminate middle position between the acceptance and negation of what is laughed at. Humor sustains this position by demonstrating negativity through the logic of acceptance. In doing so, it avoids producing edgy or pointed effects. But when the negative impulse of laughter prevails over the logic of acceptance, abolishing an indeterminate middle position and becoming the principal drive of laughter, humor takes on the form of irony or satire.[71] It transforms humorous laughter of absurdity into a laughter of social criticism. Tosaka concludes, "The most important condition of laughter lies in its function of exposing and critiquing."[72] Following Tosaka's dialectical formulation, we are reminded of how in Gennai's *The Biography of Elegant Shidōken*, paradoxical messages such as absurdity and seriousness or nonsense and illumination created the effect of humor. But we are also reminded that when strong negativity, that is, satirical and ironic messages, came to the foreground of the semantic landscape, Gennai's social criticism began to appear as the key component of this travesty. Or consider Shikitei Sanba's profanation of Confucian virtues and Buddhist doctrine and Hokusai's pointed satire of samurai rituals. All these examples of comic realism contain the element of what Tosaka calls the "aggressiveness of negation" (*hitei no kogekisei* 否定の攻撃性), a focal shifting point from the comic as humor to the comic as criticism.[73] This is exactly what Freud also meant by negation—a sign of cognizance and exposure of what is repressed. Indeed, the essence of laughter engendered through comic realism lay precisely in its function of exposing and critiquing what was repressed in the official discourse on the social reality.

But was the townspeople's laughter of exposing and critiquing aimed only at the powerful figures and elites or their insistence on the unconditional necessity of social hierarchy and the division of labor? In his best-seller comic series, *Shank's Mare* (*Tokaidōchū hizakurige* 東海道中膝栗毛; 1802–9), Juppensha Ikku created a protagonist, Yaji, who represented a prototype of an Edoite. Yaji figured, rather paradoxically, as both a witty and ignorant, compassionate and dishonest, and unpretentious and vain man. One scene from the story exemplifies this: "Yaji is a very caring father. One day he takes his son out to pay a visit to a shrine. His son asks him, 'There are two guardian statues on both sides of the gate, and I hear that one is called *Yadaijin* and another *Sadaijin*. Can you tell me which one is which?' Yaji answers with a serious look, 'Son, remember this! The one that is not *Yadaijin* is *Sadaijin*, and the one that is not *Sadaijin* is *Yadaijin*'."[74] The laughable element can be clearly found in absurdity effected by the paradox or the hopelessly unbridgeable gap between Yaji's inability to answer the question and his vain conviction that he passed down wisdom to his son. Yet, at the same time, this very same line also presents Yaji as a loving and caring father. Laughter emerges from the humorous effects of reading the phrase that points to the paradoxical character of Yaji. This type of comical story was the very popular genre called "Funny Stories" (*warai banashi* 笑い話) among the townspeople during the late Tokugawa period.[75] Its thrust was, without exception, the townspeople's self-mockery of their foolishness, vanity, and ignorance. But this act of humorous self-mockery of folly rarely developed into bitter criticism and poignant satire. Indeed, aggressive negation seemed to accompany laughter only when it was directed toward the abusive, exploitative, and hypocritical authority figures.

As shown in the above examples, laughter in Edo popular culture worked as both self-mockery and a critique of the powerful. Laughter unhinged all transcendental claims and pretensions and submitted them to ridicule and relativism. Nothing escaped this convulsion of laughter. Recognizing and exposing incompleteness and finitude in all human beings, laughter dissolved all limits, boundaries, and inhibitions. Conversely, although the Tokugawa rulers and elites also acknowledged the deficiencies of humanity, they saw them mainly as the exclusive attribute of the commoners. By representing them as the natural manifestations of the commoners' "lowly" (*hi* 卑) and "stupid" (*gu* 愚) propensities, the official ideology promoted a belief that it was the commoners' unfortunate but inevitable providence to be regulated by a handful of elites who possessed extraordinary moral capacity and exceptional wisdom. Commoners' laughter, however, defied this claim by dissolving the division between high and low into the egalitarian vision of humanity's finitude.

How this particular view of humanity came about relates back to the discussion of Nishikawa Joken (1648–1724) presented in chapter 1. At the turn of the eighteenth century, townspeople found themselves torn between great social strictures and the possibility of agency. Self-confidence grounded in their rapid rise to prominence as a result of cultural and economic innovations conflicted fundamentally with the dominant structures—social, economic, political, and ideological—that sustained the hierarchical configuration of Tokugawa order. However, at the same time, the awareness that their remarkable ascendancy was actually enabled by the very socioeconomic structures that seriously constrained their agency made it difficult for them to articulate openly their confidence. Their resultant consciousness of ambivalence, or "in-betweenness," gave rise to the view of life as split and oscillating. This conflicted ontological consciousness provoked a keen awareness of society as a composite of disunity, disharmony, and contradiction and encouraged varying expressions of such awareness in art and literature. The rise of this new historical consciousness should not be taken, however, as an instance of the Hegelian dialectic, or sublation, in the manner, for example, of Lukács's theory of the rise of revolutionary class consciousness whereby the reified existence of the proletariat would lead to self-awareness of the wretched conditions (commodification) of their lives, a desire to overcome those conditions, and a will to fully restore their authentic selfhood.[76] Rather, the consciousness of townspeople in eighteenth-century Tokugawa Japan was manifested primarily in concern with how to negotiate and survive, not overcome, the conflicted existence originating from contradictory historical conditions. The tragic dramas of double suicide in the early-eighteenth-century puppet and kabuki theaters exemplified such a consciousness precisely because they portrayed death not as a complete closure to the agonizing negotiation between norms and passions, nor as a means to attain a tranquil state of happiness in the afterworld, but as the undesired yet inevitable path to *survival* in afterlife. The drama of double suicide was not a story, in short, that ended with a happy synthesis. From the mid-eighteenth century onward, comic parody replaced the trope of tragic death as a new form of articulating in-betweenness as the primary condition for survival. But terms of survival were configured more exclusively within the frame of life in this world. "The floating world" (*ukiyo*), as it was called, now referred to the condition of existence suffused with growing dissonance between the rigid formalism on which Tokugawa social order was premised and the dispersion and diversification of lived experience. Accordingly, human beings came to signify an existence torn apart by that dissonance and thus full of contradiction and incompleteness. Comic realism became the most expressive means of articulating the new vision of society, humans, and historical conditions, because it was capable of addressing, via the literary and artistic techné called *ugachi*, the very nature of the dissonance. Laughter was a phenomenon that occurred precisely at the moment when comic realism executed the *ugachi* performance to full extent. In this regard, laughter elicited by comic realism could also be considered to be the most symbolic materialization of historical consciousness specific to the latter half of the eighteenth and the early nineteenth centuries.

The authorities believed that laughter signified dissipation and disorder precisely because of its ability to crystallize and critically evaluate the socially discernible dissonance, which they hoped to repress. That *gesaku*, ukiyo-e, and other genres of representation filled with the spirit of wit and satire became the target of the shogunate 's regulation largely because they achieved the scandalous relativization of authority—thus invalidating any monopoly of moral and intellectual power—by announcing a vision of contradictory and imperfect humanity as universal. Charles

Baudelaire's observation regarding laughter—that it tends to be despised by the powerful as "generally the attribute of madness" and as always implying "a greater or lesser degree of ignorance and weakness"—aptly captures the Tokugawa authorities' attitudes toward the popular culture of Edo.[77] By disparaging laughter as no more than an instantiation of ignorance, weakness, and madness, they hoped to muffle its antidogmatic, plural, and open-ended proclivities.[78]

The Potency of Comic Realism and Its Significance

Comic realism was not a form of protest or resistance in the ordinary sense of these words. It neither initiated an organized political activism nor produced a collective mentality based on a shared political vision of change and reform. What made it political in the eyes of the Tokugawa authorities and elites was its attempt to reveal the *inner mechanism* of the symbolic system of Tokugawa power by defamiliarizing it. This defamiliarization disclosed the overdetermination of contradictions that nullified the binary sign system's reductive configuration of social reality. The late eighteenth and early nineteenth century was indeed a time when Tokugawa society was undergoing sharpened social fragmentation and cultural and economic contradictions; subject positions—status and labor—prescribed by the symbolic system appeared increasingly to be disjoined from those realities. Comic realism's articulations of disjuncture between the symbolic and the experiential acted both as a symptom and as a catalyst of the dynamism of historical transformation. In this regard, comic realism resembles what Peter Stallybrass and Allon White have called, following Bakhtin, "carnival": it does not produce "noticeable transformative effects but, given the presence of sharpened political antagonism, it may often act as catalyst and site of actual and symbolic struggle."[79]

That the body surged forth as the primary site of symbolic struggle between power and popular culture has important implications. For the shogunate, as seen in chapter 1, the body—more precisely, the body of the common person—needed to be contained by the requirements of productivity and the moral imperative of societal harmony. The bodies of common people became objects of official scrutiny and regulation largely because of the shogunate and its ideologues' shared assumption that, because of their relative moral and mental weaknesses, commoners were susceptible to the alluring power of corporeal desire and thus needed to be made dependent on the moral injunctions of the ruling elite. With this assumption providing the logic for social hierarchies, the shogunate sought to secure the hegemonic position of samurai in Tokugawa Japan.

In contrast, the urban popular culture of late-eighteenth-century Edo began to valorize the body by suffusing it with carnal desire, or "folly" and "idleness," reflecting the world of play and pleasure. Defying the official ideal of the productive body as moral and claiming the "idle" body to be far more productive and innovative than the intellectual labor of the ruling elite, popular writers and artists exposed the hypocrisies and contradictions of the presumed social hierarchies through which the ruling elite preserved its power and privileges.

Perhaps it was no coincidence that both the official and the popular discourses often converged in the rhetorical battle over the meaning of "productivity." This signaled the fact that eighteenth-century Tokugawa Japan underwent an epochal transformation, occasioned by the emergence of a social condition in which multiple modes of production came to coexist and compete—a condition which Louis Althusser refers to as the "overdetermination of a contradiction" and Ernst Bloch as "the synchrony of the nonsynchronous."[80] From the eighteenth century on, both the feudalistic mode of production (centered on rice) and the commercial economy (centered on money) worked as driving forces for social formation, and, as time passed, the latter seemed to have supplanted the former by undercutting the principle of economic production that had been designed to sustain the Tokugawa social order. Under this new economic principle, consumption was no longer viewed as detrimental to production but as an essential element of it. Therefore, the fact that common people's transgressive imaginations were grounded in and enabled by the spaces governed by the economy of spectacle and its consumption carried serious political implications for the Tokugawa authorities. In these milieus, it was not the moral principle of austerity, hard work, and loyalty-duty, but the production and consumption of play and pleasure that served as the basis for subsistence.

All sorts of people were drawn into the sphere of new economic and cultural forms that celebrated the possibility of identities, or subject positions, that had not existed within the received political and ideological paradigm. These spaces for heterogeneous social formation paralyzed the principles of distinction and made possible literary and visual imaginings of dialogic encounter between high and low. Popular literature and art brought the decorum of the samurai class into relativizing and contestatory dialogue with the "vulgar" discourses of the market and entertainment districts, thereby achieving the dramatic displacement of the ostensibly inviolable primacy of mind over body. It was in such "a dynamic state of low-ascending and high-descending" in semiotic fields, according to Geoffrey Harpham, "a state in which the established order of things began to disintegrate," that new figures of the body emerged prominently as the site where the disjuncture and contradictions between ideological premise and socioeconomic reality were forcefully articulated.[81]

V. N. Volosinov explicates the political implications of this kind of semiotic operation. He argues that all signs have two faces: "Any current curse word can become a word of praise, any current truth must inevitably sound to many other people as the greatest lie." "This *inner dialectic quality* of the sign," he continues, "comes out fully in the open only in times of social crises or revolutionary changes."[82] It was indeed no accident that the inversion of dominant categories and values through the idle and carnal body appeared as one potent mode of negation at a time when a deepening sense of crisis beset Tokugawa Japan. It was against this social, cultural, economic, and political reality that the symbolic system of Tokugawa power came under scrutiny, and those who held on to it were increasingly criticized for their refusal to recognize new realities. The verbal and visual play of inversion materialized complex reorderings of the dominant social order and the categories of social thought that legitimized such an order, supplying a possibility of directing criticism, albeit allusive, against those who safeguarded them. In this regard, the playful symbolic action was rarely mere play: it articulated cultural and political meanings that subjected to ridicule and relativism the authoritarian solemnities of monologue fashioning the powerful as the custodian of wisdom, morality, and intelligence.

It was indeed one of the most powerful ruses of the dominant to assume that meaningful articulation could only come from the language of "reason," "pure knowledge," and "seriousness." The humorous and satiric words and images of Edo popular culture should not be understood as part of a benign and apolitical realm of escapist activities, as Maruyama Masao and others have argued.[83] They need to be reconceived as a discursive field in which the reified conception of "cosmic-human unity"—the fundamental form of reification under the Tokugawa regime—was confronted, negotiated, and contested through articulations of the idle and useless body as a site of radical difference.

FOUR

Grotesque Realism: A Strategy of Chaos

Grotesque is a word for this paralysis of language.
GEOFFREY HARPHAM, *ON THE GROTESQUE*

People's penchant for the grotesque (*iyō* 異様) poses a serious problem for public morals. A TOKUGAWA GOVERNMENT DECREE OF 1841

In May 1804, the city magistrate of Edo apprehended a comic writer and illustrator, Juppensha Ikku (1765–1831), and placed him in handcuffs for fifty days for creating *The Chronicle of the Battles of Demons* (*Bakemono Taiheiki* 化け物太平記; 1804), a burlesqued adaptation of *An Illustrated Story of Hideyoshi* (*Ehon Taiheiki* 絵本太平記; 1797–1802). *An Illustrated Story* itself, together with *Demons*, was banned in the same year for parodying *The Story of Hideyoshi* (*Taikōki* 太閤記; 1625), a "biographical" work about the sixteenth-century warlord Toyotomi Hideyoshi (1537–98). Two popular woodblock artists, Kitagawa Utamaro (1753–1806) and Utagawa Toyokuni (1769–1825), were also arrested along with Ikku for making prints that ridiculed the key samurai figures of the Toyotomi era (1585–1603), including Hideyoshi.[1] Furthermore, Tadasuke (dates unknown), the publisher responsible for printing and selling copies of Ikku's book, as well as Utamaro's and Toyokuni's prints, was punished with a heavy fine.

This series of apprehensions carried out by the shogunate in 1804 was targeted at various parodic versions of *The Story of Hideyoshi*.[2] Oze Hōan (1564–1640), a Confucian scholar and a physician who served Hideyoshi, wrote *The Story* after his master's death to idolize him as a paragon of such Confucian moral values as loyalty and righteousness and thus to help create a narrative conducive to preserving the legacies of his rule. According to a historian, Minami Kazuo, these parodies fueled the trend in which ordinary townspeople from young to old, from women to men, grew enamored with talking about the history of the warring period (the late fifteenth to the late sixteenth centuries), especially about the rise and fall of Hideyoshi, which greatly disturbed both Hideyoshi's close relatives and the Tokugawa authorities.[3] Hideyoshi was a quintessential figure of the civil war strife in that he rose from a humble background of poor peasantry to become the most powerful warlord ever, but his heirs were only to be betrayed and destroyed in 1615 by Tokugawa Ieyasu (1542–1616), a close ally of Hideyoshi and the founder of the Tokugawa shogunate. The parodies placed an emphasis on this tumultuous, treacherous, and sordid process of power struggle, in sharp contrast to Oze's original work. The uneasiness felt by Hideyoshi's descendants and the Tokugawas as a result of this scandalous reminder of their historical origins was reflected in the indictment announcing Tadasuke, Ikku, and the others' arrest and the ban on the books:

> This [Tadasuke] ignored the city ordinance by printing and selling the prints [by Toyokuni and Utamaro], which depicted the [eminent samurai] figures of the Toyotomi period. . . . The descendants of the families illustrated here demanded that the copies of the prints be confiscated and banned from further circulation. Moreover, [Tadasuke] also sold another illustrated book [by Juppensha Ikku], which showed the same samurai figures as grotesqueries (*ikei* 異形) along with their family crests [that would help disclose their identities]. This is clearly a violation of the ordinance that prohibits references to the names and crests [of important samurai families]. Those who made, published or sold the illustrated book are to be punished according to the degree to which they defied the law.[4]

The indictment shows that Ikku and the others were all punished on the basis of the same criminal charge: violation of a Tokugawa law that prohibited references to eminent samurai figures. Although the prints and the illustrated book did not specify the names of the samurai, they used family crests to allude to their identities. Since the middle of the seventeenth century the shogunate had customarily reiterated to the townspeople the ordinances that proscribed any discussions of or references to important samurai families and their historical origins. It also used this law as the rationale for implementing censorship against books, prints, theatrical performances, and speeches designed to recall, often in a form

4.1 Juppensha Ikku (1765–1831), *Taiheiki of Demons*, 1804. Woodblock print. (Courtesy of the Tokyo Metropolitan Museum)

of ridicule or satire, the history of those samurai's ignominious rise to power.[5] It is yet to be ascertained, unfortunately, exactly what prints of Utamaro and Toyokuni incited the Edo authorities' charges against them, but Ikku's *Taiheiki of Demons* was intended unmistakably to bring about such a satiric effect. It portrayed as grotesque demons all the important warriors of the late sixteenth century who strove to bring an end to the warring period and to become the supreme leader in the realm (figure 4.1). Oda Nobunaga (1534–82) was rendered as a sluglike monster, Akechi Mitsuhide (1528–82) as a frog-shaped monster, and Toyotomi Hideyoshi as a snake. The story develops as a satire of the historical account of how these samurai actually fought each other in their struggle for power: the frog eats the slug, only later to be devoured by the snake.

It is unclear if each of these hideous, yet somewhat humorous-looking, creatures carried a specific symbolic meaning for the people of late Tokugawa times, but the shogunate was evidently apprehensive about the prospect that such dishonorable depictions of ruling samurai figures would demystify their self-fashioning of sacrosanct stature by turning them into the objects of public mockery. Potential defamation and degradation through popular discourse seemed to be the main reason for the authorities' sustained concern about and persistent interference with popular cultural texts of this sort.

Grotesque representation as a particular mode of political satire became more visible in the popular culture of Edo from the late eighteenth century onward.[6] Even anonymous commoners frequently deployed this method of representation to call into question what they perceived as unjust and abusive doings of the powerful. An Edo townsperson created the illustration (*Monster of Seven Eyes*; figure 4.2) in 1786, which was circulated in hand-copied and printed forms throughout the city when the highest-ranking shogunal advisor, Tanuma Okitsugu (1719–88), was

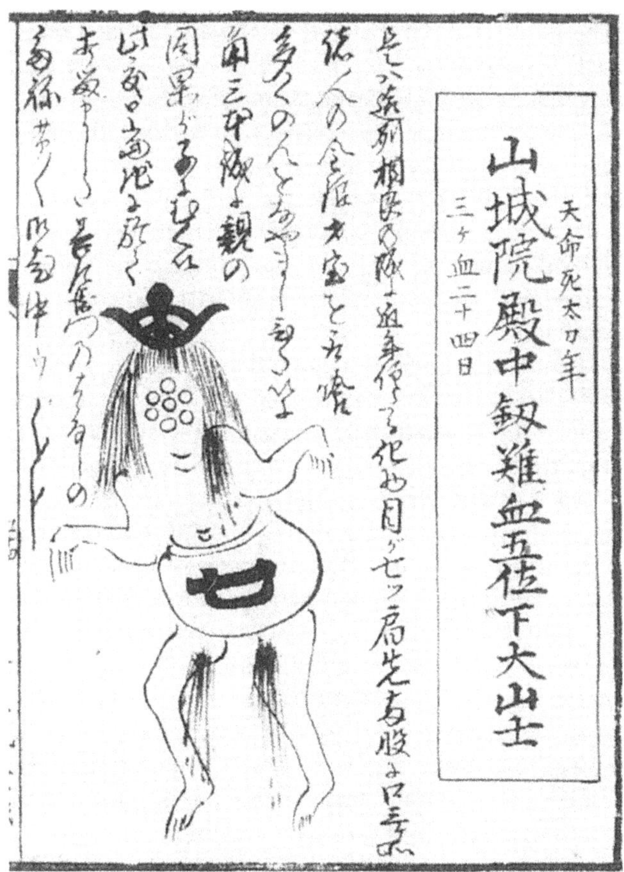

4.2 Anonymous, *Monster of Seven Eyes*, 1786. Illustration. (Courtesy of the National Diet Library, Tokyo)

forced to step down after twenty years in office. His notoriously corrupt administration had failed dismally to cope with one of the most devastating famines caused by natural disasters, the Tenmei Famine (1782–87). The caption of the illustration says, "This monster inhabited the castle of Enshū [present-day Shizuoka prefecture], having seven eyes on its face and bearing three sword cuts on its thighs. It gobbled up people's gold and silver, and this led to much suffering. As a result of its evil doings, [Sano] Zenzaemon avenged the people by destroying the monster's child, and at the same time slaying the monster itself."[7]

Here, "seven eyes" implied the Tanuma's family crest, "Enshū" was their home domain, and "the monster's child" meant Okitsugu's son, Okitomo (d. 1786), who was murdered by Sano Zenzaemon (dates unknown). The monster's "three sword cuts" were the fatal scars left by Sano's attack. Sano's motive was never disclosed, but some contemporaries speculated that he had a personal grudge against Okitomo because Okitomo had failed to keep the promises Sano had bought with bribery. Others argued that Sano was an assassin dispatched by an anti-Tanuma faction. In any case, this representation of the Tanumas echoed the fury of the Edo townspeople toward Tamuna's politics; they welcomed Sano's act as heroic, called him "Savior," and paid respects at his tomb. It is also said that some townspeople threw stones at Okitomo's coffin during his funeral procession.[8]

The representational method mobilized by both Ikku and the anonymous townsperson was a widely shared tactic of astute camouflage designed to perform a veiled criticism against the authorities. It seems plausible that the shogunate took relatively harsh penal actions against what appeared to be a politically inconsequential satire by Ikku as a measure to impede the further proliferation of popular practices of this sort. Whatever the shogunate's intention, the cases of Ikku and the others attested to the truism, as Daniel Botsman has shown, that the Tokugawa state regarded anyone belittling and questioning its self-imposed respectability and its efforts to bolster and sustain its authority as fundamentally its enemy and thus considered it vital to criminalize such an act for its own survival.[9] Moreover, they demonstrated the shogunate's intent to make people aware through exemplary punishment that even the slightest critique of the authorities might be considered to be an act of disrupting social order and thus be met with punishment. After all, the Tokugawa state not only recognized no obligation to explain why it regarded the ruling samurai status groups' monopoly and use of violence as legally legitimate but also insisted on the right to punish at will any who would question the legitimacy of that monopoly.[10] Like any other autocratic government, the Tokugawa shogunate presumed to personify law without any rational basis, except for the claim that the preservation of social order was the foremost ethical matter and that samurai must perform the task of ensuring it as the ruling elite born with the moral and intellectual endowment that qualified them to instruct and govern the people.

Conceptualizing *Iyō* (異様), *Ikai* (奇怪), or the Grotesque

Yet, while pointing out the autocratic dispositions of the Tokugawa state and the censorship policy reflecting such dispositions may suffice to explain why the authorities took Ikku and the others' parodies as an irremissible offense, much remains to be clarified in regard to grotesque representation as a parodic form of aesthetic negation and the political implications of its use. How do we explain the explosive proliferation of grotesque images in popular woodblock prints and kabuki plays in the late Tokugawa period? When viewed within the context of the cultural politics of late Tokugawa Japan, what were the connotations of the townspeople's grotesque representations of acclaimed and powerful samurai figures? Were there any unanticipated effects, besides that of covert criticism, that the use of these imageries alone was capable of creating?

"The grotesque" is a rendering of the Tokugawa terms, *iyō* (異様), *ikei* (異形), and *kikai* (奇怪). *Iyō* literally denotes something "strange, odd or uncanny," *ikei* something "deformed, abnormal or monstrous," and *kikai* something "mysterious, weird or fantastic." Numerous images described as "grotesque" in woodblock prints and kabuki plays made their marked appearance at the moment when the established world of status hierarchies and its carefully maintained decorum seemed to be crumbling under the volcanic pressures of social, economic and cultural contradictions. The widely recognized reversal of power relations between samurai and townspeople in the areas of economy, cultural innovation, and societal influence had rendered the ideological premise of the high/low distinction more palpably insubstantial, and the ruling samurai status groups' ineffectiveness in resolving calamities suffered by common people contributed to the diminution of their moral authority. "Samurai can no longer command people's respect," an Edo official lamented in 1812.[11] Echoing this observation, Buyō Inshi noted around the same time, "Not only have commoners stopped looking to their leaders for matters that require the important distinction between good and evil, right and wrong, but also they often hold sneering attitudes toward them."[12] "Nowadays,"

Buyō went on, "the whole world adores townspeople and idlers [instead of samurai] such that everyone wants to emulate or be acquainted with them. Even samurai, forgetting their stations, unabashedly try hard to win a cordial relationship with townspeople while vagabonds seek to learn prodigal arts [street entertainments] so as to take up the life of a townsperson. Peasants look up to the city life and send their children to Edo to have them take service under townspeople."[13]

What were the relationships between the perceived inversion of the structure of authority (respectability and influence) inscribed in social relations and the salient emergence of the grotesque in the early nineteenth century? Put more precisely, how was the grotesque's rise as a principal mode of symbolic negation related to the perceived disarray of social order and the decline of the samurai's stature and moral authority? M. M. Bakhtin, Geoffrey Harpham, and others have formulated "grotesque" as a word for anomalousness, ambiguity, or ambivalence.[14] The anomalous stands, in Susan Stuart's words, "between the categories of an existing classification system. . . . The ambiguous is that which cannot be defined in terms of any given category. . . . The ambivalent is that which belongs to more than one domain at a time."[15] In other words, grotesque speaks to a zone of unstable or indeterminate signification—be it word or image—wherein a professed unity of meaning authorized by given categories for classification and structured thought that underlies the categories is proven to be untenable as it reveals its own representational limitations or ineptitude: meaning is incapable of, in Harpham's words, "organizing the world, dividing the continuum of experience into knowable particles."[16] Grotesque is, in this regard, a figure of speech that signifies "the paralysis of language."[17]

Indeed, in late Tokugawa Edo the use of the grotesque form showed that the dominant mode(s) of representation, which supplied the rationale for status distinctions and the division of labor, was incapable of accommodating rapidly diversifying social realities or restructuring the disintegrating social order. The deployment of the form also stimulated the acute sense, as in the case of townsperson's caricature of the Tanumas, that the discourse authorizing samurai's moral and intellectual ascendancy was hardly defensible in light of its apparent failure to fulfill its promises of benevolence and righteousness. The grotesque thus served as a mode of critique not only of deficiencies but also of duplicities in the official representation of the ideal of totality. Grotesque form visualized most efficaciously both the paralysis of the official representation of reality and the unsustainability of the ideological claim upon which samurai's inviolable stature was premised.

Grotesque imageries rose to prominence during the late Tokugawa period. For example, take the various iconographic images of the popular gods called "the gods of harmonious union" (*wagōshin* 和合神; figure 4.3). According to Shikitei Sanba (1776–1822), a best-selling writer of comic and satiric stories, the iconography of *wagōshin* enjoyed wide circulation and adaptation in Edo during the early 1800s, through which the gods took on the meaning of auspicious omens for married and unmarried heterosexual couples.[18] Viewed by the townspeople as promising "a harmonious marital relationship [that] would naturally result in inviting good fortune and long life,"[19] *wagōshin* pictures were sought after and displayed on living room walls as a decoration or object of worship. According to Hattori Yukio, an eminent specialist in kabuki and Edo popular culture, this image's popularity was due not only to its secular promise of fertility, heterosexual love, successful marriage, and material prosperity but also to the somewhat anomalous quality created by the ingenious marriage of incongruities: the gods' short and corpulently childish bodies despite their aged appearance, their strong pronouncement of harmonious heterosexual relationships despite their lack of discernible gender differentiation, and, above all, their hermitlike casualness and transcendence despite their unconditional celebration of secular desire (treasures underneath their feet and in their hands, as well as clothes designed with coin images).

Katsushika Hokusai (1760–1849), a renowned ukiyo-e artist, further underscored the anomalous features of this *wagōshin* image. Hokusai, among writers and other ukiyo-e artists, responded to the popularity of *wagōshin* by making two different adaptations of it. One (figure 4.4; 1816) is believed to have become the standardized image and contributed to the further popularization of the image within and beyond Edo. The other (figure 4.5; 1822) is a drastically appropriated image that exhibited the "harmonious union" in terms of overt libidinal symbolism. In the first illustration, the tension between the sacred and the profane was accentuated by the sharp contrast between shabby and vulgar appearances of the gods' bodies and their transcendental power to bring about the happiness of intimate unity. In addition, as in figure 4.4, the couple's physiological features do not clearly demarcate a male or female identity despite the received knowledge that the gods represent a promise of prosperity and happiness primarily for heterosexual relationships. But in Hokusai's second illustration (figure 4.5), this gender distinction is rather bluntly and unmistakably proclaimed as the gods' faces are drawn as sexual organs. Moreover, with treasures no longer at their bare feet, nor boxes of gifts in their hands, the iconography is reduced to that of erotic and fertile

4.3 Anonymous, *Wagōshin* (*Gods of Harmonious Union*), 1820s. Woodblock print. (Courtesy of the Victoria and Albert Museum, London)

4.4 Katsushika Hokusai (1760–1849), *Wagōshin* (*Gods of Harmonious Union*), 1816, in *Hokusai manga*. Woodblock print. (Courtesy of the Division of Rare and Manuscript Collections, Cornell University Library)

energy, celebrating life energy itself in an image bearing a most explicit sexual symbolism. From the perspective of mainstream Tokugawa arts, especially that of the samurai and aristocratic arts that privileged grace and sublimity as the essential qualities of the highest form of aesthetic expression, this was clearly one of the most anomalous representations of sacredness. It violated the sacrosanct division between the upper and lower parts of the body in such a way that the lower took over the entire body in an unabashed endorsement of abundant erotic pleasure and energy.

The last image of *wagōshin* to be discussed here is an 1852 work by Utagawa Toyokuni (1769–1825) (figure 4.6.). This print took on the ambiguity of the gods' sexuality as a central motif by parodying them in the image of popular kabuki actors, Ichikawa Danjurō, the eighth (1823–54),

4.5 Katsushika Hokusai (1760–1849), *Wagōshin* (*Gods of Harmonious Union*), 1822, in *Hokusai manga*. Woodblock print. (Courtesy of the Division of Rare and Manuscript Collections, Cornell University Library)

and Bandō Shuika (1813–55), who were idolized by theater goers for their performance of a dear and handsome couple. The figure on the right is Danjurō impersonating a husband, as on the stage, and the one on the left is Shuika, a wife. Toyokuni wittingly superimposed the ambiguity of sexuality in kabuki performance onto that in *wagōshin* iconography so

4.6 Utagawa Toyokuni III (Kunisada; 1769–1825), *Wagōshin* (*Gods of Harmonious Union*), 1852. Woodblock print, ink and color on paper. (Courtesy of the University of Michigan Museum of Art; gift of Dr. James Hayes 2003/1.483)

as to provoke a perspective that dislocated the normative understanding of the gods as those promising the material and spiritual well-being of heterosexual couples. It was well known that Danjurō and Shuika were close friends in their personal life, and kabuki spectators were drawn to their performance partly because they enjoyed seeing how the actors converted their friendship into heterosexual love in the play. Clearly, what this transmutation conjured up was the prevalent rumor about their "male-male love" relation in their personal life and thus the possibility that their performance of "fictive" love was actually an enactment of that concealed actual relation. The evocation of such a possibility blurred, even disrupted, the diametrical configurations of the private and the public, the everyday and the theatrical, the real and the fictive, and the hetero- and homosexual relations—demarcations that defined the moral economy of everyday life in Edo. The more Danjurō and Shuika's heterosexual love was idealized and idolized in the print (and in the play), the more it deconstructed itself through the ironic reminder that it was their "homosexual" romance that imparted an impeccable impression to their exalted heterosexual relation. The ambiguity of sexuality emanating from kabuki's aesthetic form—female impersonation—was superimposed onto the indeterminate and anomalous quality of *wagōshin*'s sexual identity. Through this form of parody, Toyokuni's print brought to light what the normative reading of *wagōshin* tended to exclude or repress.[20]

As in all the illustrations above, grotesque form made no distinction between high and low; everything exuding from the bodies—the bodies of *wagōshin*—meant at once sacredness and profanity, and transcendence and secularity. All the base elements of their bodies carried sacred meanings in the crudest and most contradictory forms as the figures combined unavaricious appearances with love of treasure and money, and aging and deformed flesh with the fertile energy of the flesh—the energy of abundant life, or heterosexuality with homosexuality. Grotesque form neither sought to reconcile this contradiction nor did it force it into a perfect union. Instead, by contravening the putative correspondence between signifier and signified, it pluralized and multiaccentuated the image and meaning of the subject, dismantled its unity into a heterogeneous and internally contradictory signifier, and ceaselessly transgressed and disrupted representational economies. In other words, grotesque form placed an enormous strain on the fusion of incongruent form and content by foregrounding them both, so that they appeared not as a stable and static unity, but as mobile or shifting parts. Compared with the Kano or Tosa schools' paintings, grotesque form bore no trace of the perfect unity between form and content. *Confucius and His Disciples* (figure 4.7;

4.7 Kano Tanyū (1602–74), *Confucius and His Disciples*, mid-seventeenth century. Three panels, ink and light color on silk. (Photograph © 2013 Museum of Fine Arts, Boston)

mid-seventeenth century) by Kano Tanyū (1602–74),[21] for instance, effects and holds up the idealism of the universal and timeless Truth of Confucius's superlative morality, righteousness, and wisdom. The permeating solemnity realized through the hierarchical configurations of the figures, the stillness and rigidity of expressions and postures, and the harmonizing execution of colors induces the perception of the dominant and unassailable stature of Confucius as the "Enlightened." These representational methods placed an emphasis on thematic coherence and aesthetic integrity—the ideality of the subject matter. The grotesque was the opposite: it was the least ideal form. It was marked by structural confusion, thematic incoherence, or the unspeakable copresence of incongruent images such as that between the normative, fully formed, "high" or ideal, and the abnormal, unformed, degenerated, "low" or material.

Kuniyoshi's *He Looks Scary, But He Is Actually a Nice Guy* (figure 4.8; 1830s), which is another parodic version of the Asahina image discussed in chapter 3, would serve the objective here of further underscoring the particular characteristic of grotesque form. Beholders of this print are aware that the scary-looking yet nice guy is Asahina, a legendary warrior hero, but with his face and body made up by numerous other bodies of commoner laborers (firefighters) and thus with his original identity completely effaced, the new "Asahina" is furnished with images of structural irregularity and thematic confusion. This Asahina constantly defers its unequivocal identification because the various body parts making up his body assert their distinct presence without amounting to the unitary

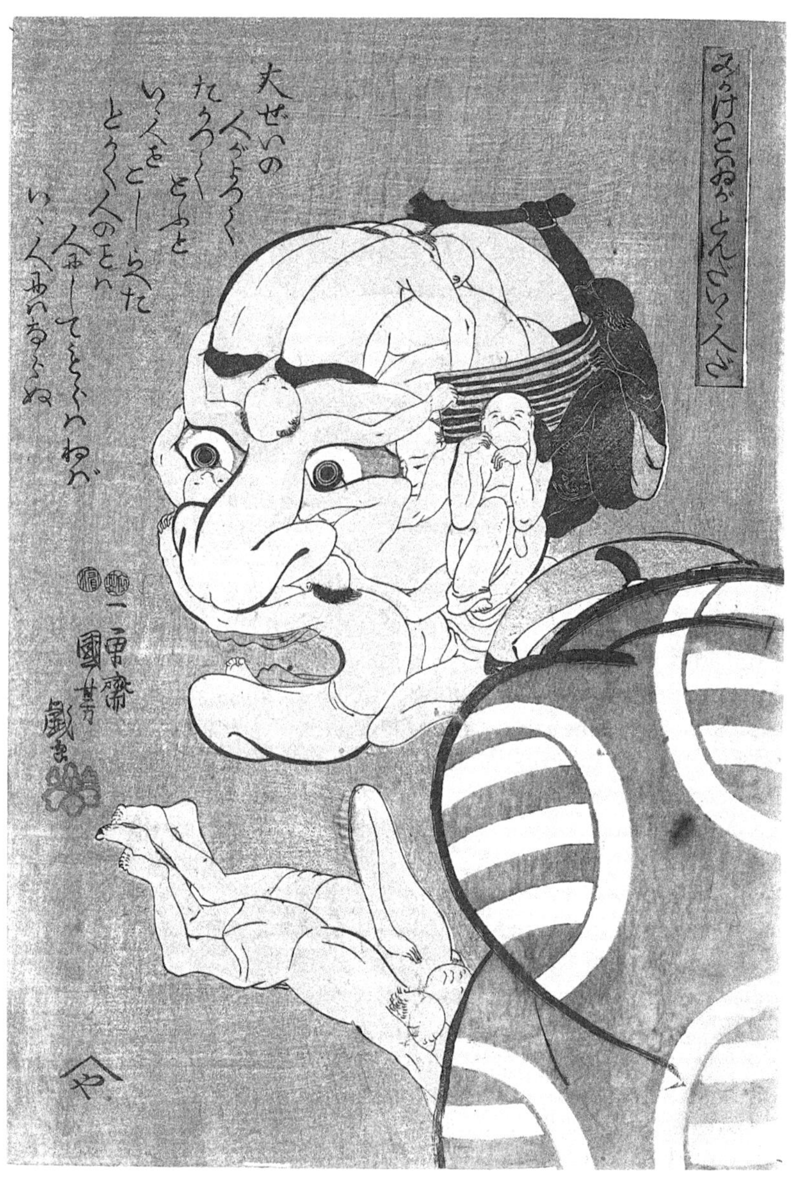

4.8 Utagawa Kuniyoshi (1797–1861), *Tonda, iihitoda* (*He Looks Scary, But He Is Actually a Nice Guy*), 1830s. Woodblock print. (Owned by the author)

image of Asahina (originary or otherwise). Asahina's presence, in turn, appears to depend entirely on the fluid and contingent relationality of the body parts, not vice versa, thus rendering "Asahina" itself part of the relationality. The seemingly random assemblage of body parts makes it difficult for beholders to determine whether the real subject matter is Asahina, bodies, or their relationality, leaving them in the circuit of multiple interpretive possibilities. What can be concluded, then, from Asahina and *wagōshin* iconography is that the grotesque form prevalent in late Edo culture consisted of an indeterminate relationality of parts that induced structural irregularity and thematic confusion as opposed to the aesthetic theory of identity that presupposed the fixed relation of parts making up a unitary whole or a totality.

This particular aesthetic composition of grotesque form was made possible by a literary and artistic method of parody called *naimaze* (ないまぜ)—intermixing incongruities to dismantle the integrity of the original form and to provoke the visual sensation of irregularity or strangeness. Just as Kuniyoshi's "Asahina" was the creation of mixed signifiers of the legendary warrior hero Asahina and Edo's popular firefighters, *wagōshin* iconographies created by Hokusai and others were a parodic appropriation of the images of Daoist sages, Kanzan and Jittoku (Chinese: Hanshan and Shide, respectively), which symbolized the Daoist ideal of unceremonious playfulness representing detachment or transcendence from the world steeped in secular desire for fame, status, and money. As in figure 4.9, the ideal was often transcribed into the similes of Kanzan and Jittoku's jovial mien and the happy grin on their faces. Edo popular culture appropriated this ideal by incorporating symbols of secular desires, such as, for wealth or sexual union. The method of *naimaze* further amplified or underscored the anomalous and incongruent sensations of *wagōshin* images, dislocating the hallowed and spiritual meanings attached to the Daoist sages.

It would be meaningful to point out, for the purpose of comparison, that this characteristic of late Tokugawa grotesque form corresponds to that elaborated by Geoffrey Harpham in his etymological analysis of "grotesque" in the European context. According to Harpham, the original connotations of "grotesque" were related to architectural ornaments in Renaissance Europe. These ornaments combined human figures with parts of animal bodies or natural plants, which came to carry the meanings of the anomalous and the ambivalent.[22] These figures appeared to inhabit the borders between the human world and the world of nature because they bore the physical features of both. Harpham argues that the anomalousness or ambivalence of their images would later become

4.9 Kano Shunsen Akinobu (1800–1816), *Hanshan (Kanzan) and Shide (Jittoku)*, first half of nineteenth century. Hanging scroll, ink and light color on paper. (Photograph © 2013 Museum of Fine Arts, Boston)

the symbol of the liminal world—a sphere that destabilized the clear demarcation between humanity and nature. It was in this effect of dissolving the normative division and order, he continues, that the grotesque revealed its distinct feature: it created aesthetically and perceptually disruptive sensations toward the perceived integrity of normalcy. Thus, the grotesque was (and continues to be) synonymous with the indefinable and the in-between that were not only irreducible but also counter to what was received as ordinary, regular, and natural.

How does an analysis of *kikai, iyō, ikei,* or the grotesque as a signifier of anomaly, multiplicity, or indeterminacy inform the symbolic meaning of grotesque form in Edo popular culture? As seen above, grotesque form bore no idealism of absolute coherence, center, authenticity, and wholeness, and disclosed irreconcilable disjuncture, split, or contradiction in images and meanings that supplied unity and integrity to a subject. The grotesque forms' ability to visualize contrary qualities in one and the same subject or within a single representation brought forth the perspective that human thought, desire, and aspiration consisted of irreconcilably multiple and conflictive elements, thus always remaining split and nonunitary. We clearly see this perspective materialized in *wagōshin*'s accommodation of copresent affluence/raggedness, youth/age, sacredness/vulgarity, and heterosexuality/homosexuality. *Wagōshin* was not the sacred symbol of the ideal of purity and perfection, but a metaphor for the irreconcilable contradiction of humanity.

Effecting a New Vision of Humanity

It is tempting to hypothesize how this view of humanity came to dominate the popular cultural scene in late Tokugawa society. My conjecture here is consistent with the overall argument that I have been presenting throughout this work. The Tokugawa state organized and represented differences—status identities and a division of labor—as unchanging in hope of instituting the stasis of social relations as the essential condition for its long-lasting existence. However, with the proliferation of a money economy and the vibrant confluence and interaction of ideas, commodities, people, and images enabled by the economy, there emerged new articulations of "differences"—conflicting feelings, diversifying lifestyles, tastes, and self-expressions—that were not consonant with institutionally organized differences. These articulations ignored, transgressed, and even violated the privileged logic of social stasis and encouraged new and heterogeneous social formations. The social order predicated on the perpetual reproduction of organized differences and thus on the negation of the transformativity of social relations appeared neither self-evident nor viable because the new articulations of "differences" seemed to speak more to the daily sensibilities of people, especially urbanites. A divergent consciousness of reality thus came into being. The ideologically projected image and rhetoric of eternality came to be contested and nullified by the awakening of a consciousness of social formation and transformation—history—provoked by the production and circulation of "differences."

A consciousness of history was imprinted in many aesthetic expressions that placed an emphasis on the here and now—the valorization of instantaneity (speedy mutation), as I have discussed in chapter 2—as opposed to the official conception of eternality. From the late eighteenth century onward, kabuki, ukiyo-e, *gesaku*, and *misemono* organized representations around this concept of temporality. As Thomas Looser argues in his penetrating reading of the implication of the money economy for new cultural formation in late Tokugawa society, this intense interest in instantaneity in popular culture was inseparably bound up with an increasingly prevalent sense of uncertainty or precariousness about the present, a sense engendered in part by a particular characteristic of the new economy.[23] There was emergent awareness among townspeople at the turn of the eighteenth century that money as a form of wealth operated on a paradoxical logic: money as general expression of wealth might appear to be "a private possession," but it was actually "a social one" because [it could] "not remain stationary in a single place for any length of time" in order for it to exist as a form of wealth.[24] Money in itself, in other words, embodied no value, and it could assume a status of value and thus become wealth only with the assumption that it could be disposed by the possessor for it to be acquired, accumulated, and parted with by others. This recognition of money as incessantly circulating and thus fantastic—possession simultaneously signifying dispossession—was exactly what Marx has also observed about money's distinctive characteristics:

> *As material representative of general wealth,* [money's value] is realized only by being thrown back into circulation, to disappear in exchange for the singular, particular modes of wealth. It remains in circulation, as medium of circulation; but for accumulated individual, it is lost, and this disappearance is the only possible way to secure it as wealth. To dissolve the things accumulated in individual gratifications is to realize them. The money may then be again stored up by other individuals, but then the same process begins anew. I can really posit its being for myself only by giving it up as mere

being for others. If I want to cling to it, it evaporates in my hand to become a mere phantom of real wealth.[25]

As intellectuals and commoners alike began to see money mediating all aspects of social relations by the early eighteenth century, this new perception of reality rendered the sense of the present as constantly in motion, hence dynamic, accidental, and precarious. The fate of the present depended largely on its unpredictable relation to the future as a market-driven economy was sustainable only through an investment in the ultimately unknowable future. If the future could not be foretold with certitude, the present remained uncertain as well. The indeterminacy stemming from this future-oriented sense of the present impelled desire for epistemological certitude in mid-eighteenth-century Tokugawa Japan, yielding deluge in scholarly inquiries into mathematics, astronomy, medicine, geography, ethics, and political economy among intellectuals including some merchants, as the history of the Kaitokudō Academy of Osaka exemplified.[26] But, for ordinary Edoites, the issue was less epistemological than ontological. The incertitude of the present led them to see their conditions of being not as frozen in eternity but as continually shifting in time, which therefore gave rise to the generic vision of human life as being subject to the vicissitudes of history. As people like Nishikawa Joken (1648–1724) came to believe, any person, regardless of a given status, could rise and fall, depending on his/her fortuitous relation with the unpredictable link between the present and the future. Popular literature and art were captivated by the realization of life as being in constant flux—*ukiyo* or the floating world—and took keen interest in capturing the fleeting moment of the here and now through their representations.

What was spurred by the new perception of life was the question of desire. The vision that life was the continual unfolding of fleeting and uncertain moment without a law or a telos generated sharp dissonance with the official theory of the cosmic-human unity that determined life to be the perpetual reproduction of the same or the instantiation of the timeless principle. Life in this regard featured as the process of deferral of a moment of fulfillment in a dual sense: life was an experience of constraint, laid by the formal theory and social structures, on the latitude for fully exploring the newly felt dynamics of social formation; but it also pointed to the impossibility of reaching the state wherein one could feel completely satiable because of its proclivity for constant vacillation. Desire to fulfill or express, not circumvent, the "lack" generated by the deferral took on different forms of fantasy. The tragic trope of double suicide, as discussed in chapter 1, supplied ordinary townspeople a fantasy of transgression of social norms via "illicit" love and its fulfillment by death, the fetishism of money (chapter 2) afforded wealthy merchants a fantasy of attaining everlasting happiness through pure materialism, and the comical satire (chapter 3) provided townspeople, both wealthy and poor, with a way to verbalize heterogeneous and contradictory realities repressed or unacknowledged by the authoritative discourses. In all these fantastic manifestations of desire, humans appeared as creatures driven and possessed by impulse to behave in a way that did not fit with regulatory norms and social structures.

It comes as no surprise that the conception that human life was essentially precarious and humans were intrinsically contradictory supplied a ground for grotesque form to operate as a popular mode of aesthetic negation against the official discourses that authorized people of samurai status as born with infallible moral and intellectual integrity, as well as with an exclusive aptitude for ruling society. In foregrounding the view that human beings were often self-contradictory and finite creatures, as described below, grotesque form proved to be potent in accentuating what the townspeople considered the samurai class's untenable claim: social hierarchies were the direct and truthful reflection of innate differences in people's moral and intellectual competence. Furthermore, from the late eighteenth century onward in particular, as exemplified in both the Kansei and Tenpō reforms, the ruling samurai appeared to the townspeople increasingly hypocritical in not admitting their inability to understand and accommodate the new and massive socioeconomic and cultural changes on the one hand, while on the other almost entirely attributing the causes of society's predicaments to the townspeople's "reprehensible" propensities toward wasteful expenditure and their "abominable" penchant for vulgar and immoral activities. Grotesque form surged forth as an aesthetic mode of visualizing this hypocrisy. Its political potency came precisely from this contestatory ability to perform the scandalous disclosure of realities that were vexing to the ruling elites.

But the grotesque form's performative potency was not limited to the disclosure of the samurai world's hypocrisies and contradictions. Through the disclosure of the reality unacknowledged or masked in the official discourse, the form went a step further to make a resolute statement that the principal moral virtues defining and legitimating the samurai's inviolable stature were literally bankrupt. From around the 1810s on to the end of the Tokugawa period, grotesque representations brought to the fore images of gruesome, horrible, and extreme sensory-graphic violence, which became more prominent than humorous ones like Ikku's, as a way to render the degeneration of samurai morality.[27] Betrayal, malice, grudges, and bloody frenzy—the deleterious refractions of avarice and self-delusion haunting degenerate samurai—became the principal motifs of aesthetic expression and ran rampant through an entire range of grotesque imagery in kabuki plays and ukiyo-e prints. This particular representational mode played a decisive role in evoking the most inconceivable trait of samurai, which was selfishness or egoism (as samurai identity was defined by the negation of it), especially in its vivid depictions of impoverished samurai desperately seeking to regain through criminal acts their long lost prestige and respectability. Self-delusional or delirious as they seemed, samurai failed to recognize and accept the reality that their status bore no more than a nominal value and tried to force the world of fantasy or mirage onto that of reality, even at the risk of violating the most fundamental moral codes that gave them a sense of distinctive identity. Overtly violent images that permeated late Tokugawa kabuki and ukiyo-e prints symbolized the deep irony of the self-destruction—degenerate samurai trying to reclaim bygone respectability by becoming even more degenerate—of the ruling class.

The ironic portrayal of the elites as having no choice but to commit the act of self-destruction as a result of the mirage in which they had trapped themselves seemed to echo the popular culture's assessment of the deteriorating economic conditions of the ruling elites. Samurai's insistent refusal to acknowledge irreparable cleavage between perception (their self-image) and reality (actual living conditions) resonated with their obstinate defense of the premise that rice and the social values—that is, eternity, harmony, propriety, and frugality—attached to it had guided and would continue to guide economic life in Tokugawa society. If the irony targeted the samurai's mirage about the possibility of redeeming their power and of resuscitating the viability of the status structure, it also implied criticism of another related mirage or misplaced confidence that the perpetual reproduction of the social relations of production still dominated the first order reality of Tokugawa Japan. Samurai's horror of and thus persistent attack on the scandalous ascension of money as the first-order reality corresponded to their extreme paranoia about the overwhelming stature of townspeople in social, economic, and cultural life in Edo, in comparison with their own fall. Just like the symbolic value of status as the key determinant in structuring social hierarchies was on the wane, the socioeconomic value of rice as the material representation of general wealth also weakened. The ironic representation of samurai in popular culture as those who were perpetually trapped in self-delusion was of great significance in that it called attention to the fundamental cleavage that existed between objective (structural) and subjective (perceptual) realities surrounding the samurai class.

The sense of irony central to the late Tokugawa grotesque form elicited dark and chilling laughter among kabuki audiences and ukiyo-e lovers. A literary critic, Hirosue Tamotsu, for example, once rendered such laughter as "black humor" in his discussion of the predisposition of late Tokugawa cultural texts.[28] Although the humorous and satiric laughter engendered by *comic realism* overlapped significantly with the dark laughter elicited by *grotesque realism*, their differences should be clarified here for the sake of understanding the latter's distinct potency as a form of aesthetic negation. As discussed in the previous chapter, the defining feature of laughter elicited by comic realism was its ability to acknowledge and unveil contradictions, limitations, and imperfections in all human beings regardless of their social status and background. Laughter transgressed and dissolved all limits, boundaries, and inhibitions—whether moral, political, or social—which the Tokugawa shogunate designed in order to sustain the system of samurai rule. In doing so, laughter relativized, even trivialized any truth claims made to impart legitimacy to the given order of things. Grotesque form was also capable of dissolving the normative division and hierarchical order through the overt revelation of self-contradiction and incompleteness.

But what separated grotesque realism from comic realism in terms of their manners of negation was the former's capacity to *deconstruct all principal values that supported binary forms* through the exposure of contradiction that appeared to bespeak the self-destruction of the subject it addressed. In chapter 3, I described comic realism as a mode that contested the official doctrine that organized and represented different types of subjects according to the hierarchical ordering of the status system. All those of samurai status were portrayed as noble, moral, and righteous, while subordinate social groups were described and sometimes decried as base, immoral, and devious. This classificatory schema was contrived to lend legitimacy and stability to the Tokugawa regime, allowing the ruling elites to retain both an aristocratic disdain toward, and political and social domination of, the nonsamurai population. The official representation of "reality" was predicated on the conception that beneath the official decorum of moral significance and nobility, there existed another "reality": earthy and potentially unruly, it consisted of the unfiltered sensory life of the everyday and was inhabited by a morally and intellectually inferior populace. Accordingly, the regime argued that this "vulgar" reality ought to be subjected to strict regulation and surveillance by the high moral order.

Although grotesque realism shared the same mode of semiotic operation as comic realism in calling into question what the authorities promoted as "real," it posed a different possibility of contestation. It went a step further to demonstrate the figurative denial of the regime's conception of reality by adamantly deconstructing the core moral values that sustained the given structures of binary classification. Comic realism tended to rely on the logic of inversion—turning the world upside down, that is, turning the terms of binary opposition against themselves by celebrating the lower terms of a diacritical pairing vis-à-vis the higher. For all its political potential, comic realism retained the existing binary categories of high and low in its attempt to suggest and underscore a point of view from a perspective counter or contradictory to a dominant one.[29]

Grotesque realism, on the other hand, negated the very terms of the binary system itself—for example, good and evil, high and low, and beauty and ugliness—in interrogating and nullifying the categories of fundamental moral values—that is, righteousness, loyalty, compassion, wisdom, and propriety—which constituted the terms. It not only made visible anomalous and contradictory reality repressed or unacknowledged under the binary terms of reality, therefore, but also symbolically foregrounded the untenability of the terms on which the hierarchical order of society was configured. The systematic negation of the categories of fundamental moral values was then crucial for this semiotic operation, since this negation was not simply meant to point out the increasingly untenable position of status hierarchies (comic realism also achieved this to a certain extent through its tactics of playful inversion). Its distinct effect, whether intended or unintended, was to bring to consciousness the decay or disintegration of the ruling class by underlying the total bankruptcy of the categories of moral values that had supported that class's dominant stature. Grotesque realism, then, contained the elements of genuine break or ruptures with the formal reality and could be considered to be constituting a legitimate occasion for social conflict.

Central to the operation of grotesque realism was the tactic of hybridizing or intermixing binary pairs such as good and evil that served as a normative basis for moral and aesthetic judgment. Hybridization displaced the purportedly inviolable demarcation between the two in such a way that it dissolved them into an unthinkable and unrecognizable form. By unsettling the most commonly used dictum "Promoting Good, Chastising Evil" in Tokugawa literary and artistic discourse, the form re-presented the reality hidden, repressed, and spurned under the official discourse of societal normalcy and harmony in aberrant, even loathsome images. For example, late Tokugawa kabuki placed a heavy weight on plotlines and techniques that engendered the disquieting sensation of cognitive and perceptual chaos by way of demonstrating the instantaneous mutation of beauty into hideousness, kindness into brutality, righteousness into wickedness, and loyalty into duplicity. This unsettling disarray of moral and aesthetic distinction became most manifest through the dramatic impressions of abysmal shock and horror. We will examine this in detail below.

It is important to clarify here that we have been discussing thus far two interrelated, yet often quite distinct kinds of grotesque form in the context of late Tokugawa Japan. The first is a humorous variety, evident in Ikku and the others' satirical prints, and in the various images of *wagōshin*; the second is a gruesome variety, which is best discussed via the cases of late Tokugawa kabuki and ukiyo-e. If both represented a boundary phenomenon of hybridization in which incongruities become enmeshed in an inclusive, heterogeneous, and dangerously unstable zone and produced the effects of what might be called "dis-identification"—a semiotic operation counter to that of identity or identification on which Tokugawa social order was built and maintained—their differences demonstrated the varying degrees to which the deranged reality of the ruling status groups in the late Tokugawa world were accentuated. The humorous grotesque carried in it a critical, yet nonvenomous, assessment of humanity's contradiction, whereas the gruesome kind performed an aggressive and affirmative negation of the contradiction through the inexorable exposure of the dreadfulness of wicked realities. Both modes drew most frequently on the depiction of excesses of inconsistency or irregularity; in particular, the form of monstrous and hideous bodies without definite shapes, order, sequence, or recognizable proportions. But they differed in the degree of intensity with which they created the sensory and perceptual effect of deformity.

Representations of deformity were dominated by the problematics of the degeneration of the ruling class's moral integrity. From the 1820s on, the problematics were anchored to narratives and images of abominable crimes committed by samurai villains and of gruesome vengeance by ghostly incarnations of women victimized by the villains (the implications of vengeful spirits being always women are discussed at some length below).[30] Whether figured as a humorous monster or as a horrific ghost, popular representations of the deformity pointed to the world deranged by the moral degeneration and bankruptcy of elites. It is important to stress here that these representations were grotesque not because they used hideous figures—demons, ghosts, and monsters were not necessarily grotesque—but because, in the midst of an overwhelming impression of monstrousness, people were able to recognize the common existence of man's speciousness and disingenuousness or, more specifically, those of the ruling class.

Sites of the Grotesque

Because the grotesque most commonly appeared in kabuki plays, ukiyo-e prints, and *misemono* shows, it is important to probe here the ways in which the special characteristics of these popular cultural media helped to engender perspectives and sensations of disorder. We have seen earlier in this book that these entertainments, and those who indulged in them, received the Tokugawa shogunate's accusations of being idle and immoral. Entertainers such as acrobats, ballad singers, storytellers, magicians, *shamisen* players, dancers, and kabuki actors were all integrated into the status of "nonhuman," the bottom rung on the hierarchical ladder. In particular, negative designations were ascribed to kabuki theaters, as manifested in their best-known official epithet, "evil places." Viewed from this perspective, it comes as no surprise that the regime regarded cultural practices such as kabuki that channeled life energies (*ki* 気) into something other than the requirement of material productivity as a dangerous excess. The regime made continuous attempts to preclude the potentially unruly energies of cultural practices from disrupting the established order of things by classifying them as base and by confining them to the peripheries of the urban space.

We have also seen, however, that despite the Tokugawa shogunate's reproving rhetoric and interventionist policies toward kabuki plays and other forms of popular entertainments, it never went as far as to totally proscribe them. In fact, the shogunate countenanced the kabuki theaters (and *misemono* show) by granting them a license to thrive, for example, even though it interdicted the use of the term "kabuki" as an official designation for the popular theaters and forced the theaters to relocate three times during the Tokugawa period—each time to the margins of the city proper.[31] Kabuki theaters, as in the case of the Yoshiwara "pleasure" quarter, were authorized to exist as licensed enclaves called the district of theater (*shibaimachi* 芝居町) within the spatial structure of Edo. This was largely due to the shogunal power's interest not only in keeping a vital component of Edo commercial economy alive but also in having ordinary townspeople comply with required duties in their everyday routine by permitting them spaces to relish the momentary pleasures of release, flight, or diversion. Indeed, for townspeople, "evil" places were places of play (*asobiba* 戯場), which offered an experience of temporary transposition or metamorphosis.[32] An anonymous commoner, expressing his or her ecstatic experience of difference as a kabuki spectator, wrote a verse, "Our hearts beat, So much so that we forget, Affairs of our everyday world."[33] Insofar as the popular entertainments observed the expected role of supplying a momentary means of escapist pleasure and did not diverge from it, the shogunal power judged their presence to be "useful" for the regulatory operation of the everyday. The authorities' derogatory discourse on and discriminatory policies toward these entertainments should then be understood as an attempt to demarcate the value of their existence only in terms of a "licensed transgression" or a safety valve. The "otherness" ascribed to these entertainments was never a neutral conception that automatically guaranteed the possibility of resistance or subversive potential. Rather it was an ideological expression deployed to support the regime's strategy of folding difference into the mechanisms of rule for the continuance of the social order.

Then, exactly what aspects of these popular cultural entertainments were deemed by the authorities as "perilous influence"? This inquiry brings us back to the genealogy of kabuki and the trajectory of its self-transformation in response to the shogunate's aggressive efforts to delineate the conception of the normative body. It is well known that from its early years, kabuki dramaturgy employed aesthetics that tended to defy and "pervert" social norms of etiquette, propriety, and morality. This nonnormative and transgressive disposition of kabuki aesthetics was evident, as briefly mentioned above, in the word "kabuki" itself. As the noun of the verb "*kabuku*" (傾く), it denoted "deviation from normalcy," "outlandish style," or "idiosyncratic behavior."[34] This term originally referred to townspeople who led their lives as drifters, exhibiting eccentric mien and audacious behavior. During the first half of the seventeenth century, the Tokugawa authorities repeatedly enforced a policy of expulsion from Edo for those called "*kabukimono*"—people with kabuki disposition—with the consequences of arrest and severe punishment if they disobeyed. An official document of 1652 described *kabukimono* as "those who belong to the lower stratum of society and are fond of outlandish clothing and hairstyles. They loiter everywhere bearing large and small swords at their waists."[35] Another official document of 1659 defined them as "idlers and villains."[36]

Kabuki performance modeled its dramaturgical and choreographic motifs after this particular group of townspeople. When it first appeared at the end of the sixteenth and seventeenth centuries, it involved a form of female dance consisting of erotic, exaggerated, and extraordinary styles of music, speech, gestures, and appearance. As these early kabuki performers enjoyed their transient way of life, traveling freely to major cities and performing makeshift shows, its popularity grew quickly in towns and nearby villages. Their mobility—indeed, their rejection of attachment to stable domiciles, quarters, or shelters—was possible largely because the Tokugawa power was still in its early formative years. But around the 1620s when the shogunate began to make concerted efforts to mold the mobile into the immobile, the licentious into the licensed, it sought to integrate kabuki into its institutional structures, first in Kyoto and in Osaka between 1615 and 1624 and then in Edo between 1624 and 1660. Under the new law, only those who domiciled and operated as permanent theaters were licensed to run businesses. In Edo, this new development in cultural politics resulted in the authorization of three major kabuki theaters, called *Nakamura-za* (中村座; 1624–1893), *Ichimura-za* (市村座; 1634–1932), and *Morita-za* (森田座; 1660–1875). Given that the shogunate's regulation of *kabukimono* and kabuki occurred simultaneously to the larger process of state-building, it was clear that the shogunate held any activities associated with *kabuku* to be the disruptive and pernicious Other of the public order.

Kabuki's assimilation of *kabuku* or *kabukimono* characteristics—nonconformist, outrageous, and licentious dispositions—became more overtly pronounced during the late Tokugawa period. First, the exhibition of extravagance or profligacy in costumes and settings, which was otherwise prohibited in public life by sumptuary laws, formed an essential feature of kabuki performance. In Buyō Inshi's words, "The extravagant beauty of their costumes is beyond words. In playing the roles of aristocrats, shoguns, and their wives, actors' clothing is made of multi-colored silk textiles embellished with real gold and silver. The attire of female impersonators is said to be worth one hundred *ryō*. Such luxury is beyond the reach even of the shoguns' real wives."[37] The authorities banned the conspicuous display of such profligacy during the Kansei Reform of the 1790s and the Tenpō Reform of the 1840s by sending officials to inspect the theaters on a regular basis. Nonetheless, whenever they were subject to official surveillance, actors escaped the authorities' watchful eyes by putting on much less elaborate costumes.[38] Furthermore, kabuki's role in shaping popular fashion was decisive. The Edo magistrate tried to curtail its influence by issuing a number of decrees warning the townspeople against imitating the appearance of the "inferior outcasts." For instance, an official edict of 1795 forbade women and girls from imitating the hairstyles and garment designs of kabuki female impersonators on the account that such practices vulgarized the social atmosphere by violating the moralities of simplicity and frugality and transgressed the status distinction between townspeople and kabuki actors.[39] The decrees, however, were never effective.

Secondly, kabuki's sensuality took on a new disposition in the late Tokugawa period. In addition to erotic choreographs, outlandish attires, and fervid music, kabuki in its early form (*onna kabuki*) offered various types of sexual "services" after the performance. Despite the Tokugawa authorities' decisions to outlaw *onna kabuki* and to license male-only performances in 1629 to uproot the "corrupt culture spreading among men of high and low," kabuki's sensual dimension did not fade away.[40] The licensed male-only kabuki used preadolescent youths as female impersonators (*onna gata* 女形), which presented a different form of libidinous allure. The shift did not mean, however, that the youth's impersonation signified a complete remapping of the body's erotic sites, redistributing the erogenous zones, and breaking of the monopoly of heterosexual pleasure. In fact, the practice of female impersonation by young male actors had existed well before the banning of *onna kabuki* as part of the well-established samurai (and Buddhist) practice of "male-male love" (*nanshoku* 男色). The wholesale shift in early Tokugawa kabuki to the male-only style meant that kabuki formed the new basis for its popularity by drawing from this tradition and that young female impersonators became objects of passion among the samurai. As a shogunate official noted in 1649, "Regional lords and their retainers are consumed by the pleasure of male-male love to an excessive degree. They invite young kabuki actors to their parties and make them provide services for their sexual pleasure."[41] The Tokugawa authorities did not wait long to make another intervention to outlaw young male female impersonators in kabuki in 1652. Kabuki quickly responded to the new regulation by substituting adults for youths and continued to build its popularity on the transgressive power of erotic performance.

The adult female impersonators' mimicry of feminine beauty and sensuality unsettled the normative conception of sexuality itself.[42] For example, two male actors' enactment of erotic scenes called *nureba* (濡場) or *irogoto* (色事) was so compellingly executed that the spectators found it "rivetingly alluring."[43] Because the "fictitious" sexuality acted out in the female impersonators' mimicry of femininity appeared as "authentic" as "real" sexuality, thus destabilizing the conception of authenticity itself, it subverted the foundational conceptions of gender categories such as masculinity and femininity. The kabuki theaters were spaces that exploded the official moral doctrine and a clear demarcation between male/female and homosexuality/heterosexuality, hence unleashing "anomalous" erotic desire and energy. Late Tokugawa kabuki added a new twist to this non- or antinormative disposition by focusing on the themes of immorality, that is, reprobate, tabooed conducts—adultery and incest—as motifs central to the representation of sensuality.[44]

The last feature constituting the late Tokugawa kabuki's nonconformist and licentious disposition was closely intertwined with the two features discussed above, especially the second. Kabuki purposefully challenged the official distinction between normal and abnormal, or good and evil, by constructing what might be called the "aesthetic of deformity," wherein deranged social relations were overtly experimented with. Impoverished samurai, villains, prostitutes, beggars, and vagrants were all brought together in this imaginary world of selfish motives and heartless calculations. Terrorizing scenes of violent action and of utter cruelty were frequently used, even valorized as the legitimate mode of dramatization.[45] What needs to be stressed here is that such representations of the debauched tended to focus on the world of déclassé samurai, a world in which impoverished and depraved samurai used and abused their foundational moral virtues of loyalty, benevolence, wisdom, trust, and righteousness—virtues that legitimated their status as the ruling class of Tokugawa society—in order to carry out their egotistic pursuit of desire.

These features of kabuki all hinged on a certain aesthetic disposition: the dramatic accentuation of the body and its senses. In kabuki, the representation of reality was not only bound firmly to physical properties, be they costume or choreography, but also made a riveting appeal, via these properties, to spectators' sensuousness and sensuality. Devices for performing corporeal pleasure and pain in a most sensational way became the preoccupation of late Tokugawa kabuki's dramaturgy. This new orientation was accelerated especially from the 1810s on in popular cultural scenes. One of the plausible explanations as to how and why such forms of representation gained prominence in late Tokugawa popular culture relates to that which I have suggested with regard to the discussions of double suicide in chapter 1 and comic realism in the previous chapter—that is, the official system of binary classifications and the social thought legitimating the system lost their credibility as they appeared to suffer growing disjuncture from the reality of the everyday. This perceived chasm between the normative and the everyday opened a space for the new cultural articulation of the real—reality as inarticulate within the institutionalized discourse of reality (the first- and the second-order reality)—that privileged corporeality as a ground for understanding and relating to the rapidly changing world. Early nineteenth-century kabuki's privileging of extreme corporeal sensations as the site where realities could be acutely perceived rendered the conception of the "real" articulated through the ideological discourse of status hierarchy, moral order, and division of labor as abstract and hollow.

Late Tokugawa kabuki's "profligate" display and its dramatic evocation of sensual and horrible sensations certainly inspired grotesque images and violated the official virtues of frugality and propriety, but the ways in which kabuki's provocative renditions of the body affected people's daily life ultimately constituted the major source of the shogunate's concerns. Late Tokugawa kabuki's role in shaping new fashions and practices greatly disturbed the authorities. The edict issued by the city magistrate during the 1810s exemplified such a concern: "In recent years, many townspeople encourage their daughters to imitate and perform kabuki, or the *jōruri* (ballads) closely associated with it, to make some money. This behavior is unspeakably shameless because kabuki and *jōruri* are the business of outcasts."[46] Another edict issued in the 1830s further attests to the way the authorities saw the popular entertainments' overwhelming influence among ordinary townspeople, especially women: "Those [townspeople] who make their daughters learn the skills of vulgar entertainments and dancing spend a large amount of money on useless costumes and tools. Instead of learning the daily tasks required of proper girls, their daughters find delight in mimicking kabuki actors and lowly [street] entertainers and will soon learn the ways of desire, passion, and lascivious pleasure. This should never be allowed."[47] Buyō Inshi echoed the city authorities' accusations of the entertainments' "venomous" influence on public mores as follows:

> (T)ownspeople and idlers all adore kabuki, and ladies and girls in particular are very passionate about it. . . . Their pleasure starts and ends with kabuki, as do their admirations. For them, a day hardly passes without thinking about it. . . . As the popular saying goes, 'there are no girls who dislike men and kabuki,' and they are happy to skip three meals to save money for a kabuki performance. Young ladies are in particular so exhilarated by the performance that they forget about [their duties] to their parents and husbands.[48]

Buyō goes on to describe how the popularity of kabuki also galvanized other forms of street entertainments and how this trend drew more people to the entertainment businesses:

> The popularity of theater is so great that there are numerous [street] performances that mimic choreography and voices of actors. They too enjoy enormous popularity among

idlers. There are also makeshift theaters [*yoseba* 寄場] all over the [low] city where people entertain crowds with storytelling, the impersonation of actors, magic, female dancing, and ballads. If poor commoners dwelling in backstreets [*uradana* 裏だな] happen to have girls, they encourage them to become someone's mistress, [street] performers or dancers, following the popularity of the lowly culture of play . . . Even some people of venerable samurai status have begun to follow such a worldly trend. They have their daughters learn this vulgar art, and their wife and mistresses take delight in singing with the *shamisen* [a string instrument made popular among commoners around the beginnings of the eighteenth century] and drums by intermingling with the outcast performers.[49]

In *A Report on the Prosperity of Edo* (*Edo hanjōki* 江戸繁昌記), Terakado Seiken (1796–1868) observed how *yoseba* (sometimes called *yoseseki*) became a new cultural phenomenon promoting the commingling of people of all sorts of status:

In recent years, it's become a vogue that amateur entertainers gather in ordinary people's houses, calling their meeting places *yoseba*, and collect some fees from spectators. *Yoseba* repertoires include magic shows, ballads, comic storytelling, impressions of kabuki actors, and shadow play [*kageshi* 影紙]. The shows normally run seven days a week with actors appearing alternately for day time or night time performances. . . . Audiences are newcomers from the countryside such as ordinary folks and [low-ranking] samurai retainers, as well as young courtesans, retirees, clerks, and shopkeepers. . . . Women are particularly sold at *yoseba* shows.[50]

What is clear from the above statements is that a number of informal, new spaces of entertainment called *yoseba* emerged in the low city of Edo, a space where outcast performers were invited to show off their skills of mimicking kabuki actors and playing or singing its music through *jōruri*, impressions, and storytelling.[51] Furthermore, *jōruri* performed by young girls won enormous popularity beyond status boundaries, as briefly mentioned in chapter 1, and they began to exert notable influence over the daily practices of samurai, as well as ordinary people. Clearly, Edo authorities apprehended that the popularity of this new genre endangered society's moral values and habits, in particular those of women. Following the 1798 regulation of the female *jōruri* performance, the Edo authorities outlawed in 1805 the performance:

In recently years, female *jōruri* has enthralled people's mind to such an extent that that girls in the town joined the people of outcast status in learning the skills and performing at *yoseba* in a group of five to seven. After being reproached by the authorities for the inappropriateness of the gathering, the performance temporarily disappeared. But not long after that, it returned as a response to the townspeople's frequent request. It is said that among them there are several lecherous and immoral women who act like prostitutes. Their parents should be ashamed of allowing their daughters to comingle with the outcasts. Such an intermingling of different statuses is indeed an unabashed conduct. The girls must stop acting like outcasts and beggars. If this continues to occur, city officials must immediately report it to the magistrate."[52]

The fact that the authorities' concerns about moral degeneration often focused on women is of central importance for an understanding of what I have called "the economy of culture" in chapter 1—the logic that accommodated the presence of the culture of play and pleasure as a mechanism for sustaining social order. Why was it that the shogunate and intellectuals saw women being drawn to places of entertainment such as *yoseba*, or women performing in those places, as having perilous consequences for the moral integrity of society? Let us return to Buyō Inshi's words to probe this question:

Songs, musical instruments, choreography, and plotline are combined to engender the pleasure of lewd sensation. They exhilarate female passions by encouraging lecherous affairs of men and women in which the age-old virtues of faithfulness and righteousness are blatantly violated, filial piety is discarded, and the crimes of passion [double suicide] are enacted.[53]

The statement posits that each and every component of popular entertainment is dangerous precisely because it imbues women with "lewd" emotions and desires. The confusion of their "age-old" virtues is then seen as the cause of degeneration of public mores, in particular, that of marital and familial relations. Buyō goes on to say that this has negative consequences even for the polity:

The Way of man and woman constitutes the basis for ethics. It is the pivotal ethic for governing oneself, family, and the polity. When the Way is not in order, the Way of the polity is confused. The vogue for theaters and [street] entertainments is responsible for the current confusions. Townspeople, idlers, and peasants are all lured into a penchant for luxury and immorality whereby they disturb the Way of the Polity.[54]

The idea that ethics of man and woman were the foundation for societal peace and order was predicated on the premise that the kernel of this ethics resided ultimately in women's abilities to remain loyal to their marriages and families, as well as to follow the virtues of simplicity and frugality. Townswomen's contact with the culture of play and pleasure that exposed them to "lewd" sensations and desires was hence judged to be detrimental to social order.

That premise reflected the Tokugawa shogunate's body politics as a whole: the strategies of containing female desire and sexuality played a crucial role in constructing and maintaining the order of Tokugawa society, as exemplified by the history of kabuki. Prevalent moral discourse among such intellectuals as Kaibara Ekken (1630–1714), who articulated the need to understand the female body and sexual intercourse exclusively in terms of the function of biological reproduction, was intrinsically correlated to the state's policies to impose bans on *onna kabuki* as a dangerous sexual excess and deviation.[55] Observing extraordinary erotic aura and power of captivation in *onna kabuki*'s music and choreography, Miura Jōshin (1577–1644), an ex-samurai literati who lived in Edo during the early decades of the Tokugawa period, described women as devils who artfully beguiled men into self-destruction and praised the shogunate's decisions to outlaw it.[56] This compulsion to extirpate female sexuality pointed to the official fear that the self-expression of female sensuality would invoke the reality that must be kept inarticulate—a reality that women's sexuality was irreducible to the reproductive function. Once unleashed, female erotic energies would enthrall and corrupt all men, regardless of high and low, disrupt the unity of family, and disturb the peace of the polity; they would throw moral codes that specified the matrices of distinction—status, gender, and occupation—into disarray. It was not a coincidence then that Edo popular fiction often fantasized the Yoshiwara pleasure quarter as the space where status and gender hierarchies were suspended or dissolved, even though the female "sexuality" licensed by the authorities was in reality highly commodified and patriarchic.

The birth of an "inverted" culture in which man or the male body alone represented femininity was largely attributable to the shogunate's containment of female sexuality. Male writers such as Ihara Saikaku assumed the privilege of impersonating female voices and thus depicting women's romance in *Five Women Who Loved Love*, whereas female impersonators of kabuki performed feminine beauty and passion by transmuting their bodies into an impeccably feminine physique. Depicting the feelings of women who were driven desperately to double suicide demanded, for instance, the consummate mastery of femininity through the effacement of masculine traits. Yoshizawa Ayame (1673–1729), a popular impersonator of the Genroku period (1688–1704), articulated most vividly the culture of female impersonation by asserting that the female body, in particular, the sexually attractive aura (*iroke* 色気) exuding from the body, could be replicated only if he lived his daily life as a woman.

> Sexual attractiveness is fundamental to the female impersonator. Even though you are born to be a beautiful impersonator, if you reveal any traces of masculinity in scenes, such as when you confront the enemies [of your samurai husband], this will ruin feminine attractiveness. Or if you consciously try to show off feminine grace, it ends up being pretentious. That is why you must live as a woman in every moment of your daily life. Otherwise, you cannot become [a proper] impersonator. If you try hard to be a woman only on the stage, your masculinity will become even more pronounced.[57]

To live a quotidian existence as a woman meant inscribing femininity on his body in a manner that naturalized female identity as his authentic self. By completely effacing all traces of fictitiousness in feminine beauty, the female impersonator was to attain the ultimate ideal, that is, to cease to be an impersonator and to attain womanhood itself. Ayame's vision of the female impersonator as embodying the beauty of the feminine body and mind without any masculine trace can be said to have represented a classic prototype of kabuki aesthetics. "The art of kabuki's female impersonator was to demonstrate the beauty of ideal femininity in both body and mind," as Yokoi Yasuko puts it.[58] Moreover, it accepted the premise of a moral dualism that corporeal beauty (physical attractiveness) came necessarily with goodness of heart (unconditional loyalty and affection toward her lover/husband), and physical deformity or ugliness reflected wickedness (a short-tempered, jealous, and incredulous character). These assumptions regarding ideal femininity supplied the tragic aura surrounding female protagonists of double suicide—beautiful courtesans who, despite their profession of selling the fantasy of "love," remained absolutely loyal to their lovers by choosing death.

Female impersonators began to play the role of "ugly ladies" (*shūjo* 醜女) for the first time in the 1730s, according to Yokoi, and audience's response was not at all enthusiastic. [59] It took half a century for the Edo spectators to fully embrace the new type of impersonator, and by the early nineteenth century, the aesthetics of deformity completely superseded the classic prototype of female impersonator. The spectators were less captivated by the beauty of the impersonator than by the scenes in which the ugliness intensified or the beauty transfigured into a hideous form as a result of accumulated grudges and rage against injustices and treacheries inflicted on her. Her ghostly incarnation—a vengeful spirit or *kasane* (累)—flashing horrifying looks became one of the staples of popular kabuki productions. From the early nineteenth century on, the crisscrossing of beauty and hideousness that brought about the aesthetics of perceptual confusion and chaos characterized the distinct feature of the grotesque form of late Tokugawa kabuki.

The new aesthetics signaled the emergence of a new kind of female subjectivity available to both female impersonators and women themselves in artistic and literary imaginations. The female protagonist no longer possessed a persona that could be easily classified according to the binary typologies of beauty and ugliness or goodness and wickedness. She exhibited the subjective will to vengeance and exercised the other-worldly power of "affliction" (*tatari* 祟り) or "curse" (*noroi* 呪い) against the Tokugawa patriarchal system that brought her tribulations. In medieval literature, this supernatural power was typically an exclusive attribute of heroes, high-ranking samurai, or the nobility, such as Sugawarano Michizane (845–903), Tairano Masakado (?–940), and Kusunoki Masashige (1294–1336), but in late Tokugawa kabuki, women became the bearers of such power.[60] "Hair-raising," "lurid," or "scary" were the words often used to refer to the early-nineteenth-century kabuki performance, in particular, that of enraged female spirits, due largely to the novel articulation of female agency represented by their horribly destructive power.[61] (It goes without saying that the magnitude of the spirits' rage and grudge visualized in the images of brutal death, bloodshed, and extreme physical deformity contributed further to the effect of horror.)

Illustrations of the wretched realities underlying the seemingly well-ordered Tokugawa society carried a "realistic" quality because nineteenth-century kabuki scripts married popular stories of a historical kind with actual crimes and incidents that terrorized the Edo populace. This method of parody, called *Stories of the Contemporary World* (*tōseimono* 当世物 or *imayō* 今様), in which contemporaneous events were injected into the narratives of familiar historic tales, supplied the possibility for spectators to take a critical distance from the present as well as the past. Even though the plot was set in the distant past, spectators might find it directly relevant to the conditions of their own times. Likewise, even if its contemporaneous quality seemed to be unrelated to the past, it offered a fresh perspective on received knowledge. Parody, as argued in chapter 2, created the dynamic of dialogic contestation between the past and the present, the familiar and the unfamiliar, thus radically relativizing the established conceptions of "reality" by offering alternative perspectives.

The fact that female ballad singers of the *yoseba* adopted the same method of parody and articulated the reality in the image of a degenerate world—the image that revealed a repressed, yet clearly extant reality—made the authorities anxious about the entertainment.[62] For the first time since the banning of female kabuki actors in the early seventeenth century, female entertainers—arguably the ultimate figure of "extraneous" existence called nonhuman within the structure of the Tokugawa status hierarchies—took the lead in expressing subjective feelings, such as "passion," "grudge," "sorrow," and "indignation," through their own voices (it should be noted that many of them chose to use pseudonyms to disguise themselves as male performers).[63] This meant not only that the new female subjectivity found effective expression independent of male performers and patriarchal structures but also that the articulation of repressed degenerate realities went beyond the spatial confines of kabuki theaters and spilt over into the streets, the spaces of the everyday. The popularity of female ballad singers signified one of the striking symptoms of the early nineteenth century—the collapse of the regulatory boundaries delineating the everyday from the extraordinary.

The shogunate's aggressive measures against ballad singers during the Tenpō Reform of 1841–43 were hardly accidental.[64] Despite the earlier regulations and bans against the singers, in 1815 there were seventy-five *yoseba* in Edo alone where female *jōruri* was performed regularly, and in 1825 the number grew to one hundred twenty-five.[65] By 1841, two hundred thirty-eight *yoseba* were in business, but after the city magistrate arrested sixty people, the majority of whom were female ballad singers and their hosts, only thirty *yoseba* were permitted to continue in business on the condition that their repertoires were to be limited to ideologically unproblematic genres, such as didactic Shinto sermons, the teachings of the Mind Study School (*Shingaku* 心学), war tales, and folk stories. It is telling that of thirty *yoseba*, only seven were allowed to operate in popular entertainment places such as Ryōgoku and none were in townspeople's residential quarters.[66] However, even these draconian policies of redemarcating the borders of male and female, as well as everyday and noneveryday, spheres did not last for a long time. Within two years after the setback of the Tenpō Reform in 1843, seven hundred *yoseba* flourished, and female *jōruri* and kabuki impressions returned as their popular fixture.[67]

Representations of the World of Chaos

A determination of how grotesque form produced the perspective and sensation of chaos—especially in relation to the samurai's moral degeneration—and what such a representation meant requires a brief genealogical reflection on the particular literary and artistic genre of ghost tale known as *Kasane-mono* (累物). The narrative structure of this genre—a vengeful spirit returning repeatedly to afflict the living—had existed long before the Tokugawa period, yet informed the form and contents of other ghost stories until the middle of the Tokugawa period.

Kasane was born from a medieval Buddhist theology that aimed to teach ordinary people about the Buddhist law of causality (*karma* or *in'ga* 因果). The tales conveyed the simple and didactic message that it was in people's best interest to follow the Buddha's teaching of honesty and compassion because evildoings such as murder and treachery would surely be met with horrific retribution, a punishment enacted by the ghostly incarnation of the victims of the evil. Not only would the doer be tormented by the punishment, but his/her families and descendants would also be subjected to a series of misfortunes. The curse of affliction would last forever unless the spiritual power of Buddhist prayer could tame the sorrowful and enraged spirit.

The Nirvana of the Vengeful Spirit (*Shiryō Gedatsu Monogatari* 死霊解脱物語; 1690) was a popular tale representative of the *kasane* narrative structure.[68] Yoemon, who married a woman with a child by her former marriage, was averse to his new wife's young son Suke for his being handicapped and having an unpleasant appearance. By finding Suke useless and unsightly, Yoemon demanded his wife give Suke to someone or leave home with him for good. Feeling desperate, the wife drowned Suke in the river. Soon after, she gave birth to a baby named Kasane (this name is said to be the origin of the genre), who resembled Suke like a twin (thus Kasane was the incarnation of Suke). Kasane, being lazy, bad-tempered, and ugly, finally managed to marry a man who felt no love for her but only held the avaricious scheme of murdering her and taking all her possessions and properties. As soon as Kasane fell victim to his conspiracy, her husband took a new wife. His marriage did not last for long as the wife died of a mysterious illness. The same misfortune followed all his wives, until the sixth marriage brought him a baby girl. The girl, Kiku, was possessed by Kasane's spirit when she turned twelve, however, and began to speak in Kasane's voice about the violent deaths of both Suke and Kasane. Because the villagers had not known the horrific causes of Suke and Kasane's demises until this point, they were so frightened by the Kiku/Kasane revelation that they decided to ask for help from the renowned Buddhist monk, Yūten Shōnin.[69] Kasane's spirit was tamed and put to rest in peace by Yūten Shōnin's prayer, as depicted in a print by Hokusai (figure 4.10; 1820s).

The Nirvana's narrative followed the clear-cut Buddhist logic of causality—an evil deed always invites evil consequences. Because of the

4.10 Katsushika Hokusai (1760–1849), *Kasane's Vengeful Spirit and Yūten Shōnin*, 1820s, in *Hokusai manga*. (Courtesy of Dan Mckee)

unspeakably brutal acts committed by Suke's parents and Kasane's husband, the curse of affliction beset the family. And this causal chain of evil and affliction could not be broken because Kasane's grudge continued to loiter in the present. What was significant about this logic of causality was the way it established a particular conception of vengeance. Although

Kasane's husband was clearly the perpetrator, her spirit instead subjected the husband's wives, the innocent women, to her violent reprisals. This ostensibly illogical substitution was possible only if vengeance figured as a matter of jealousy—a "bad temperament" peculiar to women—instead of as "reprisal" against the real perpetrator. Indeed, the thrust of the *Nirvana* consisted in the plot that Kasane's spirit entrapped the wives in the endless chain of curse, whom she considered to be taking her place unrightfully. The spirit explained in rage through Kiku to her husband that it took the lives of his six wives because he loved them. Vengeance was thus an expression of jealousy. Alternatively, Suke/Kasane's untamed spirit could be possibly read as vengeance against her husband if viewed from the perspective that it denied him a chance to have his heir, thereby destroying the succession of his family. But the notion that vengeance could be fulfilled only through the destruction of family lineage itself indicates the patriarchal assumption held by the Buddhist law of causality, which regarded women merely as reproductive beings. The women's affliction and demise bore no causal relationship with their own actions, but only with their derivative status as the one responsible for enabling the succession of familial lineage. Therefore, in *The Nirvana*, vengeance was never about seeking "justice," punishing "evil," or "avenging" oneself. It was never about questioning the patriarchal values on which such violence was conceived and acted out. Vengeance functioned as a metaphor, instead, for the logic of causality that bound women to the chain of misfortunes.[70]

The first kabuki adaptation of *Kasane* appeared in 1731. In this production of *Kasane* (*Ōzumō fujito genji* 大角力藤戸源氏), the novel concept that the female protagonist could be featured as having an "ugly appearance," "short temperedness," and a tendency to become "jealous" was introduced.[71] It marked an important chapter in the history of female impersonators, as mentioned above, in that the impersonator departed from the classical prototype of beauty to play the role of the "ugly lady." This did not imply, however, that the 1731 production made a notable break with the traditional aesthetics of kabuki and its patriarchal assumptions—the "morphology" that produced conformity with the normative conceptions of beauty and authority.[72] It actually followed it. The plotline that Kasane's husband felt entitled to cheat her out of her possessions because of her "defects" in appearance and personality might have invited sympathy from audiences, but hardly called into question kabuki's traditional aesthetics and the patriarchal values associated with them: the "ugly woman" tended to fall prey to villains; her ugliness prefigured the monstrousness of her ghostly incarnation; her vengeance featured as jealousy; and jealousy was an inner reflection of the ugliness of the exterior.

This morphology was affirmed once again in the 1778 version of *Kasane*. The new version portrayed Kasane as a "beautiful lady" who underwent a dramatic transfiguration. She became a "hideous creature" as a result of her body being possessed by the spirit of Takao, her elder sister who was in love with, but for some reason was murdered by, a samurai, Kinukawa Yoemon.[73] After Takao's death, Kasane and Kinukawa fell in love. Feeling jealous and betrayed, Takao's spirit sought vengeance by defacing her younger sister. Kasane was unaware of her deformed appearance, and out of a sense of guilt and sympathy, Kinukawa married her. Being ignorant of her own "monstrous" looks, Kasane lived as an "ideal" wife—unconditionally loyal and loving to Kinukawa, but after realizing her altered appearance, Kasane was completely overtaken by shame, disgust, and insecurity, and quickly metamorphosed into a person of suspicion, jealousy, and indignation. As her soul and body grew monstrous and their marriage began to crumble, Kinukawa eventually decided to murder Kasane. Kasane returned as a vengeful spirit to torment Kinukawa's family.

The novelty of this production consisted in its dramatic presentation of the transformativity of beauty into hideousness, as well as the possibility of their coexistence. It was not until Kasane realized her own disfiguration that she lost her mind and became consumed by burning rage. The disjuncture or discordance between her self-perception (beauty) and others' (hideousness) produced grotesque effects, provoking tragic and horrific sensations far greater than in any earlier versions of *Kasane*.[74] But such dramatic effects of transformation and juxtaposition were not intended to dislocate the simple opposing categories of the ugly and the beautiful. Nor were they meant to forsake the patriarchal values of attractiveness and loyalty as primary female virtues. Rather, these effects were made viable precisely because the production relied heavily on such categories and maintained its conformity with the patriarchal values that undergirded them. The 1778 production's compliance with the morphology of traditional kabuki was most clearly evinced in its repetition of the narrative formula of vengeance as jealously. The question of patriarchy was once again shunned, only to be replaced by the question of woman's "temperament."

It was with Tsuruya Nanboku (1755–1829) that the *Kasane* story diverged from, even subverted, the said morphology when the conception of vengeance was rearticulated not as an expression of women's negative attributes but as a repudiation or negation of the Tokugawa patriarchal system itself. Furthermore, by recasting vengeance as a mode of addressing the system, Nanboku's work extended beyond the problem of patriarchal domination to confront another ideological matrix of the Tokugawa power: the status system. Creation of the overwhelming impression of the verisimilitude of claims of samurai's moral supremacy (selfless devotion to greater causes such as peace and order, as expressed in the moral categories of loyalty, righteousness, and benevolence) was a prerequisite, as seen in chapter 1, for the maintenance of the system. Nanboku's new articulation of vengeance shattered such an impression altogether by powerfully portraying an image of the samurai's self-destructive contradictions. Samurai protagonists—especially female ghosts representing that status—converged on the common tendency to claim vengeance as a way of achieving moral rectitude while actually pursuing selfish or heartless calculation and murderous schemes. The power of Nanboku's work consisted precisely in its ability to problematize, through the rearticulation of vengeance, the guile underlying the Tokugawa norms of gender and status. He masterfully illustrated the ways the norms interacted to produce the nexus of fundamental contradictions. The dual identity of the female ghost, as samurai (a status of the ruling class) and woman (an abject subject under patriarchy), played an extremely important role in this rearticulation, because traversing status and gender exposed the murky zone where the logics of both the ruling and the ruled augmented and incapacitated each other.

The Ghost Story of Yotsuya (*Yotsuya kaidan* 四谷怪談; 1825) was the most representative and popular example of this new articulation, and since Nanboku drew key inspirations from *Kasane*'s narrative motifs, it is appropriate to discuss *Yotsuya* here in some length.[75] The most important compositional feature of *Yotsuya* was its attempt to fuse *Kasane* with the famed story of righteous samurai retainers, *The Treasury of Loyal Retainers* (*Chūshingura* 忠臣蔵; 1748). *The Treasury* itself was a literary rendering of the historic event, as is well known, that occurred in 1703, in which forty-seven samurai retainers avenged their master's wrongful defamation and subsequent death at the expense of their lives. *The Treasury* made this historic event into an illustrative story of the samurai virtues of loyalty and righteousness. Although there were other exemplary tales of this kind, the shogunate was particularly keen on authorizing performances of *The Treasury* for popular theaters—kabuki and *ningyō jōruri*—because of its popularity and thus its efficacy in publicizing samurai virtues.[76] With *Yotsuya*, Nanboku produced a novel play by ingeniously fusing this supposedly honorable story with that of the ignoble—the vengeful ghost. This parodic composition was further reinforced by the clever incorporation of the contemporaneous element of actual murderous incidents that had horrified the Edo populace. Nanboku transformed *The Treasury*, which is supposed to portray the retainers' selfless acts of sacrifice for their master, into a story in which a group of degenerate samurai betray and murder one another in pursuit of their own self-interests. Unmitigated violence, ferocious desire, and heartless calculation run rampant in Nanboku's play, becoming the underlying principles that guide the thought and actions of the samurai protagonists. Righteousness and propriety emerge as sheer disguises for self-interested schemes. Wisdom is used to only pursue malicious and often murderous conspiracy, and compassion is a deceptive ploy used to settle a score. All the characters are consumed by abysmal frenzy and fear, imprisoned in an unceasing repetition of sheer evil until the moment of violent destruction. (Unlike the other versions of *Kasane*, this story does not end with a scene in which Buddhist prayers bring peace to the vengeful spirits.)

It is necessary to look more selectively at some aspects of this rather complex story in order to understand how and to what extent *Yotsuya* succeeded in foregrounding the guile and thus the bankruptcy of the samurai's moral world. The story begins with Naosuke, a samurai turned peddler, attempting to flirt with and seduce Osode, the daughter of a samurai family fallen into decline, who ekes out a living working as a waitress by day and a prostitute by night. Naosuke served Osode's father as a servant until her father lost his high-ranking position after his own lord, Lord Enya, committed malfeasance leading to the disbanding of the entire clan. This opening scene, in which a former samurai/peddler/servant seeks an intimate relation with the daughter of his former master, is clearly intended to signal the collapse and confusion of the established status order in late Tokugawa society. As a matter of fact, as in *The Treasury*, the main protagonists of *Yotsuya*—except Kohei, a commoner servant of Iemon and Oiwa, and Ito Kihei, a doctor serving Lord Kō no Moronao—are all born into the samurai class and once served Lord Enya in different capacities. After the disbandment of the clan, they decide to settle in Edo with the pledge that they would avenge their master. But because of their lack of practical skills, which is held to typify all samurai of the Tokugawa period who due to their status lived off the labor of those beneath them, they are forced to merge with townspeople of the lowest status and become prostitutes, beggars, and peddlers themselves. Despite their wretched realities, their pride and conceit as samurai persists in their dealings with one another, and they demand absolute respect and decorum from those of lower status. Hence, for example, in response to Naosuke's initial overture, Osode remarks, "How dare you! You were my father's servant and you still belong to the lower status no matter what happened to my father and my family. Don't presume to even imagine you can pursue me!"[77] (The irony is that they do not know that they are brother and sister.) The narrative returns repeatedly to the disparity between the samurai's unchanging self-image grounded in status consciousness and their current miseries that force them to live as outcasts: it is as if the story seeks to accentuate that, after their power and authority have been stripped away, the only thing left to samurai is their illusory, petty pride.

The tragedy of the story begins when two dark desires conjoin. Tired of poverty and the low life, Tamiya Iemon—another ex-samurai retainer of Lord Enya—begins to seek an opportunity to regain a position in samurai officialdom. His neighbor, Ito Kihei, a doctor serving the enemy of Lord Enya—Lord Kōno Moronao—schemes to poison Oiwa, Iemon's wife, as well as Osode's elder sister, not only because his granddaughter, Oume, has fallen in love with Iemon but also because he is desperate to keep his family lineage alive after losing his male heir. Immediately after Oiwa delivers her first child with Iemon and falls ill, Kihei sends Oiwa a "medicine"—actually a poison that will soon disfigure Oiwa's face—with the lie that it will help rejuvenate her frail body. Oiwa takes it, and her face begins to hurt and burn. While Oiwa is in excruciating pain, Iemon is at the house of Kihei who has told him to separate from Oiwa and marry his granddaughter. Iemon accepts Kihei's proposal on the condition that he will be granted an official position in return (which means that Iemon betrays his master by seeking an employment in his enemy's clan). At Iemon's residence, Takuetsu, a masseur and an owner of a low-end brothel, attempts to seduce Oiwa into adultery upon Iemon's request. Iemon arranged this scheme so that he could press false charges against Oiwa for adultery and thereby break up with her. (Iemon was not aware, however, of Kihei's plot to deface Oiwa with a poison.) Oiwa rejects Takuetsu's advance in anger, and Takuetsu is so frightened that he confesses Iemon's ruse to Oiwa and inadvertently remarks, "(E)ven a poor wretch like me wouldn't want a woman with your awful face. How unpleasant! I don't know why this was fated to happen, but on top of your sickness, now your face. How pitiful you are!"[78] To prove his point, Takuetsu goes on to confide Kihei's secrets to Oiwa: "It is a woman's fate to be deceived. That miracle drug for your circulation you got from Kihei was all a trick. It was a poison for changing people's faces, an extraordinary poison. When you took it, your face changed and now you look like an ugly, evil woman!"[79] Takuetsu forces Oiwa to look at her own reflection in the mirror, and upon seeing herself, Oiwa shouts aloud in shock,

"Is this my face? Have I really turned into such an ugly woman? Is this truly my face?"[80]

Being told everything about Iemon and Kihei's cold-blooded conspiracies and that Iemon, Kihei and his family are celebrating at this very moment the engagement between Iemon and Oume over sake at Kihei's residence, Oiwa prepares in fury to visit Kihei's house to "thank" Kihei for his "kindness." As she combs her hair, it comes out with blood in great handfuls and a grotesque swelling above her right eye is totally exposed. The makeup further underscores Oiwa's monstrous defacement. Despite Takuetsu's efforts to stop her from going out, Oiwa raises her body and howls, "Now I have nothing but hatred for you, Iemon, and hatred for the house of Kihei, hatred for the Ito family. None of you shall ever escape to a life of peace. . . . . My fury will not rest until it reaches its goal!"[81] But Oiwa is too weak to walk and staggers and then accidentally slits her throat on a sword stuck in a pillar. Oiwa instantaneously metamorphoses into a ghost fuelled with revengeful indignation and begins to haunt and torment Iemon, Kihei, their families, and the cronies who helped or condoned in one way or another their heartless ruses. She exacts pitiless and murderous revenge convinced that her acts are righteous, because they avenge loyalty betrayed and punish faithlessness. Indeed, Oiwa evokes the highest samurai virtues of righteousness, faithfulness, and loyalty in carrying out this malicious revenge.

The Ghost Story of Yotsuya represented a radical break with earlier versions of the *Kasane* tale. Unlike the 1730s' and 1770s' productions of *Kasane* that presented the chain of events according to karma, the Buddhist law of causality, *Yotsuya* forsook the law by articulating the protagonists' motives and actions as springing from dynamic interactions between personal (desire) and institutional (patriarchy and status) determinants. The story was not about the horror of affliction as an unbreakable causal chain of misfortune. The story was about the crucial way in which human action mediated between person and institution, disavowing the idea of fatalism and foregrounding (personal) desire (for status, money, power, prestige, and revenge) as the powerful and capricious force that both shaped and was shaped by the institution. Iemon's scheme to recuperate lost power and prestige was unthinkable without considering how the institution of status hierarchy generated the desire for such a scheme. Iemon's ill-treatment and deception of Oiwa was unthinkable without considering how the institution of gender hierarchy made such behavior possible. Kihei's conspiracy could not have been conceived if the Tokugawa society's preoccupation with familial succession and patriarchal authority did not exist as the nexus of social organization. Similarly, Oiwa's rage and vengeance would have made no sense if the violence of patriarchy were not felt and observed at a societal level.

At the same time, the way the story showed human action as mediating between person and institution was never univocal and unidirectional (i.e., institution determining a person's desire, motive, and action). Indeed, the protagonists' desire and action figured as capricious forces, not as automatic and passive reflections of institutional determinants. Much as Iemon and Kihei's malicious desire and action were the products of existing patriarchy and status structures, they were also the results of their subjective choice, decision, and judgment (not every man living in Tokugawa society would follow the same course of action). Iemon's cruelty could appear exceedingly cruel because it exhibited ruthlessness peculiar to his personality. Kihei's craftiness could magnify its viciousness because it demonstrated the incredible magnitude of heartless calculation unique to his personality.

Likewise, just as Oiwa's vengeance was the product of (i.e., a response to) the exploitative system of patriarchy, it was also the outcome of a *willed* and *chosen* action. Her rage was as objective (as an institutional expression) as it was subjective (as a personal expression). Oiwa's vengeance and rage thus indicated an intricate connection between the working mechanism of patriarchy—the direct source of misery and violence—in which all women were inescapably implicated, and singular instances of Oiwa's personal experiences—how she experienced misery and violence and how she responded to them—which were particular to her.

The power of *Yotsuya*'s narrative—or of how it represented rage, vengeance, monstrousness, and cruelty—devolved from this asymmetry, a noncausal, nonidentical, and indeterminate relation between the institutional and the personal. The story refuses to resolve this relation into causal law or traditional kabuki morphology, in which case all motives and actions could be understood simply as parts of the whole, as instantiations of Law, or as a predetermined "sequence of events like the beads of a rosary."[82] This powerful articulation of the protagonists' agency as radically overdetermined—that is, as an agency that both conditioned and was conditioned by a constellation of motives and actions formed contingently by the asymmetrical relation between the institutional and the personal—injected into the story a logic of history that invoked the *eventfulness* of human action—lie, deception, murder, affliction, vengeance, rage, and grudge.

Illustrating the dynamics of agency by injecting a dramatic concept of time as disintegration or chaos with a focus on the world of degenerate samurai was a way of historicizing late Tokugawa society in terms that belied the reified image of the society as a reflection of cosmic order. *Yotsuya* deployed a number of dramaturgical methods to perform this effect, one of the most arresting of which was its symbolic use of the crying voice of Oiwa and Iemon's newborn baby. Making salient appearance whenever the scene was dominated by violent confrontation between Iemon and Oiwa, the cry functioned as a subtext for Iemon's egregious personality and the cruelty of patriarchal norms that accommodated such a personality. It also represented a reason for Oiwa to hold on to the life that was otherwise filled with suffering and humiliation.

As their poverty becomes grave and Oiwa's health deteriorates, Iemon starts blaming Oiwa for giving birth to their child: "The brat is nothing but a nuisance, and a baby is just another mouth to feed. . . . How could you give birth to the brat when we have no money? Marrying an amateur woman [as opposed to a courtesan] gives me a headache."[83] After making up his mind to leave Oiwa and marry Oume for prestige, comfort, and power, Iemon returns home in need of money for the wedding and snatches the mosquito netting from Oiwa and the baby. Oiwa struggles to take it back, only to be kicked by Iemon and have her nails be torn away. Iemon curses Oiwa, "This still isn't enough, you stingy bitch!" Oiwa screams in desperation,

> "Iemon! Iemon! I can't let you have the mosquito net. He's already gone. He took the only thing I could not give up. Even though I'm as weak and sick as I am, I hung on to it for dear life for the sake of my child. Nothing could have made me agree to part with that net. How violently, violently, the net and my fingernails were torn away. Iemon, you are so cruel. How sorry I feel for my poor baby when I think about his being your flesh and blood."[84]

During this exchange, the baby's cry continues to intensify, accentuating the sense of the wretchedness of the life Oiwa and the baby have to endure. And it reaches the climax in the subsequent scene wherein Oiwa undergoes a monstrous metamorphosis. The most intense cry cannot reach Oiwa's ears, however, as she becomes overtaken by fury and begins to bear a horrendous otherworldly appearance. Oiwa's deafness to the cry marks the decisive moment when she begins to cross beyond the sphere of sanity and reason, the everyday, to that of insanity or madness, the noneveryday. Without anyone capable of being caring and attentive enough to hear the baby's cry, the cry's violent yet solitary reverberations symbolize the total collapse of the everyday and its moral order in the samurai world (see figure 4.11).

4.11 Utagawa Kuniyoshi (1797–1861), *Yotsuya Kaidan*, 1840s. Woodblock print, ink and color on paper (owned by the author). This print dramatizes the sorrowful yet fuming spirit of Oiwa and Kohei with the baby, which confronts Iemon in the house where Iemon poisoned and drove Oiwa into madness and death and brutally murdered Kohei.

The baby's cry followed the trajectory in which official norms that endowed the institutions of status and family with the value of eternity are shattered by violence. Iemon and Kihei's fixation with institutional values (Iemon with status and Kihei with family) gave rise to the scenario in which the lives of Oiwa and the baby were converted into disposable objects. *Yotsuya* brought into light the concept of time—disintegration or chaos—precisely at this very juncture when the institutions embodying the value of eternity exploded into a form of violence.

Men exploiting women was only one obvious dimension in *Yotsuya*. It would be mistaken to assume, however, that Oiwa was simply a victim of patriarchy and her vengeance represented the righteous indignation of the wretched, or an act of protest and derision, or an expression of the collective rage of the downtrodden. Even though Oiwa was undoubtedly a victim of the system and her vengeance was the explosive effusion of cumulated rage against the evils of the system, she too was filled with ideas of her former greatness, or the honor and respect of her father. It was her aristocratic (status) consciousness that made it possible for her to commit, under the name of justice, callous and abominable crimes such as devouring Iemon's mother, Okuma, strangling Iemon's crony, Akiyama Chōbei, and having Oume killed by Iemon. Her cruelty, especially her ironic conjuring of moral rationales for her atrocious acts, appeared to surpass Kihei's and Iemon's wickedness. Oiwa's vengeance drenched the world completely in horror, brutality, and madness, in a manner that was guided only by boundless hatred. Distinctions between morality and immorality, perpetrator and victim, were dissolved into this malevolent maelstrom. In this regard, understanding Oiwa and Iemon's relation as that of victim and perpetrator is less important, even less valid, than understanding it in terms of the samurai's self-destruction and the destruction of their moral world. As Oiwa's spirit cried out to Iemon, they were destined to "fall together into the abyss of sin."[85]

The resonance, rather than divergence, that existed between Oiwa and Iemon becomes clear when their malicious deeds are compared with the comportment of their commoner-servant Kohei. Before being hired by Iemon to look after Oiwa, Kohei served the most respected samurai in Lord Enya's house (Iemon's former master). Because his former master had recently fallen ill and his family was too poor to do anything for the master, Kohei decides to enter Iemon's service to help support his master. Out of a desperate impulse to do whatever he can to cure his master's illness, Kohei steals a precious Chinese medicine from Iemon, a medicine that has been passed down in his house for generations. After Iemon and his cronies discover Kohei's theft, they beat him hard and confine him in the closet where he happens to hear Iemon's plot against Oiwa. Kohei is murdered by Iemon with a false accusation that he committed adultery with Oiwa. Kohei and Oiwa's bodies are nailed on a wooden door and thrown into a river, but their spirits return repeatedly to haunt Iemon. Unlike Oiwa's spirit, however, Kohei's is never violently vengeful: it is rather pitiful and sorrowful. Whenever he appears in front of Iemon, he sadly reiterates the words to him, "Master, master, please give me the medicine!"[86] His demeanor contrasts strikingly to Oiwa's indignant spirit. Kohei's fixation about the medicine seems to underscore the contrast between his virtues of loyalty and affection toward his master and Iemon's lack of them. When Kohei offers Iemon an explanation that his misconduct was born of his loyalty to his master, Iemon dismisses it as an absurdity. The malice draws Oiwa and Iemon closer to each other while it separates the two from Kohei. And the difference between the two and Kohei seems to originate from the formers' delusional and baneful consciousness of self-importance rooted in aristocratic origins.

Tsuruya Nanboku's dramaturgical technique conjured the concept of time—the disintegration of the samurai's moral world—through a tingly atmosphere of dread and repugnance. In his theatrical representations, all familiar forms disappeared, yielding to deformity and disorder. Nanboku achieved this effect, as Maeda Ai pointed out, by associating the ostensibly honorable samurai world with a particular sociocultural topos—the so-called fringes of the world—the filthiest slum quarter in Edo. There, all sorts of outlaws with dubious backgrounds and occupations swarmed to row houses in backstreets. In *Yotsuya*, all the murderous events were set against this underworld of Edo. "The story makes a circle, starting from the left along the outer fringes of Edo proper," as if it followed the trajectory of moral degeneration that gradually permeated the entire city.[87] Every important twist and turn was marked by the symbolism of violence and vice, as the former samurai villains left mounds of corpses and lakes of blood at every corner of this underworld. Nanboku's plot that purposely associated déclassé samurai with these fringe spaces and portrayed the gradual interpenetration of the samurai and underworld spheres, threatened the principle of social distinction and symbolically signaled the beginning of the end of social order built on the premise of the samurai's moral integrity and superiority.

The strategy of visualizing a state of perversity and abnormality by collapsing the distinctions of high and low, morality and immorality, the everyday and the noneveryday, the real and the fantastic into unspeakable forms was central to Tsuruya Nanboku's dramaturgy. It fused diametrically opposite senses and sensibilities, such as gratitude and malice, beauty and hideousness, simultaneously, into one form, without any attempt to unify or harmonize them. Such a strategy was also deployed by ukiyo-e artists in early-nineteenth-century Tokugawa Japan. The first example is a woodblock print by Utagawa Kuniyoshi, which I discussed at some length in chapter 2 (figure 2.1). I will focus here on how the grotesque form of representation produced images germane to the samurai's moral degeneration. What Kuniyoshi achieved in this illustration was an astute marriage of the fantastic and the real, the world of phantoms and that of shogunate politics. The upper part of the picture represents the world of the fantastic where people in the form of grotesqueries appear to seek revenge against the shogun and his advisors who fined or arrested them during the Tenpō Reform for engaging in "immoral" entertainments or by selling and buying "luxurious" goods. The lower part representing high politics depicts the shogun and his advisors who pass the time sleeping or playing chess. The print's layout that divides the composition into the two spheres also signifies the division between the shogun's dream and the real world that he governs. Even though the grotesqueries appear riotous and frenzied, they seem to simply reflect the shogun's nightmare, having no consequences for the real world. But on a closer look, these divisions are not as impermeable as they seem initially. The legendary demon, Earth Spider, summoning the riotous and enraged spirits in the upper right corner, is gradually intruding into the sphere of the real as the Earth Spider spreads the web over the shogun's head. One advisor on the far left appears to be alerted to the overwhelming phantasmal presence, although the others continue to play chess in a state of total apathy.

The townspeople's interpretations of this print diverged over the symbolic meaning of each grotesquerie, yet they all agreed that, although the illustration was based on a famous, mythic story about the battle between a tenth-eleventh century shogun, Minamoto Yorimitsu (948–1021), and a Earth Spider, it conveyed an allegorical and thus veiled message critical of the Tokugawa rulers who, in the face of increasingly problematic social and economic conditions, did nothing but resort to far more stringent control of and all-encompassing intervention into people's everyday world.[88] The townspeople in Edo interpreted the overwhelming presence of the incensed spirits as an indication of political chaos and as the absence of righteous and compassionate rulers in Tokugawa society. To them, the image of samurai rulers who continued to sleep and play chess in the presence of enraged spirits further attested to the lack of the rulers' moral commitment to just and benevolent governance. Their interpretation shared a perspective, similar to that evoked by *Yotsuya*, that Kuniyoshi's grotesqueries portrayed the complete paralysis of Tokugawa politics.

Another illustration by Kuniyoshi, *Princess Takiyasha Summons a Skeleton Specter to Frighten Mitsukuni* (1849; figure 4.12), applied the same tactic of allegory in generating apparitional sensations of chaos.[89] There is no record suggesting that this illustration inspired Edo townspeople's critical interpretations of contemporary Tokugawa politics, but it is not farfetched to theorize such a possibility since it seemed to make an allegorical reference to the present in the guise of the past. The theme of this illustration was inspired by a Nanboku's play based on the well-known mythistorical tale of the lord of the Heike clan, Taira no Masakado (~940), whose insurrection against the court was defeated. After his execution, his head was displayed to the public as a warning, which enraged his daughter, Princess Takiyasha. She prayed at a shrine to have his father's spirit summoned, and Masakado returned as a ghost to take revenge on the court's vassals. Given that the Tokugawas claimed to be the descendants of the Genji clan (despite their obscure origins and the lack of evidence for such a claim), which eventually destroyed the Heike clan upon the request of the imperial court in the series of historic battles in the late twelfth century, Masakado's vengeful spirit against the court conceivably might have been rendered by the townspeople of Edo as an anti-Genji and thus anti-Tokugawa position or a unrealized history that would explode the legitimacy of the present.

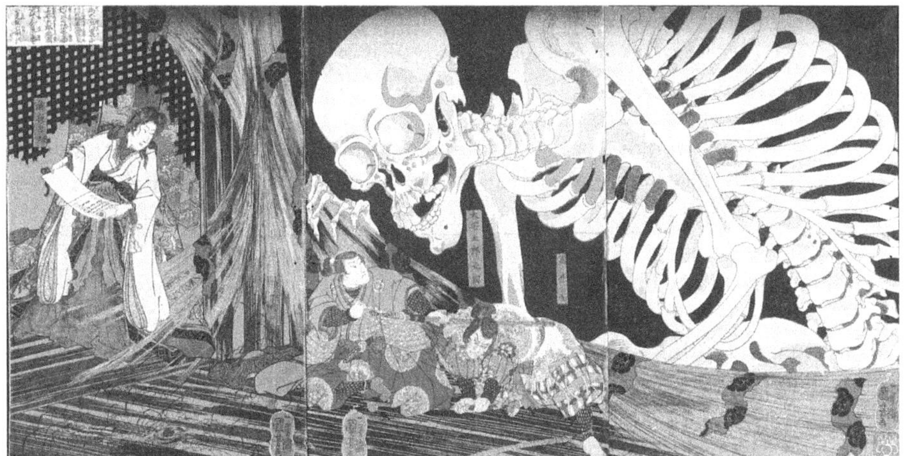

4.12 Utagawa Kuniyoshi (1797–1861), *Princess Takiyasha Summons a Skeleton Specter to Frighten Mitsukuni*, 1849. Woodblock print, ink and color on paper. (Courtesy of the Victoria and Albert Museum, London)

If the subject matter of Kuniyoshi's illustration stirs up the images of chaos through the use of historical allegory, his representational method further accentuates them. It combines a purely stylized and fantastic mode with a technique that allows for precise accuracy and fidelity to the anatomical details of the skeleton. Anatomical descriptions and depictions of the human body were easily available at that time, owing largely to the proliferation of Western medical knowledge enabled by the rapid spread of Dutch Studies. Kuniyoshi is said to have owned a collection of copies of European illustrations and prints, among them anatomical illustrations, which mighty have prodded him to draw this skeleton. Kuniyoshi's realistic depiction of the skeleton plays a crucial role in creating a horrific sensation as the world of samurai appears to be completely overpowered by the realm of the phantasms. A reed screen reminiscent of a spider web or the circulation of ghostly air also reinforces the vision of turmoil caused by the pungent presence of the ghost.

The Potency of Grotesque Realism and Its Significance

Grotesque representation of reality in the late Tokugawa culture was a mimesis that estranged and subverted the consciousness anchored to the official hierarchy of the first- and the second-order reality. In mimesis, to follow Herbert Marcuse's words, "Language [and vision were] tightened or loosened, forced to yield insights otherwise obscured."[90] Mimesis made it possible for spectators and beholders of popular arts to perceive the world demystified. It intensified the perception by re-presenting reality as distorted and perverted "so that the unspeakable [was] spoken, the otherwise invisible [became] visible, and the unbearable explod[ed]."[91] The aesthetic of deformity thus turned into a mode of negation and indictment.

The negativity unique to the grotesque representation arose from the paradoxical principle that only an immaterial or fantastic existence—the figure of haunting—was capable of unearthing the actual conditions of material realities. The immaterial body of the haunting ghost was a metaphor for realities consigned to a marginalized status, an unarticulated existence beneath the overwhelming impressions of the reality of the existing arrangements of power. But it was also a figure of speech for extraordinary mobility and eloquence in terms of a potency to transgress and traverse the carefully guarded borders between the orderly appearance of reality and the unarticulated reality of wretchedness. Through the power to transgress and traverse, the immaterial body forced the two spheres of reality into a contestatory dialogue. Such dialogical dynamics abolished the borders and exposed the limits and limitations of the symbolically dominant reality—the empty formalism of the regime's ideological projection of reality.

The grotesque bodies of monsters and ghosts were most effective in accentuating the perversions of reality through their capacity to produce sensations of contradiction and chaos. This semiotic operation corresponds to M. M. Bakhtin's insight about the grotesque: it frequently foregrounds not only the actual conditions of ideological production but also the mechanisms of domination that the ideology seeks to conceal or naturalize. Grotesque in late Tokugawa Japan not only revealed that social boundaries and subjects (status) were artificially constructed by and for the ruling samurai class but also visualized that these boundaries and subjects functioned as the instruments for naturalizing the mechanisms of power and masking the mechanisms' vice. This unique potency of grotesque forms was largely due to their tendency to privilege the anomalous and the unspoken that displaced given social categories and normative aesthetic judgments. By hybridizing the established binary categories and engendering a formless form, the grotesque gave novel expressions—chaos, disintegration, paralysis, and contradiction—to realities that were kept unarticulated under the existing symbolic order of things. To understand the grotesque as a process of hybridization, however, is not to define its role as a prerequisite for contestation. Rather it is to acknowledge that the grotesque *tended to operate* as a demystification of a dominant symbolic order that had set the terms of "reality." The logic of the grotesque could unsettle given social positions and interrogate the rules of inclusion, exclusion, and domination that structured the social ensemble of the Tokugawa order. In kabuki theaters or ukiyo-e prints, the place of high and low or good and evil was never a simple given: the images of decorum and enormity "peered into each other's faces" in such a way that they were immediately thrown into dialogical contestation.[92] In such a heterogeneous encounter of images that were normally kept separate, any truism could be made subject to interrogation. The truism promoted by the Tokugawa regime was no exception.

The most scandalous revelation occasioned by grotesque form was the confused moral state of the ruling class. By foregrounding the samurai's use and abuse of loyalty, wisdom, righteousness, and benevolence, the grotesque form called attention to their self-destructive desire, duplicity and contradiction.

Late Tokugawa kabuki's and ukiyo-e's use of haunting, especially in its grotesque manifestation, the disfigured body, indicated the most extensive degree of conjunctural moment, of an overdetermination of the contradictions in the scenes of cultural politics. The dramatic narrativization and/or visualization of horrific corporeal deformity signified a radical mutation of the possibility of negation suggested by the tragic motif of double suicide in the early eighteenth century. The grotesque also signaled a significant shift from the late eighteenth century, when a mode of humorous parody posed such a possibility through the deployment of "vulgar" bodily images. If double suicide represented the moment of negation of reality in its recognition of the hard truth that only death—self-destruction of corporeal existence—could promise an experience authentic to feeling, and if comical satire—assault on established decorum and the respectable body—did so by cleverly performing the nullification of official hierarchical distinctions, this new mode, the grotesque, exposed the kernel of the Tokugawa system's contradictions in the image of horrific disfigurement representing the breakdown of fundamental moral values upheld by ruling elites to lend support to the existing mechanism of power. With their valorization of and the penchant for the grotesque, late Tokugawa kabuki and ukiyo-e prints might have appeared to confirm the authorities' claim that popular entertainments were nothing but "vulgar," "idle," and "immoral" and that those celebrating them were engaged in folly. Yet, it was precisely their representational capacity to *de-form* the formal reality through the disquieting figures of haunting that underscored the unarticulated reality—the paralysis and insolvency of the Tokugawa system—and thus supplied the potential moments of criticism and mutinous intervention.

FIVE

Reconfiguring the Body in a Modernizing Japan

Pure competition is not a primitive given. It can only be the result of lengthy efforts and, in truth, pure competition is never attained. Pure competition must and can only be an objective, an objective thus presupposing an indefinitely active policy. Competition is therefore an historical objective of governmental art and not a natural given that must be respected.

MICHEL FOUCAULT, *THE BIRTH OF BIOPOLITICS*

The urgent task for the state is to educate [ordinary people] to rid themselves of idleness and to guide and supervise them to be able to work for and persevere in building modern industries.

ŌKUBO TOSHIMICHI, *A 1875 REPORT SUBMITTED TO EMPEROR MEIJI*

This final chapter looks into fundamental shifts in body politics, which took place under the Meiji's state's policies of constructing the modern capitalist nation. Late Tokugawa cultural politics had amply demonstrated, as seen in the previous chapters, that early modern Japan's social order and moral economy came to experience fundamental fragmentation and bankruptcy beginning in the late eighteenth century, with the majority of the populace disregarding or questioning the formal arrangement of social relations based on the decorum of loyalty and deference to authorities. The dissolution of societal cohesion presented the grave and imminent concern to the new Meiji government established in 1868, which saw the transformation of Japan into a strong and competitive modern nation as the only solution to the country's semicolonial status imposed by Western imperialists in the 1850s. Therefore, as soon as the Meiji leaders took power by overthrowing the Tokugawa government, they began to work on the reorganization of heterogeneous social groups, which possessed neither a shared consciousness of "national" belonging nor a conception of the modern nation-state, into individual subjects willing without hesitation to identify their destinies with that of the country. Convinced that the early modern regime's cosmological projection of totality authorizing the hierarchical division of society could not produce the desired effect, the government turned to an egalitarianism grounded in patriotic sentiment as the new organizing principle of the social order. Japan's teenage emperor, Emperor Meiji (1852–1912), announced in the first year of his rule the Charter Oath, a statement of national policy that called for the unity of high and low as a necessary condition for all to pursue the common goals of national power, independence, and prosperity. In 1871, Yamagata Aritomo (1838–1922), one of the oligarchs who dominated Meiji politics, spoke in favor of the oath, "By all innovations, the rulers and the ruled will be put on the same basis, the rights of the people will be equal, and the imperial way will be cleared for the unity of the soldiers and peasant. Therefore, neither the samurai nor the common people will have the status to which they were accustomed in the past. Nor will there be any distinction in the service they render to their country, for they will all be alike as subjects of the Empire."[1]

Although the Oath and Yamagata's pronouncement might have signified a radical, even liberatory, break with the Tokugawa power that sought to contain people within the structure of fixed hierarchies, the majority of the populace remained skeptical about how joining the new ruling elite in pursuit of these goals would improve their livelihood. (Indeed, from 1871 to 1887, a number of popular protests and uprisings erupted against new educational and tax policies, conscription laws, and imposed reforms of daily customs.[2]) Meiji leaders understood that the production of a cohesive national community—impelling heterogeneous populations into embracing a shared sense of national belonging—necessitated more elaborate strategies than mere verbal slogans and imperial proclamations. The new government moved swiftly in 1869 to dismantle the old Confucian-based social order, as well as the privileges and restrictions that had defined different social groups, and introduced a new governing principle of liberalism founded upon the idea of universal egalitarianism or egalitarian humanism (*ningen byōdō* 人間平等). Under the new order, former peasants, artisans, and merchants, who made up almost 90 percent of the country's population, were all classified together as *heimin* (平民), ordinary citizens. Two years later, outcasts—who had occupied the bottom rung of the status hierarchy during the Tokugawa period—also gained *heimin* status through the emperor's Emancipation Proclamation (although this did not mean that prejudice and discrimination against them disappeared, as Hirota Masaki's study shows).[3] As part of the demolition of status hierarchies, restrictions on occupation, travel, and location of residence were all lifted in 1871. However, these liberal reforms were not intended to guarantee citizens' freedoms of speech, thought, and association, or to create a legal and political framework for civil disobedience. Rather, the state intended reform to yield social mobility and prompt individuals to pursue their ambitions tirelessly and to participate aggressively in the intense competition according to the Darwinian law of the survival of the fittest.

A New Body Politics

What lay at the heart of the Meiji government's new ideological orientation was a strategic objective of establishing Japan's full sovereignty and advancing its status as an imperial power within the global system of capitalism and nation-states. Producing ambitious, competitive attitudes among the citizenry was deemed essential to this objective precisely because these new attitudes would unleash energies that could propel the country toward economic and military might (*fukoku kyōhei* 富国強兵).[4] The new government firmly believed that a competitive ethos of self-motivated individuals was the key to the Western nations' dominance in wealth, military strength, and technology, and that Japan's successful transformation into a modern nation-state worthy of the respect of Western counterparts depended on the creation of such an ethos at home. On the basis of this conviction, the government launched a universal education program (*gakusei kōfu* 学制公布) in 1872, arguing that "the country's stability, prosperity, and strength depended entirely on the degree to which common people, not select men of intelligence, are civilized." The government's announcement of the program defined the ultimate goal of the program as supplying every individual with the most basic "capital" (*zaihon* 財本) to "establish oneself, acquire one's means of life, and prosper in one's vocation."[5] It also stipulated the "establishment of oneself" (*mi o tateru* 身を立てる) by way of learning as a "duty of every human being (*hitono tsutome* 人の努), regardless of gender and class," and reasoned that "homelessness, poverty, downfall, and degradation" were the natural consequences of the individual's deficiencies in living up to this duty.[6] By attributing individuals' success entirely to their personal aptitudes and efforts, the Meiji state sought to implant in every individual citizen competitiveness and self-responsibility, not only as a new way of life to accept but also as a positive value to embrace, so that each citizen would become an industrious and productive subject.

Accordingly, human desire, which the Tokugawa powers had viewed entirely negatively, was now said to be a positive force for propelling individuals toward success—and, ultimately, the nation toward progress. Leading liberal intellectuals such as Fukuzawa Yukichi (1834–1901), Katō Hiroyuki (1836–1916), and Nishi Amane (1829–97) joined this governmental call for ordinary people to compete, succeed, and prosper by pursuing new knowledge and excelling in learning (see figure 5.1). The Meiji government thus spent the first half of its reign (1868–87) trying to institute and disseminate liberal values and behaviors under the slogan "Civilization and Enlightenment" (*bunmei kaika* 文明開化).

But, like any liberalism, early Meiji liberalism contained within itself an aporia that could potentially fragment state power. Producing self-motivated and ambitious individuals constantly posed the danger of generating tensions and chasms between society and the state as it might encourage what the state saw as "excesses" of individualism: namely, the audacious pursuit of personal gain and success without patriotic concerns and commitments. The state intended its liberal principles to unify the infant nation in a manner that consolidated the economic and military foundation of the country. Universal education prioritized utilitarian subjects, such as world geography, physics, and mathematics, as well as the acquisition of literacy and communication skills based on the "standard" language (not languages that were classified by the state as dialects), reflecting the government's desire to create people who were capable of making the country unified and stronger with practical knowledge and a shared sense of belonging.[7] In this vein, while Itō Hirobumi (1841–1909), one of the most influential architects of modern Japan, insisted on the urgent need to create a "common folk" who were rational, ambitious, and assiduous, he never forgot to emphasize that the folk must at the same time be ready and willing to sacrifice their individual rights for the sake of the Emperor and the country. For Itō, the common folk were the "splendid material with which to build up a strong nation."[8] It was therefore essential for the state to succeed in effectively channeling the energies unleashed by individualism into the efforts of nation-state building.

This balancing act was most vigorously articulated by Meiji enlightenment thinkers, such as Fukuzawa and Katō, in their theories of popular

5.1 Utagawa Toyokuni III (Kunisada; 1769–1825), *Nine-Year-Old Boy Studying Hard in Osaka*, 1870s. Woodblock print (Courtesy of the University of Michigan Library). This print praises the boy as a model student whose unwavering commitment to academic achievement helped him to overcome his belated entrance to primary school. It underscores how he manages to find time to study even when he is in the middle of running errands for his parents. It was also around this time that many multicolored prints of "genius children" were made and circulated widely among people.

rights that expounded the importance of striking a balance between state power and individual rights in the country's ascension to a modern civilization, while deemphasizing, if not completely disregarding, potential tensions and confrontations that might surge forth between them at any given moment. "Excessive state power brings suffering to the people while people having too much right gives trouble to the state . . . This is why the popular rights theory has too many defects to be implemented. The unity of the government and people should be achieved," as Fukuzawa wrote it in 1878.[9] Katō went a step further, announcing in 1882 that the theory of natural rights was a myth or fallacy, because it was the state—not some immaterial divine authority—that should claim the ultimate power to confer rights to happiness and privileges on individuals, according to their levels of education and intelligence. Only those who possessed sufficient aptitude should be involved in state affairs, Katō contended, and it was only through the effective work of these select elites that the well-being of the "ignorant crowds" would be also guaranteed.[10]

The theories of the unity of the government and people and meritocracy were responses to an unintended historical conjuncture where the new government was faced with the lack of an effective resolution to the problems emanating from the aporia inherent in liberalism. In addition to "egotistic" individualism, the new liberal principles inadvertently incited the popular political movement known as the Popular Rights Movement (1874–83), which called for the immediate establishment of parliamentary democracy, universal suffrage, and a democratic constitution. Faced with the rising momentum of the movement, the Meiji state grew exceedingly anxious about the unintended consequences of liberal theory and identified the movement's proponents as a cause of "social maladies," and hence as a grave danger to its visions of new social order.[11] In 1876, the state announced the law *The Prohibition of Radical Opinions* (*Kagekiron Yokuseihōjō* 過激論抑制法条) to suppress the discourses calling for the popular right to "overthrow the government which denied their natural rights to freedom and obstructed their security and happiness."[12] Four years later, the state started consolidating a new ideological framework through which political dissents inspired by the movement could be silenced. It issued in 1880 an ordinance (*shūkai jōrei* 集会条例) that granted the police the power to regulate and dismiss political assemblies at will and revised it to enhance its power in 1882. Furthermore, educators were told to deemphasize liberal values and to guide pupils through a discourse of national ethics based on the newly reified stature of Emperor Meiji as a divine ruler. Nishimura Shigeki (1828–1902), a cofounder with Fukuzawa and Katō of the Meiji Enlightenment group the "Meiji Six Society" (*Meirokusha* 明六社), was arguably one of the earliest intellectuals to advocate resuscitating the Confucian ethics of loyalty and filial piety as the basis of "national morality." By forming the Tokyo Moral Training Society (*Tokyo Shūshingakusha* 東京修身学社) in 1876, he hoped to decouple Japan from its liberalist path by curtailing the supposed excesses of individualism expressed in the popular call for democracy, as well as in "egotistic" individualism.[13] This new ideological orientation would quickly gain support among the ruling elite and shape the core conceptions of the Imperial Constitution (1889) and the Imperial Rescript on Education (1890). They proclaimed the emperor to be the sovereign of the nation, whereas the people were "imperial subjects" (*shinmin* 臣民) whose ultimate duty was to give up their lives voluntarily to defend the body of imperial institutions—the incarnation of the putatively unchanging essence of the national body (*kokutai* 国体)—should some exigencies befall the nation. This clear master-subject formulation was naturalized in terms of a quasi-familial structure—the emperor as the ultimate patriarch and the people as his children (*kazoku kokka* 家族国家).

Numerous scholarly works in both Japanese and English have sought to explain the process of imperial subject formation. The modernist school, represented by Maruyama Masao and his students, and the Marxist historical school, called the Lecture School (*Kōzaha* 講座派), argued that the remnants of feudalistic mentalities, such as submissiveness to and blind faith in authorities, that persisted in village communities after the Meiji *Ishin* allowed the emperor system to penetrate into and dominate the psyche of ordinary people. Students of People's History (*Minshūshi* 民衆史) have placed an emphasis on the process by which indigenous popular religions were co-opted into the ideology of emperor worship (*tennō sūhai* 天皇崇拝).[14] More recent works inspired by the invention of tradition theory have begun to look at the symbolic functions of various rituals—processions, pageantry, schooling, national holidays, and so on—invented to produce and naturalize the affective and empathetic relationship between emperor and people.[15]

Despite their different approaches, the modernists, Marxists, and *Minshūshi* scholars all rely on what I would like to call mobilization theory: a perspective that it was through the state's ability to appropriate the common people's preexisting mental and spiritual universe (tradition or *dentō* 伝統) that the emperor system succeeded in infiltrating all corners of society. What makes this viewpoint possible are two problematic assumptions: first, that there existed a unitary subject called "people" and a cohesive mental or spiritual universe prior to the emergence of the modern nation, and second, that this universe persisted as a historical continuum from the Tokugawa to the Meiji periods. These assumptions not only fail to recognize and articulate the multiple layers of break between the two periods but also promote an ahistorical understanding of the production of ideology. Because the collective mental makeup and its subject, the "people," are posited as always already present in a manner consonant with the emperor system, they remain outside of the historical process or their historicity figures only in disembodied form.

The symbolic analysis of the emperor system on the contrary makes an important break with mobilization theory in its attempts to explain how the imperial subject and its "traditional" cultural values were *invented* in modern times through the institution and ritualistic repetition of national holidays, spectacles, and educational indoctrination. The invention theory effectively reveals that what has often been considered to be modernity's opposite, "tradition," is itself constitutive of and constituted by modernity. However, because the theory tends to rely on an exclusively cultural approach to the process of national subject formation, it ignores how the production of nation and the national subject were related to the state's program of restructuring society based on the emerging capitalist mode of production. The Tokugawa shogunate's efforts to naturalize the immutability of status identity through an insistence on the eternality of time and the immobility of space had been inextricably linked to sustaining the existing division of labor, which ideally served the rice-centered Tokugawa economy. Similarly, the Meiji government's introduction of "competitive individual" based on the new principle of social mobility was undeniably correlated with its attempts to create a new division of labor capable of launching Japan into capitalist competition for wealth and power on the global stage. In this respect, modern subject formation must be examined in terms of its duality—as the formation of national *and* capitalist subjects. If this duality is not acknowledged, our understanding of Japan's modern transformation will continue to be circumvented by the invention theory's perspective that the dialectic of the traditional and the modern congealed without much clamor and tumult into the creation of a homogeneous national subject while overlooking the precarious process in which the uneven developments of socioeconomic formation incessantly generated antagonism, conflict, and ruptures. The ostensive conflict of the traditional and the modern was in fact a dialectical rhetoric deployed by the state and the leading intellectuals to maneuver the country's overdetermined process of modern capitalist transformation, allowing the state to build political and economic mechanisms necessary for its meteoric ascension to imperial power. Much as the traditionalist rhetoric of patriotic devotion worked to prevent excesses of individualism prompted by the capitalist mode of production and consumption from fragmenting the state's program of building a unified nation, the capitalist ideology of liberalism worked to ensure that the stasis and inelasticity of feudalistic social relations would not impede the state's drive toward imperial power. The both traditionalist and liberalist impulses were part of the modern process of social formation. It was crucial for the Meiji state to convince its subjects, therefore, that striving for personal success must be ultimately affixed to building Japan's stability, prosperity, and strength. It was no coincidence that eminent industrialists, such as Shibusawa Eiichi (1840–1931) and Iwasaki Yatarō (1834–85), echoed the government's call for patriotic individualism in their claims that their entrepreneurship was a means to strengthen the country's position in the world.[16] Although the invention theory can offer insight into the process by which newly contrived "traditional" discourses and rituals served to bring heterogeneous peoples to see themselves as bearing a unitary identity, it remains insufficient as an explanation of how and why the traditionalist strategies were contrived in conjunction with the creation and management of a capitalist society.

Critical examination of the process of Japan's nineteenth-century transformation demands another level of inquiry—beyond the invention theory—regarding why and how the production of a collective ethos came to constitute a crucial branch of the state's efforts to create the imperial subject. Historians have long posited that indoctrinating the popular mind was an essential part of imperial subject formation from the very beginnings of the Meiji period, but in doing so they overlooked the question of when ethos—human interiority—*itself* became a primary strategic target of interpellation. This question is of great significance because Tokugawa powers harbored no desire to appropriate, regulate, mold, or homogenize human interiority. For the Tokugawa shogunate, interior disposition was never a matter of state intervention. So long as the bodies (of peasants, artisans, merchants, and outcasts) fulfilled public obligations, such as producing rice, paying taxes, and behaving according to laws and moral codes, Tokugawa authorities showed little interest in intervening in each individual's interior space. The state's incessant efforts to control the body through sumptuary laws and various modes of punishment, as well as its scant attention to the people's mind-set confirms that the idea of molding human interiority never occupied a significant place in Tokugawa strategies for constructing and sustaining the social order. This particular feature of shogunal politics was predicated on the theory that people's dispositions were innately "different" and unalterable (what could be called an essentialist theory of diversity). This view of difference derived from the Confucian concept of nature or character (*sei* 性) as preordained by Heaven. The crucial difference that separated commoners from elites, according to this theory, was the common folk's decisive lack of an intellectual and moral capacity to resolve the body's antagonistic relations with the mind. It was precisely this assumption of essential and immutable differences between samurai and commoners' interior qualities that authorized the erection of the hierarchical system of social order and the division of labor based on the system. Put differently, a view that articulated human interiority in an undifferentiated manner would contradict and undermine the very foundation of Tokugawa social order.

Meiji Japan renounced the Tokugawa theory of innate difference and adopted a view that human interiorities possessed the same universal qualities. This new postulate worked, of course, as a basis for the liberal theory of egalitarian humanism and thus for legitimating the Meiji state's policies of spurring people into social mobility and competition. Making ethos a focal point of the state strategies of imperial subject formation did not constitute a coherent policy, however, until the middle of the Meiji period.[17] Until the mid-1880s, the state concentrated its efforts and resources on "reforms of popular culture or customs" (*fūzoku kairyō* 風俗改良; or *kyōsei* 矯正), by which the state meant an attempt to reshape people's "vulgar appearance, demeanor, taste, life-style" into a culture consistent with its vision of a civilized and enlightened nation.[18] It appeared as if the state were more concerned with forms (exteriority) of popular culture than with their contents (interiority), as people like Fukuzawa expressed their frustrations with the superficiality of the government's policies of westernization (*ōka* 欧化). But during these first two decades of the Meiji period, the ideas of an ethos of civilization and a morality of the nation were constant subjects of public debate, with government participation. A more affirmative official definition of the desired mind-set would emerge in the late 1880s and early 1890s, when the concept of culture became increasingly dominated by the fetishism of the traditional, signifying folk culture or national culture (*nihon no fūzoku* 日本の風俗).[19] The strategies of imperial subject formation began to exert a de facto impact on the populace through the forces of interior homogenization. It is no coincidence that the new *fūzoku* discourse began to gain currency between 1895 and 1910, when ordinary people were for the first time absorbed in jingoistic patriotism through Japan's victories over China (1895) and Russia (1905) and witnessed the country's aggressive colonial expansion into Asia—the colonization of Taiwan (1895) and Korea (1910). Together with such new genres as wartime reporting and travelogues from the colonies, a number of books entitled Japanese *fūzoku*, Ryukyu *fūzoku*, Ezo *fūzoku*, Korean *fūzoku*, Chinese *fūzoku,* and Russian *fūzoku* were published during this period.

The mutation of Emperor Meiji's symbolic image followed the same trajectory as Meiji body politics. During the first half of the Meiji period, as Takashi Fujitani explains in *Splendid Monarchy: Power and Pageantry in Modern Japan*, the emperor's visible corporeal presence was instrumental in spreading among the masses his image as the new leader of a civilizing Japan, but in later years, the explicit public display of his body was halted to enhance his sacred and divine aura. The crucial turning point arrived with the Imperial Constitution in 1889 and Imperial Rescript on Education in 1890. These documents emphasized the image of the emperor as the spiritual leader who embodied the timeless virtues of Japan passed down from the ancient ages. In place of his physical presence, Emperor Meiji's mythicized portrait was distributed to every elementary school around 1890. Fujitani rightly argues that the emperor's invisible presence proved to be far more effective than his corporeal presence in fetishizing him as the incarnation of eternal Japanese virtues in the minds of the masses. What Fujitani's explanation leaves unaddressed, however, is how the strategies of imperial pageantry were linked to the larger processes by which premodern conceptions of mind and body were negated and their relations were reconfigured in modern times. Why did the Meiji state find it necessary to carry out such a drastic reconfiguration? What did it hope to achieve? How did the new mind-body configurations change the notion of subject and subjectivity during the early years of Japan's encounter with modernity? These issues are essential to our genealogical reflection on imperial subject formation and, more broadly, to uncovering the historical implications of the emergence of modern ontology during the Meiji period.

Fūzoku as the Body

Our inquiries start with a short summary of the arguments I have presented thus far in this book about the history of Tokugawa popular culture in order to shed some light on how and when the shift from the body to the mind as the locus for subject formation took place. By assigning a specific meaning and function to the body, the Tokugawa shogunate sought to create a subject whose actions were devoted to the task of providing for material needs, thus preserving the established social order. The body, especially that of the common person, was conceptualized exclusively in terms of material contribution, and the ruling samurai class measured commoners' moral and existential worth by how—and how much—they supplied through industrious devotion to the social whole. The official designation of the body as productive labor constituted the central moral principle by which the Tokugawa shogunate constructed and maintained social order. Within this context, the body that privileged play—especially a play that incited corporeal pleasure—over work signified no more than the unwanted, even scandalous, digression of the official moral order. What should be noted here is the Tokugawa shogunate's view that the body always already possessed an unruly and disruptive potential to the economy of morality and the preservation of social order. For the elite, the relationship between body and mind was never symbiotic, but rather perpetually disjunctive, conflictive, and antagonistic. Suzuki Shōzan's (1579–1655) insistence that the body was a "bag of desires" and thereby disruptive and contaminative to man's spiritual self was emblematic. This particular configuration of the mind-body binary provided the Tokugawa state with powerful ideological language for formulating high and low hierarchies and dominating ordinary people. Because the authorities regarded ordinary people as innately lacking the moral and intellectual capacities to control and contain their indocile bodies, they took the policing of peoples' everyday lives as an essential component of effective governance. Instead of entirely quelling the popular culture of play and pleasure, however, the shogunate allowed for momentary diversion and flight by allocating it to particular districts at the margins of Edo proper. Such lenience granted the state the ability and plasticity to maintain a stable social order by providing a safety valve. This was a strategy of containment, in short, rather than suppression.

By the early eighteenth century, the strategy of containment had failed, as numerous cultural activities emerged, with networks that extended beyond the spatial confines established by the Tokugawa state. Supported by vibrant publishing businesses and the proliferation of print media and entertainments, popular writers, artists, and playwrights were drawn to the task of representing diversifying tastes and lifestyles associated with the new aesthetics of play and pleasure, which the state condemned as "idle" and "immoral." These representations celebrated the body in an infinitely heterogeneous way. They affirmed the social function and meaning of the body in all its aspects—including farting, fighting, drinking, laughing, making love, rioting, and murdering—and, in doing so, served as the motor force for the endless play of imagination and signification, supplying new values, perspectives, and modes of social interactions that ignored, trivialized, and subverted the official insistence on the primacy of mind over body. These imaginings juxtaposed and intermixed high and low through the "vulgar" materialism of the body, revealing the primacy of mind over body as an ideological expression that legitimated social hierarchies and hid the ruling elite's deficiencies, hypocrisies, and illegitimacy. The Tokugawa official doctrine of status hierarchies and division of labor was unable to accommodate the growing diversity of playful and contestatory imaginings and lost its persuasiveness by the mid-nineteenth century.

Even after the new Meiji government overthrew the Tokugawa shogunate in 1868, the official perception of *fūzoku*—popular culture—as the site generating moral and social disorder did not appear to have changed significantly. Following the Charter Oath's statement, "Base customs of the past shall be abandoned," the new government issued a series of laws aimed at separating spaces of popular entertainment from those of everyday life. From 1868 to 1872, kabuki, storytelling, puppet plays, and other forms of street shows (*misemono* 見世物) began to appear as primary targets of the new government's strict regulation. In 1868, the government delivered an ordinance under the name of Emperor Meiji:

> Despite the fact that both Kyoto and Tokyo are the capitals of the imperial nation and centers for virtuous cultivation, we have situations in which irreverent and licentious sentiments among the populace are being encouraged. Because their poisonous influence will likely reach all corners of society, we must enforce our policies of purging any activities promoting such sentiments. In recent years, there are people who openly sell and buy erotic and obscure multicolored prints, and there are others whose show tents carry offensive and unsightly signboards depicting naked men and women. These prints must be confiscated and businesses banned.[20]

In 1870, following the prohibition of erotic prints and street shows, the Meiji government ordered kabuki actors, storytellers, and puppeteers to limit their repertories to only war tales, old fables, and sermons, specifically excluding stories of double suicide, adultery, murder, and vengeful ghosts (subject matters and motifs discussed extensively in the previous chapters), which sent the public clear moral messages, carrying on the Tokugawa dictum "Promote Good and Chastise Evil" (*kanzen chōaku* 勧善懲悪).[21]

A year later, the administration issued an ordinance in which newspapers were ordered to promote the dictum and to commit to the task of enlightening and civilizing people with factual information about Japan and the world. "Stories about ghosts and irrational happenings," as well as "comical and lascivious fads," were prohibited.[22] The government established the Ministry of Education (*kyōbusho* 教部省) in 1872 as the agency responsible for overseeing popular entertainers and supervising

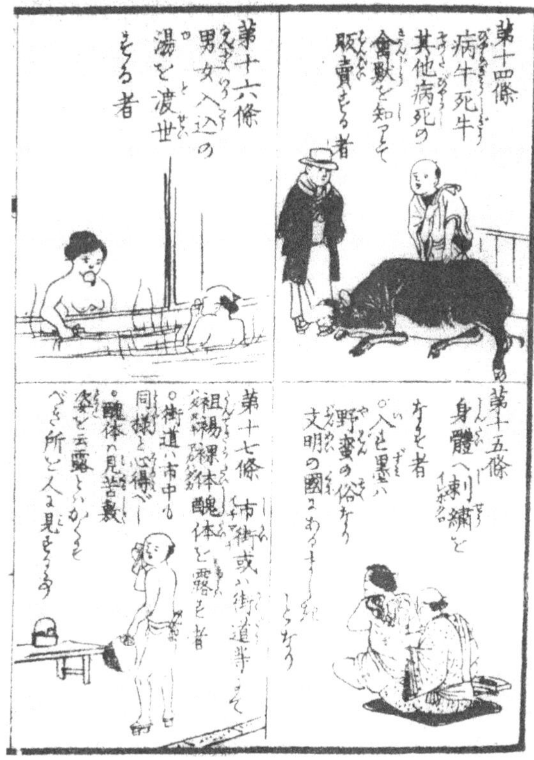

5.2 Anonymous, *Banning Mixed Bathing, Tattooing, Walking Naked, and Selling Dead Animals*, mid-nineteenth century. Illustration for public announcement. (Owned by the author)

religious affairs. In August of the same year and again in 1875, the ministry reiterated that theaters and other forms of spectacles and shows—especially storytelling (*yose* 寄席 or *yoseba* 寄せ場)—must recognize it as their primary *duty* to "Promote Good and Chastise Evil"; they must help cleanse "old evil customs" (*kyūhei* 旧弊) and enlighten the "ignorant" populace by stripping their performances of "licentious dispositions and disgraceful bearing" (*in'fūshūtai* 淫風醜態) that disturbed public mores and customs.[23] In conjunction with the regulations of popular entertainments, the governor of Tokyo (formerly Edo) announced in November 1873 an ordinance (*ishiki kaii jōrei* 違式詿違条例) that those who tattooed their bodies, walked naked, urinated in public, ran mixed bathing houses, entertained dog fighting, performed transvestism, sold erotic prints, and held mixed sumo wrestling were all subject to punishment (figure 5.2.).[24] The ordinance became effective in other prefectures in 1875 and in Osaka in 1877. In December 1873, the Tokyo government began a concerted effort to raze entertainment spaces in Asakusa and Ryōgoku, building modern facilities, such as the office of telegraphic communication in their place, and evicting entertainers from the areas.[25] In 1877, performances of burlesque, impression, and storytelling were banned by the Tokyo government as promoting disorderly and disgraceful comportment.[26] These draconian policies did not eradicate entertainers from the squares and street corners of Tokyo: they remained visible and popular throughout the city until the Meiji government resorted in 1891 to the Ordinance of Security (*hoan jōrei* 保安条例), which was originally targeted at popular rights activists, as a rationale for ousting street entertainers, such as acrobats, storytellers, singers, and dancers. They were rounded up and moved to the sixth district of Asakusa in the same year.[27]

The Meiji state based these laws and ordinances on three major assumptions: first, there were intrinsic connections between popular entertainments and "ignorant people's immoral and lascivious tendencies"; second, these connections must be broken in order to spread values of modern civilization and encourage ordinary people to embrace them; and third, the entertainments should be allowed to exist only if they contributed to "promotion of the distinction of good and evil."[28] The government continued its efforts to regulate popular culture on the basis of these assumptions until, in the 1880s, it increasingly turned to a compulsory education system as a mechanism for disciplining and edifying the public.

A New Modality of Power, A New Subject

While it may seem as if the new government had inherited its predecessor's conviction that successful governance must rest on the effective containment of the body (*kakomu* 囲む), early Meiji politics in fact marked a radical departure from Tokugawa politics in that it rejected a negative conception of the body as indocile. As exemplified by the notion of reforming (*kairyō* 改良 or *kyōsei* 矯正) popular customs, the Meiji government adopted the logic of improving or reshaping—but not containing—the body. The notion of containment implied that Tokugawa elites saw the body as the target of regulation precisely because they recognized the body as possessing its own agency, or an untamable power, not only independent of but also subversive to the power of mind or reason. However, the Meiji notion of reform implied that the new leaders took the body as a site for "transmutation through indoctrination" (*kyōka* 教化) because they saw the body as a constitutive part of a universal and uniform value system. The Meiji view of the body signaled the birth of a new modality of power, a power that operated by drawing corporeal agency into a new conception of human interiority, which Meiji leaders called the "ethos of civilization" (*bunmei no seishin* 文明の精神).

Hence, during the early Meiji period, the mind-body relation was radically reconfigured. If the Tokugawa conception of the relation can be understood as metaphorical (as it was never assumed to be identical, but disjointed and conflictive), the Meiji state transformed it into a synecdochical relation, rendering the body into part of the progressive ethos of a civilized nation. Through this new configuration, every individual's appearance and behavior became a symbol of "national character" (*kokufū* 国風).[29] The body was no longer seen as the site where desire engendered by heterogeneous social formations and relations incessantly generated excessive energies that deranged the power of mind. Rather, it became an empty homogeneous form to be permeated by the positive values of the civilized nation. This synecdochic rendering—and the negation of corporeal agency—was consistent with early Meiji Japan's liberal view of egalitarianism in that it posited the body as invariably capable of expressing the progressive ethos of the nation. The Tokugawa state never assumed such universal and uniform predisposition of the body. In fact, it regulated the body precisely because it recognized its contingent and divergent proclivity. And, on the basis of this premise, it built and maintained the regime of difference in the form of hierarchy. Sumptuary laws were implemented only to police and contain commoners' excessive transgressions of difference with conspicuous display of play and pleasure and violations of moral codes. Street entertainers and poor commoners were never forced to take on homogeneous dispositions, nor were they demanded to ameliorate their comportment even though their "lowly" or "vulgar" appearance and conduct were occasionally objects of scorn and reproach by many elites. Meiji Japan's decision to abolish status hierarchies and adopt liberalism completely altered the Tokugawa politics of difference. The principles of equality and uniformity began to dictate the politics of the everyday.

It has been argued that this dramatic change in cultural politics during the early Meiji period was brought on by the critical gaze of Western visitors and imperialists who often commented on the practices of ordinary people—including *misemono* sideshows, a man waking half-naked, mixed bathing, travesty, tattooing, and public urination—in Meiji Japan as backward and barbarous.[30] A British journalist, John Black, wrote in his Japanese daily newspaper that

> there are all sorts of misemono-shows in crowded areas like Asakusa and Ryōgoku, and some of them reflect barbarous customs that gravely disturb basic morality. They display the private part of female body, or disabled people, like pleasurable objects. Treating humans like an animal in this way reflects Japan's dreadful culture. The people of civilized nations will surely be disappointed. Since the evil customs cause national humiliation, I am greatly concerned if the civilized people would view Japan in a friendly or disdainful manner.[31]

"In a matter of 3 or 4 days [after I published the article about the misemono]," wrote Black in another article, "all the show tents were wiped out [from the area]. Since then, there has not been a single show in entire Tokyo, which entertains the crowd with unpleasant performances."[32] Merely one month before Black's articles appeared, the Tokyo government issued the ordinance to the major kabuki theaters: "Because nobles and foreigners began to make visits [to kabuki theaters] in recent years, lewd spectacles that embarrass parents and children must be prohibited so that [kabuki] could start to promote edifying stories and win the respect of these new audiences."[33] For a government whose immediate goal was Japan's sovereignty and rapid rise to a respectable status within the global hierarchy of nations, the West's critical and discriminatory gaze was certainly a source of serious concern. With the body standing as a synecdoche of the nation's progress and prestige, the body in popular entertainments and customs appeared as a sign of backwardness and vice to be surmounted, and the state began resolute campaigns to stamp marks of civilization onto the body.

This received theory that identifies the West's gaze as the primary cause of the dramatic changes in Meiji cultural politics is correct to a certain degree, but it needs to be supplemented by considering the Meiji state's incessant efforts to produce a national subject whose thought and behavior were consistent with the requirements of a capitalist mode of production. The state's declared goals of uprooting "old evil customs" and transforming "ignorant" people into a civilized populace was no less motivated by its program of making people competent and competitive entrepreneurs and workers for capitalist production. In a 1875 report to the new government in which he discussed numerous challenges Japan faced in building modern industries, Ōkubo Toshimichi (1830–78), an architect of Meiji Japan, wrote that Japan's relative economic weakness was largely due to the lack of people's industrious ethos. The urgent task for the state, according to Ōkubo, was to educate common people to rid themselves of idleness and to guide and supervise them as they would work for and persevere in building modern industries. Nobody would be excused from this endeavor, insisted Ōkubo.[34] Ōkubo's conviction reflected the perspective presented in the government's declaration of a universal education program in 1872, discussed earlier in this chapter. The official dictation's pronouncement that "the country's stability, prosperity, and strength depended entirely on the degree to which common people, not select men of intelligence, were civilized," was followed by the claim that a compulsory education was the best means to lead people to renounce "vacuous and uncivilized customs," embrace practical learning, and become industrious.

The government believed, in particular, in shaping youths' mien or comportment for their acquisition of new mental faculties: rational conduct gained through an industrious ethos. Disciplining pupils' behavior thus became a pronounced component of the compulsory education system during the 1870s. In 1873, the Ministry of Education ordained seventeen rules for pupils to follow at home and school. Particularly noteworthy were the directives that encouraged them to (1) develop the habit of getting up early, washing faces and hands, brushing teeth, combing hair, greeting parents respectfully, having a proper breakfast, and remembering to prepare books and pencils; (2) pay respect to teachers every morning; (3) sit and wait quietly for teachers to arrive in the classrooms; (4) remember that teachers are benefactors who provide an opportunity to learn, and therefore do not lose respect and gratitude; (5) enter and exit classrooms and use textbooks with utmost care and respect; (6) be mindful of avoiding rude behavior and being laughed at by peers for such behavior; (7) keep faces and hands always clean; (8) refrain from soiling toilets and clothes in bathrooms; (9) go straight home after school; (10) never neglect learning even though progress is slow, because one will eventually learn as long as one try his/her hardest.[35] Guiding all these directives were three core principles that revealed the state's vision of the desirable modern subject: respect for order, self-discipline, and diligence. The first two were designed to equip students with the abilities to understand and follow a specific tempo or flow of daily life through the mastery of self-control, while the last one required them to learn an attitude of industriousness. The state repeatedly stressed that the ability to pattern one's life in a manner that honored hard work and orderly conduct would bear positive results in academic performance and would eventually lead to success in one's career.[36] Meritocracy—the kernel of the liberal principle of social organization and an ideology that introduced the naturalized concept of self-help and self-responsibility, which, in turn, justified inequalities as the expression of merit—was thus instituted at the level of compulsory education.[37]

The body in this sense became the primary site where the Meiji government sought to inscribe liberal values through disciplinary measures. Even mere appearance mattered to the extent that it must reflect these values. Cleanliness was seen as an expression of one's competence in self-discipline and industriousness, and a polite mien became an emblem of respect for order. The state initiated this new politics of the body from the top down by mobilizing the imperial authorities. The emperor's demonstration of the nation's will and determination to carry out a program of civilization and capitalism not only offered Western powers a vivid impression of a new Japan but also exerted the power to motivate and mobilize his own people to embrace the program. Indeed, the bodies of Emperor and Empress Meiji played a decisive role in leading the reform of popular culture. In 1873, when the Meiji emperor announced that he had a Western-style haircut and urged ordinary men to follow his lead, the Meiji empress also followed suit by ceasing to shave her eyebrows and blacken her teeth.[38] Their lead was effective. By 1880, two-thirds of the men in Tokyo had the Western-style haircut, called "randomly chopped heads" (*zangiri atama* 散切り頭). The figure had reached ninety percent a scant six years later, and by 1889, only the rare eccentric still wore his hair in the old fashion.[39] The women of the court quickly followed the empress's lead, and the new fashion spread downward, taking the better part of a century to reach the last peasant women in the remotest corners of the land. Praising the new appearance of women as epitomizing the values of civilization, a leader of the Meiji Enlightenment movement, Fukuzawa Yukichi, wrote a short story in which he described women who preserved old habits of blackening teeth and shaving eyebrows as "crippled" and as an "embarrassment" for the nation.[40]

A similar initiative came from one of the most influential kabuki managers, Morita Kanaya (1846–97), who had the ambition to make Shintomiza (formerly Moritaza; 1660–1872) a national theater. Echoing the government's calls for theaters capable of promoting positive mores reflecting values of modern civilization, Morita began a movement to "improve" the kabuki in 1873. He wholeheartedly accepted the Meiji leaders' charge that the kabuki performance centered on frivolous and salacious pleasure and their demand that it edify. In 1879, Ichikawa Danjūrō (1838–1903), a leading actor and exponent of improvement at Shintomiza, read a statement on behalf of his fellow actors:

The theater of recent years has drunk up filth and reeked of the coarse and the mean. It has discredited the beautiful principle of rewarding good and chastising evil, it has fallen into mannerisms and distortions, it has been going steadily downhill. Perhaps at no time has the tendency been more marked than now. I, Danjūrō, am deeply grieved by these facts, and in consultation with my colleagues, I have resolved to clean away the decay.[41]

Before many years passed, the Shintomiza's endeavor to raise kabuki to the status of a national art and make it a symbolic center of edification was met with a reward. In 1886, under the leadership of Counselor of the Department of the Interior, Suematsu Kenchō (1855–1920; who studied at Cambridge University and was an ardent admirer of British theaters), Itō Hirobumi, Inoue Kaoru (Minister of Foreign Affairs), Okuma Shigenobu, and Mori Arinori (Minister of Education) joined the group of eminent industrialists and bankers such as Shibusawa to initiate the movement of "Reforming Theaters" (*engekikairyō undō* 演劇改良運動). The movement aimed at "transforming the culture of theaters into an institution that is conducive to promoting the progress of society and cultivation of intelligence," since they found the culture to be "still upholding the obsolete ways of the uncivilized age."[42] "The people of knowledge and intelligence should plan," Suematsu argued, "the reform, and have the theaters imitate those in the West, and implant new ideas of civilization in the minds of women and children."[43] In 1887, this new initiative led to the official decision to have the emperor attend a kabuki performance for the first time in the art form's history. Kanaya was in charge of the arrangements, and Danjūrō headed the cast. The emperor stayed on from morning to midnight to view the performances. He was aloof in his reactions, leaving the remark that he found kabuki unusual. Yet the empress had a different kind of reaction when she had her viewing the next day: she wept so profusely at a play about the murder of a child that Kanaya, alarmed, urged the actors to tone down their performances. The emperor and empress's attendance produced the effect hoped for by both kabuki and the state. For Kanaya, the imperial presence helped efface the kabuki's stigma as "outcast art," allowing it to publically declare the clear break with the past and embellishing it with the badge of respectability, whereas the state completed the interpellation of kabuki by conferring on it membership within the civilizing Japanese nation.

The "reform" of kabuki demanded radical changes in dramaturgical arrangements, especially the representation of the corporeal.[44] Tokugawa kabuki's formalized and stylized representation of facial appearance and choreography was replaced by a more individualistic and subjective mode. As Itō Sei remarks:

> Ichikawa [Danjūrō] was scorned as a poor actor in those days because of his innovative technique. He stopped applying powder to his face in the exaggerated manner of the traditional theater and resuscitated patterns of ordinary speech. Furthermore, rather than employing spectacular acting techniques which involved ridiculously grandiose bodily movements, he struggled to develop expressions that would convey a sense of psychology to the audience. All these efforts were in perfect accordance with the philosophy for the reform of drama developed later by Morita Kanaya. The new intelligentsia of the Meiji period gradually became acclimated to the realist, humanistic appeal of Ichikawa's technique, accepted him, and came to see him as the foremost actor of the day.[45]

Kanaya's view that the representation of the psychological dimension of figures enabled a more realistic and humanistic theater was consistent with the one held by the leaders of the "Reforming Theaters" movement:

> The major repertoire of the theaters is still dominated by feudal remnants and people of civilized worlds never appreciate it. It goes without saying that vengeful ghosts and supernatural happenings must be completely taken out from their performance, but even the depiction of human relationship must not reflect [such feudal values as] unconditional loyalty to one's lord epitomized by the act of ritual suicide. Instead, it should communicate the righteousness of nation's independence epitomized by the men of high purpose [patriotic revolutionaries during the end of the Tokugawa era]. Or, if it comes to the relationship between man and woman, it must avoid the topics like lovers' double suicide and eloping which speak only of the absurdity of lust and physical relations. Instead, it should focus on the grace, beauty and warmth of affective interaction that resonates with the current climate of enlightenment.[46]

Kanaya's and the movement's privileging of insight into human interiority—psychological dimension of a person's feeling and sentiment—as the essential condition for modern theater to be able to communicate universal humanism and modern aesthetic realism would be further underscored by modernist literary critics such as Watsuji Tetsurō in the 1920s. Watsuji characterized the Tokugawa kabuki's mode of stylized representation of the corporeal to be the negation or lack of persona or individuality and saw in this absence vivid imprints of a feudalistic, backward mentality that failed to manifest the complex inner world of the individual psyche.[47] The modernist critique's psychologizing and individuating perspective precisely mirrored the new configuration of the mind-body relation that began to appear during the Meiji period. What this perspective deemed a lack or negation of persona in Tokugawa kabuki's representation of the body functioned, in fact, as an open-ended social text offering a multitude of interpretive and imaginative possibilities and the joy of transcendental change and reincarnation, as described in chapter 4. Depersonalized presentation did not produce identical, archetypal, and monolithic views of the world, as modernist critics charged. Instead, it worked as a "concept,"[48] as Karatani Kōjin so aptly puts it—a sign capable of provoking multilayered and heterogeneous interpretations of the social meanings among its audiences, which were often deviant from and dissonant with established social norms and morals. It was because of the body's potency as a social text in Tokugawa kabuki—its ability to inspire possibilities of diverse and divergent imaginings and signification—that the shogunate never overcame its paranoia about the art's subversive and transgressive potential.

The Meiji kabuki's condemnation of the Tokugawa mode of representation and its voluntary subjection to the requirements of the "civilized" nation were based on an insistence on the primacy of "spirit" (*seishin* 精神) or human interiority (*kokoro* 心) as the locus where modern subjectivity or authentic Self could be identified. As the interior space of individual gained a privileged status as the ontological foundation, the body came to be reconfigured as a pure form, or an empty shell devoid of its contents, that simply reflected that interior space and thus ceased to exist as a social text. Karatani argues that Danjūrō's decision to expose "the naked face" of the kabuki actor by removing the heavy and boldly patterned makeup from his face signified the new conception of the body as an unmediated form of representation.[49]

This reconceptualization of the mind-body relations in aesthetic thinking and production corresponded to the shift in Meiji government policies for molding people into national subjects during the 1880s. During the first decade of the Meiji period, as argued earlier, the government concentrated its efforts on engendering social mobility based on liberal principles. Early Meiji liberal egalitarianism meant a utilitarian idea of freedom and equal opportunity for competition, as egalitarian policies were implemented to create a mass of human capital (*jinzai* 人材)—labor power—for capitalist production. But, as it turned out, the government could not delimit the use of this new egalitarian principle in strictly economic terms. It also inadvertently incited vibrant public debates about political freedom, a democratic constitution, and universal suffrage. Popular rights activists such as Ueki Emori (1857–92) openly challenged the Meiji government for being despotic, called for the immediate establishment of a parliamentary system, and demanded a constitution that guaranteed the popular right to revolt against tyrants. In this political climate, diverse and competing meanings of a civilized ethos arose in the public sphere. For the government, it meant Japan's mental aptitudes to achieve political, economic, scientific, and military parity with the Western industrial powers, whereas leading intellectuals such as Fukuzawa saw the ethos as people's internal drive to seek innovation and new knowledge for the independence of the country. And for thinkers like Ueki and Nakae Chōmin (1847–1901), a leading theoretician of the popular rights movement, the ethos meant a critical, independent, and democratic spirit for individual freedom.

Faced with this overdetermined political landscape originating from the aporia of liberalism, the Meiji state remained highly inconsistent in its policies, if not in its ideological goals. Its commitment to building a strong and competitive nation based on patriotism and capitalism remained unchanged, but the strategic approach to this objective varied from time to time. The 1880s were exemplary of such inconsistent maneuverings. In 1880, a new ordinance called the Order of Educational Reform (*kaisei kyoikurei* 改正教育令) was issued to deemphasize Enlightenment values, counter the popular rights movement, and legitimate the state's total control of education.[50] The government moved swiftly to ban nearly one-quarter of the textbooks in use at the primary school level for their critical assessment of monarchy, government, and officials, as well as their favorable description of constitutional government, people's freedom and sovereignty, and rightful resistance against corrupt politics. A year later, the government officially announced in the name of the emperor that education would be devoted to the restoration of traditional moralities such as loyalty, filial piety, and compassion, which were deemed endangered by the rapid pace of westernization, while school curriculums were nationalized and every school textbook became subject to state censorship and authorization. The moral education class (*shūshin kyōiku* 修身教育) topped the list of required subjects, with its central tenet resuscitating and exalting the Confucian ethics of filial piety and loyalty. Filial piety was especially emphasized as the moral foundation of the nation. Students were taught to revere and serve the emperor just as they would their parents. The Western history class became secondary, while Japanese history rose to top priority. In 1882, all school teachers received governmental instruction through their principals that they must be aware of the role of education in "awakening patriotic sentiments and fostering reverence and loyalty to the Emperor" among pupils.[51]

However, the state's drive for the aggressive indoctrination of interiority did not last for long. In 1886, Minister of Education Mori Arinori (1847–89), one of the founders of the Meiji Six Society, which promoted the cause of liberal education, announced that education must return to a more liberal principle. Mori's advocacy of reviving liberal education came from the observation that overly disciplinary education would be counter to the state's goal of building a unified and strong nation. First, Mori wrote, teaching students to imagine their relations with the distant, divine emperor in terms of the filial piety and loyalty that were usually reserved for their own parents might be perceived as an imposition; second, because Japan was still an infant capitalist nation and needed more self-motivated, enthusiastic, and talented youths to advance the welfare of the nation, education must function as a way to nurture and assist these youths. In the same year, Mori announced a new educational policy that loosened state control of education, gave teachers rights to manage their own schools, and abolished the moral education class. This drastic shift in educational policy did not mean, however, that the Meiji government totally abandoned the cultivation of certain moral values under Mori's leadership. Mori embarked in 1886 on a series of official visitations to a number of cities, towns, and villages to deliver lectures on what he called three cardinal principles of education: deference (*jūjun* 従順), fraternity (*yūai* 友愛), and dignity (*igi* 威儀). It is clear that Mori wanted to replace the Confucian moral concept of "loyalty" with deference, and "filial piety" with fraternity, while reclaiming the value of self-respect or dignity privileged during the early 1870s as part of the liberal ideology. The reintroduction of liberal values was intended to deemphasize the feudalistic formulations of morality, yet it also sought to create national unity and harmony without completely invalidating the relevance of authority and hierarchy. In elaborating on deference, for example, Mori evoked the importance of carrying out orders from above as a way to contribute to the stability and unity of the nation.[52]

The dramatic oscillation of educational policy during the 1880s revealed the lack of consensus and consistency in the state's strategies for building a wealthy and strong nation. In fact, even after the promulgation of the Imperial Constitution in 1889 which placed a heavy weight on the duty of imperial subjects far more than on their rights, there continued the intense public debates over how to reform people's custom and culture into a more civilized one. In July 1891, an anonymous columnist of Yomiuri newspaper expressed the opinion that "there is no noticeable difference between the deplorably confused and degenerate state of popular customs and culture of the feudal period and that of the present days" and that "a cohesive and punitive measure of carrying out the reforms through the police authorities has proven far less effective than using compulsory education for inculcating people with more civilized manners and values."[53] The author emphasized that the state power—policing and severe punishment—should be used to discipline the populace only when there were violent riots and disturbances, and education was the best approach to motivating people to understand the new ways of life. In July 1899, the same paper reported that the government's continued failure to eliminate various popular entertainments that displayed immoral dispositions led the government to consider implementing severe punishments against the violators of the law.[54] Despite all these divergences and oscillations in opinions and policies, there was one common ideological premise on which the Meiji state and leading intellectuals envisioned and carried out the formation of a new subject: human interiority was where power could and should effect an individual's fundamental transformation into a desirable national-capitalist subject. This alone signaled a radical epistemic and ontological shift from Tokugawa to Meiji Japan.

This exclusive focus on the interior space of a person as the principal site for modern subject formation was symptomatic of the advent of the new conception of the social brought about by the nation-form and modern capitalism. It posited a person as the individual monad, an alienated and isolated entity responsible for its own destiny, which made up the most rudimentary unit of society. The social came to be theorized as a relationship between these atomized individuals and thus society as their aggregation. For instance, Natsume Sōseki's (1867–1916) advocacy of individualism or the "Ego" as the inevitable, yet tragic, consequence of the modern required precisely the category of the individual monad—a symptomatic figure of the modern, which was imaginable only in relation to the problematic of the nation and capitalism.[55] Individualism worked, for Sōseki, both as the basis for person's conscience and independence from the unwarranted requirement of the state and the disproportionate temptation of money (capitalism) and as the basis for solitude and anxiety as an atomized being. As Fredric Jameson points out in his discussion of Munch's *Scream*, this figure in the painting, while enjoying "freedom" and one's own will, "has to pay the heavy price for the precondition of autonomous self which dramatizes the unhappy paradox that when it constitutes its individual subjectivity as a self-sufficient field and a closed realm, it thereby shuts itself off from everything else and condemn itself to the mindless solitude of the monad, buried alone and confined to a prison cell of without egress."[56] This quintessential form of bourgeois ego, or monad, was the image of anomie of the autonomous subject overridden by anxiety and "loneliness" that Sōseki saw as "the price [people] have to pay for being born in this modern age, so full of freedom, independence, and our own egotistical selves."[57] Sōseki has been thus celebrated by the scholars of modern Japanese literature as the true champion, a modern thinker and writer who recognized and grappled with the irresolvable tensions between self and society, as well as individual and the state. However, this dichotomy belies the deeper problematic of the formation of modern subject, into which Sōseki himself was deeply subsumed, within the schema of the cofiguration of the nation and capitalism. It was via the premise of the autonomous, "fee-willed" individual that the state could successfully forge an alliance with bourgeois society in materializing the "vitality" of capitalist production and in articulating the vitality as the prerequisite for the survival of the nation. In this way, the state could carefully steer the excesses of individualism (i.e., egotism), an inseparable component of bourgeois society, which would potentially result in conflicts and contradictions with society. In his speech *My Individualism* (1914), Sōseki proposed the importance of symbiotic relationship between the individual and the state while reiterating the importance of individual's autonomy:

> Japan is not a country that is about to collapse. Nor is it at all threatened by annihilation. Therefore, it is not necessary for us to go around making a noise about it and chanting "The country, the country!" This is like running about town in fire-proof clothing and being uncomfortable when there is no fire. When all is said and done, it is a matter of degree. If war comes or if the country falls into crisis, people whose mental faculties allow them to think, those who have created for themselves, through education and culture, a personality that obliges them to think, naturally direct their attention to the national situation. Then they put all their efforts into working for the good of the country, if necessary restricting their individual freedom and reducing their personal activities. We see here no more than simple operation of natural laws. This is why I firmly believe that the two ideologies are not in any way involved in a conflictory process, in which they would contradict each other and engage in mortal combat.[58]

Sōseki's theory of the harmonious coexistence of the state and the individual is far more efficacious than a theory of statist or autocratic rule in supplying an intellectual ground for a hegemonic politics—rule based on consent rather than coercion. It foregrounded the logic of inculcating people with an idea of "freedom" in terms of voluntary participation in national affairs by establishing the *natural* link between a civilized personality and his/her ability to think, direct attention to the national affairs, and limit his/her freedom for the sake of the country when a palpable threat to the nation was felt. This symbiotism of individual freedom and responsibility for the nation offered the much-needed articulation of hegemonic politics. The alliance between the state and society became a defining characteristic of late Meiji and Taishō politics as Carol Gluck has shown in her analysis of Meiji ideology.[59] Therefore, Sōseki's figure of individual monad was not that of resistance par excellence, as has been argued by many, but was in fact one of the most salient symptoms of an emergent capitalist social order under the modern state, which many Meiji political leaders and intellectuals worked hard to install from the beginning of the era.

Conclusion

In *Origins of Modern Japanese Literature*, Karatani Kōjin portrays the emergence of the new form of literary representation called *genbun itchi* (言文一致, a phonetic system of writing) in the late Meiji period as the point when the phonetic came to be privileged over the scriptural as the system of writing capable of expressing the inner world of the individual.[60] This new literary realism—"phonocentrism"—is significant, argues Karatani, for it marked the ascension of the modern subject or subjectivity through its announcement of interiority as the ontological basis of "true self." In Karatani's own words:

> The illusion that there is something like a "true self" has taken deep root. It is an illusion that is established when writing has come to be seen as derivative and that voice which is most immediate to the self, and which constitutes self-consciousness, is privileged. The psychological person, who begins and ends in interiority, has come into existence.[61]

Karatani goes on to argue that the valorization of voice as the direct reflection of human interiority gave birth to the new form of ideology that reified the transparent and the immediate over the heterogeneous, while repressing script as a form that refracted the former, thus consigning "modes of expression in which thought [was] recorded through radial structures" to oblivion.[62]

My analysis of modern subject formation presented above corresponds roughly to Karatani's critical analysis of phonocentrism in late Meiji

Japan. But because my approach situates this problematic in a broader social, economic, and cultural process, it diverges from Karatani's claim that "far more than readily apparent introduction of modern science or the systems of the modern state, it was *genbun itchi* that had profound implications for Meiji Japan."[63] As a result, it also questions his somewhat limited observation that it was this literary form that brought "interiority" into being. The profound implications of the emergence of the modern subject in Meiji Japan can be properly gauged, I argue, when the analysis of the state, especially its strategies of producing a new modality of power or the new grid of power, is taken into account. The literary discourse on interiority constituted only one aspect of the larger process of what Louis Althusser calls interpellation.[64] A more holistic understanding of this process is necessary.

Just as phonocentrism worked as a catalyst for the birth of the modern conception of human interiority, the early Meiji state's preoccupation with reforms of the corporeal was indissolubly correlated to the discovery of the primacy of the universal ethos. The real significance of the state's reforms lay in the fact that the desire to reform the body according to the conception of the universal ethos indicated the body's fall into a status derivative of interiority, the loss of its singular potency of offering a vast array of surplus and heterogeneous meanings and imaginations. The fact that the body occupied the central place in the politics of subject formation from 1868 to the 1880s did not imply that early Meiji politics replicated its predecessor. The Tokugawa modality of power had been designed to purge opportunities for social mobility—an overwhelming surge of divergent modes of existence, identity, and subject position—by regulating desire expressed through and by the body, whereas Meiji Japan sought to decouple desire from the body and rendered it, via the production of "the individual" as the rudimental unit of society, into the new conception of mental attitude—ambitious and competitive drive for success—so as to mobilize it for nation-building and capitalist production. This new orientation of desire firmly grounded liberalism as the ideological framework that shaped a particular kind of human interiority—civilizing and civilized ethos—and subjectivity exemplifying that ethos. Intense and extensive debates over the content of the ethos of civilization erupted during the 1870s, drawing in the Meiji oligarchs, leading intellectuals, and popular rights activists. Unable to command an authoritative definition of what constituted the ideal mind-set of a modern subject, the Meiji state found itself oscillating between a liberal and a traditionalist notion of ethos during the 1880s. The capitalist mode of production clearly demanded a much more flexible and free flow of population, as well as a new type of competitive and industrious behavior—what Michel Foucault calls *homo œconomicus*—to create a vibrant labor market and spur the much-needed accumulation of capital for industrialization.[65] Consequently, even though the state was concerned about the so-called excesses of liberalism represented by the popular rights movement or the rise of "egotistic" individualism, it could not afford to do away entirely with its liberal ideological line. The state recognized that its objective of building a unified, strong nation could not be achieved without industrious and entrepreneurial individuals who would push capitalist development forward of their own *free* wills. It was precisely for this reason that, despite its oscillation between a liberal and a traditionalist position, the Meiji state consistently devoted itself to the cultivation and promotion of competitive behavior as a matter of human nature through compulsory education. "Competition" was brought into being during the early Meiji period as "an historical objective of governmental art," and its natural appearance was actually an effect of that art.[66] "*Homo œconomicus*" was thus born and became "the interface of government and the individual."[67]

In this regard, the early Meiji body politics, especially the elementary school's directives for pupils' self-discipline in the matter of industriousness, cleanliness, and hygiene as the essential prerequisite for becoming the desirable (competitive, productive, and patriotic) national subject, can be seen as the prefiguration of what Giorgio Agamben calls "the production of biopolitical body."[68] One of the earliest discussions of the link between nation-building and creation of a person's physical health and strength can be found in one of Fukuzawa Yukichi's writings (1878). Asserting that "vital spirit resides in the healthy body"—"*kattatsu na seishin wa kenkōnaru shintai ni atte yadosu*" (闊達な精神は健康なる身体にあって宿す)—Fukuzawa established the necessary correlation between the "nurturing of individuals' health" (*yōjō*) and the nation's progress and independence.[69] Whether through leisurely sports or hard labor, Fukuzawa averted, one "should sweat by spending one or two hours using the body every day" so that "it strengthens muscle and nurtures the spirit necessary for times of war."[70] The new ideology that commenced the mental or spiritual tie between person's life and politics through corporeal discipline would be implemented in a fuller scale from the late Meiji onward with the introduction of an amalgam of new technologies of subject formation, such as physical education, social reform, psychology, psychiatry, and national health. The realm of life would be made more deeply intertwined with the governmental affairs by the state whose ultimate objective was to produce a population equipped with physical, mental, and emotional capacity to function as the motor force for national capitalist development. That capacity called for the people to acquire both mental and bodily discipline in a way that they learned to become conscious of their existence no longer as the object but as the subject of country's destiny. Cultivating one's ability to voluntarily identify with the rise and fall of the country to a degree that one would operate within a zone of complete inseparability between his/her life and the politics of the country was exactly the effect that only liberalism—a national(list) liberalism propounded by people like Fukuzawa—could promise and deliver. Liberals such as Fukuzawa, Nishi, and Sōseki were far more effectual than statists such as Katō and Nishiyama in naturalizing and disseminating the secret tie uniting the politics and life through the advocacy of individualism and patriotic identification and voluntarism.[71]

This articulation of the relations between life and politics would supply from the 1890s on a new epistemology and language of biological fitness for Japan's capitalist imperial development and colonial conquest of its neighboring societies. This topic exceeds the scope of the study under discussion, but it is worthwhile probing it in some length. The theory of the civilizational hierarchies of the world contained within it the assumption that race or ethnicity was the given rudimental unit and substantive reality constituting the heart of national community. Because the theory was in itself an already racialized discourse, the formation of nation impelled by the theory was also a racialized practice. The Meiji leaders' wholehearted embrace of the assumption as the new ideological framework for the country's transformation propelled them into the project of forging the imaginary unity called Japanese (racialized and ethnicized "people") through various state apparatuses and policies, including the reform of popular culture and custom, as the subject of national-capitalist development. The concerted push, albeit inconsistently, for a speedy construction of a modern nation mirrored the leaders' acute concern and anxiety about the real possibility of falling short of the universal standards of civilization, outlined by the Western imperialist nations, and tumbling down the path of extinction or enslavement by the nations. It suffices to recall Fukuzawa's and Ito's mantra that the striving toward a civilized Japan was an absolutely necessary means for securing the country's independence and achieving the equilibrium with the Western counterparts.

However, acting on the recognition of racial stratification of the world was not simply a matter of escaping or internalizing discriminatory perception or an attitude of disdain for another social group as defined by genetic criteria or by cultural criteria. Disdain and discrimination were probably ancillary to what defined the practice of racism in the operational schema of national capitalism. They were the surface phenomena of the racism's deeper presupposition of mental aptitude seen as determined by genetic criteria. What Meiji leaders called the "ethos of civilization" was simply another way of expressing this premise. And their concerns with popular custom and culture—sphere of the body—originated from the notion that culture or custom was a religious, historical, and linguistic pattern formed by the level of mental aptitude—the strength of mind and intelligence—of the nation. The concept of mental fitness or aptitude required of civilization became the absolute ideological fulcrum for imperial Japan to build the relations of colonial domination in East Asia.

The Ainu people, who inhabited the island of Ezo (renamed as Hokkaido in 1869 by the government), became the first experimental ground for imperial Japan to put this logic into practice and launch the project of modern colonialism. The first policy toward the Ainu was the "reform" of their custom and culture, which was implemented in 1871 exactly at the time it was also applied to the people on Japan's main island. It banned the tattooing of female infants and piercing of men's ears, both of which carried important religious and symbolic meanings for the Ainu for many centuries. In 1876, the government became more determined to enforce the policy by imposing stricter measures of punishment. Defining Ainu's customs of tattooing and piercing as the "one to be cleansed" for "these ill customs will inhibit their path to enlightenment and baffle their will to become enlightened people," the government called for a need of "educating" them in a way that would help them "enter the way of humanity."[72] There was a profound irony, which was shared by all late imperial powers, in this universal conception of "humanity." The Meiji state itself was troubled by and learning hard how to implement and enforce this universalism against its own people in order to elevate the country to the rank of the universalism while behaving in its assumed superiority toward the Ainu as if the country represented the rank. How this dual enactment of inferiority and superiority in face of universal humanity transmuted into a much more racially affirmative and hierarchal bifurcation of the Japanese-and-their others, as well as how the transmutation was intertwined with the advent of capitalist project, require a separate and more extensive treatment.[73] It suffices to say here that the force of universal humanity that dictated the reforms of people both on the mainland and Ezo/Hokkaido would congeal into the amalgamate of sharper bifurcations of developed/undeveloped, progressive/primitive, and rising/vanishing ethnicities. And the process of bifurcated ethnicization precipitated the process of expropriation of Ainu's rights to their basic means of subsistence—fishing, hunting, land, and modes of social life. The forced transformation of the Ainu ("Ainu" meaning "humans" in Ainu language) into the derogatory name "natives" (*dojin* 土人), as expressed officially in Hokkaido Former Natives Protection Law in 1899, happened simultaneously with the government policy that forced them to abandon their long-established means of subsistence—fishing and hunting—and become farmers instead under the name of protection. The government's introduction of the Regulation for the Sale of Hokkaido Land (1886) and the Law for the Disposal of Undeveloped Land in Hokkaido (1897), which worked as the legal lynchpins that enabled the Japanese systematic expropriation of Ainu lands, played the decisive role in consolidating the relations of colonial domination.[74]

That racial classifications according to the scale of mental aptitude emerged in conjunction with the programs of nation-state building was no coincidence at all. Racial rerendering of the heterogeneity of history into the hierarchical division between national and "tribal" communities marked the rise of the new regime of power that "projected historical and social differences into the realm of an imaginary nature."[75] This regime differed from Meiji's predecessor in that it articulated the naturalized concept of historical and social differences as biologically determined rather than cosmologically ordained. Racial classifications and hierarchies were "operations of naturalization *par excellence*."[76]

Clearly, the biological conception of difference served the capitalist organization of hierarchy or unevenness in socioeconomic relation (class) from which capitalist production derived its energies and profit. Although the right to "free" competition was granted to Japanese subjects, racialized social minorities such as the Ainu were given a limited right as a full member of imperial Japan and yet as a permanently inferior existence within the hierarchies of biological aptitude. This dual status of Ainu meant a limit to their rights to "freedom" to compete and become independent at the same level with Japanese subjects in light of their putative lack of the civilized and civilizing ethos. Pure competition posited in the liberal theory was therefore nothing but an imaginary construct that hid massive social, economic, and cultural inequalities. If class hierarchy was justified by its meritocratic assumption that it was a natural expression of merit, or an inevitable consequence of free competition among equal individuals, biological determination of racial hierarchy constituted an exception to this assumed pure competition of liberalism. Ainu were included in the national capitalist operation as a social existence excluded from its competitive mechanism. This aporia of national capitalism enabled the state and capitalists to expropriate their land or resources and keep them afloat to mobilize and exploit their labor to a maximum degree. It was this mechanism of inclusion through exception or exclusion that made possible the normal operation of capitalist free competition under the Japanese imperial rule. In this regard, the universalism of liberal humanism represented by meritocracy was not contradictory or a challenge to the particularism of racism. The modern capitalist state pursued the doctrine of meritocracy and racism simultaneously as the secret mechanism of mutual supplement, in the same way that it pursued liberalism and traditionalism. Liberalism's universal principle—competition based on equality—made the commodification of social relation, especially labor, possible. Yet, inherent inequality in terms of wage for the creation of surplus value and thus the accumulation of capital necessitates "fictive ethnicity," as Balibar puts it.[77] The early Meiji body politics toward the Ainu prefigured the coming of this new modality of power.

However, the new modality of power that linked life and politics remained highly rudimental and fragmentary in the early Meiji. The government's primary goal was still focused on how to establish the firm foundation of sovereign power itself (i.e., to create the strong center through which men and women's energies and natural resources could be mobilized for the objective of nation-state building through patriotic sentiment and imaginaries). This is evident in the fact that in order to deal with the irresolvable ambiguity or aporia inherent in liberalism, which reached its peak in the overdetermined political landscape of the 1880s, the Meiji government resorted aggressively to a more reactionary traditionalist rhetoric from 1889 on by promulgating the Imperial Constitution and the Rescript on Education a year later. In these documents, the emperor figured as the divine sovereign representing the unbroken continuity of the Japanese nation from a mythical time to the present, as embodied in the emperor's portrait in figure 5.3, while people's duties to the emperor were accentuated in a deliberately archaic tone. The virtues of loyalty and filial piety were defined as the nation's spiritual tradition passed down from ancient times. Societal harmony was valorized as an age-old Japanese moral characteristic. Using rhetoric that represented human interiority as a unitary ethnic ethos, the government sought to contain and overcome the excesses of liberalism—and capitalist production—that appeared to be hindering its drive to produce a unified nation.

Yet, by the early twentieth century, these moral imperatives articulated in the traditionalist rhetoric faced their own limitations and thus sought to reassert their viability as a response to increasing social unrests and fragmentations caused by consequences of the full-fledged development

5.3 Artist unknown, *True Portrait of His Majesty, the Commander-in-Chief* (*Daigenshi heika goshin'ei*), about 1889. Lithograph based on a drawing by Edoardo Chiossone and mounted as a hanging scroll; ink, silver and bronze printing (photograph © 2013 Museum of Fine Arts, Boston). This lithograph establishes Emperor Meiji as a direct descendant of the mythical first emperor of "Japan," Jinmu, an heir of the sun goddess, Amaterasu.

5.4 Kobayashi Kiyochika (1847–1915), *Hurrah for Japan! The Victory Song of Pyongyang* (*Nihon banzai, Heijō no gaika*), October 1894. Woodblock print, ink and color on paper. (Photograph © 2013 Museum of Fine Arts, Boston)

of capitalism, such as rural and urban poverty, huge wealth differentials, and relentless exploitation of the working class and colonized people, as well as a new mass culture of possessive individualism exemplified by the emergence of nouveaux riches and an urban middle class immersed in the material pleasure of consumer society.

Japan's imperialist wars with China (1894–95) and Russia (1904–5) and colonial expansionism into Taiwan (1895) and Korea (1910), both spurred by the same capitalist development, also appeared to intensify societal division, rather than solidarity, as experiences of unprecedented brutality of war and violence of colonial rule were brought back to Japan in the form of news and memoirs. The Meiji government was quick to glorify sacrificial death—as well as belligerence—for the Japanese empire by enshrining the war dead as national heroes. The government made every effort to remind people of the body of self-sacrifice and triumph, rather than the body of hardship and exploitation found under the capitalist-imperialist enterprise. By disseminating soldiers' experiences as inspirational and exemplary tales of heroism and courage, the government turned the cruelty of war and colonial rule into the sublime object of community admiration and desire. Ukiyo-e artists such as Kobayashi Kiyochika (1847–1915) and *nishikie* (錦絵) news media (a precursor of modern newspapers) joined the government's strategies of the "fantasy-construction which serve[d] as a support for [the new] 'reality' itself," in Slavoj Žižek's words.[78] "Hurrah for Japan!" (figure 5.4; *Nihon banzai*;

1894), by Kobayashi, depicting Japanese victory in the Sino-Japanese War, turns horrific scenes of violence into an object of aesthetic joy: indeed, the soldiers' barbarity becomes an ecstatic moment of victory and a symbol of military might and national strength—remarkable achievements of the country's rapid metamorphosis into a modern state. The aestheticization of violence masked "some trauma," an "insupportable, real, impossible kernel" by calling on each and every individual to participate in the clamor of jubilation and thus in the collective fantasy of the sublime—the glory of nation.[79]

Accordingly, politics in Meiji Japan was dominated by the problematic of how to navigate the overdetermined historical situations brought about by the contradictory—complementary *and* discordant—impulses of traditionalist *and* liberalist enterprises. It had to maneuver the contradiction in such a way as to prevent it from threatening the ultimate objective of ensuring the survival of the nation-state through economic and military might. The Meiji state made attempts, be it ideological or practical, to keep the overdetermined realities under control; to do so effectively, it often relied on the rhetoric of such binary epistemologies as modernity versus tradition and West versus (East) Japan. Although these binary pairs appeared to present diametrically opposite value systems, they actually served, to a certain degree, the objectives of ensuring both the unity and the capitalist prosperity of the nation-state. If traditionalist rhetoric was promoted as the way to impede the fragmentation of the nation-state by constructing mythologies of its unchanging unity sustained by an ethos particular to the Japanese ethnos, modernist rhetoric worked to safeguard a free market system to allow for the continued accumulation and circulation of capital that was indispensable to the creation of national wealth. The traditional and the modern kept each other in check so as to prevent the excesses engendered by liberalism and capitalist development from imperiling the power and integrity of the nation-state. The Japanese state's accelerating turn from the end of the nineteenth century to the tropes of the "ancient and timeless virtues"—loyalty and filial piety—of the Japanese nation then should be understood as a testament to the extent to which capitalism infiltrated all aspects of Japanese society and constituted the central, knotty problem of the state project.

It is crucial to understand the Meiji reform of popular culture within the historical contexts summarized above. Only after its decisive break with the Tokugawa view that figured body and mind as substantially autonomous, even antagonistic—a view that gave birth to the conception of the human body as having a dynamic of its own, as the scene of an excess that defied set norms and thus the mind—could the state call on each and every individual to make voluntary sacrifices for it. The Meiji power renounced the nonidentitarian view of the relationship of the body and mind by assigning agency exclusively to the latter. The "ethos" became the focal point in the discourse on a new modern (national capitalist) subject, while the body was assumed to be the unmediated externalization of the "ethos." The body was stripped of its agency, being emasculated through the valorization of interiority, and ceased to function as a "concept" that inspired infinite possibilities of imaginations, interpretations, and praxis.

From the 1890s on, this new configuration of the mind-body relationship was further reinforced by what Karatani calls "the discovery of interiority" discussed above. The Imperial Constitution and the Rescript on Education supplied this synecdochic view of the mind-body relationship with a much more authoritative thrust in that the body was articulated as no more than an object or an instrument to enact "national morality" inscribed in the mind of every individual. Japan's first modern wars with China and later with imperial Russia also played the role in consolidating a morality that glorified voluntary death in the name of emperor as a honorable act preserving the ageless virtues of the Japanese nation.[80] By the early twentieth century, bodily sacrifice was firmly established as the emblem of the highest moral integrity. In schools and homes, Meiji children were taught that "patriotic death was the way to achieve the immortality of soul."[81] Meiji Japan's transformations from its immediate past were indeed fast and profound, as many have pointed out. But the degree of these transformations can be properly gauged only by considering the fact that common people—who had never before been called on to die and kill for rulers, governments, or domains—were suddenly expected to offer voluntarily their very lives as a matter of moral and ontological imperative. That the radical reconfiguration of mind-body relations underwrote this dramatic shift reveals the disquieting implications of the discovery of interiority and the politics of modern subject formation.

Notes

INTRODUCTION

1. Frederic Jameson, *The Prison-House of Language: A Critical Account of Structuralism and Russian Formalism* (Princeton: Princeton University Press, 1972), 14.
2. Here I am not positing the dichotomy between history and theory in a way that positivistic empiricists often do. I agree with the new historicist assertion that any "primary" documents are always already mediated by a certain mode of conceptual and interpretive operation that existed at the time when they were written, and in this sense there is no pre-interpretive or pre-discursive document that reveals the past as it was. The reason I would like to recognize the difference between history and theory is then that I consider the extremely fragmentary and accidental nature of the former as inassimilable and thus open-ended to *our own* interpretive/theoretical intervention. Thus, I understand interpretation as necessarily a conceptual and theoretical activity, and historical interpretation as that of interpretation performed by actors of the past that I am addressing. Our own reading of the past then must probe premises and assumptions that informed and regulated the mode of the interpretation that existed in the past. But it also means that a self-reflexive engagement with our own premises and assumptions is essential. Since premises and assumptions traverse both conscious and unconscious realms, the critical examination of an ideology of the past, by which "documents" were shaped, *and* an ideology of the present, in which we are inescapably embedded, constitutes an integral component of our interpretive practice. Historical interpretation requires the simultaneous operation of both inquiries not to integrate

the past and the present into a unity to achieve a "true" understanding of the time and place that historians are investigating but to keep them in a critical tension so as to probe the historical conditions of the present and a potentiality of the future. Therefore, my interpretive approach differs from Gadamerian hermeneutic in a crucial way. Gadamer sees the ultimate objective of historical study as the realization of what he calls the "fusion of horizon"—overcoming the "prejudice," or the particularity, of the present, which originates from one's being embedded in a tradition, and reaching a higher truth or universality through the mediation of an understanding of the other, the past. The binary of prejudice and truth, particularity and universality, is predicated on the premise about his understanding of the existential condition of human being: there exists a coherent and unitary "tradition" that determines our self-understanding of the world and we demand the possibility of transcendence towards the future via the realization of a pure and authentic (universal) meaning of the past. Gadamer believes that the recovery of a true meaning of the past leads dialectically to the disclosure of authentic self, and thus it is in the fusion of horizon where an authentic understanding of the past and the present can be realized. This desire for authentic understanding or a higher universality through the unity of the past and the present, the other and the self, seems to be a more self-conscious and theoretical re-articulation of an empiricist interpretivist desire for the disclosure of a true meaning of the past, which ultimately serves the creation and reinforcement of an image of history as the continual remaking of a unitary tradition [i.e., national tradition] in the anticipation of the future. By assuming the concept of "tradition" as a given ontological condition, Gadamer and empiricists fail to reckon with the fact that any discursive activities of the past and the present, including the very notion of "tradition," are both the cause and the effect of a certain regime of power and ideology. Gadamer and empiricists' position is in the final analysis to accumulate knowledge for the renewal of the tradition of a nation and therefore perpetuate the legitimacy of the received paradigm of national history, which is in itself a product of modern ideology and power relations (i.e. capitalism, colonialism, and imperialism). See Hans Gadamer, "The Problem of Historical Consciousness," in Paul Rabinow and William M. Sullivan eds., *Interpretive Social Science* (Berkeley: University of California Press, 1987) 82–140.

3. Fredric Jameson, *The Political Unconscious: Narrative as a Socially Symbolic Act* (Ithaca: Cornell University Press, 1981), 97.
4. Those phrases are borrowed from William Sewell's discussion of the concept(s) of culture in his *Logics of History: Social Theory and Social Transformation* (Chicago: University of Chicago Press, 2005), 172. Sewell also argues that it is important to understand "those dispersed everyday acts" in conjunction with powerful institutional nodes where "much cultural practice is concentrated." I take this point as meaning that focusing exclusively on

the dispersed sites of resistance does not help us understand how politics works in culture, whether in the form of domination, normalization, subjectivization, transgression, or resistance, and therefore as calling for a more holistic or structural analysis of cultural politics.

5. M. M. Bakhtin, *The Dialogic Imagination: Four Essays*, trans. Caryl and Michael Holquist (Texas: University of Texas Press, 1981).
6. Louis Althusser, *For Marx* (London: Verso, 2005), 211 and 250. Althusser reformulates Lenin's concept of "weakest link" as "conjunctural moment" to "denote the exact balance of forces, state of overdetermination of the contradictions at any given moment to which political tactics must be applied."
7. Raymond Williams, *Marxism and Literature* (Oxford: University of Oxford Press, 1977), 130.
8. Ibid. 216.
9. Althusser, *For Marx*, 211, 216.
10. My theorization of *sakasama* is largely indebted to Peter Stallybrass and Allon White, *The Politics and Poetics of Transgression* (Ithaca: Cornell University Press, 1986), 56–57.
11. "Gakusei jisshi saimokunitsuki dajoukanshirei," in *Nihon kindai shisō taikei*, ed. Yamazumi Masami, vol. 6, *Kyōiku no taikei* (Tokyo: Iwanami Shoten, 1990), 27 and 31.
12. Ibid., 29 and 31.
13. Althusser, *For Marx*, 116.
14. Ibid.
15. Ibid., 101.
16. Ibid., 102.
17. Ibid., 103. Italics in original.
18. For Maruyama's role in and intellectual contribution to the debate on Japan's modernity, in particular the problem of political subjectivity, see J. Victor Koschmann's *Revolution and Subjectivity in Postwar Japan* (Chicago: University of Chicago Press, 1996), chap. 4.
19. Maruyama wrote in the English version that "in terms of overt political doctrines the two and a half centuries were really a barren, impoverished period. There was not even a trace of the medieval European theory of the *right* of resistance [italics in original], let alone any hint of a social contract theory or notions of popular sovereignty. . . . Right up to the end of the period there was not a trace of any fundamental ideological rejection of the class structure of Tokugawa society itself." See Maruyama Masao, *Studies in The Intellectual History of Tokugawa Japan* (Princeton: Princeton University Press, 1974), xxix.
20. Georg W. F. Hegel, *The Philosophy of History* (New York: Prometheus, 1991), 17.
21. Maruyama, *Intellectual History of Tokugawa Japan*, 126.
22. Ibid., 330.
23. Ibid., 329.

24. Maruyama Masao, "Rekishi ishiki no Kosō," in *Rekishi shisō shū*, ed. Maruyama Masao (Tokyo: Chikuma shobō, 1972).
25. Maruyama Masao, *Thought and Behavior in Modern Japanese Politics* (London: Oxford University Press, 1963), xvi. In clarifying his position, Maruyama says that he was interested in the Hegelian thesis of history as progression toward the consciousness of freedom, but not his theory of the state as the embodiment of Reason. See also Tetsuo Najita, *Doing Shisōshi*, ed. and trans. Katsuya Hirano, Osamu Mihashi, Akifumi Kasai, and Hiroshi Sawada (Tokyo: Misuzu Shobō, 2008), 130–31. He talked about his faith in the universal history of mankind centered on the model of Western European history in his interview with Tsurumi Shunsuke in "Maruyama Masao: Fuhenteki Genri no Tachiba," in Tsurumi Shunsuke, ed., *Kataritsugu sengoshi*, vol. 1 (Tokyo: Shisōno kagakusha, 1969), 93.
26. Hegel, *Philosophy of History*, 25.
27. Harry Harootunian, *The Empire's New Clothes: Paradigm Lost, and Regained* (Chicago: Prickly Paradigm Press, 2004), 3.
28. William C. Dowling, *Jameson, Althusser, Marx: An Introduction to the Political Unconscious* (Ithaca: Cornell University Press, 1984), 48–49.
29. Robert Neelly Bellah, *Tokugawa Religion: The Cultural Roots of Modern Japan* (New York: Macmillan, 1985).
30. Thomas Smith, "Japan's Aristocratic Revolution," in Thomas Smith, *Native Sources of Japanese Industrialization* (Berkeley: University of California Press, 1988), 134.
31. Ibid., 135. Even though Smith did not acknowledge it, the same reasons had been pointed out by Marxist historians such as Noro Eitarō (1900–1934) as early as the late 1920s. See Noro Eitarō, *Nihon shihonshugi hattatsu-shi*, vol. 1 (Tokyo: Iwanami Shoten, 1983).
32. Ibid., 146.
33. Althusser, *For Marx*, 228.
34. Ibid.
35. Ibid., 103. Althusser writes in a phenomenological and deconstructivist manner that "the simplicity of Hegelian contradiction is never more than a reflection of the simplicity of this internal principle of a people [an ethno], that is, not its material reality but its most abstract ideology."
36. Smith, "Japan's Aristocratic Revolution," 136.
37. Ibid., 135.
38. Ibid., 145.
39. It is important to note that Smith seemed to become troubled by his own conclusion in "Japan's Aristocratic Revolution." A few years after he wrote this piece, Smith would attempt to openly distance himself from the scholars of modernization theory (such as Albert Craig and Marius Jansen) and propose a more nuanced and inclusive understanding of the Meiji *Ishin* in "Discontented." Smith calls attention to ordinary people and people at the bottom of the status hierarchy as *active* participants in the dramatic

transformations of late Tokugawa society, contradicting his earlier claims of the aristocratic revolution. See Thomas Smith, *Native Sources of Japanese Industrialization*, 148–55.

40. Tetsuo Najita, "Introduction," in Tetsuo Najita and J. Victor Koschmann, eds., *Conflict in Modern Japanese History: The Neglected Tradition* (Princeton: Princeton University Press, 1982), 5–6.
41. Ibid., 4.
42. Ibid., 9.
43. Ibid., 6.
44. Ibid., 9.
45. Ibid.
46. Ibid., 10.
47. Nam-lin Hur, *Prayers and Play in Late Tokugawa Japan: Asakusa Sensōji and Edo Society* (Cambridge: Harvard University Press, 2000), 192.
48. There are numerous works that belong to this category. To name a few, Konta Yōzō, *Edo no Hon'ya san: Kinsei Bunkashi no Sokumen* (Tokyo: Nihon Hōsō Shuppan Kyōkai, 1976); Yoshiwara Kenichirō, *Rakusho to yū media: Edo minshū no ikari to yūmoa* (Tokyo: Kyōiku Shuppan, 1999); and Minami Kazuo, *Edo no fūshiga* (Tokyo: Yoshikawa Kōbunkan, 1997).
49. Althusser, *For Marx*, 108. I use the concept of "built environment" defined by William Sewell, *Logics of History: Social Theory and Social Transformation* (Chicago: University of Chicago Press, 2005), 362–69.
50. Yasumaru Yoshio, *Nihon no kindaika to minshū shisō* (Tokyo: Heibonsha 1999), 458. See also 12–24, 93–98.
51. Spivak's argument that the nationalist narrative or historiography, which claims to uncover the authentic experiences of marginalized people, is still trapped within the Hegelian paradigm is suggestive for our critical reflection on the Japanese historiography called *people's history* (*minshūshi* 民衆史). I do not regard every work written in the name of *people's history* as a nationa*list* project, but in so far as *people's history* assumes the people to be the given homogeneous entity (ethno) and continues to operate on the premise that there is a way to access directly their "lived experiences," I would argue that it reproduces the national(ist) epistemology as the basis of historical inquiry. See Gayatri Chakravorty Spivak, *A Critique of Postcolonial Reason: Toward a History of the Vanishing Present* (Cambridge: Harvard University Press, 1999), 62–63.
52. Tosaka Jun, *Shisō to fūzoku* (Tokyo: Heibonsha, 2001), 15, 16, 20, and 21.
53. Antonio Gramsci, "The Study of Philosophy," in *Selections from the Prison Notebooks of Antonio Gramsci*, ed. and trans. Quintin Hoare and Geoffrey Nowell-Smith (New York: International Publishers, 1971), 325–33; and Althusser, *For Marx*, 233.
54. Tosaka, *Shisō to fūzoku*, 27 and 28.
55. Althusser, *For Marx*, 99.
56. Ibid., 253.

57. Ibid., 215.
58. Ibid., 205.
59. Ibid., 254–55.
60. Ibid., 147–51.
61. Ibid., 209.
62. Ibid., 232.
63. Ibid., 233. Althusser limits the possibility of this move from the unconscious to the conscious, the exercise of critical faculty, to an intellectual dialectical process from Generality 1, to 2, and to 3. G1 refers to the state of the unconscious in which we are all deeply embedded in ideology, G2 means the intellectual labor through which we come to grasp and historicize the forms of ideology to which we are subject, and G3 is the moment in which the labor transforms those forms into critical knowledge. By calling it "science" as opposed to "ideology," Althusser privileges materialist dialectic as the only intellectual praxis capable of actualizing this process. See Althusser, "Materialist Dialectic," in *For Marx*.
64. Ibid.
65. Ibid., 233–34.
66. Ibid.
67. Terry Eagleton, "Ideology and Its Vicissitudes in Western Marxism," in *Mapping* Ideology, ed. Slavoj Žižek (London: Verso, 1994), 217.
68. Stuart Hall has also made a penetrating critique of Althusser's concept of ideology and overdetermination in "Signification, Representation, Ideology: Althusser and the Post-Structuralist Debates," *Critical Studies in Mass Communication* 2:2 (June 1985): 91–114.
69. V. N. Volosinov, *Marxism and the Philosophy of Language* (Cambridge: Harvard University Press, 1973), 28.
70. Ibid., 22.
71. Ibid., 11, 23.
72. Ibid., 23
73. Ibid.
74. Ibid.
75. Ibid.
76. Raymond Williams, *Marxism and Literature* (Oxford: Oxford University Press, 1977), 130.
77. Ibid., 132.
78. Ibid., 133.
79. Fredric Jameson, *Postmodernism, or, The Cultural Logic of Late Capitalism* (Durham: Duke University Press, 1991).
80. Ibid., xvi.
81. Ibid., 211.
82. Ibid., 47.
83. The perspective, which I have proposed above, is not entirely novel in the field of Tokugawa cultural and intellectual history. Harry Harootunian's

pioneering work on the late Tokugawa culture has been clearly one of the greatest inspirations for my historical and theoretical approach to the subject. His works have suggested a possibility of radical rethinking and articulation of the political beyond the Hegelian idealist paradigm by showing the multifarious sites of politics in uneven relations of socioeconomic transformations and divergent articulations refracting those transformations without positing stable and self-conscious political subjects. See his "Cultural Politics in Tokugawa Japan," in *Undercurrents in the Floating World: Censorship and Japanese Prints*, ed. Sarah E. Thompson and Harry Harootunian (New York: Asia Society Galleries, 1991). Eiko Ikegami has also recently written an important work on the history of Edo popular culture. Her *Bonds of Civility* (Cambridge: Cambridge University Press, 2005) pays attention to the material and structural conditions of late Tokugawa society in analyzing the associational pattern of popular cultural practices which were distinct from the official ones. Her narrative, however, relies on the functionalist dichotomy of vertical (official) and horizontal (popular) principles of association to foreground the "subversive" nature of Edo popular culture. By pitting popular culture's horizontal principle against the government's vertical principle, Ikegami tends to present the possibility of subversion as existing almost automatically and everywhere in the former as if horizontality itself guaranteed a radical political potential. My argument differs from her position in three ways. First, I see the intensification of contradictions of the dominant structures and the rise of diverse articulations of those contradictions, which were manifested in divergent identities, subject positions, and ways of life condemned by the state and intellectuals as "idle," as the ground for the political. Second, I do not think that societal tensions and contradictions in the late Tokugawa period can be defined in terms of the clash between vertical and horizontal principles of associational pattern. In this respect, cultural practice of subversion is secondary to the politics that emerged from the culture's efficacy of representing the overdetermined social reality. Finally, I see the form, dynamics, and effects of what I call dialogical hybridization and contestation of different ideological signs, voices, and perspectives as the primary arena where Tokugawa society's contradictions were most forcefully articulated. This form is not necessarily subversive in itself. Rather it should be seen as the symptom of the dissolution of the assumed unity of the Tokugawa social order and was therefore an effect and catalyst of conjunctural moment.

CHAPTER ONE

1. Miura Jōshin, *Keichō kenmonshū* (Tokyo: Shinjinbutsu Oraisha, 1969), 197–202.
2. Gunji Masakatsu, *Kabuki hasseishi ronshū* (Tokyo: Iwanami Gendai Bunko, 2002), 247–52.

3. Masakatsu, *Kabuki hasseishi ronshū*, 253–77; and Miura Jōshin, *Keicho kenmonshū*, 197–202.
4. Amino Yoshihiko, *Chūsei no hinin to yūjo* (Tokyo: Akashi Shoten, 1994), 190–95; Nam-lin Hur, *Prayer and Play in Late Tokugawa Japan: Asakusa Sensōji and Edo Society* (Cambridge: Harvard University Asia Center, 2000), 88.
5. Tokyo Daigaku, *Dai Nihon kinsei shiryō: Shichū torishimari ruishū*, vol 1 (Tokyo: Tokyo Daigaku Shuppan, 1959), 68 and 435–36.
6. My views correspond to Harry Harootunian's observation that "Late Tokugawa culture and practice seemed to converge upon the body . . . Despite the variety of forms of verbal fiction that proliferated in the late eighteenth century to meet the rapid diversification of tastes, pleasures, and demands for greater "consumption," the content of playful culture invariably focused on the activities of the body." See Harry Harootunian, "Late Tokugawa Culture and Thought," in Marius B. Jansen, John Whitney Hall, Madoka Kanai, and Denis Twitchett, eds.,*The Cambridge History of Japan*, vol. 5 (Cambridge: University of Cambridge, 1989), 173.
7. See Harry Harootunian, *Things Seen and Unseen: Discourse and Ideology in Tokugawa Nativism* (Chicago: University of Chicago Press, 1988); J. Victor Koschmann, *The Mito Ideology: Discourse, Reform, and Insurrection in Late Tokugawa Japan, 1790–1864* (Berkeley: University of California Press, 1987); Maruyama Masao, *Studies in the Intellectual History of Tokugawa Japan* (Princeton: Princeton University Press, 1974); Tetsuo Najita, *Visions of Virtue in Tokugawa Japan: The Kaitokudō Merchant Academy of Osaka* (Chicago: University of Chicago Press, 1987); and Toshinobu Yasunaga, *Ando Shoeki: Social and Ecological Philosopher of Eighteenth Century Japan* (New York: Weatherhill, 1992). The authors mentioned here focus on different intellectuals of the mid- to late eighteenth and the early nineteenth century (except Maruyama) whose voices raised fundamental questions about the ideological premises upon which the Tokugawa shogunate constructed and maintained social order.
8. "Social tattoo" is a phrase used by Herman Ooms in "Forms and Norms in Edo Arts and Society," in *Edo: Art in Japan 1615–1868*, ed., Robert T. Singer (New Haven: Yale University Press, 1998), 26.
9. Ogyū Sorai (1666–1728), an eminent Confucian scholar residing in Edo, observed in 1725 that the blurring distinctions between peasants and merchants were becoming common and called for a reform designed to restore the status order modeled after the system of ancient China. See Ogyū Sorai, *Seidan* (Tokyo: Iwanami Shoten, 1987), 13–14; see also Hiroshi Shimbo and Akira Hasegawa, "The Dynamics of Market Economy and Production," in Akira Hayami, Osamu Saito, and Ronald P. Toby eds., *Emergence of Economic Society in Japan 1600–1859* (Oxford: Oxford University Press, 2004), 183–85.
10. David Howell shows in *Geography of Identity in Nineteenth-Century Japan* (Berkeley: University of California Press, 2005) that the status system was the foundational principle that organized and regulated social, economic,

political, and cultural boundaries in Tokugawa Japan, despite the fact that status was rather a fuzzy concept and status hierarchies were not always strictly observed. Particularly noteworthy is his argument that in the realm of occupation (a particular kind of social function assigned to each individual according to his or her status), not livelihood (the means of subsistence that was often devised by individuals for their personal gains besides their occupations), status was a determining factor in dividing Tokugawa Japan into different social groups and assigning them particular kinds of labor.

11. Yokota Fuyuhiko points out that during the Tokugawa period, the idea of productivity functioned as an organizing principle for configuring the hierarchical order of society, whereas purity had played the same role during medieval times. While I agree with Yokota's recognition of the idea of productivity as key to the shogunate's structuring the status order, he seems to misrecognize or overlook the primary role played by the shogunate's moralistic view of the world in the formation of a view of political economy. People in power regarded production and consumption as essentially a moral issue. See Yokota Fuyuhiko, "Geino, bunka to mibunteki shuhen," in *Mibun o toinaosu*, ed. Kurume Shimahiko, Takano Toshihiko, Tsukada Takashi, et al. (Tokyo: Yoshikawa Kōbunkan, 2000), 29–48.
12. Suzuki Shōzan, *Selected Writings of Suzuki Shozan*, trans. Royall Tyler, Cornell East Asian Papers (Ithaca: China-Japan Program, Cornell University Press, 1977), 26–32.
13. Herman Ooms, *Tokugawa Ideology: Early Constructs, 1570–1680* (Princeton: Princeton University Press, 1989), 139.
14. Suzuki Shōzan, *Selected Writings of Suzuki Shōzan*, 67.
15. Ibid., 71–73.
16. Ibid., 32.
17. Ooms, *Tokugawa Ideology*, 280.
18. Ibid., 275–86.
19. Yoshikawa Kōjiro, "Jinsai, Tōgaigaku," in *Itō Jinsai, Itō Tōgai*, vol. 33, *Nihon shisō taikei*, Yoshikawa Kōjiro, and Shimizu Shigeru, eds. (Tokyo: Iwanami Shoten 1971), 565–621. See also Ooms, *Tokugawa Ideology*, 226.
20. The official dictum of the samurai code called *bunbu ryōdō* (Respecting the two Ways—literary cultivation and martial training) expressed precisely this ideal of disciplining the body by the power of will and intellect. Equal weight placed on literary and martial cultivations in this dictum might lead to the conclusion that the shogunate viewed the body as no less important than the mind, but it must be remembered that the body it privileged was the one that stood for order, discipline, and self-constraint deemed essential for performing the samurai duty, namely, fighting battles. Thus, *bunbu ryōdō* expressed the ideal that both literal and martial activities were guided by the power of mind. Suzuki Shōzan, e.g., often used the phrase "assault both body and mind by the mind itself" or "torment both body and mind by the mind itself" to explicate the way for samurai to attain enlightenment

as a ruler. Here, we can see that Suzuki saw the mind as capable of regulating itself by way of transcendence, whereas he never recognized such a possibility in the body. For Suzuki, what enabled the mind to transcend itself was precisely the power of will and intellect.

21. Suzuki Shōzan, *Selected Writings of Suzuki Shōzan*, 45–60.
22. Yamaga Sokō, "Shidō," in *Sources of the Japanese Tradition*, comp. Ryusaku Tsunoda, William Theodore De Bary, and Donald Keene (New York: Columbia University Press, 1958), 399.
23. Like many Confucian intellectuals during the Tokugawa period, Yamaga Sokō saw the creation of four statuses as that of "natural process," or as a "Heaven's mandate," and identified labor or occupation as an instantiation of status identity. We can see here another instance in which social order came to be reified as a second Nature. See Kurachi Katsunao, *Kinsei no minshū to shihai shisō* (Tokyo: Kashiwa Shobō, 1996), 46–47.
24. Daniel V. Botsman, *Punishment and Power in the Making of Modern Japan* (Princeton: Princeton University Press, 2005), 10.
25. Ibid., 20 and 83.
26. *Chū* (loyalty) and *kō* (duty or filial piety) were often paired and used as an idiom in the official discourse of social values deemed essential for realizing and maintaining proper social relations during the Tokugawa period. The very pairing of these two terms seemed to represent the official view that one's loyalty to superiors could be demonstrated only through the performance of one's duty to the social whole. On sumptuary laws, see Donald H. Shively, "Sumptuary Regulation and Status in Early Tokugawa Japan," in *Harvard Journal of Asiatic Studies* 25 (January 1964): 123–64; and Park Jin-han, "Kinseizenki ni okeru ken'yakurei no zengokutekitenkai to sono tokuchō," *Shirin* 86 (May 2003): 141–59.
27. Botsman uses a materialist approach in a Foucauldian sense, and what I am suggesting by "interrogating the complex relations of the symbolic and the material" is an approach grounded in the marrying of cultural and Marxian materialist analyses. This approach aims to investigate the intertwined relationship between the production of cultural forms, and that of economic and political circuits of power by taking the two as semiautonomous yet mediated by the relations between them. My perspective is largely inspired by Fredric Jameson's critical reworking of Louis Althusser's concept of base and superstructure relations in his attempts to reinvigorate cultural analysis within a materialist epistemology. See Fredric Jameson, *The Political Unconscious: Narrative as a Socially Symbolic Act* (Ithaca: Cornell University Press, 1981), chap. 1.
28. György Lukács, "Reification and the Consciousness of the Proletariat," in *History and Class Consciousness: Studies in Marxist Dialectics* (Cambridge: MIT Press, 1997), 83–222.
29. These are wordings used by William C. Dowling to explain Marx's view of ideology in *The Eighteenth Brumaire*. It is my understanding that Lukács's

theory of ideology as reified consciousness is identical with the formulation put forward by Marx in this work. William C. Dowling, *Jameson, Althusser, Marx* (Ithaca: Cornell University Press, 1984), 53.

30. Jameson, *Political Unconscious*, 54–55.
31. Ibid., 53.
32. Jameson's concept of ideology finds resonance, not dissonance, with poststructural philosophies that repudiate such "totalizations" in the name of difference, flux, dissemination, transgression, or heterogeneity, because these concepts can be articulated only when one recognizes some ideology of unification already in place, which it is the poststructuralists' mission to rebuke and to shatter. I find this formulation of the dialectical relationship between "totality" and "heterogeneity" useful particularly for our understanding of the interplay between power/ideology and urban popular culture during the late Tokugawa period. See Jameson, *Political Unconscious*, 52–54. It should also be noted that the term *heterogeneous* indicates, to follow Georges Bataille's formulation, that "it concerns elements that are impossible to assimilate" or reduce; see Georges Bataille, *Visions of Excess: Selected Writings, 1927–1939* (Minneapolis: University of Minnesota, 1985), 140–41.
33. Ooms, *Tokugawa Ideology*, 91.
34. Herman Ooms, "Neo-Confucianism and the Formation of Early Tokugawa Ideology: Contours of a Problem," in *Confucianism and Tokugawa Culture*, ed. Peter Nosco (Princeton: Princeton University Press, 1984), 57.
35. Herman Ooms, "Forms and Norms in Edo Arts and Society," 29.
36. Ogyū Sorai, *Seidan*, 102.
37. Ibid., 103.
38. Ooms, *Tokugawa Ideology*, 145.
39. Shively, "Sumptuary Regulation and Status in Early Tokugawa Japan," 154.
40. Ibid., 155.
41. Park, "Kinseizenki ni okeru ken'yakurei no zengokutekitenkai to sono tokuchō," 149.
42. Shively, "Sumptuary Regulation and Status in Early Tokugawa Japan," 154.
43. For the term "unproductive expenditure," I draw on Georges Bataille's formulation in "The Notion of Expenditure," in Bataille, *Visions of Excess: Selected Writings, 1927–1939*, 118. Another important essay for my discussion of expenditure, consumption, and waste is Thorstein Velben's "Conspicuous Consumption," in *The Consumer Society* ed. Juliet B. Schor and Douglas B. Holt (New York: New Press, 2000), 187–204.
44. Ooms, *Tokugawa Ideology*, 119–20.
45. Uramoto Yoshifumi, *Edo, Tokyo no hisabetsu buraku no rekishi: Danzaemon to hisabetsu minshū* (Tokyo: Akashi Shoten, 2003), 119–25.
46. For more detailed accounts on the workhouse, see Kato Takashi's excellent essay "Governing Edo," in James L. McClain, John M. Merriman, and Ugawa Kaoru, eds., *Edo and Paris: Urban Life and the State in the Early Modern Era* (Ithaca: Cornell University Press, 1994), 60–61.

47. Takayanagi Shinzō and Ryōsuke Ishii, eds., *Ofuregaki Tenpō Shūsei*, vol. 2 (Tokyo: Iwanami Shoten, 1958), 439.
48. This phenomenon had been already observed by Ogyū Sorai as early as the 1720s. Asked by the shogun's advisors to offer his opinions about the most imminent problems of Tokugawa society and his political prescriptions for them, Sorai submitted the lengthy thesis titled *On Politics* (*Seidan*) in which he warned of the dangerous implications of the rising influence of townspeople and their culture among villagers and even samurai. Buyō Inshi's work, *The Records of Worldly Affairs* (*Sejikenbunroku*), indicated the extent to which the problem discussed by Sorai had evolved almost a century later.
49. Buyō Inshi, *Sejikenbunroku* (Tokyo: Iwanami Shoten, 1994), 281–84. Buyō wrote this treatise in 1816.
50. "Empty formalism" is a phrase used by Herman Ooms to describe the increasingly unsubstantial quality of the Tokugawa state's ideological structure. Ooms, "Forms and Norms in Edo Arts and Society," 35.
51. Ogyū Sorai, Buyō Inshi, and the Tokugawa shōgunate all used these derisive adjectives to refer to the entertainments in the districts. For a detailed account of "misemono" (shows or exhibits) spectacles in Edo, see Andrew L. Markus, "The Carnival of Edo: Misemono Spectacles From Contemporary Accounts," *Harvard Journal of Asiatic Studies* 45:2 (December 1985): 499–541.
52. Hiraga Gennai (1728–79), whom I will discuss later in the chapter, made this astute observation about the market and entertainment district *Ryōgoku* in his uniquely playful way. The rest of his statements can be found in *Rootless Weeds*, trans. Chris Drake, in Haruo Shirane, ed., *Early Modern Japanese Literature* (New York: Columbia University Press, 2002), 474–75. See also Takeuchi Makoto, *Edo no sakariba kō: Asakusa Ryōgoku no sei to zoku* (Tokyo: Kyōiku Shuppan, 2000), 12–14.
53. Mikhail Bakhtin uses the term in *Rabelais and His World* (Bloomington: Indiana University Press, 1984) to demonstrate social dynamics in creating (or imagining) "contact zones" where dialogic (interpenetrating) interactions of high and low unfold. See also Peter Stallybrass and Allon White, *The Politics and Poetics of Transgression* (Ithaca: Cornell University Press, 1987), introduction and chapter 1. My argument differs from the perspective put forward by people such as James Scott that privileges marginality as an essential condition for generating counterculture. This theoretical position posits that marginality in itself guarantees the possibility of the culture of dissent, which, of course, ignores many historical cases demonstrating that marginalized social groups tend to develop an ambiguous, even ambivalent relationship with dominant culture and its norms. James Scott, *Domination and Arts of Resistance: Hidden Transcripts* (New Haven: Yale University Press, 1990).
54. Buyō, *Sejikenbunroku*, 362.

55. Nam-lin Hur, *Prayer and Play in Late Tokugawa Japan: Asakusa Sensōji and Edo Society* (Cambridge: Harvard University Asia Center, 2000), 77–81. Hur offers an interesting account of how the Sensoji temple came to assume the dual function of prayer and play in this book. Sensoji was originally appointed by Tokugawa Ieyasu (1542–1616), the founder of the Tokugawa shōgunate, as its official guardian temple because of its long history and influential stature among the populace in the Edo area. But with the construction of the Kanei temple in 1625 as the new religious center for the Tokugawas, it was made subordinate to this new temple and lost the large bulk of its income, which led it to a decision to lease its land to shops and entertainment business as a means to collect rents and attract more visitors. Also see Timon Screech's fascinating analysis of the same episode in *Edo no ōbushin: Tokugawa toshi keikaku no shigaku*, trans. Masaaki Morishita (Tokyo: Kōdansha, 2007), 121–30.
56. Mikami Sanji, *Shirakawa Rakuō-kō to Tokugawa jidai* (Tokyo: Yoshikawa Hanshichi, 1892), 85–87.
57. Takeuchi Makoto, *Edo no sakariba kō*, 118–20.
58. Ibid., 41.
59. Nam-lin Hur, *Prayer and Play in Late Tokugawa Japan*, 75–80 and chap. 3.
60. Ibid., 117–19.
61. Screech applies the term "the iconography of absence" (*fuzai no zuzōgaku*) used in the field of art history to the analysis not only of visual materials but also of city planning. See Screech, *Edo no ōbushin*.
62. This wording is taken from Terry Eagleton's discussion of the revolutionary potential of Bakhtin's formulation of carnival in *Walter Benjamin: Or, Towards a Revolutionary Criticism* (London: Verso Editions and NLB, 1981), 150.
63. Clearly, to risk an overgeneralization, Buddhists, who saw corporeal desire in an absolutely negative light, adapted a much harder tone toward the matters of desire in general than Confucians who understood desire as an essential component of humanity. The difference was not essential, however, as far as their conflictive view of mind and body was concerned.
64. One might ask then whether Tokugawa ideology underwent some mutation over two hundred years. My view is that what made certain assumptions about the Tokugawa social order ideological was precisely their assumed formalism, or the logic and appearance of the immutability of the established social relations. The well-known Tokugawa practice of issuing the same ordinances repeatedly over two hundred years, regardless of the changing historical circumstances, epitomized this formalism that functioned as the ideology. I believe that Oom's analysis of early Tokugawa ideology also shows the persistence of the formalism throughout the Tokugawa period. This does not mean, however, that Tokugawa ideology was immune to any appropriation or modification by different social groups and actors. In fact, as Victor Koschman shows, Mito ideology was a

great example of how this ruling ideology came to be re-worked and appropriated dialectically by late Tokugawa patriotic revolutionaries who sought to (re)install emperor as the central political authority. See Koschmann, *Mito Ideology*.

65. Kato Takashi, "Governing Edo," 41–67.
66. Ibid., 67.
67. Tokugawa Ieyasu's predecessor, Toyotomi Hideyoshi (1537–98), implemented the policy of the separation of the military and agricultural classes. He strengthened status distinctions between samurai and peasants, and forbade the latter from possessing weapons. The same laws were applied to artisans and merchants as well. Ieyasu further consolidated Hideyoshi's policies.
68. Kato Takashi, "Governing Edo," 68.
69. Five-family groups consisted of five households as a unit. The system was set up by the shogunate to make all members of the group responsible for the good conduct (paying taxes and not committing crimes) of other members, including their dependents.
70. Ibid., 66.
71. James L. McClain, "Edobashi: Power, Space, and Popular Culture in Edo," in McClain, Merriman, and Ugawa, eds., *Edo and Paris*, 127.
72. McClain makes the same argument by using the term "negotiated autocracy" in his "Edobashi," 131.
73. I found the following article useful for my discussions of the status of money economy and its dramatic rise in eighteenth century Tokugawa Japan: Matao Miyamoto, "Quantitative Aspects of Tokugawa Economy," in *Emergence of Economic Society*, 68–82.
74. Constantine Vaporis, *Tour of Duty: Samurai, Military Service in Edo, and the Culture of Early Modern Japan* (Honolulu: University of Hawai'i Press, 2008), 103.
75. Dazai Shundai, "On the Political Economy," in *Tokugawa Political Writings*, ed. Tetsuo Najita (Cambridge: Cambridge University Press, 1998), 144.
76. Ogyū Sorai, *Seidan*, in *Nihon shisōshi taikei*, vol. 36, ed. Maruyama Masao, Yoshikawa Kōjiro and Tsuji Tatsuya (Tokyo: Iwanami Shoten, 1973), 307. This translation is that of David J. Lu in *Japan: A Documentary History* (Armonk: M. E. Sharpe, 1997), 229.
77. Kitahara Susumu, "Hōreki–Tenmeiki no Edo shōgyō to fudasashi," in *Edo chōnin no kenkyū*, vol. 1, ed. Nishiyama Matsunosuke (Tokyo: Yoshikawa Kōbunkan, 2006), 247–336; and Buyō Inshi, *Sejikenbunroku*, 243.
78. Donald Shivery made the same characterization of "evil place" as a safety valve ("Bakufu versus Kabuki," *Harvard Journal of Asiatic Studies* 18 [1955]: 326–56), while Abe Jirō suggested that the evil place palyed a crucial "historial role" in the formation of culture, which could not be reduced to the function of sutaning the social order (*Tokugawa jidai no geijutsu to shakai*

[Tokyo: Kaizōsha, 1931], 44–45). My attempt here is to further expand his thesis by relating the question of cultural formation to that of the social and economic formation.

79. Harry Harootunian, "Cultural Politics in Tokugawa Japan," in Sarah E. Thompson and Harry Harootunian, eds., *Undercurrents in the Floating World: Censorship and Japanese Prints* (New York: Asia Society Galleries, 1991), 26. My discussion of *tsūjin* here owes much to Harootunian's insightful analysis in this chapter.
80. Ibid., 26.
81. Abe Jirō uses in *Tokugawa jidai no geijutsu to shakai* the term "hankōshiki" (semi-official) to refer to the status of "evil place" within the Tokugawa system. Based on this notion, Hirosue Tamotsu calls such a place a topos where the noneveryday existed as an everyday affair; see Hirosue, *Henkai no akusho* (Tokyo: Heibonsha, 1973), 13. My characterization of it as a "necessary evil" is an attempt to explain why the shogunate decided to integrate the non-everyday into the structure of the everyday.
82. Buyō Inshi, *Sejikenbunroku*, 346.
83. My discussion of street performers' social status and association with the outcast groups is based on Uramoto Yoshifumi, *Edo, Tokyo no hisabetsu buraku no rekishi*, chaps. 4 and 5.
84. Ibid., 355–56.
85. Mizuno Yūko, *Edo/Tokyo musume gidayū no rekishi* (Tokyo: Hōsei Daigaku Shuppan Kyoku, 2003), 20.
86. Tamenaga Shunsui ran a booklending business and was also a storyteller before gaining a fame as a writer of romantic love stories that were exclusively focused on the pleasure quarters and courtesans. He was punished for confusing public mores in 1842 and died the following year. The most explicit reference to a female ballad singer appears in his famous *Shunshoku umegoyomi* published in 1832 and 33. For the 1837 ranking of the *jōruri* performers, see Geinōshi kenkyūkai, *Nihon shomin bunkashiryō shūsei*, vol. 8 (Tokyo: San'ichi Shobō, 1985), 420.
87. Nishikawa Joken, "Chōnin bukuro," in *Nihon shisō taikei Shinsōban: gei no shisō, michi no shisō*, vol. 5, *Kinsei chōnin shisō*, ed. Nakamura Yukihiko (Tokyo: Iwanami, 1996), 95.
88. Ibid., 87–88.
89. Ibid., 134.
90. This reading of townspeople's reflections on their conditions of being was enabled by Judith Butler's theorization of subject/subjection; see Butler, *The Psychic Life of Power: Theories in Subjection* (Stanford: Stanford University Press, 1997), introduction and chaps. 1 and 3. And my use of the term "overdetermination" is based on Louis Althusser's formulation of the term in his "On Contradiction and Overdetermination," in *For Marx* (London: Verso, 2005), 78–128. It also resonates with Stuart Hall's use of the concept;

see Stuart Hall, "Signification, Representation, Ideology: Althusser and the Post-Structuralist Debates," *Critical Studies in Mass Communication* 2:2 (June 1985): 91–114.

91. Donald Keene, "Preface," in *Four Major Plays of Chikamatsu* (New York: Columbia University Press, 1998), 22.
92. I do not discuss Chikamatsu's plays in detail here as my purpose is to present a structural analysis of his narratives as a case to probe townspeople's articulations of in-betweenness. It should suffice to note that my discussions are based on a close reading of two of his most representative works, *The Love Suicides at Sonezaki* (*Sonezaki Shinju*) and *The Love Suicides at Amijima* (*Shinju Ten no Amijima*). For the English translations, see Donald Keene, *Four Major Plays of Chikamatsu*.
93. Chikamatsu Monzaemon, "Kyo jitsu himaku ron," in *Chikamatsu*, ed. Okube Tadakuni (Tokyo: Kadokawa shoten, 1970), 333–50.
94. As Naoki Sakai has brilliantly argued, the compositional form of *ningyō jōruri* itself operated on the copresence of different performative subject positions—puppets, puppeteers, narrators, and musicians—and disjunctive interactions between them. It would be absurd to apply the dichotomous notion of the real and the unreal at the superficial level—puppet as synthetic and puppeteers or narrators as authentic—to the understanding of their roles in plays as spectators often saw the real in the movement of "soulless pieces of wood" conjoined disharmoniously with narration and music. Naoki Sakai, *Voices of the Past: The Status of Language in Eighteenth-Century Japanese Discourse* (Ithaca: Cornell University Press, 1992), 148–76.
95. Chikamatsu Monzaemon, "Kyo jitsu himaku ron," 346.
96. Gunji Masakatsu, "Kabuki and Its Social Background," in Chie Nakane and Shinzaburo Ōishi, eds., *Tokugawa Japan: The Social and Economic Antecedents of Modern Japan* (Tokyo: University of Tokyo Press, 1987), 203.
97. "Kyōhō genreishū," in *Edo bakufu no kenkyu*, ed. Kukita Kazuko (Tokyo: Gannandō Shoten, 1980), 435.
98. Naoki Sakai uses the phrase "textual materiality" in his discussion of a Confucian scholar and a founder of *Kogaku* (the ancient studies), Ito Jinsai (1627–1705)'s view of the body as the topos of the heterogeneous. I see much resonance between Sakai's view of Ito and my own understanding of the popular cultural articulation of the body; see Sakai, *Voices of the Past*, 76.
99. Raymond Williams, *Marxism and Literature* (Oxford: Oxford University Press, 1977), 132.
100. Ibid., 130.
101. Ibid., 133.
102. Hashimonto Mineo, *Ukiyo no shisō: Nihonjin no jinseikan* (Tokyo: Kōdansha gendai shiso, 1975), 94–117. Eiko Ikegami offers a different interpretation of *ukiyo* as connoting necessarily "hedonistic perspective" and "amorous activity" in her *Bonds of Civility: Aesthetic Networks and the Political Origins of*

Japanese Culture (Cambridge: Cambridge University Press, 2005), 266. Her interpretation is less about ontological implications of the term than for social networking and associational activity.

103. The word "bubbles" was used by Ihara Saikaku in his "The Story of Seijiru in Himeji," in *Five Women Who Loved Love*, trans. Wm. Theodore de Bary (Boston: Tuttle, 1956), 72.
104. Ihara's representative works of this kind are *Honchō nijūfukō* (1686) and *Nihon eitaigura* (1688).
105. Ihara Saikaku, "The Story of Seijuro in Himeji," 72. I made minor changes to de Bary's translation.

CHAPTER TWO

1. Simon Dentith, *Parody* (London: Routledge, 2000), 20.
2. Ibid., 21–32.
3. The phrase "expansion of evaluative purview" is taken from V. N. Volosinov, *Marxism and the Philosophy of Language* (Cambridge: Harvard University Press, 1973), 106.
4. Tetsuo Najita, "Method and Analysis in the Conceptual Portrayal of Tokugawa Intellectual History," in *Japanese Thought in the Tokugawa Period*, ed. Tetsuo Najita and Irwin Scheiner (Chicago: The University of Chicago Press, 1978), 26.
5. Ibid., 27–28.
6. Hiraga Gennai, *Rootless Weeds*, trans. Chris Drake in Haruo Shirane ed., *Early Modern Japanese Literature* (New York: Columbia University, 2002), 474–75.
7. Gilles Deleuze, cited in *Niiche wa, konnichi?* (*Niezsche Aujourd' Hui?*) (Tokyo: Chikuma, 2002), 109, and 117–18.
8. M. M. Bakhtin, *Problem of Dostoevsky's Poetics* (Minnesota: University of Minnesota, 1984), 185.
9. The most recent and thorough work on this subject is Suzuki Toshiyuki, *Edo no dokushonetsu: Jigakusuru dokusha to shoseki ryūtsū* (Tokyo: Heibonsha, 2007). For the larger societal implications of the expansion of readership, see Mary Elizabeth Berry, *Japan in Print: Information and Nation in the Early Modern Period* (Berkeley: University of California, 2006).
10. LaCapra makes this point as a critique of Ginzburg's tendency to posit a clear division between elite and popular cultures in *The Cheese and the Worms: The Cosmos of a Sixteenth-Century Miller* (Baltimore: Johns Hopkins University Press, 1980). The same critique can be applied to the studies of Edo popular culture which ground their arguments of the politics of the culture on such a binary. See also LaCapra, *History and Criticism* (Ithaca: Cornell University Press, 1985), 59.
11. Suzuki Toshiyuki, *Edo no dokushonetsu*, 37.
12. Nakamura Hirotake, *Fushikun*, vol. 1 (Kyoto: Iwasaki, 1811), 18.

13. In *Japan in Print*, Berry uses the concept of "information revolution" to underscore the significant transformation in the flow and range of information that became available to common people by the turn of the eighteenth century.
14. Konta Yōzō, "Edo no shuppan shihon," in *Edo chonin no kenkyu*, ed. Nishiyama Matsunosuke, vol. 3 (Tokyo: Yoshikawa kōbunkan, 2006), 136–37.
15. Konta Yōzō, *Edo no hon'ya san: Kinsei bunkashi no sokumen* (Tokyo: Nihon Hōsō Shuppan Kyōkai, 1987), 95–108; and Suzuki Toshio, *Edo no hon'ya*, 2 vols. (Tokyo: Chūō Kōronsha, 1980).
16. Ibid., 108–33.
17. Cecilia Seigle, *Yoshiwara: The Glittering World of the Japanese Courtesan* (Honolulu: University of Hawaii Press, 1993), 167.
18. For the details of the Baba Bunkō incident, see Katsuya Hirano, "Social Networks and Production of Public Discourse in Edo Popular Culture," in *Acquisition: Art and Ownership in Edo-Period Japan*, ed. Elizabeth Lillehoj (New York: Floating World Editions, 2007), 111–28.
19. Konta, "Edo no shuppan shihon," 152–53.
20. Katsuhisa Moriya, "Urban Networks and Information Networks," in *Tokugawa Japan: The Social and Economic Antecedents of Modern Japan*, ed. Chie Nakane and Shinzaburo Ōishi (Tokyo: University of Tokyo Press, 1985), 117.
21. Tatsuro Akai, "The Common People and Painting," in Nakane and Ōishi, *Tokugawa Japan*, 184–89.
22. Maeda Ai, "Shuppan to dokusho-Kashihon'ya no yakuwari wo chushin to shite," in *Maeda Ai chosaku shū*, vol. 1, *Bakumatsu ishinki no bungaku: Narushima Ryūhoku* (Tokyo: Chikuma Shobō, 1989), 23–36; and Konta, *Edo no hon'yasan*, 152.
23. Nagatomo Chiyoji, *Kinsei kashihon'ya no kenkyū* (Tokyo: Tokyodō, 1982), 167–71.
24. Quoted in Nagatomo, *Kinsei kashihon'ya no kenkyu*, 170.
25. Ibid.
26. Paul Ricoeur, "The Hermeneutical Function of Distantiation," in Paul Ricoeur, *Hermeneutics and the Human Sciences: Essays on Language, Action, and Interpretation*, trans. and ed. John B. Thompson (Cambridge: Cambridge University Press, 1981), 131–44.
27. For more on this triptych, see Melinda Takeuchi, "Kuniyoshi's Minamoto Raikō and The Earth Spider: Demons and Protest in Late Tokugawa Japan," *Ars Orientalis* 17 (1987): 5–40; and Sarah E. Thompson and H. D. Harootunian, *Undercurrents in the Floating World: Censorship and Japanese Prints* (New York: Asia Society, 1991), 62–63 and 82–83.
28. Minami Kazuo, *Bakumatsu Edo no bunka: Ukiyoe to fūshiga* (Tokyo: Hanawa Shobō Yūzankaku, 1998), 80–82.
29. Other media that arose in eighteenth-century Edo and supplied a new

social space for collective interpretation were numerous. But there were two noteworthy social media: "graffito" (*rakusho* 落書) and early forms of "newspaper" (kawaraban 瓦版). Their common features were as follows: (1) free (*rakusho*) or inexpensive (*kawaraban*), (2) mobile, (3) fast, (4) disposable, and (5) mass produced. These features imparted free-floating and guerrilla-like fluidity and flexibility to them in social communication. The shogunate often regarded these media as responsible for spreading "rumor" (*ryūgen* 流言, *fūsetsu* 風説, or *fusetsu* 浮説) or "false" discourse (*kyosetsu* 虚説). All these official denominations indicated the authorities' awareness of the *"free-floating"* (as expressed in the ideograph 浮 and 流) and *"guerrilla-like"* (as in 風) characteristics of the media. *Rakusho* and *kawaraban* were indeed extensively used by the townspeople to spread their mockery and satirical critique of the officials because of their *anonymity* and *fleetness*. In particular, they were indispensable for disseminating "rumors" prohibited by the authorities, which contained (1) governmental affairs, (2) natural disasters, (3) rioting and protest, (4) famine, (5) the family lineage or ancestors of important daimyo including the shogunate family, and (6) arson. These topics reflected the government's concern about its legitimacy in the public eyes and the media's possibility of disrupting social order. See Yoshihara Ken'ichirō, *Rakusho toyū media* (Tokyo: Kyōiku Shuppan, 1999) and *Edo no jōhōya: Bakumatsu shominshi no sokumen* (Tokyo: Nippon Hōsō Shuppan Kyōkai , 1977).

30. Barbara Babcock, ed., *The Reversible World: Symbolic Inversion in Art and Society*, (Ithaca: Cornell University Press, 1978), 32.
31. My reading of popular fantasy as capable of articulating the inarticulable within the ideological structure of Tokugawa society is inspired in part by Salvoj Žižek's observation of desire as "a hard kernel," "leftover" that breaks the power of the "ideological dream": "there is always a hard kernel, leftover which persists and cannot be reduced to a universal play of illusionary mirroring (ideology) . . . the only point at which we approach this hard kernel of the Real is indeed the dream. . . . The only way to break the power of our ideological dream is to confront the Real of our desire which announces itself in this dream." Salvoj Žižek, *The Sublime Object of Ideology* (London: Verso, 1989), 47–48.
32. Henri Lefebvre, *The Production of Space* (Oxford: Blackwell, 1992), 39.
33. Ibid., 41.
34. Ibid., 42.
35. Buyō Inshi, *Sejikenbunroku* (Tokyo: Iwanami Shoten, 1994), 304.
36. Ibid., 304–5.
37. Hiraga Gennai, *"Furyūshidōkenden,"* in *Hiraga Gennai shū*, ed. Tetsuzō Tsukamoto (Tokyo: Yūhōdō Shoten 1926).
38. Asai Ryōi, *Edo meishoki*, ed. Haruhiko Asakura (Tokyo: Meicho Shuppan, 1971), 56–60.

39. Ibid., 61–63.
40. Haga Noboru, *Edogo no seiritsu* (Tokyo: Kaitakusha, 1982), 9–45. Mizuhara Akito, *Edogo, Tokyogo, Hyōjungo* (Tokyo: Kōdansha, 1994), 8–43. For the extensive linguistic analysis of the language of the townspeople, see Yuzawa Kōkichirō. *Edo kotoba no kenkyū* (Tokyo: Meiji Shoin, 1959).
41. Mizuhara, *Edogo, Tokyogo, Hyōjungo,* 15–16.
42. Shikitei Sanba, "Ukiyoburo," in *Sharebon, kibyōshi, kokkeibon,* ed. Nakamura Yukihiko and Keisuke Hamada (Tokyo: Kadokawa Shoten, 1968), 222–23.
43. Tao Yuanming (365–427) was a Chinese poet of the Eastern Jin dynasty (317–420). He was revered by the Tokugawa elites as a principal poet to emulate and learn from. Tanshin (1653–1718) was the son and successor of Tanyu, the founder of the Kano school. Tanshin's picture accentuates the learned and venerated image of Tao by embellishing him with a scholarly appearance and placing two young disciples beside him. Watanabe Kazan, *Issō hyakutai: Shomin fūzoku* (Tokyo: Iwasaki Bijutsusha, 1969), 1–3.
44. Nagata Seiji, ed., *Hokusai Manga,* vol. 1 (Tokyo: Iwasaki Bijitsusha, 1987), 125.
45. *Dai Nihon kinsei shiryō: Shichū torishimari ruishū* (Tokyo: Tokyo Daigaku Shuppankai, 1994), 169.
46. Kuniyoshi's *Shasei Hyakumen sō,* cited in Tsuji Nobuo, *Kisō no keifu; Matabē-Kuniyoshi* (Tokyo: Perikansha, 1988), 130.
47. Hattori Yukio, *Kabuki* (Tokyo: Heibonsha, 1971), 53.
48. Nakamura Yukihiko, *Gesakuron* (Tokyo: Kadokawa Shoten, 1961), 49–50.
49. Ibid., 41–42.
50. Ibid., 43–44.
51. Ibid., 44–45.
52. On the social meanings of *bunjin,* see also Karaki Junzō's *Muyōsha no keifu* (Tokyo: Chikuma Shobō, 1960), 202–62.
53. To be a masterless samurai meant to relinquish all samurai privileges such as receiving a stipend (rice) and having an official position within the establishment.
54. Iwasaki Haruko also explored the community of *gesaku* writers in her dissertation *The World of Gesaku: Playful Writers of Late Eighteenth Century Japan* (Harvard University, 1984).
55. Nakamura Yukihiko, *Gesakuron,* 49.
56. Gion Nankai, *Nankai shiketsu,* in *Edo shijin senshū,* ed. Yamamoto Kazuyoshi and Yokoyama Hiroshi, vol. 3 (Tokyo: Iwanami Shoten, 1991), 89.
57. Minakawa Soen, *Shiwa,* quoted in Karaki, *Muyōsha no keifu,* 210.
58. Ibid., 226.
59. Paul Ricoeur, "Appropriation," in Ricoeur, *Hermeneutics and the Human Sciences: Essays on Language, Action, and Interpretation,* 186–87.
60. Amino Yoshihiko, *Muen, kugai, raku: Nihon chūsei no jiyū to heiwa* (Tokyo: Heibonsha, 1996), 80–92.

61. Ibid., 290–301.
62. Victor Turner, *The Ritual Process: Structure and Anti-Structure* (New York: Aldine De Gruyter, 1995), 128
63. Victor Turner, *Dramas, Fields, and Metaphors; Symbolic Action in Human Society* (Ithaca: Cornell University Press, 1974), 274; and Jinnai Hidenobu, *Tokyo no kūkan jinrui gaku* (Tokyo: Chikuma, 1992), 132–50. Drawing on Amino's concept of "detachment," Jinnai argues that these liminal spaces occupied by entertainers and markets offered Edo townspeople anarchic freedom.
64. Harootunian's important work differs in this regard and offers an exemplary reading of Edo culture though a Bakhtinian perspective; see Harootunian, "Cultural Politics in Tokugawa Japan," in Sarah E. Thompson and H. D. Harootunian, eds., *Undercurrents in the Floating World: Censorship and Japanese Prints* (New York: Asia Society Galleries).
65. Shikitei Sanba, *Ukiyodoko* (Tokyo: Tenbōsha, 1974), 44.
66. Ibid., 46.
67. Cecilia Seigle, *Yoshiwara*, 131–32.
68. Shikitei Sanba, *Ukiyodoko*, 58–9.
69. Ibid., 59.
70. Inaka Rōjin Tada no Jijii, *The Playboy Dialect*, trans. Herschel Miller, in *Early Modern Japanese Literature*, ed. Haruo Shirane (New York: Columbia University, 2002), 633–55.
71. M. M. Bakhtin, *Rabelais and His World* (Bloomington: Indiana University Press, 1984), 10.
72. Harry Harootunian, "Cultural Politics in Tokugawa Japan," 22–23.
73. Ibid.
74. Santō Kyōden, *Grilled And Basted Edo-Born Playboy*, in Haruo Shirane, ed., *Early Modern Japanese Literature*, 687–710.
75. Thomas Looser, *Visioning Eternity: Aesthetics, Politics and History in the Early Modern Noh Theater* (Ithaca: East Asia Program, Cornell University, 2008), 77–78.
76. See especially Abe Jirō's critique of Santō Kyōden, 333–34. It is noteworthy that their critique of late Edo culture and its forms of representation were part of their larger concerns with the problem of the deficiency or shortcomings of Japanese national spirit. Their works were indeed written primarily for the purpose of evaluating the particular and universal qualities of Japanese ethnic culture in comparison with the putatively superior and unitary western culture. This essentially nationalist concern or organicist perspective that informed their mode of analysis deserves a separate analysis, which this work, unfortunately, cannot take up. For an important critique of this line of academic discourse during the 1920s and 1930s, see Leslie Pincus, *Authenticating Culture in Imperial Japan: Kuki Shūzō and the Rise of National Aesthetics* (Berkeley: University of California Press, 1996). In

many ways, my work is an attempt to propose an alternative reading of late Tokugawa culture to those of the modernist and nationalist writers, which remain very influential in Japan.

77. Fredric Jameson, *Postmodernism or, The Cultural Logic of Late Capitalism* (Durham:Duke University Press, 1991), 17. Interestingly, Santō Kyōden has been compared on several occasions by Japanese literary scholars with a postmodern Japanese writer, Tanaka Yasuo, especially for his 1980 novel *Somehow, Crystal* (*Nantonaku Kurisutaru* なんとなくクリスタル). Although I am not at all endorsing the fashionable ahistorical discourse, which swept 1980s and '90s Japan, that Tokugawa Japan had already lived a "postmodern" epoch because of the striking resemblances between Edo and postmodern cultures, the method of blank parody used by Kyōden and Tanaka hint at some degree of similitude. See Nobuhiro Shinji and Tanahashi Masahiro, eds, "Taidan: Gesaku kenkyū no shin chihei e," in *Edo bungaku* 19 *Gesaku no Jidai 1* (Tokyo: Perikan, 1998), 8. For a critical introduction of Tanaka's work, see Norma Field, "Somehow: The Postmodern as Atmosphere," in Masao Miyoshi and Harry Harootunian, eds., *Postmodernism and Japan* (Durham: Duke University Press, 1989), 169–88.
78. Jameson, *Postmodernism or, The Cultural Logic of Late Capitalism*, 17.
79. Dentith, *Parody*, 155.
80. Santō Kyōden, *Yonoue sharemiezu*, cited in Karaki Junzō, *Muyōsha no keifu* (Tokyo: Chikuma Shobō, 1960), 232–33.
81. "Tendential alignment" is a phrase used by Stuart Hall to explain a historically contingent relation between class position and ideology, economic conditions, and consciousness. Obviously Hall uses the words to overcome the mechanistic determinism of a Marxist theory of correspondence or reflection between base and superstructure while reinforcing Althusser's crucial formulation of "overdetermination" or Gramsci's conception of "hegemony." What is important here is Hall's effort to retain the validity of the concept of "determination"—thus a structural understanding of sociohistorical formation—without reducing it to the mechanistic formula or completely renouncing the concept, which is simply an inversion of the former as epitomized by a poststructuralist privileging of discourse. Hall argues that there is some tendency for material conditions and ideas to resonate with each other at a specific historical moment (often at the time of intense and explosive crisis), but such resonance is never guaranteed by any predetermined law. Interpretation of social formation then requires, I believe, an effort to unpack complex and dynamic structural relations that are historically singular and contingent. My use of the phrase here is meant to suggest the cultural logic of the political, in particular political implications of the comic or humor, as an instance. See Stuart Hall, "The Problem of Ideology: Marxism without Guarantees," in David Morley and Kuan-Hsing Chen, ed., *Stuart Hall* (London: Routledge, 1996), 42–43.

CHAPTER THREE

1. For an insightful analysis of parody as a form of defamilialization with a focus on language, see Naoki Sakai, *Voices of the Past: The Status of Language in Eighteenth-Century Japanese Discourse* (Ithaca: Cornell University Press, 1991), especially chap. 6.
2. Buyō Inshi wrote, "心情を狂わすなり," in *Sejikenbunroku* (Tokyo: Iwanami shoten, 1994), 359.
3. Ibid.
4. Michel Foucault, "Theatrum Philosophicum," *Critique* 282 (November 1970): 885–908.
5. Robert Phiddian, *Swift's Parody* (Cambridge: Cambridge University Press, 1995), 13–14.
6. Ibid.
7. Simon Dentith gives a clear definition of metafiction as follows: "Fiction which has built into it a moment of self-reflection, or which alludes to its own, or others,' fictional practice. Parodic novels which include parodies of other fictions tend to have a metafictional aspect, since they draw attention to the nature of story-telling in suggesting the inadequacy of the styles that they parody." See Dentith, *Parody* (London: Routledge, 2000), 192.
8. M. M. Bakhtin, *Problems of Dostoyevsky's Poetics*, trans and ed. Caryl Emerson (Minneapolis: University of Minnesota Press, 1984), 194.
9. Ogata Tsutomu, et al., ads., *Kinsei no bungaku*, vol. 2. (Tokyo: Yuhikaku sensho, 1977), 78.
10. My theorization of "inversion" in the context of Edo popular culture is largely indebted to Peter Stallybrass and Allon White, *The Politics and Poetics of Transgression* (Ithaca: Cornell University Press, 1986), 56–57.
11. Henri Bergson, "Le rire," in Wylie Sypher, ed., *Comedy* (New York: Doubleday, 1956), 118.
12. There are many comparable instances of "negation" as a performance of the world upside down in early modern Europe, the US, Latin America, and Africa. The best anthology on this subject is Barbara Babcock, ed., *The Reversible World* (Ithaca: Cornell University, 1978).
13. Herbert Marcuse, *The Aesthetic Dimension: Toward a Critique of Marxist Aesthetics* (Boston: The Beacon Press, 1978), 54.
14. Sigmund Freud, "Negation," in Richard, A. and J. Strachey eds.,(tr. J. Strachey), *The Pelican Freud Library*. Vol. 11, *On Metapsychology*. (Harmondsworth: Penguin Books , 1984), 437–38.
15. Marcuse, *Aesthetic Dimension*, 54.
16. Ryūtei Tanehiko said in the original, "Kono kō no e shin wo hanarete shin wo utsusunari—この翁 [北斎] の絵、真を離れて真 を写すなり," in Katsushika Hokusai, *Hokusai manga*, vol. 3 (Tokyo: Seigensha, 2011), 287.

17. Honda Yasuo, *Ukiyoburo ukiyodoko: Sekenbanashi no bungaku* (Tokyo: Heibonsha, 1994), 44–84.
18. Maurice Charney, *Comedy High and Low: An Introduction to the Experience of Comedy* (New York: Oxford University Press, 1978), 51.
19. Nakamura Yukihiko, *Gesakuron* (Tokyo: Kadokawa Shoten, 1966), 214–39, and his "Gesaku nyūmon," in Nakamura Yukihiko and Hamada Keisuke eds., *Sharebon, kibyōshi, kokkeibon* (Tokyo: Kadokawa Shoten, 1978), 5–14.
20. Santō Kyōden, "Kyōden ukiyo no suisei" and "Terako jo," in *Santō Kyōden zenshu*, vol. 3 (Tokyo: Perikansha, 2001) 15.
21. Nakamura Yukihiko, *Gesakuron* (Tokyo: Kadokawa Shoten, 1966), 219–22. Nakamura identifies Shikitei Sanba as the one who theorized *henchi* as a literary theory.
22. See Hiraga Gennai's *Hōhiron* (On Farting), *Fūryūshidōkenden* (A Biography of Elegant Shidōken), *Nenashigusa* (Rootless Weed), and *Tengusharekobe mekiki engi* (Judging the Authenticity of Tengu's Scull), in *Hiraga Gennai shū*, ed. Tetsuzō Tsukamoto (Tokyo: Yūhōdō Shoten, 1926).
23. Peter Duus, "Weapons of the Weak, Weapons of the Strong—The Development of the Japanese Political Cartoon," in *Journal of Asian Studies* 60:4 (Ann Arbor: University of Michigan, 2001), 971.
24. Haruo Shirane, *Early Modern Japanese Literature: An Anthology, 1600–1900* (New York: Columbia University Press, 2002) 462.
25. For the purpose of conceptual comparison, *naimaze* is almost identical with metaphor. But *henchiki* and *chakashi* bear resemblance to neither metaphor nor metonymy, not to mention synecdoche. In fact, metaphor, metonymy and synecdoche are quite opposite to *henchiki* and *chakashi* in that their primary function is to create specific forms of sameness with difference, whereas that of *henchiki* and *chakashi* is to create or expose the different in the same. Metaphor connects the different by way of suggesting similarity and metonymy connects the different by way of making two elements contiguous to each other, most commonly by treating them as elements of an encompassing category. Synecdoche connects the different by integrating parts into a whole, suggesting an organic relationship.
26. Shikitei Sanba, *Ukiyoburo*, in *Sharebon, kibyōshi, kokkeibon*, ed. Nakamura Yukihiko and Keisuke Hamada (Tokyo: Kadokawa Shoten, 1978), 209–12.
27. Hiraga Gennai, *Fūryūshidōkenden*, 281.
28. The translation is that of Adriana Delprat taken from her unpublished dissertation "Forms of Dissent in the Gesaku Literature of Hiraga Gennai (1728–1780)" (Princeton University, 1985). My analysis here benefited from her interesting discussion of Gennai's wordplay, although my approach and interpretation differ.
29. Gennai, *Fūryūshidōken*, 281.
30. Ibid., 282. The translation is that of Adriana Delprat.
31. Ibid., 292.
32. Ibid., 276–77.

33. Ibid.
34. V. N. Volosinov, *Marxism and the Philosophy of Language* (Cambridge: Harvard University Press, 1986), 102–3.
35. Ibid.
36. I owe much of this understanding and formulation of social texts to Umberto Eco's discussion of "open texts." See his *The Role of the Reader: Explorations in the Semiotics of Texts* (Indiana: Indiana University Press, 1984), chaps. 1 and 3.
37. Hiraga Gennai was born into the family of a low-ranking samurai in Sanuki but renounced his hereditary rights in his late twenties to move to Edo and lived there as a townsperson until the end of his life. He described his lack of a stable status within Tokugawa social hierarchies as "a privilege that allows me to live freely without any masters to serve, that is, to be able to say 'yes' and 'no' as I want." Hiraga Gennai, *On Farting, Part 2,* in Haga Tōru, ed. *Nihon no meicho,* vol. 22, *Sugita Genpaku, Hiraga Gennai, Shiba Kōkan* (Tokyo: Chūō Kōronsha, 1984), 391.
38. The *Classic of Changes, Book of Changes* or *I Ching,* is one of the oldest Chinese classics, which contains the method of a divination based on the vision centered on the dynamic balance of opposite forces of yin and yang.
39. Hiraga Gennai, *Naemara Itsuden,* in Haga, *Nihon no meicho,* 22:401.
40. Fung Yu-Lan, *A Short History of Chinese Philosophy,* ed. Derk Boddle (New York: Macmillan, 1948), 300.
41. Gennai, *Naemara Itsuden,* 402–3.
42. Ibid., 403–4.
43. Volosinov, *Marxism and the Philosophy of Language,* 105.
44. Slavoj Žižek, *The Sublime Object of Ideology* (London: Verso, 1989), 157.
45. The earliest record about this entertainment was written in the 1770s, the time when Hiraga Gennai wrote *Hōhiron.* There were also several folk stories and urban legends about flatulence and the "fartist" printed and reprinted between the 1810s and the 1840s by publishers in Edo. The entertainment of flatulence itself remained popular until the early Meiji period, the 1880s, in the Asakusa-Ryōgoku area. Satō Tamio, "He no saho ni tsuiteno kosatsu," in *Edo to Tokyo,* ed. Ishizumi Harunosuke and Ogi Shinzō, 28 vols. (Tokyo: Akashi Shoten, 1991), 4:25; and Honda Seika, "Asakusa okuzan jidai no misemono," in Ishizumi and Ogi, *Edo to Tokyo,* 1:16.
46. Hiraga Gennai, *On Farting,* trans. William Sibley, in *Readings in Tokugawa Thought,* ed. Tetsuo Najita (Chicago: University of Chicago the Center for East Asian Studies, 1998), 171.
47. Ibid.
48. Ibid., 172.
49. Ibid.
50. Ibid., 172–73.

51. Ogyū Sorai, *Benmei*, in *Tokugawa Political Writings*, ed. and trans. Tetsuo Najita (London: Cambridge University Press, 1998).
52. Gennai, *On Farting*, 173.
53. Hiraga Gennai, *Soshirigusa* [*Slandering*], in *Hiraga Gennai shū* (Tokyo: Tokyo shoi'n, 1923).
54. Hiraga Gennai, *Hōhiron kōhen* [*On Farting, Part 2*], 22:388.
55. There were two categories of outcast, the defiled (*eta*) and the nonhuman (*hinin*), in Tokugawa society. *Setta* belonged to the latter, together with the various entertainers mentioned in this book.
56. Hattori Yukio, *Sakasama no yūrei: "Shi" no Edo bunkaron* (Tokyo: Heibonsha 1989), 46–68.
57. Quoted in Kurushima Hiroshi, *Kuniyoshi* (Tokyo: Asahishinbun 1998), 57.
58. For a historical account of the *yakko* (*hatamoto yakko* and *machi yakko*) and their relation to popular culture in the late seventeenth and early eighteenth centuries, see Gary Leupp's fascinating essay "The Five Men of Naniwa: Gang Violence and Popular Culture in Genroku Osaka," in *Osaka, the Merchant's Capital of Early Modern Japan*, ed. James McClain and Osamu Wakita (Ithaca: Cornell University Press, 1999), 125–55.
59. Gunji Masakatsu, *Kabuki hasseishi ronshu* (Tokyo: Iwanami Shoten, 2002), 151–62.
60. Leupp, "Five Men of Naniwa," 146.
61. Kurishima, *Kuniyoshi*, 54–56.
62. Utagawa Sadahide's print, *A Giant Asahina* (1847), depicted the actual bamboo doll of Asahina, which was removed from the fair. Clearly, Kuniyoshi's print was a parody of the samurai Asahina. His *yakko* bears no swords and samurai attire unlike Sadahide's.
63. Anne Walthall makes a similar observation regarding the shogun's invisibility in public space in her "Hiding the Shoguns: Secrecy and the Nature of Political Authority in Tokugawa Japan," in Bernhard Scheid and Mark Teeuwen, eds., *The Culture of Secrecy in Japanese Religion* (London: Routledge, 2006).
64. Arakawa Hidetoshi, ed., *Tenpo kaikaku machifure shiryō* (Tokyo: Yūzankaku Shuppan, 1974), 155–58.
65. Tosaka Jun, "Warai, Kigeki, oyobi Yûmoa," in *Tosaka Jun zenshū*, vol. 4. (Tokyo: Keisōshobō, 1974), 76.
66. M. M. Bakhtin, *Rabelais and His World* (Indiana: Indiana University Press, 1984), 90.
67. Ibid., 92.
68. Henri Bergson, *Laughter: An Essay on the Meaning of the Comic* (København: Green Interger, 1999), 11–12.
69. Ibid., 34.
70. It should be noted that Bergson's notion of personality refers specifically to the problem of automatism in the positivistic intellectual current of the late nineteenth century. Although Edo society's conventionalized behavior

had nothing to do with this problematic, it had the problem of automatism under the different kind of register: rigid norms and rituals.

71. Tosaka Jun, "Warai, Kigeki, oyobi Yūmoa," 75. For a more extensive discussion of Tosaka's theory of laughter, see my "The Dialectic of Laughter and Tosaka's Critical Theory," in Ken Kawashima and Robert Stolz, eds., *Tosaka Jun: Critical Reader* (forthcoming from Cornell East Asian Series). The full English translation of Tosaka's essay on laughter is included in this volume.
72. Ibid., 76.
73. Ibid., 75.
74. Jippensha Ikku, *Tōkaidō-chū hizakurige* (Tokyo: Perikan, 1996), 78–81.
75. For a comprehensive anthology of *warai banashi*, see Tokuda Susumu, *Edo no warai banashi* (Tokyo: Kyōiku Shuppan, 1983).
76. György Lukács, "Reification and the Consciousness of the Proletariat," in *History and Class Consciousness* (Cambridge: MIT Press, 1971).
77. Charles Baudelaire, *Selected Writings on Art and Literature*, trans. P. E. Charvet (London: Penguin Books, 1992), 143.
78. For an interesting discussion on the political and critical potential of laughter, including that on Edo, see Iizawa Tadasu, *Buki to shite no warai* (Tokyo: Iwanami shinsho, 1977).
79. Stallybrass and White, *The Politics and Poetics of Transgression*, 14.
80. Althusser, *For Marx*, 211, 216; and Ernst Bloch, "Nonsynchronism and The Obligation to Dialectics," *New German Critique* 11 (Spring 1977): 22–38.
81. Geoffrey G. Harpham, *On the Grotesque: Strategies on Contradiction in Art and Literature* (Princeton: Princeton University Press, 1982), 74.
82. Volosinov, *Marxism and the Philosophy of Language*, 23.
83. Maruyama Masao, *Studies in the Intellectual History of Tokugawa Japan* (Princeton: Princeton University Press, 1974), 329–30.

CHAPTER FOUR

1. Toyokuni was placed in handcuffs for one hundred days, whereas Utamaro was said to be imprisoned. Some historians speculate that his early death—two years after his arrest—was a result of poor health conditions he developed while in prison. See Minami Kazuo, *Edo no fūshiga* (Tokyo: Yoshikawa Kōbunkan 1997), 78–91.
2. The comprehensive account of the parodies of *Taikōki* is found in Miyatake Gaikotsu, *Miyatake Gaikotsu chosakushū*, vol. 4, in *Hikkashi*, ed. Tanizawa Eiichi and Yoshino Takao (Tokyo: Kawade Shobō Shinsha, 1986), 100–103.
3. Minami, *Edo no fūshiga*, 99–100.
4. Fujita Noboru and Satō Takayuki, eds., *Dai Nihon kinsei shiryō: Shichū torishimari ruishū* (Tokyo: Tokyo Daigaku Shuppan, 1988), 18:243.
5. Under this law, Utagawa Yoshitora was also handcuffed for fifty days in 1838 for publishing *Midai no wakamochi* (*A Rice Cake of the Reign*), in which

he depicted Tokugawa Ieyasu's rise to power as a result of his cunning maneuvering. See Miyatake, *Miyatake Gaikotsu chosakushu*, 4:118–19.

6. I make this claim based on the following works: Minami, *Edo no fūshiga*; Yokoyama, *Edo Tokyo no kaidan bunka no seiritsu to hensen: Jūkyūseiki o chūshin ni* (Tokyo: Kazama Shobō, 1997); and Adam Kabat, *Edo kokkei bake-monozukushi* (Tokyo: Kōdansha, 2003).
7. Minami, *Edo no fūshiga*, 60–63.
8. Ibid., 49–50. For a lengthy treatment of the Tanuma incident, especially how Edo townspeople ridiculed the Tanumas through poetry, see Anne Walthall, *Social Protest and Popular Culture in Eighteenth Century Japan* (Tucson: University of Arizona Press, 1986), 207–9.
9. Daniel Botsman, *Punishment and Power in the Making of Modern Japan* (Princeton: Princeton University Press, 2005), chaps. 1 and 2.
10. Katsuya Hirano, "Social Networks and the Production of Public Discourse in Edo Popular Culture," in *Acquisition: Art and Ownership in Edo-Period Japan*, ed. Elizabeth Lillehoj (Warren: Floating World Edition: 2007), 111–28.
11. Konta Yōzō, *Bakumatsu shakai kōzō no kenkyu* (Tokyo: Hanawa shobō, 2003), 73.
12. Buyō Inshi, *Sejikenbunroku* (Tokyo: Iwanami Shoten, 1994), 20.
13. Ibid., 283–84.
14. M. M. Bakhtin, *Rabelais and His World* (Bloomington: Indiana University Press, 2009); Geoffrey G. Harpham, *On the Grotesque: Strategies on Contradiction in Art and Literature* (Princeton: Princeton University Press, 1982); and Susan Stewart, *Nonsense: Aspects of Intertextuality in Folklore and Literature* (Baltimore: Johns Hopkins University Press, 1979). For a work related to the grotesque in Japanese history, see Michelle Osterfeld Li, *Ambiguous Bodies: Reading the Grotesque in Japanese Setsuwa Tales* (Stanford: Stanford University Press, 2009).
15. Stewart, *Nonsense: Aspects of Intertextuality in Folklore and Literature*, 61.
16. Geoffrey G. Harpham, *On the Grotesque: Strategies on Contradiction in Art and Literature* (Princeton: Princeton University Press, 1982), 3.
17. Ibid., 6.
18. Haga Noboru, "Edo no bunka," in *Kasei bunka no kenkyū*, ed. Hayashiya Tatsuzaburo (Tokyo: Iwanami Shoten, 1976), 183.
19. Quoted in Hattori Yukio, *Sakasama no yūrei: "Shi" no Edo bunkaron* (Tokyo: Heibonsha, 1989), 174.
20. Hattori also discusses Toyokuni's print in *Sakasama no yūrei*, 278.
21. I choose Kano Tanyū's work here although he was not a cotemporary of Hokusai. The reason for this is that Tanyū set the standard of for the artistic style of the Kano School, which remained unchanged until the end of the Tokugawa period. It was also Tanyū who gained patronage from the Tokugawa family and other powerful samurai for the Kanos' artistic production. Timon Screech writes that "the school of Kano painted motifs of ethical rule, either in the form of narratives or of auspicious flora and

fauna, for disposition by the shogunate." Screech continues to discuss how the motifs and styles of the Kano, especially that of Tanyū, continued to be important for the elite, despite the intensified criticism that their work had lost relevance to the late-eighteenth- and nineteenth-century world. See Screech, *The Shogun's Painted Culture: Fear and Creativity in the Japanese States, 1760–1829* (London: Reaktion, 2000), 125–40.

22. Harpham, *On the Grotesque*, chap. 2.
23. Thomas Looser, *Visioning Eternity: Aesthetics, Politics and History in the Early Modern Noh Theater* (Ithaca: Cornell University Press, 2008), chap. 2.
24. Tetsuo Najita, *Visions of Virtue in Tokugawa Japan: The Kaitokudō Merchant Academy of Osaka* (Chicago: University of Chicago Press, 1987), 49. Also see his discussion of Kusama Naotaka (1753–1831), in Najita, *Visions of* Virtue, 227–48.
25. Karl Marx, *Grundrisse*, trans. Martin Nicolaus (London: Penguin Books, in association with New Left Review, 1993), 233–34.
26. Najita, *Visions of Virtue.*
27. Yokoyama Yasuko shares my observation that, from the 1810s on, ghostly images that appeared in kabuki and ukiyo-e were designed or choreographed with unsightly and often unthinkable forms of violence and deformity to shock and horrify spectators; see Yokoyama Yasuko, *Edo Tokyo no kaidanbunka no seiritsu to hensen: Jūkyūseiki o chūshin ni* (Tokyo: Kazama Shobō, 1997), 8.
28. Hirosue Tamotsu, *Henkai no akusho* (Tokyo: Heibonsha, 1973), 233.
29. My critical assessment of inversion is inspired in part by Althusser's discussion of the term in his reexamination of Marx's conceptual relationship with Hegel and Feuerbach. See Althusser, "Feuerbach's 'Philosophical Manifestoes'," in Althusser, *For Marx* (London: Verso, 2005), 43–49.
30. Gunji Masakatsu, *Gisei no bun* (Tokyo: Hakusuisha, 1991), 187.
31. Gunji Masakazu, "Edo bunka ni okeru kabuki no ichi," in *Edo jidai to kindaika*, ed. Nakane Chie and Ōishi Shinzaburō (Tokyo: Chikuma Shobō, 1986), 356.
32. Hattori Yukio, *Hengeron: Kabuki no seishinshi* (Tokyo: Heibonsha, 1975), 24.
33. Quoted in Hattori Yukio, ed., *Kabuki* (Tokyo: Heibonsha, 1971), 15.
34. Hirosue Tamotsu, *Yotsuya kaidan* (Tokyo: Kage Shobō, 2000), 12. For a thorough historical study of kabuki, see Hattori, *Kabuki*, 7–147; and Nishiyama Matsunosuke, *Edo kabuki kenkyū* (Tokyo: Yoshikawa Kōbunkan, 1987), 305–71.
35. Kuroita Katsumi, ed., *Tokugawa jikki*, vol. 3 (Tokyo: Yoshikawa Kōbunkan, 1998), 131.
36. Nishiyama, *Edo kabuki kenkyū*, 332.
37. Buyō Inshi, *Sejikenbunroku* (Tokyo: Iwanami Shoten, 1995), 341.
38. Ibid., 342–42.
39. Takayanagi Shinzō and Ryōsuke Ishii, eds., *Ofuregaki tenpō shūsei*, vol. 2 (Tokyo: Iwanami Shoten, 1958), 437.

40. Ibid., 439.
41. Kuroita, *Tokugawa jikki*, 3:90.
42. Hattori, *Kabuki*, 30–42.
43. Nakayama Mikio, "Kabuki nureba kō," in *Fukugan no kisai: Tsuruya Nanboku* (Tokyo: Shintensha, 2001), 208–30. Nakayama introduces instances in which spectators found themselves sexually aroused by *nureba* scenes. Intimate sexual scenes were performed behind folding screens or sliding paper doors. Spectators "saw" the scenes through blurry silhouette of the actors projected on the paper door or simply through the actors' vocalization.
44. Ibid., 174–77. Gregory Pflugfelder makes an important point that official ideology did not identify sexual desire—including male-male love—as pernicious in itself. Rather the shogunate's regulations were aimed at the problem of "excess" such as "unsolicited sexual advances" and "*wakashūgurui*" (going crazy over youths). This confirms my overall argument in this book that official ideology was built on the recognition of the body as the site of autonomous agency including a sexual kind, and the regime's primary concern was not the negation but the regulation or containment of it for the preservation of social order. The policies against kabuki also reflected this ideological position. See Gregory Pflugfelder, *Cartographies of Desire: Male-Male Sexuality in Japanese Discourse, 1600–1950* (Berkeley: University of California, 1999), 105–24.
45. Together with "erotic scenes," "murderous scenes" (*koroshiba* 殺し場) was considered to be a defining feature of late Tokugawa kabuki; see Nakayama, "Kabuki nureba kō."
46. Takayanagi and Ishii, *Ofuregaki tenpō shūsei*, 2:442 and 2:444–45.
47. *Dai Nihon kinsei shiryō: Shichū torishimari ruishū*, vol. 1 (Tokyo: Tokyo Daigaku Shuppankai, 1959), 35.
48. Buyō Inshi, *Sejikenbunroku*, 346.
49. Ibid., 354.
50. Terakado Seiken, *Edo hanjōki*, vol. 2, ed. Haruhiko Asakura and Kikuji Andō (Tokyo: Heibonsha, 1975), 244.
51. Yoshida Nobuyuki, "Yose to manabi," in *Shūhen bunka to mibunsei*, ed. Wakita Haruko, Martin Collcutt, and Taira Masayuki (Kyoto: Shibunkaku Shuppan, 2005), 106.
52. Mizuno Yūko, *Edo Tokyo musume gitayū no rekishi* (Tokyo: Hōsei Daigaku Shuppankyoku, 2003), 21.
53. Buyō, *Sejikenbunroku*, 347.
54. Ibid., 356.
55. Susan Burns, "The Body as Text: Confucianism, Reproduction, and Gender in Early Modern Japan," in *Rethinking Confucianism: Past and Present in China, Japan, Korea and Vietnam*, ed. Benjamin Elman, Herman Ooms and John Duncan (Los Angeles: UCLA Asia Pacific Monograph Series, 2002).
56. Miura Jōshin, *Keichō kenmonshū* (Tokyo: Shin Jinbutsu raisha, 1969), 199–200.

57. Hirosue Tamotsu, *Henkai no akusho*, 164.
58. Yokoyama, *Edo Tokyo no kaidanbunka no seiritsu to hensen*, 112.
59. Ibid., 113–25.
60. On the stories of these figures and their curses, see Yamada Yūji, *Bakkosuru Onryō: Tatari to chinkon no Nihon shi* (Tokyo: Yoshikawa Kōbunkan, 2007).
61. Yokoyama, *Edo Tokyo no kaidanbunka no seiritsu to hensen*, 221.
62. Kurata Yoshihiro, *Shibaigoya to Yose no Kindai* (Tokyo: Iwanami, 2006), 96. From the 1810s onward, one of the most popular repertoire of many *Yose* was ghost stories such as *Yotsuya* and *Kasane*. They were performed in many different forms raging from puppet play to shadow play to kabuki-style performance. See also Terakado, *Edo hanjōki*, 2:248–9; and Yoshida, "Yose to Manabi," 107.
63. Yoshida Nobuyuki, *Seijukusuru Edo* (Tokyo: Kodansha, 2002), 234.
64. Ibid.
65. Mizuno, *Edo/Tokyo Musume gitayū no rekishi*, 35.
66. Yoshida, *Seijukusuru Edo*, 235.
67. Ibid., 236.
68. Hattori Yukio, *Hengeron: Kabuki no seishinshi* (Tokyo: Heibonsha, 1975), 219–64.
69. Yūten Shōnin (1637–1718) was a very famed priest of Pureland Buddhism. He was honored by and received support from the fifth shogun, Tokugawa Tsunayoshi (1646–1709). He was also responsible for the restoration of Tōdaiji in Nara and the Buddha statue of Kamakura. Later in his life, Yūten was elevated to the status of sainthood. The temple, Yūtenji, was built in his honor in 1718 and is in Meguro, Tokyo. It is possible to speculate that *The Nirvana* was written and spread by the Pureland Buddhist group to promote its teaching among commoners. But Hattori Yukio perceptively argues that its popularity cannot be explained away by its propagandic nature: its appeal was grounded in part in the harsh realities of agrarian communities, a background in which *The Nirvana* was set and from which many Edo residents originated (Hattori, *Hengeron*, 139). I would like to add that the story's popularity was also largely due to its extraordinary ability to reveal the power dynamics of patriarchy and gender. The later versions of the story gradually deemphasized the possibility of salvation offered by the Buddhist prayer and imparted a new dimension of the power dynamics of status by bringing the déclassé samurai into the story. This is one of the key points I am arguing with regard to *Yotsuya* in this chapter.
70. Yokoyama, *Edo Tokyo no kaidanbunka no seiritsu to hensen*, 108–9.
71. Ibid., 111–13.
72. I borrow the concept of "morphology" from Judith Butler's discussion of how pain of guilt produces conformity with the ideas of a proper body enforced by social taboo in her *Bodies That Matter: On the Discursive Limits of "Sex"* (New York: Routledge, 1993).
73. Yokoyama, *Edo Tokyo no kaidanbunka no seiritsu to hensen*, 116–22.

74. References such as "scary" and "hair-raising" to the performance of ghost stories began to appear around this time. See Yokoyama, *Edo Tokyo no kaidanbunka no seiritsu to hensen.*
75. Tsuruya Nanboku, *Tōkaidō Yotsuya kaidan* (Tokyo: Iwanami Bunko, 1956). Hereafter I refer to this text as TYK.
76. The Tokugawa authorities insisted that the play should be set in the Kamakura period. This is another example of how any reference to contemporaneous events was discouraged and prohibited during the Tokugawa period.
77. TYK, 25–26.
78. TYK, 131.
79. TYK, 132. The translation is that of Mark Oshima in *Traditional Japanese Theater: An Anthology of Plays*, ed. Karen Brazell (New York: Columbia University Press, 1998), 475.
80. Ibid.
81. TYK, 134; Brazell, *Traditional Japanese Theater*, 478–79.
82. Walter Benjamin, *Illuminations*, trans. Harry Zohn and ed. Hannah Arendt (New York: Random House, 1988), 267.
83. TYK, 111; Brazell, *Traditional Japanese Theater*, 465.
84. TYK, 128–29.
85. TYK, 250.
86. TYK, 145, 161, 228.
87. Maeda Ai, *Toshi kūkan no naka no bungaku* (Tokyo: Chikuma Shobō, 1992), 106.
88. These diverse interpretations are introduced and analyzed by Minami Kazuo in *Bakumatsu Edo no bunka: Ukiyoe to fūshiga* (Tokyo: Hanawa Shobō, 1998). The analysis of these interpretations offered here is mine.
89. Asano Shūgō and Yoshida Nobuyuki, eds., *Kuniyoshi*, vol. 6 (Tokyo: Asahi Shinbunsha, 1997), 17–18.
90. Herbert Marcuse, *The Aesthetic Dimension: Toward a Critique of Marxist Aesthetics* (Boston: Beacon Press, 1978), 45.
91. Ibid.
92. M. M. Bakhtin, *The Dialogic Imagination: Four Essays*, trans. Caryl and Michael Holquist (Austin: University of Texas Press, 1981), 171.

CHAPTER FIVE

1. Ishii Ryōsuke, ed., *Japanese Legislation in the Meiji Era*, trans. William J. Chambliss (Tokyo: Pan-Pacific Press, 1958), 724.
2. James W. White, *Ikki: Social Conflict and Political Protest in Early Modern Japan* (Ithaca: Cornell University Press, 1995). See chaps. 5–7 where White discusses the dramatic rise in peasant protests and the greater degree of violence they engendered in the first ten years of the Meiji period.

3. Hirota Masaki, *Sabetsu no shisen: Kindai Nihon no ishiki kōzō* (Tokyo: Yoshikawa Kōbunkan, 1998).
4. Hirota Masaki, *Bunmei kaika to minshū ishiki* (Tokyo: Aoki Shoten, 1980). 37.
5. "Gakusei jisshi saimokunitsuki dajōkanshirei," in Yamazumi Masami, ed., *Nihon kindai shisō taikei*, vol. 6, *Kyōiku no taikei* (Tokyo: Iwanami Shoten, 1990), 27 and 31
6. Ibid., 29 and 31.
7. Arakawa Shōji, "Kiritsuka sareru shintai," in *Kindai Nihon no bunkashi*, ed. Komori Yōichi et al., vol. 4, *Kansei no kindai 1870–1910* (2) (Tokyo: Iwanami Shoten, 2002), 176–77.
8. Ito Hirobumi, "Some Reminiscences of the Grant of the New Constitution," in *Fifty Years of New Japan*, comp. Count Shigenobu Okuma and trans. Marcus B. Huish, vol. 1 (London: Smith, Elder, and Company, 1910), 124–25.
9. Fukuzawa Yukichi, "Tsūzoku kokkenron," in *Fukuzawa Yukichi Shū*, ed. Tomita Masafumi (Tokyo: Chikuma Shobō, 1966), 40.
10. Katō Hiroyuki, *Jinken shinsetsu* (A Reconsideration of Human Rights), trans. Victor J. Koschmann, in *From Japan's Modernity: A Reader*, ed. Tetsuo Najita (Chicago: Center for East Asian Studies, University of Chicago, 2002), 1–43.
11. Ito Hirobumi wrote to Emperor Meiji in 1880 that "those who agitate people's minds with angry rhetoric undermine our national polity and incite rebellions. . . . They are nothing but social maladies. We must move promptly to carry out educational reforms to solve them." See Ito, "Kyoikugi," in Yamazumi, *Nihon kindai shisō taikei*, 6:80.
12. Miyatake Gaikotsu, in *Miyatake Gaikotsu chosakushū*, ed. Tanizawa Eiichi and Yoshino Takao, vol. 4, *Hikkashi* (Tokyo: Kawade Shobō Shinsha, 1985), 188–93. Popular right activists such as Komatsu Eitaro, Yamawaki Ryo, and Yokose Fumihiko wrote in the paper called *Hyōron shinbun* during the late 1870s to express the idea of people's natural right to overthrow the autocratic government. This view resonated with that of more eminent activists such as Ueki Emori, Komatsu, Yamawaki, and Yokose were all arrested in 1877.
13. Nishimura Shigeki, "Daini daigakuku jun'shi hokoku," in Yamazumi, *Nihon kindai shisō taikei*, 6:53. On the Meiji intellectual discourse on "national morality," see Richard Reitan's *Making a Moral Society: Ethics and the State in Meiji Japan* (Honolulu: University of Hawaii Press, 2009), chaps. 2 and 3.
14. See Yasumaru Yoshio, *Nihon no kindaika to minshū shisō* (Tokyo: Heibonsha, 1999); and Irokawa Daikichi *Meiji no bunka* (Tokyo: Iwanami Shoten, 1970)
15. See Taki Kōji, *Tennō no shōzō* (Tokyo: Iwanami Shoten, 2002); and Takashi Fujitani, *Splendid Monarchy: Power and Pageantry in Modern Japan* (Berkeley: University of California Press, 1998).
16. Nakamura Masanori, Ishii Kanji, and Yutaka Kasuga, eds., *Nihon kindai shisō taikei*, vol. 8, *Keizai kōsō* (Tokyo: Iwanami Shoten, 1988), 480.
17. For the emergence of a more coherent policy from the middle of the Meiji

period, see Carol Gluck's seminal work, *Japan's Modern Myths: Ideology in the Late Meiji Period* (Princeton: Princeton University Press, 1985).

18. *Ishiki kaii jōrei* was a series of decrees issued in Yokohama, Osaka, and Tokyo in 1873, 1874, and 1876, respectively; see Ogi Shinzō, Kumakura Isao, and Ueno Chizuko, eds. *Nihon kindai shisō taikei*, vol. 23, *Fūzoku/sei* (Tokyo: Iwanami Shoten, 1990), 3–26.
19. In 1889, e.g., Doi Masataka, the founder of *the Association for the Reform of Japanese Custom* (*Dai nihon fūzoku kairyō kai*), wrote in *On Reforming the Japanese Custom* (*Nihon fūzoku kairyōron*) that "*fūzoku* refers to national custom (*kokka no shūkan*)" and was best exemplified by late Tokugawa and early Meiji revolutionaries who died for their unlimited affection and loyalty to the Emperor. See Ogi Shinzō,Kumakura Isao, and Ueno Chizuko eds., *Nihon kindai shisō taikei: fūzoku, sei*, vol. 23 (Tokyo: Iwanami Shoten, 1990), 41–42 and 45.
20. Furukawa Miki, *Zusetsu shomin geinō: Edo no misemono* (Tokyo: Yūzankaku, 1993), 292.
21. Kurata Yoshihiro, ed., *Meiji no engei*, vol. 1 (Tokyo: Kokuritsu Gekijō Chōsa Yōseibu Geinō Chōsashitsu, 1980), 22.
22. Matsumoto Sannosuke and Yamamuro Shinichi, eds., *Nihon kindai shisō taikei*, vol. 2, *Genron to media* (Tokyo: Iwanami Shoten, 1990), 410–11. "Stories about ghosts and irrational happenings" referred to the kind of stories which chap. 4 analyzes. "Comical and lascivious fads" corresponded to the kind of humorous writings discussed in chap. 3.
23. Kurata, *Meiji no engei*, 1:26 and 1:40–41.
24. Kurata, *Meiji no engei*, 1:28; and Ogi, Kumakura, and Ueno, *Nihon kindai shisō taikei*, 23:3–16.
25. Furukawa, *Zusetsu shomin geinō: Edo no misemono*, 293.
26. Kurata, *Meiji no engei*, 1:51.
27. Hyōdō Hiromi, "Meiji no pafomansu," in Komori et al., *Kindai Nihon no Bunkashi*, 4:161.
28. Kurata, *Meiji no engei*, 1:21–26, 1:51–52.
29. Momose Hibiki, *Bunmei kaika: Ushinawareta fūzoku* (Tokyo: Yoshikawa Kōbunkan, 2008), 29–30.
30. Ibid., 27–55.
31. Cited in Kurata Yoshihiro, *Geinō no bunmei kaika: Meiji kokka to geinō kindaika* (Tokyo: Heibonsha, 1999), 71.
32. Ibid.
33. Kurata, *Meiji no engei*, 1:41.
34. Ōkubo Toshimichi, "Shokusan kōgyō ni kansuru kengi," in Nakamura, Ishii, and Kasuga, *Nihon kindai shisō taikei*, 8:18–19.
35. Yamazumi, *Nihon kindai shisō taikei*, 6:476–80.
36. See ordinances issued by the central and local authorities between the 1870s and the 1880s in Yamazumi, *Nihon kindai shisō taikei*, 6:476–80.
37. Immanuel Wallerstein also sees meritocracy as the ideological kernel

of capitalist system that justifies class inequalities as the inevitable and universal expression of different levels of education and intelligence. He calls into question the liberal theory that political and economic stability can be achieved by meritocratic system, since the system follows the principle of "free" competition, not that of lineage, heritage, and tradition as in premodern times. In fact, Wallerstein continues, meritocracy is built on a politically and economically fragile basis, which is why capitalism necessitates racism and sexism to achieve a stable ground for the perpetual accumulation of capital and maximization of profit. My analysis of Meiji meritocracy resonates with his observation. See Immanuel Wallerstein, "The Ideological Tensions of Capitalism: Universalism Versus Racism and Sexism," in Etienne Balibar and Immanuel Wallerstein, *Race, Nation, Class: Ambiguous Identities* (London: Verso, 1991), 29–36.

38. Iwasaki Jirō and Shimizu Isao, *Shōwa no fūshi manga to sesō fūzoku nenpyō* (Tokyo: Jiyū Kokuminsha, 1984) 16.
39. Edward Seidensticker, *Low City, High City: Tokyo from Edo to the Earthquake* (Cambridge: Harvard University Press, 1983), 93.
40. Iwasaki and Shimizu, *Shōwa no fūshi manga to sesō fūzoku*, 16.
41. Seidensticker, *Low City, High City*, 150.
42. Kurata, *Geinō no bunmei kaika*, 261.
43. Ibid.
44. Karatani Kōjin, *Nihon kindai bungaku no kigen* (Tokyo: Kōdansha, 1988), 66–69.
45. Karatani, *Nihon kindai bungaku no kigen*, 67. The translation is that of Brett de Bary in *Origins of Modern Japanese Literature* (Durham: Duke University Press, 1993), 55.
46. Kurata, *Geinō no bunmei kaika*, 262–63.
47. Watsuji Tetsurō, *Nihon seishinshi kenkyū* (Tokyo: Iwanami Shoten, 1992), 358–74.
48. Karatani, *Nihon kindai bungaku no kigen*, 65.
49. Ibid., 67–68.
50. Nakamura Kikuji, *Kyōkasho no shakaishi: Meiji Ishin kara haisen made* (Tokyo: Iwanami Shoten, 1992), 40–60.
51. Yamazumi, *Nihon kindai shisō taikei*, 6:126.
52. Mori Arinori, "Saitama ken jinjo shihan gakko ni okeru enzetsu," in Yamazumi, *Nihon kindai shisō taikei*, 6:134–35.
53. *Yomiuri shinbun*, July 25, 1891, in *Yomidasu rekishikan*.
54. *Yomiuri shinbun*, July 3, 1899, in *Yomidasu rekishikan*.
55. Sōseki Natsume, *My Individualism; and, The Philosophical Foundations of Literature*, trans. Sammy I. Tsunematsu (Boston: Tuttle, 2004), 44.
56. Fredric Jameson, *Postmodernism, or, The Cultural Logic of Late Capitalism* (Durham: Duke University Press, 1991), 15.
57. Sōseki Natsume, *Kokoro*, trans. Edwin McClellan (Washington, DC: Gateway, 2000), 30.

58. Natsume, *My Individualism*, 56.
59. Gluck, *Japan's Modern Myths*.
60. Karatani, *Origins of Modern Japanese Literature*, 70 (English version).
61. Ibid., 69 (English version)
62. André Leroi-Gourhan, *Le geste et la parole*, 2 vols. (Paris: Albin Michel, 1964–65). This English translation is that of de Barry in Karatani, *Origins of Modern Japanese Literature*, 70.
63. Karatani, *Origins of Modern Japanese Literature*, 64–65 (English version).
64. I am not here using Althusser's concept of interpellation introduced in his well-known essay "Ideological State Apparatuses," which posits the relationship between the state and the individual as an automatic machine of subjectivation (the latter automatically internalizes the former's ideological call). Rather my use of the term is grounded in his earlier work "On Contradiction and Overdetermination," in *For Marx*, where he elaborates a nonlinear and antireductive view of subject formation by proposing the concept of multiple sites of contradiction and a historically contingent unity of contradictory forces. My analysis of early Meiji politics of subject formation presented in this chapter is informed by this perspective. See Louis Althusser, *For Marx* (London: Penguin Press, 1969), 78–128.
65. Michel Foucault defines *homo œconomicus* as follows: "considering the subject as *homo œconomicus* does not imply an anthropological identification of any behavior with whatsoever with economic behavior. It simply means that economic behavior is the grid of intelligibility one will adopt on the behavior of a new individual. It also means that the individual becomes govermentalizable, that power gets a hold on him to the extent, and only to the extent, that he is a *homo œconomicus*." As we have seen in this chapter, the Meiji government's efforts to "reform popular culture" or "people's mind-set" were intended to produce this type of economic behavior on which the individual would become both productive and governmentalizable. What Foucault does not explain is the fact that productivity and governmentalizability are never symbiotic and reciprocal but often paradoxical. It is for this reason that patriotism and national identity—egalitarian humanism defined as national citizenship—play a crucial role in containing the paradox. The Meiji government's oscillation between liberalist and traditionalist rhetoric points precisely to this strategy of maneuvering. See Michel Foucault, *The Birth of Biopolitics: Lectures at the Collège De France, 1978–1979*, ed. Michel Senellart (New York: Picador, 2008), 252.
66. Ibid., 120.
67. Ibid., 252–53.
68. Giorgio Agamben, *Homo Sacer: Sovereign Power and Bare Life*, trans. Daniel Heller-Roazen (Stanford: Stanford University Press, 1998), 6.
69. Fukuzawa Yukichi, "Tsūzoku Minkenron," in Tomita Masafumi, ed., *Fukuzawa Yukichi shū* (Tokyo: Chikuma Shobō, 1966), 18–19.

70. Ibid., 19.
71. In this sense, the birth of civil society—a democratic form of politics that posits each individual as the subject of political power—in the Taishō period (1912–26) marked a true beginning of biopolitics in the context of modern Japan. It was/is in the theory of civil society that the distinction between the realms of life and politics became/becomes indistinguishable. The aporia of liberalism reveals itself in the most sharpened manner in civil society in that it seeks to put, to borrow Agamben's phrase, "the freedom and happiness of men into play in the very place—'bare life'" that is colonized by political power (Agamben, *Homo Sacer*, 9–10). This is probably what Foucault meant by the modern modality of power-as-productive (as opposed to repressive), since the realization of freedom and happiness was simultaneously an experience of subjection, which the subjected individuals do not recognize. This aporia thus takes the form of what Lukács called "reified consciousness" or Althussuer called "ideology."
72. Momose, *Bunmei kaika de ushinawareta fūzoku*, 180–82.
73. Katsuya Hirano, *Tasha no Tōrai no Rekishigaku: "Ainu" to Posuto Koroniaru teki Kōsatsu* (Tokyo: Hōsei University Press, forthcoming).
74. The English translation of Hokkaido Former Natives Protection Law is available in Michele M. Mason and Helen J. S. Lee eds., *Reading Colonial Japan: Text, Context, and Critique* (Stanford: Stanford University Press, 2012), 57–59. Also see Komori Yōichi's analysis of it, "Rule in the Name of "Protection": The Vocabulary of Colonialism," in the same volume, 60–75. For the implication of the simultaneous operation of ethnicization and capitalist expropriation, see Katsuya Hirano, "The Politics of Colonial Translation: Ainu as a "'Vanishing Ethnicity'," *Asia-Pacific Journal* 4, March 9, 2009, http://japanfocus.org/-Katsuya-HIRANO/3013.
75. Balibar and Wallerstein, *Race, Nation, Class*, 56.
76. Ibid.
77. Ibid., 96.
78. Slavoj Žižek, *The Sublime Object of Ideology* (London: Verso, 1989), 45.
79. Ibid. From the late Meiji onward, the militarist stories that glorified "brave" soldiers who died for the nation, the genre collectively called *gunkoku bidan* (軍国美談), were included in school textbooks. They were also performed by popular storytellers and kabuki actors and made into movies and novels.
80. Arakawa Shoji argues that it was during and after the Sino-Japanese war that soldiers, solders-to-be and their families started to express their praise for those who died for the sake of "defending" (fighting for) national and imperial honors. See Arakawa, "Kiritsuka sareru shintai," in Komori et al., *Kindai Nihon no Bunkashi*, 4:198–99.
81. Those who died of "heroic death" were deified as "military gods" (*gunshin* 軍神) in the Yasukuni Shrine. See Nakamura Keigo, *Kyōkasho monogatari: Kokka to kyōkasho to minshū* (Tokyo: Nōberu shobō, 1970), 57.

Bibliography

Abe Jirō. *Tokugawa jidai no geijutsu to shakai*. Tokyo: Kaizōsha, 1931.

Agamben, Giorgio. *Homo Sacer: Sovereign Power and Bare Life*. Translated by Daniel Heller-Roazen. Stanford: Stanford University Press, 1998.

Althusser, Louis. *For Marx*. London: Verso, 2005.

Amino Yoshihiko. *Chūsei no hinin to yūjo*. Tokyo: Akashi Shoten, 1994.

———. *Muen, kugai, raku: Nihon chūsei no jiyū to heiwa*. Tokyo: Heibonsha, 1996.

Arakawa Hidetoshi, ed. *Tenpo kaikaku machibure shiryō*. Tokyo: Yūzankaku Shuppan, 1974.

Arakawa Shōji. "Kiritsuka sareru shintai." In *Kindai Nihon no Bunkashi*. Edited by Komori Yōichi, Sakai Naoki, Shimazono Susumu, Chino Kaori, Narita Ryūichi, and Yoshimi Shun'ya. Vol. 4. *Kansei no kindai 1870–1910*, 169–204. Tokyo: Iwanami Shoten, 2002.

Asai Ryōi. *Edo meishoki*. Edited by Haruhiko Asakura. Tokyo: Meicho Shuppan, 1976.

Asano Shūgō and Yoshida Nobuyuki, eds. *Ukiyoe o yomu*. Vol. 6. *Kuniyoshi*. Tokyo: Asahi Shinbunsha, 1997.

Babcock, Barbara A., ed. *The Reversible World: Symbolic Inversion in Art and Society*. Ithaca: Cornell University, 1978.

Bakhtin, Mikhail M. *The Dialogic Imagination: Four Essays*. Translated by Caryl and Michael Holquist. Austin: University of Texas Press, 1981.

———. *Problems of Dostoevsky's Poetics*. Translated and edited by Caryl Emerson. Minneapolis: University of Minnesota Press, 1984.

———. *Rabelais and His World*. Bloomington: Indiana University Press, 1984.

Bataille, Georges. *Visions of Excess: Selected Writings, 1927–1939*. Translated by Allan Stoekl. Minneapolis: University of Minnesota Press, 1985.

Baudelaire, Charles. *Selected Writings on Art and Literature*. Translated by P. E. Charvet. Harmondsworth: Penguin, 1992.

Bellah, Robert Neelly. *Tokugawa Religion: The Cultural Roots of Modern Japan*. New York: Free Press, 1985.

Benjamin, Walter. *Illuminations*. Translated by Harry Zohn and edited by Hannah Arendt. New York: Random House, 1988.

Berger, Peter L., and Thomas Luckmann. *The Social Construction of Reality: A Treatise in the Sociology of Knowledge*. Garden City: Doubleday, 1967.

Bergson, Henri. *Laughter: An Essay on the Meaning of the Comic*. Translated by Cloudesley Brereton and Fred Rothwell. København: Green Integer, 1999.

———. "Le rire." In *Comedy: An Essay on Comedy*. Edited by Wylie Sypher. Garden City: Doubleday, 1956.

Berry, Mary Elizabeth. *Japan in Print: Information and Nation in the Early Modern Period*. Berkeley: University of California Press, 2006.

Bloch, Ernst. "Nonsynchronism and the Obligation to Its Dialectics." *New German Critique* 11 (Spring 1977): 22–38.

Botsman, Daniel V. *Punishment and Power in the Making of Modern Japan*. Princeton: Princeton University Press, 2005.

Brazell, Karen, ed. *Traditional Japanese Theater: An Anthology of Plays*. New York: Columbia University Press, 1998.

Burns, Susan L. "The Body as Text: Confucianism, Reproduction, and Gender in Early Modern Japan." In *Rethinking Confucianism: Past and Present in China, Japan, Korea, and Vietnam*, edited by Benjamin A. Elman, John B. Duncan, and Herman Ooms, 178–219. Los Angeles: UCLA Asian Pacific Monograph Series, 2002.

Butler, Judith. *Bodies That Matter: On the Discursive Limits of "Sex."* New York: Routledge, 1993.

———. *The Psychic Life of Power: Theories in Subjection*. Stanford: Stanford University Press, 1997.

Buyō Inshi. *Sejikenbunroku*. Tokyo: Iwanami Shoten, 1994.

Charney, Maurice. *Comedy High and Low: An Introduction to the Experience of Comedy*. New York: Oxford University Press, 1978.

Chikamatsu Monzaemon. "Kyo jitsu himaku ron." In *Chikamatsu*, edited by Ōkubo Tadakuni, 333–50. Tokyo: Kadokawa Shoten, 1970.

Dazai Shundai. "On Political Economy." In *Tokugawa Political Writings*, edited by Tetsuo Najita, 141–53. Cambridge: Cambridge University Press, 1998.

Delprat, Adriana. "Forms of Dissent in the *Gesaku* Literature of Hiraga Gennai (1728–1780)." PhD dissertation, Princeton University, 1985.

Dentith, Simon. *Parody*. London: Routledge, 2000.

Dowling, William C. *Jameson, Althusser, Marx: An Introduction to the Political Unconscious*. Ithaca: Cornell University Press, 1984.

Duus, Peter. "Weapons of the Weak, Weapons of the Strong: The Development of the Japanese Political Cartoon." *Journal of Asian Studies* 60:4 (November 2001): 965–97.

Eagleton, Terry. "Ideology and Its Vicissitudes in Western Marxism." In *Mapping Ideology*, edited by Slavoj Žižek, 176–226. London: Verso, 1994.

———. *Walter Benjamin: Or, Towards a Revolutionary Criticism*. London: Verso Editions and NLB, 1981.

Eco, Umberto. *The Role of the Reader: Explorations in the Semiotics of Texts*. Bloomington: Indiana University Press, 1984.

Field, Norma. "Somehow: The Postmodern as Atmosphere." In *Postmodernism and Japan*, edited by Masao Miyoshi and Harry D. Harootunian, 169–88. Durham: Duke University Press, 1989.

Foucault, Michel. *The Birth of Biopolitics: Lectures at the Collège De France, 1978–1979*. Edited by Michel Senellart. New York: Picador, 2008.

———. "Theatrum Philosophicum." *Critique* 282 (November 1970): 885–908.

Freud, Sigmund. "Negation." In *The Pelican Freud Library*. Vol. 11. *On Metapsychology*. Edited by A. Richard and J. Strachey and translated by J. Strachey. Harmondsworth: Penguin Books, 1984.

Fujita Noboru and Satō Takayuki, eds. *Dai Nihon kinsei shiryō: Shichū torishimari* ruishū. Vol. 18. Tokyo: Tokyo Daigaku Shuppankai, 1988.

Fujitani Takashi. *Splendid Monarchy: Power and Pageantry in Modern Japan*. Berkeley: University of California Press, 1998.

Fukuzawa Yukichi. *Fukuzawa Yukichi shū*. Edited by Tomita Masafumi. Tokyo: Chikuma Shobō, 1966.

———. "Tsūzoku kokkenron." In Tomita, *Fukuzawa Yukichi shū*, 21–51.

———. "Tsūzoku minkenron." In Tomita, *Fukuzawa Yukichi shū*, 18–21.

Fung, Yu-Lan. *A Short History of Chinese Philosophy*. Edited by Derk Bodde. New York: Macmillan, 1948.

Furukawa Miki. *Zusetsu shomin geinō: Edo no misemono*. Tokyo: Yūzankaku Shuppan, 1993.

Gadamer, Hans. "The Problem of Historical Consciousness." In *Interpretive Social Science*, edited by Paul Rabinow and William M. Sullivan, 82–140. Berkeley: University of California Press, 1987.

"Gakusei jisshi saimokunitsuki Dajōkanshirei." In Yamazumi, *Kyōiku no taikei*, 27–33.

Geinōshi Kenkyūkai. *Nihon shomin bunka shiryō shūsei*. Vol. 8. Tokyo: San'ichi Shobō, 1973.

Ginzburg, Carlo. *The Cheese and the Worms: The Cosmos of a Sixteenth-Century Miller*. Baltimore: Johns Hopkins University Press, 1980.

Gion Nankai. *Nankai shiketsu*. In *Edo shijin senshū: Hattori Nankaku/Gion Nankai*. Edited by Yamamoto Kazuyoshi and Yokoyama Hiroshi. Vol. 3. Tokyo: Iwanami Shoten, 1991.

Gluck, Carol. *Japan's Modern Myths: Ideology in the Late Meiji Period*. Princeton: Princeton University Press, 1985.

Gramsci, Antonio, *Selections from the Prison Notebooks of Antonio Gramsci*. Edited and translated by Quintin Hoare and Geoffrey Nowell-Smith. New York: International Publishers, 1971.

Gunji Masakatsu. "Edo bunka ni okeru kabuki no ichi." In *Edo jidai to kindaika*, edited by Nakane Chie and Ōishi Shinzaburō, 354–73. Tokyo: Chikuma Shobō, 1986.

———. *Gisei no bun*. Tokyo: Hakusuisha, 1991.

———. "Kabuki and Its Social Background." In Nakane and Ōishi, *Tokugawa Japan*, 192–212.

———. *Kabuki hasseishi ronshū*. Tokyo: Iwanami Shoten, 2002.

Haga Noboru. "Edo no bunka." In *Kasei bunka no kenkyū*, edited by Hayashiya Tatsusaburō, 161–88. Tokyo: Iwanami Shoten, 1976.

———. *Edogo no seiritsu*. Tokyo: Kaitakusha, 1982.

Haga Tōru, ed. *Nihon no meicho*. Vol. 22. *Sugita Genpaku, Hiraga Gennai, Shiba Kōkan*. Tokyo: Chūō Kōronsha, 1984.

Hall, Stuart. "The Problem of Ideology: Marxism without Guarantees." In *Stuart Hall: Critical Dialogues in Cultural Studies*, edited by David Morley and Kuan-Hsing Chen, 25–46. London: Routledge, 1996.

———. "Signification, Representation, Ideology: Althusser and the Post-Structuralist Debates." *Critical Studies in Mass Communication* 2:2 (June 1985): 91–114.

Harootunian, Harry D. "Cultural Politics in Tokugawa Japan." In *Undercurrents in the Floating World: Censorship and Japanese Prints*, edited by Sarah E. Thompson and Harry D. Harootunian, 9–28. New York: Asia Society Galleries, 1991.

———. *The Empire's New Clothes: Paradigm Lost, and Regained*. Chicago: Prickly Paradigm Press, 2004.

———. "Late Tokugawa Culture and Thought." In *The Cambridge History of Japan*. Vol. 5. *The 19th Century*. Edited by Jansen, Marius B., John Whitney Hall, Madoka Kanai, and Denis Twitchett. New York: Cambridge University Press, 1989.

———. *Things Seen and Unseen: Discourse and Ideology in Tokugawa Nativism*. Chicago: University of Chicago Press, 1988.

Harpham, Geoffrey G. *On the Grotesque: Strategies of Contradiction in Art and Literature*. Princeton: Princeton University Press, 1982.

Hashimoto Mineo. *"Ukiyo" no shisō: Nihonjin no jinseikan*. Tokyo: Kōdansha Gendai Shisō, 1975.

Hattori Yukio. *Hengeron: Kabuki no seishinshi*. Tokyo: Heibonsha, 1975.

———. *Kabuki*. Tokyo: Heibonsha, 1971.

———. *Sakasama no yūrei: "Shi" no Edo bunkaron*. Tokyo: Heibonsha, 1989.

Hattori Yukio, Tomita Tetsunosuke, and Hirosue Tamotsu, eds. *Kabuki jiten*. Tokyo: Heibonsha, 1983.

Hayami, Akira, Osamu Saitō, and Ronald P. Toby, eds. *Emergence of Economic Society in Japan, 1600–1859*. Oxford: Oxford University Press, 2004.

Hegel, Georg Wilhelm Friedrich. *The Philosophy of History*. Translated by John Sibree. Buffalo: Promethus Books, 1991.

Hiraga Gennai. *Fūryūshidokenden*. In *Hiraga Gennai shū*. Edited by Tetsuzō Tsukamoto. Tokyo: Yūhōdō Shoten, 1926.

———. *On Farting*. Translated by William Sibley. In *Readings in Tokugawa Thought*, edited by Tetsuo Najita, 167–74. Chicago: Center for East Asian studies, University of Chicago, 1998.

———. *Hōhiron kōhen* [*On Farting, Part 2*]. In Haga Tōru, *Nihon no meicho*.

———. *Soshirigusa*. In *Hiraga Gennai shū*. Tokyo: Tokyo Shoi'n, 1923.

———. *Naemara itsuden*. In Haga, *Nihon no meicho*.

Hirano, Katsuya. "The Dialectic of Laughter and Tosaka's Critical Theory." In *Tosaka Jun: Critical Reader*. Edited by Ken Kawashima and Robert Stolz. Ithaca: Cornell East Asian Series, forthcoming.

———. "The Politics of Colonial Translation: Ainu as a 'Vanishing Ethnicity'." *Asia-Pacific Journal: Japan Focus* 4 (2009). http://japanfocus.org/-Katsuya-HIRANO/3013.

———. "Social Networks and Production of Public Discourse in Edo Popular Culture." In *Acquisition: Art and Ownership in Edo-Period Japan*, edited by Elizabeth Lillehoj. Warren: Floating World Editions, 2007.

———. *Tasha no tōrai no rekishigaku: "Ainu" to posuto koroniaruteki kōsatsu*. Tokyo: Hōsei University Press, forthcoming.

Hiroshi Shimbo and Akira Hasegawa. "The Dynamics of Market Economy and Production." In *Emergence of Economic Society in Japan 1600*–1859, edited by Akira Hayami, Osamu Saito, and Ronald P. Toby, 159–91. Oxford: Oxford University Press, 2004.

Hirosue Tamotsu. *Henkai no akusho*. Tokyo: Heibonsha, 1973.

———. *Yotsuya kaidan*. Tokyo: Kage Shobō, 2000.

Hirota Masaki. *Bunmei kaika to minshū ishiki*. Tokyo: Aoki shoten, 1980.

———. *Sabetsu no shisen: Kindai Nihon no ishiki kōzō*. Tokyo: Yoshikawa Kōbunkan, 1998.

Honda Seika. "Asakusa okuzan jidai no misemono." In Ishizumi and Ogi, *Edo to Tokyo*, 1:14–20.

Honda Yasuo. *Ukiyoburo ukiyodoko: Sekenbanashi no bungaku*. Tokyo: Heibonsha, 1994.

Howell, David L. *Geographies of Identity in Nineteenth-Century Japan*. Berkeley: University of California Press, 2005.

Hur, Nam-lin. *Prayer and Play in Late Tokugawa Japan: Asakusa Sensōji and Edo Society*. Cambridge: Harvard University Asia Center, 2000.

Hyōdō Hiromi. "Meiji no pafōmansu." In *Kindai Nihon no Bunkashi*. Edited by Komori Yōichi, Sakai Naoki, Shimazono Susumu, Chino Kaori, Narita Ryūichi, and Yoshimi Shun'ya. Vol. 4. *Kansei no kindai 1870–1910*. Tokyo: Iwanami Shoten, 2002.

Ihara Saikaku. *Honchō nijūfukō*. Tokyo: Meiji Shoin, 1984.

———. *Nihon eitaigura*. Tokyo: Iwanami Shoten, 1956.

———. "The Story of Seijiru in Himeji." In *Five Women Who Loved Love*. Translated by William Theodore de Bary. Boston: Tuttle, 1956.

Iizawa Tadasu. *Buki to shite no warai*. Tokyo: Iwanami Shoten, 1977.

Ikegami, Eiko. *Bonds of Civility: Aesthetic Networks and the Political Origins of Japanese Culture*. Cambridge: Cambridge University Press, 2005.

Inaka Rōjin Tada no Jijii. *The Playboy Dialect*. Translated by Herschel Miller. In *Early Modern Japanese Literature*, edited by Haruo Shirane, 633–55. New York: Columbia University, 2002.

Irokawa Daikichi. *Meiji no bunka*. Tokyo: Iwanami Shoten, 1970.

Ishii Ryōsuke, ed. *Japanese Legislation in the Meiji Era*. Translated by William J. Chambliss. Tokyo: Pan-Pacific Press, 1958.

Ishizumi Harunosuke and Ogi Shinzō, eds. *Edo to Tokyo*. 28 vols. Tokyo: Akashi Shoten, 1991

Ito Hirobumi. "Kyōikugi." In Yamazumi, *Kyōiku no taikei*, 80–83.

———. "Some Reminiscences of the Grant of the New Constitution." In *Fifty Years of New Japan* (*Kaikoku Gojunen Shi*), compiled by Count Ōkuma Shigenobu and translated by Marcus B. Huish, 1:122–32. London: Smith, Elder and Co., 1910.

Iwasaki Jirō and Shimizu Isao. *Shōwa no fūshi manga to sesō fūzoku nenpyō*. Tokyo: Jiyū Kokuminsha, 1984.

Iwasaki Haruko. "The World of Gesaku: Playful Writers of Late Eighteenth Century Japan." PhD dissertation, Harvard University, 1984.

Jacques Derrida, Pierre Klossowski, Jean-François Lyotard, and Gilles Deleuze. *Nīche wa, konnichi?* (*Niezsche Aujourd' Hui?*). Translated by Hayashi Yoshio, Honma Kunio, and Morimoto Kazuo. Tokyo: Chikuma Shobō, 2002.

Jameson, Fredric. *The Political Unconscious: Narrative as a Socially Symbolic Act*. Ithaca: Cornell University Press, 1981.

———. *Postmodernism, or, The Cultural Logic of Late Capitalism*. Durham: Duke University Press, 1991.

———. *The Prison-House of Language: A Critical Account of Structuralism and Russian Formalism*. Princeton: Princeton University Press, 1972.

Jinnai Hidenobu. *Tokyo no kūkan jinruigaku*. Tokyo: Chikuma Shobō, 1992.

Jippensha Ikku. *Tōkaidō-chū hizakurige*. Tokyo: Perikan, 1996.

Kabat, Adam. *Edo kokkei bakemonozukushi*. Tokyo: Kōdansha, 2003.

Karaki Junzō. *Muyōsha no keifu*. Tokyo: Chikuma Shobō, 1960.

Karatani Kōjin. *Nihon kindai bungaku no kigen*. Tokyo: Kōdansha, 1988.

———. *Origins of Modern Japanese Literature*. Translated by Brett de Bary. Durham: Duke University Press, 1993.

Katō Hiroyuki, *Jinken shinsetsu* [*A Reconsideration of Human Rights*]. Translated by Victor J. Koschmann. In *From Japan's Modernity: A Reader*. Edited by Tetsuo Najita. Chicago: Center for East Asian Studies, University of Chicago, 2002.

Kato Takashi. "Governing Edo." In McClain, Merriman, and Ugawa, *Edo and Paris*, 41–67. Ithaca: Cornell University Press, 1994.

Katsuhisa Moriya. "Urban Networks and Information Networks." In Nakane and Ōishi, *Tokugawa Japan*, 97–123. Tokyo: University of Tokyo Press, 1985.

Katsushika Hokusai. *Hokusai manga*. Tokyo: Seigensha, 2011.

Keene, Donald. "Introduction." In Monzaemon Chikamatsu, *Four Major Plays of Chikamatsu*, translated by Donald Keene, 1–38. New York: Columbia University Press, 1998.

Kitahara Susumu. "Horeki–Tenmeiki no Edo shōgyō to fudasashi." In *Edo chōnin no* kenkyū, edited by Nishiyama Matsunosuke, 1:247–336. Tokyo: Yoshikawa Kōbunkan, 2006.

Komori Yōichi. "Rule in the Name of 'Protection': The Vocabulary of Colonialism." In *Reading Colonial Japan: Text, Context, and Critique*, edited by Michele M. Mason and Helen J. S. Lee, 60–75. Stanford: Stanford University Press, 2012.

Komori Yōichi, Sakai Naoki, Shimazono Susumu, Chino Kaori, Narita Ryūichi, and Yoshimi Shun'ya, eds. *Kindai Nihon no Bunkashi*. Vol. 4. *Kansei no kindai 1870–1910* (2). Tokyo: Iwanami Shoten, 2002.

Konta Yōzō. *Bakumatsu shakai kōzō no kenkyu*. Tokyo: Hanawa shobō, 2003.

———. *Edo no hon'ya san: Kinsei bunkashi no sokumen*. Tokyo: Nihon Hōsō Shuppan Kyōkai, 1977.

———. "Edo no shuppan shihon." In *Edo chōnin no kenkyū*, edited by by Nishiyama Matsunosuke. Vol. 3. Tokyo: Yoshikawa Kōbunkan, 2006.

Koschmann, J. Victor. *The Mito Ideology: Discourse, Reform, and Insurrection in Late Tokugawa Japan, 1790–1864*. Berkeley: University of California Press, 1987.

———. *Revolution and Subjectivity in Postwar Japan*. Chicago: University of Chicago Press, 1996.

Kurachi Katsunao. *Kinsei no minshū to shihai shisō*. Tokyo: Kashiwa Shobō, 1996.

Kurata Yoshihiro. *Geinō no bunmei kaika: Meiji kokka to geinō kindaika*. Tokyo: Heibonsha, 1999.

———. *Shibai-goya to yose no kindai: "Yūgei" kara "bunka" e*. Tokyo: Iwanami Shoten, 2006.

———., ed. *Meiji no engei*. Vol. 1. Tokyo: Kokuritsu Gekijō Chōsa Yōseibu Geinō Chōsashitsu, 1980.

Kuroita Katsumi, ed. *Tokugawa jikki*. Vol. 3. Tokyo: Yoshikawa Kōbunkan, 1998.

Kurushima Hiroshi. *Kuniyoshi*. Tokyo: Asahishinbun, 1998.

"Kyōhō genreishū." In *Edo bakufu hō no kenkyū*, edited by Kukita Kazuko, 76–88. Tokyo: Gannandō Shoten, 1980.

LaCapra, Dominick. *History and Criticism*. Ithaca: Cornell University Press, 1985.

Lefebvre, Henri. *Critique of Everyday Life*. London: Verso, 1991.

———. *The Production of Space*. Oxford: Blackwell, 1992.

Leroi-Gourhan, André. *Le geste et la parole*. 2 vols. Paris: Albin Michel, 1964–65.

Leupp, Gary P. "The Five Men of Naniwa: Gang Violence and Popular Culture in Genroku Osaka." In *Osaka, the Merchant's Capital of Early Modern Japan*, edited by James L. McClain and Osamu Wakita, 125–55. Ithaca: Cornell University Press, 1999.

Li, Michelle Osterfeld. *Ambiguous Bodies: Reading the Grotesque in Japanese Setsuwa Tales*. Stanford: Stanford University Press, 2009.

Looser, Thomas D. *Visioning Eternity: Aesthetics, Politics and History in the Early Modern Noh Theater*. Ithaca: East Asia Program, Cornell University, 2008.

Lu, David John. *Japan: A Documentary History*. Armonk: M. E. Sharpe, 1997.

Lukács, György. *History and Class Consciousness: Studies in Marxist Dialectics*. Cambridge: MIT Press, 1997.

Maeda Ai. "Shuppan to dokusho:Kashihon'ya no yakuwari wo chushin to shite." In Maeda Ai, *Maeda Ai Chosaku shū*. Vol. 1. *Bakumatsu ishinki no bungaku: Narushima Ryūhoku*, 23–36. Tokyo: Chikuma Shobō, 1989.

———. *Toshi kūkan no naka no bungaku*. Tokyo: Chikuma Shobō, 1992.

Marcuse, Herbert. *The Aesthetic Dimension: Toward a Critique of Marxist Aesthetics*. Boston: Beacon Press, 1978.

Markus, Andrew L. "The Carnival of Edo: *Misemono* Spectacles From Contemporary Accounts." *Harvard Journal of Asiatic Studies* 45:2 (December 1985): 499–541.

Maruyama Masao. "Rekishi ishiki no kosō." In *Rekishi shisō shū*. Edited by Maruyama Masao. *Nihon no Shisō*, 6:3–46. Tokyo: Chikuma shobō, 1972.

———. *Studies in the Intellectual History of Tokugawa Japan*. Princeton: Princeton University Press, 1974.

———. *Thought and Behavior in Modern Japanese Politics*. London: Oxford University Press, 1963.

Marx, Karl. *Grundrisse: Foundations of the Critique of Political Economy*. Translated by Martin Nicolaus. London: Penguin Books, in association with *New Left Review*, 1993.

Mason, Michele, and Helen J. S. Lee, eds. *Reading Colonial Japan: Text, Context, and Critique*. Stanford: Stanford University Press, 2012.

Matao Miyamoto. "Quantitative Aspects of Tokugawa Economy." In *Emergence of Economic Society in Japan 1600–1859*, edited by Akira Hayami, Osamu Saito, and Ronald P. Toby, 36–84. Oxford: Oxford University Press, 2004.

Matsumoto Sannosuke, and Yamamuro Shin'ichi, eds. *Nihon kindai shisō taikei*. Vol. 11. *Genron to media*. Tokyo: Iwanami Shoten, 1990.

McClain, James L. "Edobashi: Power, Space, and Popular Culture in Edo." In McClain, Merriman, and Ugawa, *Edo and Paris*, 105–31.

McClain, James L., John M. Merriman, and Ugawa Kaoru, eds. *Edo and Paris: Urban Life and the State in the Early Modern Era*. Ithaca: Cornell University Press, 1994.

Mikami Sanji. *Shirakawa Rakuō-kō to Tokugawa jidai*. Tokyo: Yoshikawa Hanshichi, 1891.

Minami Kazuo. *Bakumatsu Edo no bunka: Ukiyoe to fūshiga*. Tokyo: Hanawa Shobō, 1998.

———. *Bakumatsu toshi shakai no kenkyū*. Tokyo: Hanawa Shobō, 1999.

———. *Edo no fūshiga*. Tokyo: Yoshikawa Kōbunkan, 1997.

Miura Jōshin. *Keichō kenmonshū*. Tokyo: Shin Jinbutsu Ōraisha, 1969.
Miyatake Gaikotsu. *Miyatake Gaikotsu chosakushū*. Edited by Tanizawa Eiichi and Yoshino Takao. Vol. 4. *Hikkashi*. Tokyo: Kawade Shobō Shinsha, 1985.
Mizuhara Akito. *Edogo, Tokyogo, Hyōjungo*. Tokyo: Kōdansha, 1994.
Mizuno Yūko. *Edo Tokyo musume gidayū no rekishi*. Tokyo: Hōsei Daigaku Shuppankyoku, 2003.
Momose Hibiki. *Bunmei kaika: Ushinawareta fūzoku*. Tokyo: Yoshikawa Kōbunkan, 2008.
Mori Arinori. "Saitama ken jinjō shihan gakko ni okeru enzetsu." In Yamazumi, *Kyōiku no taikei*, 132–38.
Nagata Seiji, ed. *Hokusai manga*. Vol. 1. Tokyo: Iwasaki Bijutsusha, 1987.
Nagatomo Chiyoji. *Kinsei kashihon'ya no kenkyū*. Tokyo: Tokyodō Shuppan, 1982.
Najita, Tetsuo. *Doing Shisōshi*. Edited and translated by Katsuya Hirano, Osamu Mihashi, Akifumi Kasai, and Hiroshi Sawada. Tokyo: Misuzu Shobō, 2008.
———. "Method and Analysis in the Conceptual Portrayal of Tokugawa Intellectual History." In *Japanese Thought in the Tokugawa Period, 1600–1868: Methods and Metaphors*, edited by Tetsuo Najita and Irwin Scheiner, 3–38. Chicago: University of Chicago Press, 1978.
———. *Visions of Virtue in Tokugawa Japan: The Kaitokudō Merchant Academy of Osaka*. Chicago: University of Chicago Press, 1987.
Najita, Tetsuo, and J. Victor Koschmann. *Conflict in Modern Japanese History: The Neglected Tradition*. Princeton: Princeton University Press, 1982.
Nakamura Hirotake. *Fushikun*. Vol. 1. Kyoto: Iwasaki, 1811.
Nakamura Keigo. *Kyōkasho monogatari: Kokka to kyōkasho to minshū*. Tokyo: Nōberu Shobō, 1970.
Nakamura Kikuji. *Kyōkasho no shakaishi: Meiji Ishin kara haisen made*. Tokyo: Iwanami Shoten, 1992.
Nakamura Masanori, Ishii Kanji, and Kasuga Yutaka, eds. *Nihon kindai shisō taikei*. Vol. 8. *Keizai kōsō*. Tokyo: Iwanami Shoten, 1988.
Nakamura Yukihiko. "Gesaku nyūmon." In *Sharebon, Kibyōshi, Kokkeibon*, edited by Nakamura Yukihiko and Hamada Keisuke, 5–14. Tokyo: Kadokawa Shoten, 1978.
———. *Gesakuron*. Tokyo: Kadokawa Shoten, 1966.
Nakane Chie and Shinzaburō Ōishi, eds. *Tokugawa Japan: The Social and Economic Antecedents of Modern Japan*. Translated by Conrad D. Totman. Tokyo: University of Tokyo Press, 1990.
Nakayama Mikio. "Kabuki nureba kō." In *Fukugan no kisai: Tsuruya Nanboku*, 208–30. Tokyo: Shintensha, 2001.
Natsume, Sōseki. *Kokoro*. Translated by Edwin McClellan. Washington, DC: Gateway, 2000.
———. *My Individualism; and, The Philosophical Foundations of Literature*. Translated by Sammy I. Tsunematsu. Boston: Tuttle, 2004.

Nishikawa Joken. "Chōnin bukuro." In *Nihon shisō taikei Shinsōban: gei no shisō, michi no shisō*. Vol. 5. *Kinsei chōnin shisō*. Edited by Nakamura Yukihiko. Tokyo: Iwanami Shoten, 1996.

Nishimura Shigeki. "Daini daigakuku jun'shi hōkoku." In Yamazumi, *Kyōiku no taikei*, 45–55.

Nishiyama Matsunosuke. *Edo kabuki kenkyū*. Tokyo: Yoshikawa Kōbunkan, 1987.

———, ed. *Edo chōnin no* kenkyū. Vol. 1. Tokyo: Yoshikawa Kōbunkan, 2006.

Nobuhiro Shinji and Tanahashi Masahiro, eds. "Taidan: Gesaku kenkyū no shin chihei e." In *Edo bungaku* 19 *Gesaku no Jidai* 1, 2–9. Tokyo: Perikan, 1998.

Noro Eitarō. *Nihon shihonshugi hattatsushi*. Vol. 1. Tokyo: Iwanami Shoten, 1983.

Ogata Tsutomu, et al., ads., *Kinsei no bungaku*. Vol. 2. Tokyo: Yūhikaku, 1977.

Ogi Shinzō, Isao Kumakura, and Chizuko Ueno, eds. *Nihon kindai shisō taikei*. Vol. 23. *Fūzoku/sei*. Tōkyō: Iwanami Shoten, 1990.

Ogyū Sorai. *Benmei*. In *Tokugawa Political Writings*, edited by Tetsuo Najita, 35–140. Cambridge: Cambridge University Press, 1998.

———. *Seidan*. In *Nihon shisōshi taikei*. Vol. 36. Edited by Maruyama Masao, Yoshikawa Kōjiro and Tsuji Tatsuya. Tokyo: Iwanami Shoten, 1987.

Ōkubo Toshimichi. "Shokusan kōgyō ni kansuru kengi." In Nakamura, Ishii, and Kasuga, *Keizai kōsō*, 16–19.

Ooms, Herman. "Forms and Norms in Edo Arts and Society." In *Edo: Art in Japan, 1615–1868*, edited by Robert T. Singer, 23–46. New Haven: Yale University Press, 1998.

———. "Neo-Confucianism and the Formation of Early Tokugawa Ideology: Contours of a Problem." In *Confucianism and Tokugawa Culture*, edited by Peter Nosco, 27–61. Princeton: Princeton University Press, 1997.

———. *Tokugawa Ideology: Early Constructs, 1570–1680*. Princeton: Princeton University Press, 1989.

Park Jin-han. "Kinseizenki ni okeru ken'yakurei no zengokutekitenkai to sono tokuchō." *Shirin* 86 (May 2003): 141–59.

Pflugfelder, Gregory M. *Cartographies of Desire: Male-Male Sexuality in Japanese Discourse, 1600–1950*. Berkeley: University of California Press, 1999.

Phiddian, Robert. *Swift's Parody*. Cambridge: Cambridge University Press, 1995.

Pincus, Leslie. *Authenticating Culture in Imperial Japan: Kuki Shūzō and the Rise of National Aesthetics*. Berkeley: University of California Press, 1996.

Reitan, Richard M. *Making a Moral Society: Ethics and the State in Meiji Japan*. Honolulu: University of Hawaii Press, 2009.

Ricoeur, Paul. *Hermeneutics and the Human Sciences: Essays on Language, Action, and Interpretation*. Translated and edited by John B. Thompson. Cambridge: Cambridge University Press, 1981.

Sakai, Naoki. *Voices of the Past: The Status of Language in Eighteenth-Century Japanese Discourse*. Ithaca: Cornell University Press, 1992.

Santō Kyōden. "Kyōden ukiyo no suisei" and "Terako jo." In *Santō Kyōden zenshū*. Edited by Santō Kyōden zenshū committee. Vol. 3. *Kibyōshi* 3. Tokyo: Perikansha, 2001.

———. *Grilled And Basted Edo-Born Playboy*. In *Early Modern Japanese Literature: An Anthology, 1600–1900*, edited by Haruo Shirane, 687–710. New York: Columbia University, 2002.

Satō Tamio. "He no saho ni tsuiteno kōsatsu." In Ishizumi and Ogi, *Edo to Tokyo*, 4:250–51.

Scott, James C. *Domination and the Arts of Resistance: Hidden Transcripts*. New Haven: Yale University Press, 1990.

Screech, Timon. *Edo no ōbushin: Tokugawa toshi keikaku no shigaku*. Translated by Masaaki Morishita. Tokyo: Kōdansha, 2007.

———. *The Shogun's Painted Culture: Fear and Creativity in the Japanese States, 1760–1829*. London: Reaktion, 2000.

Seidensticker, Edward. *Low City, High City: Tokyo from Edo to the Earthquake*. Cambridge: Harvard University Press, 1983.

Seigle, Cecilia Segawa. *Yoshiwara: The Glittering World of the Japanese Courtesan*. Honolulu: University of Hawaii Press, 1993.

Sewell, William Hamilton. *Logics of History: Social Theory and Social Transformation*. Chicago: University of Chicago Press, 2005.

Shikitei Sanba. "Ukiyoburo." In *Sharebon, kibyōshi, kokkeibon*, edited by Nakamura Yukihiko and Keisuke Hamada, 209–58. Tokyo: Kadokawa Shoten, 1978.

———. *Ukiyodoko: Yanagigami shinwa*. Tokyo: Tenbōsha, 1974.

Shirane, Haruo. *Early Modern Japanese Literature: An Anthology, 1600–1900*. New York: Columbia University Press, 2002.

Shively, Donald H. "Bakufu Versus Kabuki." *Harvard Journal of Asiatic Studies* 18 (December 1955): 326–56.

———. "Sumptuary Regulation and Status in Early Tokugawa Japan." *Harvard Journal of Asiatic Studies* 25 (January 1964): 123–64.

Smith, Thomas C. *Native Sources of Japanese Industrialization, 1750–1920*. Berkeley: University of California Press, 1988.

Spivak, Gayatri Chakravorty. *A Critique of Postcolonial Reason: Toward a History of the Vanishing Present*. Cambridge: Harvard University Press, 1999.

Stallybrass, Peter and Allon White. *The Politics and Poetics of Transgression*. Ithaca: Cornell University Press, 1986.

Stewart, Susan. *Nonsense: Aspects of Intertextuality in Folklore and Literature*. Baltimore: Johns Hopkins University Press, 1979.

Suzuki Shōzan. *Selected Writings of Suzuki Shōzan*. Translated by Royall Tyler. Cornell East Asian Papers. Ithaca: China-Japan Program, Cornell University Press, 1977.

Suzuki Toshio. *Edo no hon'ya*. 2 vols. Tokyo: Chūō Kōronsha, 1980.

Suzuki Toshiyuki. *Edo no dokushonetsu: Jigakusuru dokusha to shoseki ryūtsū*. Tokyo: Heibonsha, 2007.

Takayanagi Shinzō and Ryōsuke Ishii, eds. *Ofuregaki tenpō shūsei*. Vol. 2. Tokyo: Iwanami Shoten, 1958.

Takeuchi Makoto. *Edo no sakariba kō: Asakusa Ryōgoku no sei to zoku*. Tokyo: Kyōiku Shuppan, 2000.

Takeuchi, Melinda. "Kuniyoshi's *Minamoto Raikō and The Earth Spider*: Demons and Protest in Late Tokugawa Japan." *Ars Orientalis* 17 (1987): 5–38.

Taki Kōji. *Tennō no shōzō*. Tokyo: Iwanami Shoten, 2002.

Tatsuro Akai. "The Common People and Painting." In Nakane and Ōishi, *Tokugawa Japan*, 167–91. Tokyo: University of Tokyo Press, 1990.

Terakado Seiken. *Edo hanjōki*. Vol. 2. Edited by Haruhiko Asakura and Kikuji Andō. Tokyo: Heibonsha, 1975.

Thompson, Sarah E. and H. D. Harootunian. *Undercurrents in the Floating World: Censorship and Japanese Prints*. New York: Asia Society, 1991.

Tokuda Susumu. *Edo no warai banashi*. Tokyo: Kyōiku Shuppan, 1983.

Tokyo Daigaku. *Dai Nihon kinsei shiryō: Shichū torishimari ruishū*. Vol. 1. Tokyo: Tokyo Daigaku Shuppankai, 1959.

———. *Dai Nihon kinsei shiryō: Shichū torishimari ruishū*. Vol. 18. Tokyo: Tokyo Daigaku Shuppankai, 1988.

———. *Dai Nihon kinsei shiryō: Shichū torishimari ruishū*. Vol. 21. Tokyo: Tokyo Daigaku Shuppankai, 1994.

Tosaka Jun. "Warai, kigeki, oyobi yūmoa." In Tosaka Jun, *Tosaka Jun zenshū*. Vol. 4. Tokyo: Keisōshobō, 1966.

———. *Shisō to fūzoku*. Tokyo: Heibonsha, 2001.

Tsuji Nobuo. *Kisō no keifu: Matabē-Kuniyoshi*. Tokyo: Perikansha, 1988.

Tsurumi Shunsuke and Maruyama Masao. "Maruyama Masao: Fuhen genri no tachiba." In *Kataritsugu sengoshi*. Vol. 1. Edited by Tsurumi Shunsuke. Tokyo: Shisō no Kagakusha, 1969.

Tsuruya Nanboku. *Tōkaidō yotsuya kaidan*. Tokyo: Iwanami Shoten, 1956.

Turner, Victor W. *Dramas, Fields, and Metaphors; Symbolic Action in Human Society*. Ithaca: Cornell University Press, 1974.

Turner, Victor W. *The Ritual Process: Structure and Anti-Structure*. New York: Aldine de Gruyter, 1995.

Uramoto Yoshifumi. *Edo, Tokyo no hisabetsu buraku no rekishi: Danzaemon to hisabetsu minshū*. Tokyo: Akashi Shoten, 2003.

Vaporis, Constantine Nomikos. *Tour of Duty: Samurai, Military Service in Edo, and the Culture of Early Modern Japan*. Honolulu: University of Hawaii Press, 2008.

Velben, Thorstein. "Conspicuous Consumption." In *The Consumer Society Reader*, edited by Juliet B. Schor and Douglas B. Holt, 187–204. New York: New Press, 2000.

Volosinov, V. N. *Marxism and the Philosophy of Language*. Cambridge: Harvard University Press, 1973.

Wallerstein, Immanuel Maurice. "The Ideological Tensions of Capitalism: Universalism Versus Racism and Sexism." In Étienne Balibar and Immanuel Maurice Wallerstein, *Race, Nation, Class: Ambiguous Identities*, 29–36. London: Verso, 1991.

Walthall, Anne. "Hiding the Shoguns: Secrecy and the Nature of Political Authority in Tokugawa Japan." In *The Culture of Secrecy in Japanese Religion*, edited by Bernhard Scheid and Mark Teeuwen, 331–56. London: Routledge, 2006.

———. *Social Protest and Popular Culture in Eighteenth-Century Japan.* Tucson: University of Arizona, 1986.

Watanabe Kazan. *Issō hyakutai; Shomin fūzoku.* Tokyo: Iwasaki Bijutsusha, 1969.

Watsuji Tetsurō. *Nihon seishinshi kenkyū.* Tokyo: Iwanami Shoten, 1992.

White, James W. *Ikki: Social Conflict and Political Protest in Early Modern Japan.* Ithaca: Cornell University Press, 1995.

Williams, Raymond. *Marxism and Literature.* Oxford: Oxford University Press, 1977.

Yamada Yūji. *Bakkosuru onryō: Tatari to chinkon no Nihon shi.* Tokyo: Yoshikawa Kōbunkan, 2007.

Yamaga Sokō. "The Way of the Samurai" [Shidō]. In *Sources of the Japanese Tradition,* compiled by Ryusaku Tsunoda, William Theodore De Bary, and Donald Keene, 192–94. New York: Columbia University Press, 1958.

Yamazumi Masami, ed. *Nihon kindai shisō taikei.* Vol. 6. *Kyōiku no taikei.* Tokyo: Iwanami Shoten, 1990.

Yasumaru Yoshio. *Nihon no kindaika to minshū shisō.* Tokyo: Heibonsha, 1999.

Yasunaga Toshinobu. *Ando Shoeki: Social and Ecological Philosopher of Eighteenth Century Japan.* New York: Weatherhill, 1992.

Yokota Fuyuhiko. "Geino, bunka to mibunteki shūhen." In *Mibun o toinaosu,* edited by Kurushima Hiroshi, Takano Toshihiko, Tsukada Takashi, Yoshida Nobuyuki, and Yokota Fuyuhiko, 29–47. Tokyo: Yoshikawa Kōbunkan, 2000.

Yokoyama Yasuko. *Edo Tokyo no kaidan bunka no seiritsu to hensen: Jūkyūseiki o chūshin ni.* Tokyo: Kazama Shobō, 1997.

Yoshida Nobuyuki. *Seijukusuru Edo.* Tokyo: Kōdansha, 2002.

———. "Yose to manabi." In *Shūen bunka to mibunsei,* edited by Wakita Haruko, Martin Collcutt, and Masayuki Taira, 85–110. Kyoto: Shibunkaku Shuppan, 2005.

Yoshiwara Ken'ichirō. *Edo no jōhōya: Bakumatsu shominshi no sokumen.* Tokyo: Nippon Hōsō Shuppan Kyōkai, 1978.

———. *Rakusho to yū media: Edo minshū no ikari to yūmoa.* Tokyo: Kyōiku Shuppan, 1999.

Yoshikawa Kōjiro."Jinsai, Tōgaigaku." In *Nihon shisō taikei.* Vol. 33. *Itō Jinsai, Itō Tōgai.* Edited by Yoshikawa Kōjiro and Shimizu Shigeru. Tokyo: Iwanami Shoten, 1971.

Yuzawa Kōkichirō. *Edo kotoba no kenkyū.* Tokyo: Meiji Shoin, 1959.

Žižek, Slavoj. *The Sublime Object of Ideology.* London: Verso, 1989.

Index

CHICAGO STUDIES IN PRACTICES OF MEANING

Edited by Andreas Glaeser, William Sewell, and Lisa Wedeen
Published in collaboration with the Chicago Center for Contemporary Theory
http://ccct.uchicago.edu

SERIES TITLES, CONTINUED FROM FRONT MATTER

Parité! Sexual Equality and the Crisis of French Universalism
by Joan Wallach Scott

Logics of History: Social Theory and Social Transformation
by William Sewell

Bewitching Development: Witchcraft and the Reinvention of Development in Neoliberal Kenya
by James Howard Smith

The Devil's Handwriting: Precoloniality and the German Colonial State in Qingdao, Samoa, and Southwest Africa
by George Steinmetz

Peripheral Visions: Publics, Power, and Performance in Yemen
by Lisa Wedeen

Lightning Source UK Ltd.
Milton Keynes UK
UKHW020525171222
414052UK00014B/940